THE INNER CITY
Employment and Industry

The Inner City
Employment and Industry

Edited by

Alan Evans

*Reader in Environmental Economics,
University of Reading*

and

David Eversley

*Senior Research Fellow,
Policy Studies Institute, London*

 Heinemann · London

Heinemann Educational Books Ltd
22 Bedford Square, London WC1B 3HH

LONDON EDINBURGH MELBOURNE AUCKLAND
HONG KONG SINGAPORE KUALA LUMPUR NEW DELHI
IBADAN NAIROBI JOHANNESBURG
EXETER (NH) KINGSTON PORT OF SPAIN

© Alan Evans and David Eversley, 1980
First published 1980

British Library CIP Data
The inner city
   1. Labor supply – Great Britain
   2. Cities and towns – Great Britain
   3. Urban economics
   I. Evans, Alan, b. 1939
   II. Eversley, David
   III. Centre for Environmental Studies
331.1'0941   HD5765.A6

ISBN 0-435-84355-9

Printed by Richard Clay (The Chaucer Press) Ltd, Bungay, Suffolk.

Contents

Acknowledgements

Our thanks are due to the following who at one time or another were involved in the preparation of this volume:

Mrs Melanie Metcalfe, the Conference Organiser at the Centre for Environmental Studies (CES), who was responsible for arranging the original seminar series and the York Conference in 1976;

Mrs Margaret Orchard, Personnel Officer at CES, who supervised the typing of the final manuscript;

Mrs Clare Currey, who collated the footnotes and references and checked the manuscripts; and

Susan Johnson, Librarian at the Policy Studies Institute, for supplying and checking bibliographical information.

We are also grateful to the CES, of which we were formerly full time members, for underwriting the costs of the seminar series.

Thanks for permission to reprint published articles are due to the following. The chapters by Dennis and Massey and Meegan have previously been published in *Urban Studies*. The paper by Gripaios uses material previously published in *Urban Studies*. The chapter by Townsend is a shortened version of an article previously published in *Regional Studies*. The chapter by Metcalf and Richardson is a shortened version of a chapter previously published in *The Concept and Measurement of Involuntary Unemployment*, edited by G. D. N. Worswick and published by Allen and Unwin. The chapter by Keeble has previously been published in *Transactions of the Institute of British Geographers*. We thank Mrs Mary Gourlay for permission to publish the chapter by Robert Gourlay of the Inner London Education Authority, who died before his paper could be printed, and his colleagues for some emendations of the text.

Note on references: to facilitate printing and at the same time to provide an easily accessible general bibliography, the works cited in individual chapters by author and year of publication can be found referenced in a consolidated alphabetical list at the end of the volume.

ALAN EVANS
DAVID EVERSLEY

Preface

The Centre for Environmental Studies (CES) regularly reviews (separately) a whole range of economic and social planning problems in its annual residential conferences and usually publishes the main papers presented at these events.

Therefore, when it was decided in 1974 to arrange a special series of seminars under the general heading of 'Inner City Employment', this was due to a feeling that this theme had emerged as the most intractable, and possibly the most crucial, of the many subjects that were at that time being raised in the debate on the future of the inner cities. The CES also felt that its interdisciplinary approach, bringing together the specialised knowledge of physical and social planners, economists, geographers, and sociologists, might help to evolve a new approach. Traditionally working closely with government departments, especially the Department of the Environment, it was thought that such a seminar series would attract civil servants and local government officers to discuss with their academic colleagues the problems of their policy-making functions. The format of the seminars made it possible for public servants to present the results of their own research findings, or approaches to policy, in an informal manner.

It was originally thought that something like twenty or twenty-five papers would cover the field. It was planned that these should be presented in pairs between April 1975 and July 1976, and that the seminar should culminate in the residential conference held at the University of York in September 1976. In the event, more papers were offered than could be accommodated in that time. The conference not only reviewed the whole series of papers but, as might have been expected, also resulted in a new set of contributions, often incorporating original research, as well as the review papers.

Thus, we faced the task of choosing a manageable selection from, in all, some fifty papers for publication. The principles of selection cannot be spelled out very clearly since they inevitably rested on our own value judgements. Thus, some extremely interesting papers were not included because their sheer bulk made inclusion, even with cuts, too difficult. Other papers were withdrawn by their authors since, in the four years between first commissioning and final delivery to the printers, too much had changed. Some authors chose to rewrite their papers almost completely; and in the case of the Inner Area Studies, which were still in progress at the time of the seminar, we asked three active participants in the seminar, who were also leading members of the three Inner Area Study teams, to write new chapters incorporating some of their original presentation but also the ultimate findings of the exercise in which they were then engaged.

Some of the papers have already appeared elsewhere, usually in the specialist journals, but we thought these to be of such importance to our general theme that they ought to be included here, even at the expense of some papers that have now not been published at all, in order to make them more accessible to the reader wishing to obtain an overview of the whole subject.

The reader who has any knowledge of the field will no doubt recognise that many of the ideas for action thrown out in the chapters that follow formed part of the recommendations of all three Inner Area Study reports, were accepted in the government's White Paper on the Inner Areas in 1977, and were translated into legislation in the Inner Urban Areas Act 1978. This is scarcely surprising, given the fact that so many of the authors of the studies themselves were among the 100 or so rotating members of the seminars, or attended the York Conference, and that some of the civil servants who finally advised the Secretary of State for the Environment on what was to be done participated in the conference. This is not to claim undue influence for the CES. It simply means that this volume is not some remote academic exercise but illustrates a position as part of the process of policy making in Britain today – the interaction between research, experimental projects, and administrative action. Such a statement again is not complacent, as we are not saying that research always produces the correct answers nor, even if this were the case, that this would necessarily lead the government to adopt the researchers' recommendations. Still less is it the case that, when action is finally taken and funds are provided, startling results then follow.

In fact, the final answer to the question of why we should publish this volume at all must be that all the problems raised here are still with us. Nobody claims in his contribution to provide more than an approach to experiment – to suggestions for particular types of activities. Some of these have been initiated, whether entirely under government sponsorship or by private effort, within the general framework of new urban policies; but these beginnings have scarcely made an impact as yet, and many of them will no doubt fail. Therefore, the purpose of this publication, as of the seminars that preceded it, is to keep alive the informed debate on what is still one of the most intractable problems in Britain today.

ALAN EVANS
DAVID EVERSLEY

Biographical Notes on Contributors

Howard Aldrich: Professor of Organizational Behavior, New York State School of Industrial and Labor Relations, Cornell University. In 1975 he was a visiting scholar at the Centre for Environmental Studies. He is the author of *Organizations and Environments* (Englewood Cliffs, NJ: Prentice-Hall, 1979).

Catherine Avent: Careers Guidance Inspector, Inner London Education Authority.

Richard Berthoud: Senior researcher at the Policy Studies Institute. He was with Political and Economic Planning before the merger with the Centre for Studies in Social Policy (CSSP) which led to the new Institute. His study of social deprivation, *The Disadvantages of Inequality*, was published in 1976.

Glen Bramley: Lecturer in Urban Studies, School for Advanced Urban Studies, University of Bristol. Formerly, he was an economist with Shankland Cox Partnership and a full time member of the Lambeth Inner Area Study team, 1973–6.

Gordon C. Cameron: Professor of Town and Regional Planning, University of Glasgow. Before that he was a professor in the Department of Social and Economic Research, University of Glasgow.

J. T. Corkindale: Economic Adviser, HM Treasury. Formerly, he was in the Unit for Manpower Studies, Department of Employment, where he was a contributor to the London Manpower Study and carried out research into employment in metropolitan areas.

Robert Dennis: Principal Research Officer, Department of Industry's Research and Planning Unit for South-East England.

Alan Evans: Reader in Environmental Economics, University of Reading. At the time of the research he was a researcher at the Centre for Environmental Studies.

David Eversley: Senior Research Fellow, Policy Studies Institute, and Visiting Professor, Bartlett School of Architecture and Planning. University College, London. Previously, he was Professor of

Population and Regional Studies, University of Sussex; Chief Planner (Strategy), Greater London Council, 1969–72; and a member of the Centre for Environmental Studies, 1972–6.

Nicholas Falk: Director of Research, Urbed Research Trust, and of the consultancy group Urbed (Urban and Economic Development) Ltd. He left McKinsey to do a PhD at the London School of Economics on the docklands development, and to start up workshops. Publications include *Inner City* and *Think Small* (Fabian Society).

Robert Gourlay: Died in 1977. Formerly Principal Careers Officer, Inner London Education Authority.

Peter Gripaios: Senior Lecturer, Department of Economics, Plymouth Polytechnic. Formerly, he was Senior Lecturer, Department of Economics, Thames Polytechnic, and a co-leader of a group research project at Thames Polytechnic on industrial decline in London. He is the author of several published articles on urban and regional employment problems.

David Keeble: Lecturer in Geography, University of Cambridge, and Fellow of St Catharine's College. His PhD research was on industrial migration from London, and he is the author of *Industrial Location and Planning in the United Kingdom* (London: Methuen, 1976).

Doreen Massey: Principal Scientific Officer, Centre for Environmental Studies, London. She is a co-author of *Capital and Land: Land Ownership by Capital in Great Britain* (London: Edward Arnold, 1978).

Richard Meegan: Senior Scientific Officer, Centre of Environmental Studies, London.

David Metcalf: Professor of Economics, University of Kent, Canterbury. At the time that he did the research reported in this book he was Lecturer in Economics, London School of Economics.

Rupert Nabarro: Visiting Lecturer at University College, London, and a partner of Roger Tym and Partners. He is an economist and town planner who has undertaken detailed work in older urban areas, specialising on problems of economic development and land markets. He worked on the Liverpool Inner Area Study and more recently on projects in Hackney/Islington, Tower Hamlets, and Lambeth.

G. L. Reid: Director of Manpower Intelligence and Planning, Manpower Services Commission. Formerly, he was Senior Economic Adviser, Scottish Office. As Reader in Applied Economics, University of Glasgow, he carried out research in labour and regional economics.

Ray Richardson: Lecturer, Department of Economics, London School of Economics.

Lynne Russell: Research Officer for Wandsworth Council for Community Relations. Formerly at the Centre for Environmental Studies.

John Salt: Lecturer in Geography, University College, London. He is a co-author of *Housing and the Migration of Labour in England and Wales*.

Barbara M. D. Smith: Lecturer, Centre for Urban and Regional Studies, University of Birmingham, since 1970. Previously, she was in research posts in the Board of Trade Regional Office and the Faculty of Commerce and Social Science, University of Birmingham. She was a consultant to the Birmingham Inner Area Study. Publications include many on employment and industry in the Centre for Urban and Regional Studies research series, and chapters in: G. E. Cherry (ed.) *Urban Planning Problems*; F. Joyce (ed.) *Metropolitan Development and Change*; and D. Walker (ed.) *The Planning of Industrial Development*.

Alan R. Townsend: Lecturer, Department of Geography, University of Durham. Formerly, he was Director of the North-East Area Study, University of Durham, and Town Planner, Teesside Survey and Plan.

A. M. Warnes: Lecturer in Human Geography, King's College, London. Formerly, he was Secretary of the Urban Study Group, Institute of British Geographers, 1974–7.

Introduction: How the Debate Began

David Eversley

1. Traditional urban planning

In recent years town planning (or in a more specific sense, land use and transportation planning) has increasingly acquired an element of social and economic planning. Conversely, planning for welfare (which constitutes a large part of all social and economic planning) has acquired spatial dimensions – internationally, regionally, and at a local level. The two pursuits have come gradually closer together; and although they are not yet by any means integrated, there is by now a common basis. The discussion that follows this introduction is the recognition of a process that, although as yet not very well understood, is likely to be more important over time.

From the traditional planning point of view it would be said that the making of plans (development plans, structure plans, regional strategies, local plans) and the administrative processes (development control, traffic management) have never been end objects in themselves; they have had, implicitly or explicitly, welfare objectives. However, most practitioners would probably agree that these objectives often disappeared from sight. Instead, intermediate goals, e.g. 'pedestrian segregation' or 'removal of non-conforming industry' or 'green belts', became the recognised categories in planning offices. Such intermediate objectives are still an important part of planning activity and may sometimes still be mistaken for objectives themselves, e.g. 'conservation of historic townscapes' or 'curbing the motor car' or 'restoring regional balance'. Increasingly, however, certain tests have come to be applied to these planning objectives and procedures – tests now devised in relation to welfare goals. These include such desiderata as 'the maintenance of real incomes', 'the eradication of gross inequalities', 'better and equal access to social, cultural, and recreational services', 'improvement of community relations', and 'involvement and participation in the planning process'. These objectives relate to the way people live, how they feel about their environment, and how they perceive their own quality of life.

For the purposes of this explanation it is not necessary to pass any judgements as to whether those who now profess to subscribe to these objectives have totally substituted social goals for their previous purely physical aims, or whether they are merely paying lip service to what has become a fashionable preoccupation, or whether they are only seeking to forestall the criticisms of the school of radical urbanists who allege planners to be mere tools of the developers and profit-seeking entrepreneurs.

From the point of view of the makers of social policies the interest in the spatial connotations of their activities has pushed them steadily nearer the preoccupations of the traditional planners. Thus, only a decade ago total performance expressed in quantitative terms was still the touchstone of the success of national policies, whether in housing, education, the reduction of unemployment, the designation of protected landscapes, or improvements in individual or public health. Only in the field of regional policy had the need to concentrate resources on particular areas begun to dominate thinking, following a decade of debates on whether particular procedures should be applied at the narrowest local (employment exchange) or the widest (development area) scale. In the field of education the idea of the educational priority areas was just emerging. Urban renewal had always been, by definition, seen as a localised activity, typically in the form of a comprehensive development area on the Birmingham model.

2. The new factors

Why has this change come about? A number of causes may be tentatively advanced. In the first place, the early decades of the Beveridge-type welfare state saw the establishment of a National Health Service, of a universal secondary-education system on the 1944 Butler principle, and of a housing policy, under the 1948 Local Government Act, that made the provision of housing for all sections of the population mandatory. The work of the Supplementary Benefits Commission evolved from the National Assistance

Board. During these formative years nobody expected instant success, and it was commonly supposed that the incremental process of instituting new benefits and subsidies and creating new national and local organisations would in time cover the gaps. However, by the mid-1960s it was apparent that this process was not working very efficiently. Too much of the extra resources – and they did increase over time, both in real terms, *per capita*, and as a proportion of a rising gross national product (GNP) – apparently accrued to already privileged groups, while other sections of the population were consistently left out.

Second, there was in the postwar post-Keynes period an assumption of certainty about economic growth, which played an important role in the expectations of policy makers. It was supposed that growth of the GNP could, given the political will, yield improvements in the performance of public services through redistributive taxation (and local rates) and the ready availability of investment capital for the public sector. Moreover, growth normally meant demand for labour, and more skilled labour at that; and given reasonable educational, training, and labour-market organisation policies, the benefits of full employment at ever higher real incomes could be spread around. Nor were these assumptions particularly unrealistic. The supposition of improved real incomes for the vast majority, resulting from a combination of overall growth and redistributive policies, was founded on readily verifiable facts. What was perhaps unrealistic was the idea that the benefits would eventually extend to all sections of the population. It was only when the prospects of economic growth were first thrown into serious doubt that it was generally realised that, not only had some sections of the population been almost entirely left out of the general improvement, but also they were likely to have their living standards forcibly reduced if growth ceased, or inflation became chronic, or both. Whereas in the 1960s only families with more than the average number of children, the old, the handicapped, the black immigrants, the gypsies, and a few similar groups were identifiably at risk (although even these groups in total might have constituted 25 per cent of all households), the category of 'the disadvantaged' had later to be extended to low-paid workers. That is, generically, workers with low skills and low bargaining power, workers whose earnings were irregular or dependent on occasional bonuses in the shape of overtime, as well as rather better-paid or more skilled workers in plants or areas that were particularly susceptible to fluctuations in demand, had to be included. Inflation, which had once been the ally of public and private investment policies (because it made historical cost irrelevant to current expenditures), together with interest rates that would have been considered astronomical in the days of Cripps and Dalton, led to repeated severe cutbacks of public spending as well as reinforcing the apparently endemic reluctance to invest on the part of private industry.

Third, the years since the mid-1960s have seen the emergence of some more refined critiques and evaluations of the policies that had dominated postwar thinking in the field of environmental and social administration. Until the late 1960s few observers had questioned the wisdom of a vigorous decentralisation policy based on urban containment (within green belts), new and expanded towns, and the stringent control of industrial location. Measures to improve equality betwen regions, leading to the steering of a great deal of public and private investment to Northern Ireland, Scotland, Wales, and the Northern region, had been agreed policy between the political parties although they differed in the vigour of their application of such legislation.

The critique of this conventional wisdom took various forms. New towns were argued not to have benefited those who had most need of new housing and employment opportunities; green belts were seen as having protected the environment of the better-off; and policies of rural development control were judged to have kept the best environment for the sole use of those who had always enjoyed them. The administrations of the large old cities that had been denied the growth of any new employment opportunities (except offices, which played a large part only in London) began to show serious concern for the future of their economic base, as regards both individual spending power and their public finances. The pursuit of new jobs in the regions was questioned both on the grounds that the resultant distortion of the pattern of movement and locational advantages could be a cause of poor performance, and because, again, it pruned economic opportunities too vigorously in the older industrial areas.

Fourth, there emerged an increased and widespread concern with environmental quality, taking such forms as the intense desire to preserve historic buildings and townscapes and valuable landscapes, the fight against the pollution of water and air, and stronger measures to control the motor car. Fairly quickly, conservation for its own sake was seen to take the form of deep-rooted opposition to growth and new life as such, when every new development seemed to be doomed to fail, on appeal, on the grounds of a threat to some important man-made or natural feature of the existing environment. Such an attitude could, some would say, lead to petrification rather than preservation. The vigorous opposition to further landtake was identified as having been the main cause of the tendency to build economically ruinous and socially undesirable high-rise residential blocks. Total opposition to the motor car, when coupled with a failure to improve public transport, was seen to reduce the movement of persons and goods, especially within cities; and it therefore again began to be questioned as a solution to transportation problems, if it simply meant that jobs and people moved to areas where movement was relatively unrestricted.

Fifth, and probably closely connected with the other causes of changed attitudes, there emerged a preoccupation with participation, public involvement, or democratic control – whatever one likes to call the demand for a changed relationship between decision makers and those whose lives they affect. This was not by any means confined to the field of planning. In industry, in education, and in the social and medical services the idea of a paternalistic division between the activities of those with power (however well trained, motivated, and ultimately accountable they might appear to be) and the activities of those without power was felt to be unacceptable. Municipal tenants, shopfloor workers, students, patients, and clients all began to realise that they could exercise their own power to ensure that what they were given bore a closer relationship to what they wanted. This idea gained ground as the growth of performance rates slackened. At a time of apparently steady expansion, when real wages and the numbers of new housing units, university places, and hospital beds all seemed to justify the hope of eventual improvement, questions of control and allocation were perhaps not so important. The word 'perhaps' is used because there is no clear correlation between steady growth and satisfaction and because the first signs of revolt occurred in the 1960s when both public and private policies had apparently succeeded in improving performance, at least by conventional indicators (unemployment, real wages, number of student places, new and improved housing, tenancy protection, etc.). Whatever the origins of the revolt, there can be no doubt that stringency in public and private sector spending and in new investment has since aggravated the problem and that the perceived need to have a say in the allocation of scarce resources is likely to be a larger factor. When there are no serious shortages of available investment capital, and when growth ensures that the local and national taxation needed to finance new projects can be kept within bounds, the arguments against schemes like a new airport, a channel tunnel, new motorways, or new cities are likely to be largely environmental and therefore a concern of only a minority. However, when there is intensified competition, especially for public sector spending, it means that the realisation of such proposals not only may affect the existing natural and built environment but can also prejudice the prospects for the implementation of other schemes that may be judged to be of greater urgency. Then the demand for public involvement in decision making takes on another form altogether. Just as in times of severe inflation the pressures to obtain speedy settlements of apparently very large wage claims become a matter of life and death (and therefore increase the propensity to strike), so the constant threat of investment cuts and redundancies and of economies in the current spending of departments leads to more peremptory demands for the division of available funds between competing claims to be the subject of a public dialogue. Hence, there has occurred the intensification of the activities of pressure and interest groups of all kinds, which have not only changed the nature of the process of administration (including planning) but also served to highlight problems of government that might have gone unnoticed a decade earlier.

To sum up. This introduction begins the discussion of a subject that brings together the social and the physical planner at a time when certain fundamental tenets of planning thought appear to be changing in the face of altered circumstances. These are: a growing disillusionment about the capacity of traditional welfare-state policies to effect radical improvements for quite large sections of the population; an era of slower economic growth with some increase in unemployment and the unpleasant consequences of rapid inflation; increasing scepticism about the efficacy of a number of planning prescriptions taken for granted for two decades or more; an atmosphere of policy making where the relationship of decision takers and their clients is becoming strained; and the rise of a new movement for conservation and environmental protection.

For some, of course, these changed circumstances are simply evidence of the progressive and indeed inevitable collapse of the capitalistic system; and they would assume that unemployment and misery are the necessary concomitants of this collapse, so that further discussion about possible alternative policies becomes useless. This is not generally the view taken in the chapters that follow. It is assumed that Britain's problems are capable of being more clearly identified and that measures can be devised to deal with them, even in a time of slow economic growth. Britain is going through what is demonstrably not the first, and probably not the last, crisis of a mixed economy (rather than a capitalistic system *per se*), and it seems useful to continue with the process of attempting piecemeal improvements, even if it is often dismissed as disjointed incrementalism.

3. The nature of the problem

For as long as the modern industrial and commercial city has existed its growth has been considered almost inevitable. Until some North American cities began to decay in and from their centres during the 1920s and the subsequent depression, the large city was assumed to be a magnet against which there were few countervailing forces. Urbanisation was, and still largely is, considered to be the world's fate. Despite the acrimonious criticism of the city and city life that is common to British and American intellectuals, the preference of the young small-town or village dwellers and the immigrants for the city has scarcely been doubted. To be sure, this preference has often turned out to be based on illusions, because neither the jobs nor the shelter sought by the migrant has turned out to be available, and the social scientists' analyses have consistently portrayed the city as the concentration of all physical, economic, and psychological deprivation.

Nevertheless, until fairly recently the process of migration into the city hardly slackened overall. The British conurbations, as they used to be called, reached the peak of their proportion of the total population in the early 1960s, although since then they have held an ever decreasing share of the total. In Britain a process of re-ruralisation seems to have set in, in the sense that by 1974 (when local-government boundary changes made comparative analysis difficult) the proportion of people living in rural areas was actually increasing. The main shift in the growth pattern has on the whole, in Britain as elsewhere, been towards the medium and smaller size cities (Hall *et al.*, 1973). Typically, in Britain it is places like Leicester and Bristol that have gained population and places like Manchester, Liverpool, and London that have lost people. (These statements relate to settlement areas, not administrative boundaries, pre- or post-1974.)

How much does this change betoken any lessening of the attractiveness of the city? The immediate clue could be thought to be the size and composition of the urban job market. In theory cities could continue to provide more and better jobs, but lose population, provided that the size of the total labour force was maintained by a combination of rising activity rates and increasing commuting. As this book will show in some detail, neither of these assumptions now holds good. Commuting has certainly decreased, at least for London, and urban activity rates have not increased very much either since the initial sharp rise in the employment of married women in the 1960s.

The number of workplaces in cities has declined, relative to all workplaces, although at present the position of the cut-off point is doubtful. The evidence seems to show that smaller cities, especially towns of 20,000–100,000 inhabitants in the regions surrounding the metropolitan counties, are still gaining employment.

Second, the job mix in the city has altered radically with the decline of manufacturing employment and the growth of the tertiary sectors. The exact extent of these changes varies considerably; thus, Birmingham still has a very high proportion of manufacturing jobs, and the rise of office employment is proportionately less in London than elsewhere, although in absolute terms it is still high. Each city has a different pattern depending on the nature of its industries, its regional functions, its position within the central government's hierarchy of areas deserving or not deserving job encouragement, the decisions about the decentralisation of government offices, and other factors considered in this book.

In the traditional analysis of the regional planner, the extent to which an area suffered job (and income) loss was normally related to the degree to which it was dependent on industries facing a long term decline or, exceptionally, on industries subject to sharp cyclical fluctuations (textiles are an example of the first category, motor cars of the second). It is not proposed here to argue the relative severity of the deprivation of an urban area that has not enjoyed prosperity for a long time and the deprivation of one where decline has set in more recently and perhaps more selectively. Whether deprivation is greater when it is absolute and prolonged, or when it is relative and of recent origin, is a moot point. The two conditions may well require different solutions, but both command attention. The *number* of unemployed in the South-East region is larger, after all, than in any other region in the country, and there are more workless in London than in Scotland. This leads to no less hardship because the workless are surrounded by unfilled vacancies; and at the margin any increase in unemployment, or any fall in relative earnings, is just as unacceptable whether it occurs in a development area, and starts from a high level of unemployment and a low level of earnings, or in a traditionally prosperous area, where it starts from a low level of unemployment at a high level of earnings.

The decline of manufacturing industry in the big cities is a world-wide phenomenon, at least in those countries which underwent industrialisation some time ago. It is not confined to those countries which pursue active decentralisation or regional policies. Indeed, many commentators have doubted whether government policy has had such a very large influence on the situation. The factors that have led to industrial decentralisation are now so powerful that it is no longer necessary to ask industrialists, as surveys once did, why they chose to leave the big city for the smaller town; rather, it is more pertinent to inquire what it is that keeps big-city industrialists in their present locations. In many cases the true answer may well be inertia, lack of capital and of any hope for the future, especially when there is a worldwide depression, and lack of growth, from which only Japan among the major producer countries seems exempt.

Let us list some of these factors. In the first place the old reasons for locating in big cities are simply no longer there. Originally, industry concentrated on areas of water power and then on coalfields. Until about 1920 industry was tied to a railway network and, to a lesser extent, to canals. The classical model of industrial location theory enumerates all the economies of scale that the city once provided – the common services, the availability of a specialist labour force, the commercial agencies catering for particular branches of industry. This is textbook stuff. Sometimes, the reputation of a place still warrants a postal address that has some significance; cutlery should be made in Sheffield, for instance, at least so long as it is possible to sell it against the competition from Solingen or Thiers. The combination of readily available electricity and fuel oil at much the same charges wherever they are needed, the reduced significance of the transportation costs of raw materials and semi-fabricates for most final products, and the spread of professional, scientific, and commercial services to quite small places have made it relatively unimportant, from the point of view of the cost, reputation, and marketability of a product, where it is made.

If, as will be shown, most firms, when making the decision to move still, other things being equal, move not very far away, this says nothing about locational advantages in real terms, although a great deal about managerial habits. In fact, as several studies will show, the loss of manufacturing employment in big cities has not been due in the main to a physical move away from the city; rather, it has been due to the selective closure of existing concerns or of plants within a large concern. This is not the place to speculate about the role of multinational firms, nationalised industries, or mergers and amalgamations in this process (in fact only the publications emanating from the Home Office-sponsored Community Development Project have consistently claimed that the loss of workplaces has been an organised conspiracy of monopoly capital against the workers). The fact seems to be that the casualties in the big cities have been both big plants and little ones – one-man firms and huge assembly lines. In Britain the gainers from this process have sometimes been the new and expanded towns, sometimes other small towns, but always foreign competitors. Although critics often claim that too much of Britain's labour force is still locked up in unproductive manufacturing industry, the proportion of the world's manufactures now being produced in Britain has been dropping sharply. The share of imports in British consumption has been rising fast; and therefore, inevitably, the loss suffered by the big cities at a time when other areas have been gaining manufacturing employment has been even greater than the loss suffered by corresponding settlements in the United States, West Germany and France. However, whereas the background to the movement in other countries has been an overall rise in employment and real wages, and a correspondingly faster rise in the opportunities offered, for instance, by the service sector, the British process must be seen against the background of stagnation, so that one settlement's gain must be another's loss. This was true in the 1920s and 1930s; but whereas then the burden fell predominantly on the depressed areas, it is now falling to a greater extent on the formerly prosperous cities.

4. The cities face competition

It seems necessary to state this, because so many of the published subregional and local studies claim that their particular area has been discriminated against by whatever villain can be identified, just as each regional planning council believes itself to be the champion of an area uniquely neglected by the industrial managers, in the face of the obvious advantages that it can offer. The truth is that all old locations in built-up areas whether in London, Birmingham, or Tyneside, have had to compete for a share of the shrinking total employment cake, against the manifold advantages offered by the smaller free-standing towns, especially the New Towns, and semirural locations in Development Areas. On the evidence presented here it makes no difference at all whether the decision to close the old urban plant is taken by a firm owned by a British giant, a multinational firm, a single owner, or a subsidiary of a state-owned corporation; it makes no difference whether the concern has overall been operating profitably and wishes to increase these profits, or at a loss and wants to minimise them. The handicap of the urban areas consists in the higher costs, real or perceived, incurred in them; and even if this view is false or perhaps coloured by such extraneous factors as difficult labour relations, insistent and insidious government and private propaganda has created a climate of opinion where 'moving out' has become the natural action of a rational manager and 'staying put' the hallmark of a reactionary or lunatic. Connoisseurs of the publicity campaigns conducted by the Location of Offices Bureau will recognise the genre.

The attractions of the alternative locations are indeed great. Apart from the financial inducements of the regions that receive the government's largesse, there are many other long term factors at work that reduce the big city's viability as a manufacturing centre. London once attracted production because shipping from the Port of London was easy. It is now almost certainly easier to ship goods, especially in containers, from any other city in the country than from London, and its air handling capacity was not exactly brilliant even before the days of prohibitive air-freight costs. London's antiquated road system, now probably never to be improved, makes it certain that, if transport costs still play a role, almost any location is better than London; and although Manchester, Birmingham, and

Liverpool have done better for themselves in the way of linking their industrial areas to a modern road system leading to their markets and ports, the advantages are not all that great in these relatively smaller urban areas. From the point of view of managerial preferences London and Birmingham once had great attractions; but these have changed, especially given the large housing differentials, even for the highest-paid employees. For lower grades of key middle management and skilled workers, London's offer now means a choice between a long and expensive journey to work and less-than-desirable and very expensive housing. These differentials have always existed, but they have become more important with the shift in housing and transportation costs in recent years. The peripheral industrial locations score because it is one thing to drive a car 16 km from one small Hertfordshire town to another but quite another to go by public transport from Lewisham to Brent every day. The ways in which individual attitudes to travel to work, leisure, and income maximisation have changed are of great interest in this book, although unfortunately no studies that would illustrate this point were available for inclusion.

Under these circumstances it is hardly surprising that many of the cities have lost a great deal of their original *raison d'être*. Planning orthodoxy decreed that they should. Industry congests and pollutes and will function much better outside the conurbations, where workers will enjoy life more. This was, and still is, the doctrine of the new towns. It is also the philosophy behind the development areas: the workers are there; let us take the jobs to them to prevent them from flooding into the cities, as they used to, thus aggravating the housing problems. The movement of industry, so the textbooks said, will be in phase with the movement of the workers; thus, housing will be improved and congestion reduced.

This much can be taken as read. Equally, and almost certainly, the chances of promoting new industrial growth in the big cities must be adjudged minimal, at least in the foreseeable future. Liverpool, Newcastle, and Glasgow, having development area status, may still succeed; at least Merseyside has a fairly good record of new plants since 1960 or so, thus at least partially replacing the old jobs that were lost. London or Birmingham, in the 1970s, had no such chance. Overall, industrial jobs in Britain will continue to fall, most likely at an accelerating rate, and what there is by way of new or footloose plant will increasingly locate outside the old centres. To what extent new government attitudes can change this picture remains to be seen.

5. Office jobs as replacement?

What of the other sectors? Offices, as has been said, have grown in London, although not to the extent that the visual evidence of the city's skyline suggests. Replacement at more generous space standards is not a proof of real growth, and it is only in centres like Croydon that a drastic transformation of the employment market has taken place. Other cities also have their new office blocks, but in few cases has the growth of that sector been a replacement for the loss of other jobs, especially for the existing adult workforce. The jobs that the offices provide are not open to those who once worked in industry. By sex, age, and skills the new workplaces are for other people, and these other people live in the suburbs or beyond the city altogether, or they are better-qualified school leavers. The more prosperous the tertiary sector becomes, the less does it offer to the middle and older generation of workers. If the process were so managed over time that industry lost its older and less skilled workforce by natural wastage and the new employment sectors were built up by a suitable supply of school leavers, then there might be no problem; but the wastage from industry has been too rapid, and the change in the qualifications of school leavers too slow, to allow anything so orderly to take place. When it is realised that in the new office capitals of the United States and West Germany, for instance, although something like 75 per cent of school leavers have a full secondary education or more they cannot supply all demands from the office sector and that the remaining 25 per cent have problems finding jobs, the situation in Britain becomes clearer.

There are other jobs in cities. The public services, especially transportation and communications, need manual and intermediate white-collar workers. So do the personal service trades, especially, as in London, for tourism and catering. In some regional centres retailing is on the increase, although nowhere does it now require more labour; in London it is sharply decreasing, especially in the inner city, for a large variety of reasons. There is often a good deal wrong with these service jobs: pay, prospects, seasonal fluctuations. Some chapters will show how they affect earnings patterns. Until now, at any rate, the cities have often been short of labour in many of these occupations. So, in theory there ought to be opportunities for everyone; earnings should rise. Why this does not happen and why a depressed earnings sector continues to exist are things still to be explained.

Thus, at the core of this book lies the investigation of the nature of the urban labour market, the changes in its size and composition, and the changes in the labour force that is available to fill the potential jobs. The 'market' is perhaps not operating at all; there may be so many constraints that it is wrong to use the term. What role is played in this failure by the housing system, education, the lack of machinery to place people in jobs, discrimination, and many other factors will be explained in several contributions.

6. New problems of urban finance

There is another group of problems closely associated with the question of employment in the city. Although there will not be much discussion of these matters in this book, they should be mentioned here because they help to explain the rising preoccupation of those responsible for the government of large urban areas, and some beginning of an understanding of the large economic issues underlies the initiative taken by the central government since 1976.

The urban economic base is in some ways a nebulous concept, which in the past has been used as an analytical tool mainly to discuss the growth of cities. Urban concentrations achieved a certain size as the result of the growth of basic and non-basic employment, to use a once-fashionable phrase. Within this growth mechanism two important linkages stand out. First, as employment (and therefore incomes) grew, so a multiplier effect created the demand for retailing and other commercial and professional services, which in turn meant additional employment, demand for construction trades, and so on. Second, under the existing system of local government finance, enterprises supported the local tax (or rate) base; growth was self-financing. The question is sometimes asked how it came about that in the days of the London County Council, in the period of Morrison's government at County Hall, London could be so generous in its investment policies even at times of national economic difficulty. The answer lay in the buoyancy of its private and public revenues. The two are closely linked. Rising levels of personal expenditure lead to rising incomes (and profits) of population- and employment-dependent enterprises. Under such conditions the public revenue can rise relatively faster than economic activity as a whole.

If the opposite situation now occurs and the economic base is eroded, it is at least possible that public revenue will fall at a faster rate than employment and personal incomes. The decline in revenue from the rates paid by industrial enterprises is an obvious case in point. Where this decline is compensated for by an increase in commercial and domestic property, this does not matter. Where (as claimed above) this is not the case, a progressive self-reinforcing deceleration of private and public revenues can set in. The lower the real income of households are, the less they will be able to spend on goods and services. Fewer households with lower disposable incomes reduce the turnover and profitability of enterprises; this leads to a more-than-proportionate fall in the demand for new investment; therefore, there is a negative multiplier, greater than unity, associated with a fall in employment. The more households have incomes that lie below the rate (and rent) rebate line, the sharper the reduction of the public revenue will be. If, as in London, rents and rates rise sharply, just when incomes fail to keep pace with the rest of the country and consumer expenditure is subject to inflationary pressures, the results are evident. If such a reduction of revenue is not compensated for by central government, the decline of the quality of public services accelerates at a time when a higher proportion of the population requires them. This leads to both an accelerated exodus of those who can undertake the move and a reduction in the real living standards of those who remain behind.

The consequences are as yet imperfectly understood.[1] It is still sometimes assumed that the 'reduction of pressures' associated with a fall in employment yields social benefits that outweigh any possible economic costs. Whether or not this is the case will have to be discussed elsewhere, but for the purposes of this introduction it may be as well to recall that the public finance aspect of employment could be added as a third dimension to a problem normally discussed only in terms of the welfare of the individual, on one hand, and the social consequences of labour shortages, on the other.

7. Investigations and policies

The object of the Centre for Environmental Studies (CES) seminar series was to gather all available information on the inner city system as a whole, so that employment policies could be discussed in

[1] When this introduction was first written, at the end of 1975, the logic of these paragraphs was still almost universally derided by economists (as it had been three years earlier by the Layfield Report on the Greater London Development Plan). In 1979 the argument appears to be part of the orthodoxy of urban analysis.

context. To do this it was necessary to look both at the large aggregates – the national changes and the regional distribution of these changes – and at the scale of a local labour market. 'Local' is not a fixed term. In the nineteenth century British trade unionists 'tramped' regularly in search of work when they were out of their apprenticeships; it was not then considered a tragedy, nor was seasonal work for English bricklayers in Boston, or work for Irish navvies on the Staffordshire railways. Now, mobility has been much reduced, for good and bad reasons. Thus, if London were a labour market of a kind that made it immaterial where one lived and where one's job was, there might be no problem, even if most people chose to live within a reasonable distance of their work. Alternatively, if all jobs were located on a system of radial and orbital public transportation systems, as reports say is the case in some planned economies in eastern Europe, there might be no difficulties. If there were a housing market in which people could change their dwellings readily at no great cost, within the public or the private sector, or an intermediate sector, or between these, there might be fewer problems. If a very high percentage of school leavers were trained for (or educationally suitable for later training in) occupations for which there was a demand, it would be possible to see a solution over time. As it is, many educationists say that it is wrong even to think of education for 'life' having anything to do with training fodder for the capitalist labour market. Thus, the discussions took place within a framework of constraints imposed by systems (whether in housing or education) that was far too inflexible to cope with the needs created by the rapid changes in the labour market.

Again, if there were excellent and universal retraining facilities and if people could draw full wages while retraining, adaptation might be easier. Indeed, since these seminars began the government, through the Manpower Services Commission, has created a formidable armoury of instruments to deal with the situation, although precise results cannot yet be stated. If the new organisations can provide a better knowledge of employment and housing opportunities, and if, for instance, each district has its own housing- and employment-counselling service and the necessary financial support to translate aspirations into practice, the present imbalances may avert the urban catastrophes that some still fear. If the attitudes of some employers towards black workers and of some black workers towards employers could both be simultaneously changed, there might not be problems in Manchester and Lambeth.

Despite continuous criticisms there are some signs that the new legislation against racial discrimination is beginning to have an impact, although it is slow work; but it has to be recorded that many changes that seemed far away when these chapters were first presented as seminar papers had been implemented by the time the book was published.

The studies identified a number of these problems and quantified them in traditional terms where this was possible. Now something is known about the rate of disappearance – by death, retirement, or outward migration – of those who used to fill jobs; the existing vacancies and the rate of creation of new jobs have been analysed by age and skill (pretending that sex no longer matters); and something is known about the new entrants to the labour force (young people and married women not yet, no longer, or never to be bound to the home by maternity). Suppose then that it were possible to line up education and training facility schedules and to devise new ways of facilitating housing exchanges. Suppose that it were possible to invent an inner-urban transportation system to connect homes and jobs in such a way as to make the effort of going to work relatively minimal in terms of time, money, and energy. Would such policies ensure the desired improvement? This question involves some knowledge of British administrative processes – the tiers of national, regional, and local government, the relations of departments one with another, the role and accountability of non-elected authorities and statutory undertakers. It involves understanding the nature of regional strategies, structure plans, and local plans and the powers of authorities to implement what they see as desirable in policies, as opposed to wishful thinking. The Layfield panel told the Greater London Council[2] in no uncertain terms that employment and real income levels were no concern of urban planners and, if they were, that they could not influence the pattern. Since then central government has had to examine again whether this in fact is true and, if it is false, to see whose responsibility it is, and in whose power it lies, to affect employment and earnings. The partnership schemes created under the 1978 legislation appear to point the way to the answer to these questions.

This does not exhaust the list of possible topics. Once a start has been made on examining in detail the situation now facing the inner

---

[2]   Department of the Environment (1973), *Greater London Development Plan: Report of the Panel and Inquiry*, chairman Frank Layfield, (London, HMSO).

city, as the Inner Area Study and Community Development Project teams have done, it becomes clear that, just because the nature of the problems of deprivation (or relative disadvantage) are now so complex, few of the old single-policy prescriptions have any relevance. It is not because the inner city is so much more complex an organism than a new town or an agricultural region (although this may well be true), but rather because the problems of the inner city have been compounded by planning (i.e. deliberate policy interventions in an already unsatisfactory situation), that it is so much harder to change the situation. How much of the difficulty lies in the past attempts to clear slums or in the present failure to do so? How much has the situation been aggravated by the creation of one-tenure areas, and how much more difficult is it going to be made if 'colonisation' by other tenures is allowed? How much is due to the spread of the private motorcar to half of the population or how much to the failure to allow a larger part of the working population to be motorised, as it is in other countries? How much is due to excessive growth in the past and how much to failure to grow at present?

Beyond that there are genuine dilemmas of policy, now punctuated by economic failure. If it is necessary to choose between the older city and the welfare of the wider region, or between the metropolitan districts and the development areas, on what criteria should such choices be made? These questions were raised very clearly in the Strategic Plan for the North-West; they were raised again in the attempt to revise the 1970 Strategic Plan for the South-East. In 1978 the backlash against attempts to redeploy too many scarce resources from the prosperous shire counties to the metropolitan cores was beginning to be strongly felt.

Attempts to analyse the employment situation from a simplistic base will not get very far. To blame the mismanagement of the system for the difficulties that large cities face is an easy way out. Of course 'the system' is unfair, rewards are unequally distributed, and some firms still make large profits; but it should not be thought that the disappearance of income inequality, or private profit, would lead to a distribution of employment opportunities that would favour big cities more. It would of course help if a bus conductor were paid as much as a miner or a university lecturer (plus an inner-city cost-of-living allowance), but it may be necessary to contemplate the continuation both of a mixed economy and of wage differentials (to which others than the highest income strata of society may be attached). Following the 1975 Community Land Act it may be possible to take development land into public ownership and do something to equalise wealth a little more, and almost certainly more industrial firms will pass into public ownership. However, this should not misleadingly suggest that fiscal or institutional changes of this kind will necessarily do very much, even in the long run, to reverse the processes now at work; and if Britain has really come to the end of economic growth, the chances of correcting the existing imbalances and improving the existing environment will be slimmer still.

For the purposes of this book the authors have largely accepted the task of discussing what could be done quite largely within the framework of the better utilisation of existing resources, with the help of existing legislation and administrative devices. This does not of course preclude changes within this framework that have already been put into effect – such as changes in the application of Industrial Development Certificates (IDCs), or regional policy payments, or selective subsidies for urban transport and housing – which may show significant results in time. Operating within the current framework is quite consistent with the adoption of such a strategy as that advocated by the North-West or Northern region strategic-planning teams with their greater emphasis on the employment and environmental problems of existing urban areas. A radical reform of local government finance would still be a change within the present system, even if heavier national taxation were required to underwrite the reforms. The purpose of this discussion was precisely that of identifying the sort of changes in law and practice that are needed to cure the present ills. The initiative lay not in a revolutionary zeal for changing 'the system' radically, but in the attempt to consider a whole range of institutions and practices to see what relationship they bore to the central problem. This should long ago have been the outcome of the movement towards studying urban systems rather than fragmented urban pathology, and it should have been the application of corporate management that produced remedies.

The authors' self-denying ordinance in confining their discussions largely to the problems facing the politicians and administrators in the immediate future has of course prevented them from asking some important questions at a deeper level. How right is it to tackle the whole problem exclusively from the point of view of the welfare of individuals and families – the maintenance of household incomes and the social and economic prospects of youngsters? Wouldn't it be more correct, as some critics claim, equally to address questions of national well-being – the productivity and competitiveness of British industry and commerce – because a larger overall social product would achieve more results than sharper instruments of corrective policy at the level of both the individual and the community? And, on the other hand, is it permissible to plan nationally at all? Are these not matters for regional self-government and local option? Or is the whole idea of a policy an illusion in the face of the machinations of big business?

No doubt every critic of this book will say that these authors, or others, are looking at this problem in the wrong way, out of context, or, worse still, without an adequate theory. On this latter point this book will be faulted by some for not being devoted wholly, or at least mostly, to the theory of the labour market, the theory of industrial location, or transportation theory. Critics will also say that inadequate attention is paid to matters of individual and social psychology, to the revolution in communications theory and technology, and much else besides. The latest upheaval (caused by the rapid spread of microcircuit technology) had not been heard of when these chapters were drafted.

There was no expectation of being able to cover all this; but the book was started with the hope that, after an initial increase in confusion and diffusion, it might towards the end be possible to come together again in some sort of synthesis that made sense both theoretically and practically – and the only practicality would lie in planning policies that could help the inner city to overcome the appalling handicaps created by trends and deliberate policies in the last few years, short of abandoning it altogether. There is some real danger of this, as the docklands areas show, and there are examples of even more wholesale flights from the city in the United States. How to prevent this, or at least the traumatic experiences associated with this flight, was the central concern.

8. Envoi

Looking back over the four years since the seminar series was planned it can be said, on one hand, that there have been fundamental changes in inner city policies and, on the other hand, that all the problems raised here still exist.

During those four years the government has consistently diverted resources towards the inner areas, both overtly and indirectly. Local government finance has not been reformed despite a lengthy report on the need for such a reform from a committee chaired by Sir Frank Layfield. Instead, the rate support grant has been altered again (some would say manipulated) to ensure that relatively larger resources will go to the main areas of deprivation. The three Inner Area Studies were published in large volumes, together with nearly 100 supporting research and project reports. An Act of Parliament was passed giving the government large powers, in partnership with local authorities, to divert yet more resources of all kinds to the affected areas.

Some twelve such partnerships have been formed. Urban aid programmes have been vastly increased. IDC restrictions have largely been lifted in favour of inner area locations. The remit of the Location of Offices Bureau has been changed to enable it to facilitate the creation of additional office space in inner areas that need a diversification of employment. A Community Land Act is on the statute book(Community Land Act 1976), which in theory enables local authorities to acquire land needed for redevelopment at realistic costs (although to date the Act has remained almost a dead letter). Much stronger measures, e.g. to ensure equal opportunities and to outlaw discrimination, have been put in force to enhance the prospects of women, of racial minorities, and of handicapped people.

The Manpower Services Commission (MSC) has transformed the functions of the Department of Employment, with powers to create job opportunities, to subsidise employers to keep on workers who might otherwise be made redundant, to train youngsters to acquire skills, and to retrain older people, on a vastly greater scale than envisaged in the early 1970s. It is true that unemployment has also risen to levels that would have been unthinkable at any time since the 1930s; but few doubt that but for the measures taken by the MSC (described by Reid, Chapter 18), the tally would be higher still.

Alongside this official apparatus countless private and collective initiatives have sprouted, from the small enterprises referred to by Falk (Chapter 16) to self-sufficient rural communes. 'Self-help' has acquired a new meaning since the days of Samuel Smiles, and 'mutual aid' no longer refers to working man's attempts to ward off starvation; rather, it refers to voluntary community-based attempts to bypass the difficulties of bureaucratic administrative procedures. Tenants' co-operatives both improve housing and employ labour to maintain the standard of their environment.

This is not meant to be a euphoric description of a revolutionary change in attitudes resulting in the overnight disappearance of an intractable problem. We merely want to show that the dialogue between academic researchers, legislators, administrators, and practitioners continues in a climate where there need not be despair that the case of change is not heard. Rereading the original contributions to the seminar, and the revised and updated versions substituted in some cases, the editors were left with two distinct, and not necessarily mutually exclusive, impressions: that some of the authors seem now very much out of date in their analyses and prescriptions; and that others seem to be describing conditions that are still the stock in trade of current observations of the lives of the disadvantaged groups in the old industrial areas. All this means is that there is nothing homogeneous about the past, the present, or the future of urban areas, and that it is therefore unlikely that any single system of explanation can fit all cases and still more unlikely that a simple and single prescription for amelioration can solve their problems. On the other hand, it also means that the workmanlike analysis of certain phenomena *can* lead to appropriate remedial action, and that neither the official mind nor the owning and managing groups in society are monolithically opposed to change.

I The Decline of Manufacturing Industry

1 A Long Term View of Employment Decentralisation from the Larger English Cities

A. M. Warnes

1.1 Introduction

This chapter takes a broad and long term view of the changing distributions of population and employment within extensively defined metropolitan areas. Local declines of employment dislocate habitual and valued patterns of living and working. They bear most heavily on the least mobile and the least occupationally flexible and therefore particularly on the least skilled and the older working population. To ameliorate the harmful effects of change, it has been argued, not only client-based social-welfare measures need to be used but also area-based planning measures. It is by no means clear, however, what form the latter should take, partly because the level of understanding of the changes that have been affecting the inner city is low. There is a danger that local and abrupt events distort the understanding of the general processes affecting the city and a possibility that they will have an undesirable influence upon planning policies. The interests of even the most disadvantaged groups are unlikely to be best served by attempts to recreate the inner city of the recent past; of more use would be a close assessment of present trends within the entire city and an identification of feasible ways in which these could be guided in favour of inner areas and population.

1.2 The symptoms of employment decentralisation

The net outward displacement of places of work and residence is a long-established characteristic of urban areas. Population decentralisation was a clear feature of seventeenth-century London, and in the same city in the late nineteenth century there was a very strong outward movement of manufacturing employment into suburbs that are now experiencing employment decline (see, for example, Jones and Judges, 1935; Wrigley, 1967; and Hall, 1962). It is not necessary for a city to be growing for decentralisation to take place, for an equally effective cause is the modernisation or improvement of housing in a city. New houses inevitably are found mainly beyond the existing buildings; additions to the housing stock not only are generally of lower density, but also encourage a lowering of densities in the existing stock. A persistent characteristic and problem of decentralisation has been that the outward shift of employment has lagged behind the displacement of population. Postwar planning policies have aimed for the more balanced development of expanding areas, but initially rising employment deficits remain a clear feature of such areas.

Decentralisation is inevitable if population expands or the urban functions increase their space requirements. It cannot be stopped by development control except by fossilising the city, although its forms, direction, and rate can be guided. Incidentally, it is clear that a consequence of a radical change in the structure of the national or urban economy is the acceleration of decentralisation, as a result of the increasing rate of obsolescence of some areas and buildings and the switching of priorities to the provision of other facilities.

The process of decentralisation has been recognised for a much longer time than many recent studies admit. Nineteenth-century references to employment displacement are not difficult to find, as in Weber's 1899 discussion of urban 'Tendencies and remedies', which concluded his survey of urban growth during that century (Weber, 1963, pp. 468–72). Wood (1974) has recently reminded us that the phenomenon was widely discussed and analysed in the 1930s and has suggested that recent authors would have profited from study of these earlier works.[1] It is only since the mid-1950s, however, that decentralisation has received closer attention in both Britain and the United States, and increasingly it has been argued

[1] Among the works cited are Thompson (1933), Creamer (1935), Woodbury (1953), Kitawega and Bogue (1955), and Reeder (1954).

that a fundamental change has begun in the intraurban distribution of population, activities, and employment. Support for this view comes mainly from the awareness that the administrative units at the heart of the cities have recently suffered absolute declines in employment rather than just relatively slow rates of growth. One of the purposes of this chapter is to question recent interpretations of these facts and to point out that, for any inner subarea of a city, there will come a time when its employment will cease to grow and begin to decline. No particular significance need be attached to this reversal, for its timing depends entirely upon the definition of the subarea. In general it can be stated that the closer the subarea to the centre the earlier it will enter a phase of employment decline. Evidence of inner-area job losses is therefore inadequate to identify major upheavals in urban structure, and indeed commentary in these terms serves only to dilute efforts to deal with the consequences of decline.

Of the many American papers on urban decentralisation, that by Berry and Cohen (1973) is one of the most recent and succinct.[2] They have cited some of the more extreme 'presages of disaster' to be found in the daily press and news magazines and shown that these are guilty of many misconceptions, or at least oversimplifications, that have grown up about the postwar evolution of the American city. The situation in the inner and central areas is not one of unleavened decline: 'There have been some dramatic changes of a directly contrary kind. The counterpoint they place to the loss of manufacturing jobs and retail trade must be orchestrated into a balanced interpretation of contemporary urban dynamics' (p. 447). They have shown that there has been continuing large investment in inner city manufacturing and a considerable expansion of office employment at the centres. Between 1960 and 1969 private and public office space increased by 44 per cent in the twelve largest US *standard metropolitan statistical areas* (SMSAs). Even in the Manhattan central business district (CBD) the rate of increase of private office space was higher in the 1960s than in earlier decades (Table 1.1). Their concluding assessment of the conflicting evidence is nevertheless that a radical restructuring of American cities is taking place, as much from social as from economic forces, with an understandable emphasis being placed on racial divisions as both an effect and a cause of population decentralisation. They have argued that

[2]Other useful papers are by Schnore and Klaff (1972), Hartshorn (1971), Kain (1968), James and Hughes (1973), and Moses and Williamson (1967).

Table 1.1 Gross floorspace in private office buildings, Manhattan CBD, 1936–70.

	1936	1950	1960	1963	1970
Space (million sq. ft.)	126	128	160	184	226
Compound annual growth rate from earlier date (%)		0.1	2.3	4.7	3.0

Source: Berry and Cohen (1973).

American cities are becoming multinodal rather than organised around a single highly-dominant core, which is irrefutable but nothing new. Geddes coined the term 'conurbation' well over half a century ago. In the absence of any clear evidence for any American city that employment is decentralising faster than population, or that 'gradients of distance accretion are now beginning to replace those of core-centred distance-decay within the larger megalopolitan complexes', the question of what is radical in contemporary urban change is bound to be asked.

Kain (1968) has been much less extreme in his conclusions from a very valuable analysis of employment trends in forty large American cities:

> If the [identified] changes in employment distributions continue, they will bring about even more changes in the shape of the metropolitan area. The extreme peaks will steadily erode away . . . over the long haul, these processes could result in a relatively 'flat' distribution of employment and population that is sharply different from what we know today. (p. 28)

Yet, despite the evidence reproduced in Table 1.2 that population

Table 1.2 Estimated mean annual absolute changes in population and employment for central cities and suburban rings of forty large SMSAs, 1948–63 (hundreds).

	Central city			Ring		
	1948–54	1954–58	1958–63	1948–54	1954–58	1958–63
Employment:						
Manufacturing	2	−21	−35	24	13	42
Wholesaling	−1	0.6	−2	4	8	8
Retailing	−6	2	−10	9	23	19
Services	5	10	3	5	9	8
Population:	5	0.3	−46	315	367	410

Source: Kain (1968), table 5, p. 17.

increases in the suburbs (SMSA rings) continued to be several times those of employment increases between 1948 and 1963, Kain has used the fact that certain sectors of employment, particularly manufacturing, decentralised at rapid rates in the period to support the conclusion that 'employment is dispersing even more rapidly than the metropolitan population' (p. 28). However, this has not been shown and is unlikely.

Turning to Britain, many parallels to the American experience and its interpretations can be found. In many of the larger ex-county boroughs and in the Greater London Council (GLC) employment declined during the 1960s. This was of considerable concern, not least to the finances of the local authorities, but much of the resulting commentary was again couched in too cataclysmic and pessimistic terms. Some clear changes between the 1950s and the early 1960s have been clearly demonstrated by Thomas (1968, section VI) in his analysis of population and employment changes in Birmingham, Bristol, Leeds, Liverpool, Manchester, Newcastle, and Sheffield. Table 1.3 reproduces salient figures from his analysis and adds additional details for 1921 and 1971 and for other inner-city authorities in the Liverpool and Manchester conurbations. One

Table 1.3 Employment changes in selected large central and inner cities of England and Wales, 1921–71.

City	Employment (thousands)				
	1921	1951	1961	1966	1971
Manchester	414	426	418	380	321
Salford	82	84	73	68	65
Stockport	53	63	60	62	63
Stretford	32	52	58	52	48
Liverpool	327	396	388	372	312
Bootle	28	38	40	38	41
Birkenhead	46	61	55	53	50
Birmingham		624	655	647	565
Bristol		196	208	219	203
Leeds		265	273	271	245
Newcastle		175	179	173	148
Sheffield		257	271	272	256

Note: The figures refer to the county borough areas (Stretford Municipal Borough) of the authorities, and no adjustments have been made for boundary changes during the period.
Source: Census workplace statistics.

simple result of taking a wider and longer-term view of the situation is that the early 1960s become less striking as the time when employment trends reversed. For example, of the tabulated authorities, Manchester, Salford, Stockport, Liverpool, and Birkenhead already had clear declines of employment in the 1950s. Bristol and Sheffield continued to show employment increases in the early 1960s; and more remarkably, earlier employment declines have been reversed in Stockport since 1961 and in Bootle since 1966. Nevertheless, as would be expected of these central authorities, which over recent decades have constituted progressively smaller proportions of their enveloping metropolitan areas, employment declines have steadily become more prevalent.

A more extensive study, carried out as part of the Political and Economic Planning (PEP) project into postwar urban growth in Britain directed by Peter Hall, has also examined intraurban changes in employment distribution (Hall *et al.*, 1973, pp. 206–31). This was done for 100 urban concentrations or *standard metropolitan labour areas* (SMLAs), although for data reasons the emphasis was again on the period 1951–66. This analysis was also entirely by a two-zone 'core' and 'ring', which despite their well-conceived definitions (pp. 127–9) must yield a limited, and in the last resort arbitrary, picture of decentralisation. Until sufficiently detailed area data are available to enable a study of metropolitan changes to be made using shifting definitions of the city over time, which would reflect the increasing spatial extent of variously defined functional areas, these deficiencies will remain. Even so, the broad picture assembled by the analysis does not suggest that the early 1960s were a period of revolutionary change:

> The tendency is clear: population has shown a marked tendency to decentralize from the core to the ring, while employment has shown a marked stability in its patterns, at least until recently . . . between 1951 and 1966 the proportion of [metropolitan] employment fell only very marginally from 74 to 71 per cent in the cores, rising from 26 to 29 per cent in the rings . . . but a closer look shows that the larger metropolitan areas had begun to show a distinct tendency to decentralize jobs as well as people, at any rate, in a relative sense, even by the 1950s. By the 1960s this trend was more distinct, and some of the larger areas were actually recording absolute losses of jobs in their cores coupled with increases in their suburban rings. (pp. 250–51)

Similar but more recent and detailed analyses are now available from the study of 'Urban Change in Britain', directed by Roy Drewett, John Goddard, and Nigel Spence and financed by the

Department of the Environment. (Department of the Environment (1976), *British cities: urban population and employment trends 1951–71*, Research Report 10 (London: DOE).) Their analysis was extended to three zones: the SMLA cores and rings with the addition of outer metropolitan rings to form *metropolitan economic labour areas* (MELAs).[3] The SMLA ring consisted of those contiguous local authorities from which more than 15 per cent of the working population commuted to the core, and the outer ring

Table 1.4 Decimal population and employment changes by MELA zones, 1951–71 (%).

Zone	Population		Employment	
	1951–61	*1961–71*	*1951–61*	*1961–71*
Urban cores	1.9	−2.8	6.7	−3.1
Metropolitan rings	13.3	17.2	6.6	15.0
Outer metropolitan rings	3.1	9.8	−0.4	3.9

Source: Department of the Environment (1976), tables 4 and 5, p. 10.

consisted of the areas sending more workers to the particular core than to any other. Unfortunately for the purposes of this chapter the analysis was carried out by the areas defined for 126 SMLAs in 1971 and was therefore subject to the limitations applying to any longitudinal analysis of urban structure using constant subareas. Despite this, and the clear evidence assembled of employment reverses in the cores after 1961, the weight of the evidence is that, while an acceleration of decentralisation has been taking place, radical changes have now occurred. The spread of population increases into the outer rings, and the onset after 1961 of population and employment decreases in the cores, are clearly shown in Table 1.4. Although the percentage core-employment decrease was greater than the percentage core-population decrease, in the rings the ratio of population to employment increases was a higher figure. This contrast, together with the fact that during the 1960s population increased faster than employment in the MELAs of Britain, means that 'in spite of the recent onset of job decentralisation, urban cores have become increasingly dependent for labour on the rest of the daily urban system' (p. 12).

[3]See Department of the Environment (1976) in which the authors' definitions of urban zones are described on pp. 58–9.

Table 1.5 Ratios of the proportions of population and employment in urban zones, 1951–71.

Year	Urban cores	Metropolitan rings	Outer metropolitan rings
1951	0.88	1.31	1.07
1961	0.85	1.35	1.11
1971	0.81	1.40	1.14

Source: Department of the Environment (1976), table 6, p. 12.

Table 1.5, reproduced from the Department of the Environment (1976) study, compares in the form of a ratio each urban zone's share of the total MELA population and employment. Ratios less than one indicate that a zone had a larger share of jobs than population. It can be seen that the decreasing ratios in the cores were matched by steadily rising ratios in the rings. As would be expected from using 1971 definitions, the outer rings have in recent years begun to accumulate substantial employment deficits as they have increasingly been drawn into their functional urban systems. 'The immediate inference that must be drawn from these ratios is that there is on aggregate an increasing separation of homes from workplaces in urban Britain with a consistent overall increase in the length of the journey to work' (p. 12).

Britain, then, is still a long way from the situation in which jobs are decentralising faster than people, particularly if the widening extent of the functional urban area is taken into account. Although absolute declines from the central authorities are now widely established, they are not yet reversing the tendency for job surpluses to increase in more central areas, both absolutely and relative to the local resident populations (see Lawton, 1968; Westergaard, 1957; and Warnes, 1972; and the chapter by Thomas on 'Home and workplace' in Hall *et al.*, 1973). The problems of decentralisation are still as much those of the social and economic implications of the increasing separation of homes from workplaces and lengthening journeys to work, as they are those of shrinking employment opportunities in inner districts.

The latter problems are severe locally, but neither the extent or the precise nature of the problems are yet well understood, partly because local analyses of employment change have been few and far between. Little at all is known for periods before 1951, except for the very largest cities, which, being administratively fragmented, have been subdivided for census purposes. The most detailed evidence is available for London, and it is particularly instructive to examine the employment record of its inner districts since 1921.

Thomas's PEP broadsheet again provides a convenient and substantial starting point (Thomas, 1968). The London conurbation was divided into three zones: the centre (the six former Metropolitan Boroughs of Finsbury, Holborn, St Marylebone, St Pancras, Westminster, and the City in 1951, and the Registrar General's conurbation in 1966), the remainder of inner London (the London County Council area in 1951, and the same area without the London Borough of Greenwich in 1966) and the remainder of the conurbation (the conurbation in 1951, and the GLC area in 1966). His figures are presented in Table 1.6, supplemented by figures for

Table 1.6 Employment and residents in employment in London, 1921–71 (thousands).

	1921	1951	1961	1961	1966	1971
Employment						
Central London	1,139	1,241	1,307	1,415	1,304	1,241
Remainder of inner London	1,279	1,320	1,283	1,070	1,025	797
Remainder of conurbation	807	1,727	1,897	1,931	1,994	1,778
Conurbation/GLC	3,225	4,288	4,488	4,415	4,323	3,816
OMA					1,911	1,959
Residents in employment						
Central London	289	255	194	158	135	116
Remainder of inner London	1,623	1,556	1,509	1,432	1,344	1,159
Remainder of conurbation	1,213	2,413	2,484	2,505	2,496	2,373
Conurbation/GLC	3,125	4,194	4,188	4,095	3,975	3,648
OMA					2,284	2,417
Employment imbalance						
Central London:	+850	+1,016	+1,113	+1,257	+1,169	+1,125
as % of employed population	+294	+452	+574	+796	+866	+970
Remainder of inner London:	−344	−236	−226	−362	−319	−362
as % of employed population	−21	−15	−15	−25	−24	−31
Remainder of conurbation:	−406	−686	−587	−575	−503	−595
as % of employed population	−33	−28	−24	−23	−20	−25
Conurbation/GLC:	+100	+95	+300	+320	+347	+168
as % of employed population	+3	+2	+7	+8	+9	+5
OMA:					−373	−458
as % of employed population					−16	−19

Notes: The first set of figures given for 1961 are based on the definitions used for 1921 and 1951; the second set are for the same definitions used in 1966 and 1971. Following the census convention, persons with no fixed or stated workplace are assumed to work in their zones of residence.
Sources: Thomas (1968), table A4, p. 417; 1921 and 1971, census workplace tables.

1921 and 1971 taken from the census workplace statistics. Some figures for the outer metropolitan area (OMA) subdivision of the South-East region in 1966 and 1971 are also added. As Thomas has concluded:

> In central London, the decline in employment over 1961–66 . . . may have more than matched the growth over the previous decade, but population has fallen steadily. The employment surplus of 1.2 million in 1966 was about 30,000 more than in 1951 . . . . In the rest of London, the trends have been in the same direction over 1961–66 as they were over 1951–66. Employment and population in inner London, excluding the centre, have fallen steadily. Employment and population in outer London have grown rapidly. The employment deficit in both these areas has decreased. It was generally easier for residents of London to get jobs near to their homes in 1966 than it was in earlier years. (p. 400)

When changes since 1921 and within individual boroughs are also examined, the view that no radical change took place in the early 1960s is reinforced. Table 1.7 demonstrates that the decline after

Table 1.7 Employment in inner districts of London, 1921–71 (thousands).

Metropolitan borough	London borough	1921	1951	1961	1966	1971
ꞌ City of London		431	339	391	361	340
Finsbury	} Islington ·	99 } 185	82 } 174	85 } 176	166	130
Islington		86	92	91		
Holborn		81	104	119		
St Pancras	} Camden	103 } 216	123 } 259	110 } 258	213	223
Hampstead		32	32	29		
Westminster		320	457	459		
St Marylebone	} Westminster	104 } 479	147 } 655	144 } 656	596	544
Paddington		55	51	53		
Kensington	Kensington	87 } 121	84 } 115	81 } 109	102	88
Chelsea	and Chelsea	34	31	28		
Hackney		68	78	70		
Shoreditch	} Hackney	54 } 133	49 } 141	37 } 121	106	100
Stoke Newington		11	14	14		
Bethnal Green		32	25	22		
Poplar	} Tower Hamlets	66 } 210	56 } 177	46 } 153	137	113
Stepney		112	96	85		
Southwark		60	66	76		
Bermondsey	} Southwark	67 } 185	57 } 185	49 } 183	164	136
Camberwell		58	62	58		

Sources: Census reports on workplaces.

1961 of employment in the central area, far from being a completely new trend, was a reassertion and spread of a tendency established during 1921–51 in the City of London and several adjacent boroughs. Indeed, the widespread extent of employment declines, and the size of the percentage losses during 1921–51 are surprising. The following areas were most severely affected: the City (21 per cent loss), Finsbury (17 per cent), Shoreditch (9 per cent), Paddington (8 per cent), Bethnal Green (22 per cent), Poplar (15 per cent), Stepney (14 per cent), Bermondsey (15 per cent), Chelsea (9 per cent), and Kensington (10 per cent). Deptford and Hampstead also sustained small net losses of employment during the period. In the following ten years the City, Finsbury, and Paddington reversed the earlier trend and had a net employment gain of 57,000 jobs, all but 5,000 of which were in the City. The other listed boroughs all continued to lose jobs, but Holborn experienced net gains in both the intercensal periods (28 per cent in 1921–51, 16 per cent in 1961–66), as did Westminster (43 and 0.5 per cent). St Pancras and St Marylebone shared a pattern of substantial increases up to 1951 but decreases thereafter.

Given these finer details it is possible to argue that the steep rise in office employment in the City during the 1950s, in part associated with the reconstruction of sites devastated during the war, was a temporary feature that disguised more persistent employment decreases in a dozen central boroughs. When the office boom began to dissipate in the early 1960s the twentieth-century trend became apparent once more. It should also be remembered that, although the rates of employment decline in the inner authorities areas accelerated through the 1960s, they have so far remained below these of the decline in the employed population. In the whole of the inner London area, between 1961 and 1966 employment declined by 6.3 per cent and the employed resident population by 7 per cent, while between 1966 and 1971 the comparable figures were 12.5 and 20.6 per cent. It is true, however, that the continuing rise in job surpluses in the inner area has been because of the buoyancy of employment at the centre, and that after 1966 in the remainder of the inner area the 22 per cent employment loss exceeded a 14 per cent population loss. The specific and serious problems of this zone will shortly be discussed in more detail; but as evidence of a major upheaval in London's spatial structure, these exceptional employment losses must be evaluated in combination with the continuing rise in employment deficits during 1966–71 in the remainder of the conurbation and in the OMA. Overall, and at long last, employment decentralisation is beginning to approach the rate of population decentralisation, but it has not yet-matched the latter.

1.3 Stability in the gross patterns of population and employment

As has become clear, the analysis of employment decentralisation using simply cores and rings can only give a partial picture of metropolitan evolution, and it tends to put too much emphasis on the waxing and waning of totals in arbitrary administrative areas. While it has been argued that nothing radically new is happening on a metropolitan scale, but rather that long-standing trends are accelerating, the possibility remains that a more fundamental change in the intraurban distribution of employment has recently begun. If this is to be identified, however, a more subtle and detailed analysis of the evidence is required. An attempt must be made to gain more precise generalisations of the distribution of employment within cities and to see whether the generalisations need to be altered over time. The obvious approach to this task is to specify the employment density gradients of towns in an exactly similar manner to the well-established methods of describing gross population densities.

Although census data are much less comprehensive for employment than for population, it is nevertheless surprising that published studies of employment density gradients are few and for the most part disappointingly idiographic. Clark (1964–65, 1967) has reviewed the field and attempted to define the general features of these gradients. They are: first, that employment densities decline with distance from the city centre at a negative exponential rate; and second, that unlike population densities they are at an exceptionally high maximum in the city centre. This implies that the exponential gradient of employment density is steeper than that of population density.

Recently, it has been argued that the linear exponential function

$$y_x = ae^{-bx}$$

where y_x is the gross density of employment at distance x from the centre and a and b are constants, successfully models the distributions of employment in Paris, London, Manchester, and Liverpool

Table 1.8 **Linear and exponential regressions of gross employment densities per hectare and distance from centre.**

City and date	Regression coefficient a	b	r^2	$\frac{\ln a}{b}$	C(p)	F	d.f.
Manchester:							
1921	57.40	−0.164	0.938	24.70	0.0689	120.65	1,8
1951	50.40	−0.156	0.918	25.13	0.0659	89.47	1,8
1966	45.61	−0.152	0.918	25.13	0.0634	89.00	1,8
1971	39.64	−0.145	0.905	25.38	0.0603	75.89	1,8
Liverpool:							
1921	26.05	−0.166	0.633	19.64	0.0509	17.26	1,10
1951	23.05	−0.133	0.801	23.68	0.0491	40.21	1,10
1966	25.53	−0.141	0.876	22.98	0.0511	70.85	1,10
1971	26.58	−0.136	0.810	24.12	0.0600	42.71	1,10
London:							
1921	96.16	−0.153	0.894	29.84	0.0821	151.06	1,18
1951	145.04	−0.141	0.938	35.30	0.0933	271.35	1,18
1961	134.16	−0.130	0.921	37.68	0.0911	208.77	1,18
1966	88.32	−0.112	0.925	40.01	0.0799	196.40	1,16
1971	80.72	−0.111	0.891	39.56	0.0775	131.09	1,16

Notes: $(\ln a)/b$ = the radius in kilometres, R, at which estimated density is 1 per hectare

$C(p)$ = the proportion of city employment estimated to lie within the central p = 0.01 of the city area. It is given by

$$C(P) = \frac{e^{-b}R\sqrt{\rho}\,(bR\sqrt{\rho}+1)-1}{e^{-bR}(bR+1)-1}$$

Two-kilometre concentric zones of the conurbations were used for the analysis, and no separate figure for the city centres was included.

(see Bussiere, 1970; Blumenfeld, 1972; and Warnes, 1975). Moreover, as can be seen in Table 1.8, although the explanations provided by the model have slightly decreased over the period 1921–71 there is no clear sign of radical change. At each date, and in each of the three large British conurbations examined, the linear exponential function is a highly significant representation of the distribution.

On the other hand, the results from London and Manchester clearly show the steady decline of both the estimated gross density of employment at the centre (a) and the exponential rate of density decline with distance from the centre (b). Indeed, the estimated central density of employment in London has declined by about 45 per cent since 1951, and since 1921 the rate of exponential decline has fallen by 30 per cent; yet, the same basic form remains a robust representation of the distribution.

This flattening of the employment distribution does, at this level of generalisation, imply at least one other change in the characteristics of the employment distribution. If the empirically determined density gradient is used to define the extent of a city area, e.g. by identifying the radius at which employment densities fall to 1 per hectare, and if the central area is defined as 1 per cent of the total, then using integration by parts of the density function it is possible to calculate the proportion of city employment in the centre. The results of these calculations are shown in Table 1.8. In the case of London a marked shift away from the central area is indicated. However, this result is of more theoretical than practical interest, for the linear exponential function is least successful in representing the exceptionally high but very localised extremes of employment density at the centre. More analysis has shown that, if a finer division of the total city area is used, more complex exponential functions will yield superior generalisations of the employment distribution, but these have similarly shown stability during the last fifty years (for further details see Warnes, 1975).

1.4 The implications of decentralisation for inner area policies

The discussion has been concerned entirely with aggregate employment change, which in itself cannot elucidate the structure and causes of job losses. As yet few details have been established, but the surge of interest in the 'inner city problem' during the mid-1970s is now yielding through the published literature a substantial reinforcement of our knowledge.[4] Successive analyses, drawing on different sources, concur that inner-area job losses have been primarily caused by the decline of manufacturing employment at a rate exceeding the national decline of this sector (see in particular the work of Cameron, 1977b; and Lloyd and Mason, 1978; the

[4]Particularly comprehensive have been the studies based on industry data banks for Manchester (Lloyd and Mason, 1978), Manchester and Merseyside (Dicken and Lloyd, 1978), and Clydeside and the West Midlands (Firn and Swales, 1978). There are several other useful papers in the second issue of *Regional Studies*, vol. 12 (1978). Also see Bull (1978), Cameron (1977b), Dennis (Chapter 2 of this book), Foreman-Peck and Gripaios (1977), Fagg (1973), Henderson (1974), and Keeble (Chapter 5 of this book).

paper by Cameron and Evans, 1973, on the British conurbation centres is also relevant).

Mortlock's (1972) study of employment change in London found that during the 1960s, whereas trends in its service employment matched national change, its manufacturing losses had to be put down to local effects. Lomas (1974) has also singled out manufacturing as a sector for special concern, not least because it claimed 75 per cent of the notified redundancies in Greater London during 1966–73. Other conclusions of his study were that 'it is certain that the contraction of manufacturing was proceeding faster after 1966 than before' and that 'much of the decline is permanent and cannot be expected to be replaced if nationally manufacturing enjoys a resurgence' (pp. 1–6). This view was based on an inspection of Department of Employment records about the reasons given by firms for shedding workers, in which the following frequently occur: closure of plant, relocation, compulsory purchase, reorganisation including mergers, and economic difficulties and changes. Very similar conclusions, and verification that losses are closures rather than relocations, have recently been provided by Gripaios (Chapter 3) for London, Lloyd and Mason (1978) for Manchester, Bull (1978) for Clydeside, and others.

The decline in manufacturing in the inner city has only been partially compensated for by its growth in peripheral urban areas. The direct numerical importance of industrial migrations or suburbanisations is generally agreed to be a minor component of spatial change in manufacturing employment, most studies concluding that it is the high deathrates of jobs in the inner city and the favourable birthrates of the suburbs that have been much more important (see, for example, Wood 1974; Gripaios, 1977b; Foreman-Peck and Gripaios, 1977; and Lloyd and Mason, 1978). Also offsetting the decline has been the growth of tertiary sector jobs, particularly in the central area but also more widely in the case of education and local government. This trend not only reflects national structural economic change but also illustrates again the locational selectivity of different types of economic activity. Until recently at least, commercial, retail, and administrative activities have tended to favour central locations, whereas manufacturing has avoided the city centre's high land values and rents but succeeded in adjacent inner areas.

None of the analyses so far available has been able to account for the severity of the decline in inner city manufacturing by reference to national trends, and it therefore does appear that there are now locational disadvantages specific to these areas. As Keeble (Chapter 5) has summarised the most recently available evidence:

> ... in Birmingham, London and Clydeside ... the single most important element in inner-city employment decline through closures is the loss of relatively large factories; and this in turn could well reflect locational evaluation by multiplant firms of their operating costs and future potential compared with company factories elsewhere. (p. 116)

There have also been substantial contractions of employment in continuing plants, large and small.

The inner area's disadvantages are disparate and difficult to evaluate. They consist partly of environmental characteristics, notably the obsolescent or unfitted premises and the restricted availability of large plots for development, and partly of more inherent locational attributes, such as relative inaccessibility to the national road network or high land values. Many subsidiary factors can be debated. For example, do the quality and age of capital equipment in inner city plants tend to be lower than elsewhere, resulting in a lower productivity of labour and accounting for a higher propensity for closure? Rather more frequently discussed has been the fragmented land-use and ownership patterns of the inner city, as well as the comprehensive redevelopment and land-use zoning policies of local authorities. To what extent have these directly caused closures, prevented expansion, or diverted new development, and to what extent have any difficulties or restraints generated by physical planning created an unfavourable climate of opinion for industrial investment in the inner city?

Compounding the inherent problems of the inner cities has been their susceptibility to adverse national trends. Changes in industrial organisation and manufacturing processes are commonly associated with an increasing preference for larger and modern plants on larger sites. The relative decline of the small-scale private manufacturing concern has also been to the particular detriment of inner city employment. Despite the multiplicity of these influences, it is nevertheless possible that their effects would be accepted as 'normal' manifestations of the dynamism of modernising cities were it not for their exacerbation during the 1970s by Britain's lamentable manufacturing performance. Recession, structural change, and even the changing attitudes of, on the one hand, government and local authorities towards entrepreneurs and, on the other, both employers and employees towards their economic roles have all been cited as factors in Britain's manufacturing lethargy. In each case it is possible logically to deduce, if not empirically to demonstrate, that the consequences for concerns in the inner city have been particularly serious.

Given all these complexities it is questionable on practical, if not epistemological, grounds whether it is worth attempting to distinguish the inner city dimensions of employment change from either the national (and regional) factors or specific local conditions. Does more need to be done than to achieve more effective national economic management at the one scale and, at the other, to react at a local authority level to the closure of plant X, to rationalisation in company Y, and to a reluctance to take up vacancies in occupation Z?

A modest view of the advantages of evaluating recent inner-city changes from an understanding of decentralisation is therefore necessary, but some points could usefully be appreciated more widely. In the long term it is virtually inevitable that employment declines in inner areas. However, employment has traditionally been more centralised in the city than population and has normally shown a lag in its rate of dispersal. Put at a general level, the forces of inertia in the intraurban location of employment are more influential than the same forces applied to housing and population. The consequence is clear enough: adjustments in the intraurban distribution of employment tend to be abrupt rather than gradual and to occur at the most unpropitious times. They are characteristically dislocative and uncomfortable. Often they are precipitated by national changes in the structure, organisation, or volume of economic activity, such as the growth and decline of industries, a phase of the concentration of ownership, or wholesale changes in transport. The questions that arise are whether municipal authorities should do more than react to events in train. Should they attempt to detect incipient changes or anticipate even further ahead? Is it possible to plan a gradual adjustment of intraurban employment distributions? As well as considering whether public authorities can take a more positive role of this kind, an examination of existing inner-city management policies would be valuable because it might well identify ways in which the problems of the inner city have been avoidably increased.

To illustrate this last point, let us conclude by discussing the implications of inner-area redevelopment policies on local employment, using the case of Manchester. In 1977 jobs and to a greater extent industrial and wholesale firms were heavily concentrated in the innermost part of the city, itself only the core of the South-East Lancashire – North-East Cheshire conurbation (i.e. approximately Greater Manchester). Firms were characteristically very small, and nearly a third of all firms were in shared premises. Millar and Mellon (1970) have identified some of the locational disadvantages of the inner city. Approximately one-quarter of the floorspace was classified as non-conforming land use, and this was particularly pronounced with the lighter industrial types and construction, which had less than half of their floorspace in zoned industrial areas. The city's industry was widely affected by redevelopment proposals (Table 1.9): 'the number of jobs likely to be involved is over 5,000 each in clothing and wholesale distribution, 4,400 in paper printing and publishing, and 2,000 in construction'.

While the redevelopment pressures from these policies in Manchester and elsewhere may have lessened since 1966 with the cutback in slum clearance and road proposals, they have been supplemented by the pressures for commercial redevelopment on the fringes of CBDs. Overall, the difficulties created for manufacturing are known to have increased mobility rates in Manchester, and they have probably also curtailed expansion, prevented new growth, and even hastened closure. It is not just that the supply of old but cheap, flexible, and central premises has been constricted, but also that a climate of uncertainty, difficulty, and change has been created. When to these pressures is added the rigorous elimination of the traditional arterial ribbons (accommodating an unrecorded variety and volume of small units of employment), then it appears probable

Table 1.9 Floorspace affected by redevelopment proposals in Manchester, 1966.

Industrial group	By slum clearance (%)	By road and other proposals (%)	Total floorspace ('000 sq. ft)
Textiles	1.3	24.8	2,008
Clothing and footwear	13.0	20.5	2,818
Timber, furniture, etc.	34.6	23.8	998
Paper, printing, publishing	25.5	22.0	2,660
Wholesale distribution	9.1	29.4	6,225
All types	9.6	14.2	35,559

Source: Select figures recalculated from Millar and Mellon (1970), table 2, p. 386.

that the way in which redevelopment has been tackled has had a strong hand in the local rapid contraction of inner city employment. Planning for the regulated decentralisation of population by reducing densities, and planning for the improvement of inner city environments by segregating non-conforming land uses, may have been detrimental for the remaining workforce, particularly the unskilled or those requiring adjacent or part time work. In the general concern for housing and the residential environment, too little attention may have been given to the needs of small-scale employing units.

1.5 Conclusions

Population is still decentralising from the cities more rapidly than employment, and despite the falls in employment in many urban cores in the post-1951 period there is no sign as yet of a radical restructuring of the cities. As a result central surpluses and peripheral deficits of employment continue to increase. To counteract the lengthening journeys to work that these trends produce it is desirable to promote employment growth in the developing suburbs and satellite towns, and further decreases of employment in central and inner districts may be countenanced. Some other implications can be drawn from a study of decentralisation over a long period. The driving forces behind the dispersal of population and employment are so intimately bound up with the modernisation of a city's physical facilities and with improvements or changes in its inhabitants' lifestyles, and they have been so durable, that it is surely the folly of Canute's advisers in present economic circumstances to attempt to reserve or even resist them. This is not to say that decentralisation has always progressed smoothly and will continue to do so, nor that it doesn't create problems. On the contrary, periods of exceptionally rapid change have characterised the process, as with the displacement of railway termini construction during the nineteenth century, the rapid growth of suburban employment in the late 1930s, and the rapid decline of inner city manufacturing from the early 1960s. Relatively abrupt changes, particularly in individual employment sectors, are more characteristic than gradual trends. This view of decentralisation suggests that the required policy response to a new emphasis or manifestation of the process should be specific to the affected sector of employment.

More broadly conceived positive planning policies could easily achieve very little at great cost.

An argument that inner city redevelopment and other planning policies have stifled important sectors of the urban economy has been presented. If this has any force, a broader conclusion is reached about the dangers of sectional policies if the widest possible consideration is not given to their spatial or areal impact. Every effort must be made to relate and integrate housing, employment, and transport investment. Comprehensive environmental management may or may not be superior to a policy of non-intervention in the allocation of land to different uses, but perhaps the worst of all possible worlds is partial intervention without the fullest evaluation of its implications.

2 The Decline of Manufacturing Employment in Greater London, 1966–74

Robert Dennis

2.1 Introduction[1]

It has been accepted ever since the Abercrombie Plan that the continued growth of the London city region must be accompanied by the decentralisation of both people and industry to locations beyond the existing urban fringe. It was considered that the decline, first of population and later of industry, in the inner urban core was to be welcomed. It was argued, and it is still argued by some, that this decline would facilitate an improvement in environmental conditions, particularly housing conditions, for those remaining in the capital. This view was supported by central government, the Greater London Council (GLC), the Strategic Plan for the South-East, as well as the Greater London Development Plan inquiry.

However, in recent years this view on overspill has come under increasing criticism. It has been argued that the industrial decline of London arises from decentralisation, which has caused structural changes resulting in excessively high unemployment in some areas. In 1976 the GLC itself decided to withdraw, where possible, from its support of its expanding towns schemes. It now wishes to attract industry back into the capital and has begun to implement policies

[1]This chapter was first published in *Urban Studies*, vol. 15 (1978).

aimed at achieving this. The GLC and others have argued that the movement out of London is partly the result of the government's regional policies and that these policies need to be modified if London is to maintain a semblance of balance in its employment structure.

The research presented in this chapter is derived from a regional project by the Department of Industry's Research and Planning Unit for South-East England. It was undertaken to examine the nature of the fall in manufacturing employment over the nine-year period from 1966 to 1974 and in particular to assess the role of decentralisation policies, by both local and central government. After outlining the nature of the data used in this chapter, the industrial structure of London is examined to assess its role in the industrial decline. The major part of the chapter is devoted to an analysis of the components of London's industrial decline; and finally, causes are sought for the high rate of factory closures in London.[2]

2.2 The data used in examining the nature of the decline

The Department of Industry has maintained a register of all closures of manufacturing establishments in Greater London since 1966 employing twenty or more people. These have been classified into three categories: transfers to new locations (establishments that have closed in Greater London and relocated in a new establishment elsewhere); transfers to existing locations (establishments that have closed but relocated most of the production to existing establishments in the enterprise elsewhere); and complete closures (closures of establishments involving little or no transfer of production to a related plant elsewhere). The analysis in the second part of this chapter regards the first two categories as constituting industrial movement from London.

There are several problems with these data and their classification. First, our knowledge of closures is inevitably incomplete. This is particularly so for the period since 1971 when the old employment returns were replaced by the new Census of Employment as

---

[2]In fact the employment decline in London in the study period covered only eight years, because the decline was measured from the mid-year employment figures for 1966 and 1974 whereas the industrial closure data covered the full nine years.

the main source of information about factory closures. These two different records are in the process of reconciliation by the Business Statistics Office. Most of these unrecorded closures are likely to be among the smaller establishments. Second, while it is relatively easy to determine whether or not a plant has closed, it is much more difficult to assess what type of closure it was. Because of the department's national Register of Openings and Closures, in the case of the first category of closure (a transfer to a new location) the record is likely to be comprehensive. The distinction between the other two categories (transfers to existing locations and complete closures) is often a fine one because of inadequate information, and unfortunately it is frequently impossible after the closure has occurred to find out anything that will help in this assessment. There may therefore be a bias in the data in favour of classification as a complete closure rather than classification as a transfer to an existing location.

These closures are measured in terms of the total employment lost as a result of each closure, which, in order to allow for any rundown before the time of closure, is taken to be the peak recorded employment in the twenty-four months prior to closure.

The data on openings of manufacturing establishments are also derived from the department's register. As with the closure information, this also relates (in London) to establishments employing twenty people or more. The employment relating to these openings is that for the last quarter of 1974 or the nearest available to that date.

2.3 Employment decline and the industrial structure

The decline in Greater London's population has been a well-established trend over a number of decades, whereas the decline in manufacturing employment is a much more recent phenomenon beginning in the early 1960s, although the employment total was constant for a decade before that.

In the period under consideration (1966–74) London's population fell by an estimated 9.4 per cent. The decline in the inner group of boroughs (group A, shown in Figure 2.1) was, of course, much greater (17.3 per cent). Compared with this decline of 9.4 per cent in population, manufacturing employment declined by 27 per cent in the same period – a much more dramatic decline although of a

1 CITY OF LONDON
2 HAMMERSMITH
3 ISLINGTON
4 KENSINGTON AND CHELSEA
5 WESTMINSTER
6 HACKNEY
7 TOWER HAMLETS

———— Inner London (Group A Boroughs)

Fig. 2.1   Greater London boroughs

shorter duration than the fall in population.[3] Some 390,000 manufacturing jobs were lost to the capital in these eight years, leaving
only 900,000 by June 1974. Nationally, in the same period the
number of employees in manufacturing industries declined by
703,000 or 8.4 per cent (Department of Employment, 1975).

[3]Unfortunately, there is no continuous series of employment figures for the
Greater London area, nor indeed for any area below standard regional level,
which is on a comparable basis with the Department of Employment's national
and regional estimates. These continuous series take account of the discontinuities due to the change in industrial classification in 1969 and the introduction
of the Census of Employment in 1971. The method that they used to obtain these
estimates is described in Department of Employment (1975). The estimate of
390,100 manufacturing jobs lost to London over the period 1966–74, which is
used in this chapter, was obtained by the addition of the job loss that occurred in
each of the three subperiods 1966–69 (1958 Standard Industrial Classification
(SIC) insurance card count), 1969–71 (1968 SIC, insurance card count), and
1971–74 (1968 Census of Employment). This estimate of the total job loss was
used to calculate the estimated percentage job-loss by dividing it by the 1966
figure for manufacturing employment, i.e. 1,436,800 (1958 SIC, insurance card
count).

It may be thought that the decline in London's manufacturing base can be explained by an unfavourable industrial structure. If, for example, it could be shown that London's employment structure was dominated by nationally declining industries, the acceptance of a structural explanation of this change would be justified.

In order to examine the importance of industrial structure a standard shift-share method was applied to Department of Employment data for each of the periods 1966–69, 1969–71, and 1971–74 for all manufacturing sectors at Order Heading (OH) level. Briefly, the shift-share technique assumes that the total employment change in any particular local industrial sector is the outcome of three factors: first, employment change in the national economy as a whole; second, national employment change in that particular industry; and third, a residual regional or local employment change unaccounted for by the other two factors. For all manufacturing industry in the area the numerical values of the corresponding factors for each industrial sector have to be added together, so that the total manufacturing employment change can be split into a 'national' effect, an 'industrial mix' effect, and a 'local' effect. If an adverse industrial structure were the most important factor in the decline in London's manufacturing employment, the industrial mix factor would be expected to have a high negative value relative to the national effect and more especially the local effect. Table 2.1 summarises the results of the shift-share calculations.

The figures in the table show that over the whole period only 30,000 of the estimated total manufacturing job loss of 390,100 (or 7.7 per cent) can be attributed to the industrial structure of the capital. In contrast the local effect, i.e. the employment loss attributable to neither national nor industrial mix effects, accounted

Table 2.1 Shift-share analysis: Greater London manufacturing employment by OH level, 1966–74 (thousands).

Period	Total manufacturing employment change	National effect	Industrial mix effect	Local effect
1966–69	−145.0	−43.2	+15.6	−117.4
1969–71	− 97.6	−32.9	− 3.7	− 61.0
1971–74	−147.5	+31.5	−41.9	−137.1
1966–74	−390.1	−44.6	−30.0	−305.5

for 305,500 (or 78.3 per cent) of the employment decline. This pattern was repeated in each of the three subperiods. In each case the local effect accounted for over 60 per cent of the decline, whereas the industrial mix factor was relatively insignificant and even positive in the period 1966–69. The relative dominance of the local effect over national and structural effects shown by this analysis is in line with another calculation for the Greater London area over the period 1961–71 using Census of Population data (Weatheritt and Lovett, 1976).

Two further observations reinforce the conclusion that industrial structure cannot explain the extent of the decline in manufacturing employment in the Greater London area during this period. First, compared with Great Britain as a whole Greater London had a relatively favourable industrial structure. If Greater London had had the national industrial mix in 1966, total manufacturing employment would have been expected to fall by some 65,000 due to industrial mix factors alone. As has been shown (Table 2.1), the actual 1966 industrial structure accounts for the loss of only 30,000 jobs in this way. Second, the low value attributed to industrial mix factors does not appear to be due to using employment figures aggregated to OH level. It has been argued that it is futile to conduct a shift-share analysis at the OH level of industrial disaggregation because such analyses gravely underestimate the importance of structure in employment change (Buck, 1970). In order to test that the results in Table 2.1 were not due to unjustifiable aggregation, the employment data for the period 1971–74 were examined at a Minimum List Heading (MLH) level, and the identical shift-share technique was performed on them. The results of the calculation are compared with those for the same period at an OH level in Table 2.2.

The table shows that only 1,000 more of the total manufacturing job loss can be attributed to industrial structure by disaggregating to

Table 2.2 Shift-share analysis: Greater London manufacturing employment, 1971–74 (thousands)

Level of disaggregation	Change in manufacturing employment	National effect	Industrial mix effect	Local effect
OH	−147.5	+31.5	−41.9	137.1
MLH	−147.5	+31.5	−42.9	136.1

an MLH level. This result indicates that in the case of London in this period disaggregation to an MLH level does not significantly increase the importance of the industrial mix factor.

Thus, the evidence presented suggests that the decline in manufacturing employment in Greater London is caused not by an unfavourable industrial structure but by local effects or what may be termed 'conurbation factors'.

2.4 The components of industrial decline

In the period 1966–74 manufacturing employment in Greater London declined by 390,100. This net employment loss is made up of several components:
(a) employment lost through factory closures;
(b) employment created by factory openings; and
(c) employment change at plants remaining open throughout this period.

The Department of Industry's Register of Closures shows that 2,600 manufacturing establishments employing twenty or more are recorded as having closed between 1966 and 1974, with an estimated loss of 280,300 jobs or some 72 per cent of the total manufacturing employment decline of 390,100 in this period. The Register of Openings records some 3,000 jobs created by firms moving into London from elsewhere, with a further 9,900 jobs created by enterprises entirely new to manufacturing. The net loss of employment arising from the balance between the opening and closing of manufacturing establishments employing twenty or more is therefore some 267,400 or 69 per cent of the overall job loss. Clearly, therefore, it is the high closure rate, rather than a general shrinkage of manufacturing employment at plants in existence in London throughout this period, that is primarily responsible for London's industrial decline.

2.5 Industrial movement

The popular view of the closure of manufacturing industry in London is that it is primarily due to firms moving out of the metropolis (see, for example, Shepherd, Westaway, and Lee, 1974). In isolating the role of this movement in the industrial decline of London the analysis shows that the loss of 97,100 jobs may be attributed to the closure of London plants and the transfer of production to locations elsewhere. Of these closures some 41 per cent are recorded as transfers to existing locations by multiplant companies. In addition to this movement out of London it may be claimed that London suffers a decline in employment through the setting up of new branches elsewhere without any closure of the London parent plant. In examining this claim it has been assumed that all the loss of employment at the London plant since the time of formation of the new branch is attributable solely to this factor. However, with a national decline in manufacturing employment this must be an overestimate. On this basis there has been a further net loss of some 8,200 jobs attributable to this type of industrial movement. Adding together the effects on London of transfers and the creation of branches it seems that industrial movements account for the loss of 105,300 jobs or some 27 per cent of the total industrial decline in Greater London.

It may be argued that, even with the wide interpretation of the term 'industrial movement' adopted in this analysis, there is some undercounting of the role of movement in London's industrial decline, for, as Atkins (1973) has demonstrated, the related closure of the parent plant may take place many years after the opening of the new branch. In so far as these delayed transfers are known to involve some movement of production to the branch plant, account has already been taken of this. It may also be, however, that the existence of a more modern plant elsewhere ultimately threatens the viability of the parent plant without any movement of production necessarily being involved. Unfortunately, it is not possible to quantify this because of a lack of information as to the circumstances that led to the closure. An examination of all closures in this period, that were recorded as the parent plants of new branch openings in the postwar period, however, indicates that at most the employment loss was about 28,500. Most of these were already attributed to industrial movement in the calculations given above. It is possible to conclude therefore that, while industrial movement out of the metropolis is a significant factor in its decline, it is not the most important explanation.

It is interesting to see the relative importance of the different types of location to which this industrial movement has been taking place. Some 22,100 jobs have been lost in the capital due to the transfer of establishments from London to the government's Assisted Areas; of these it is estimated that 41 per cent were moves into existing plants of multiplant firms. A loss of a further 14,100 jobs could be due to declines in employment at London parent establishments when branches were opened in these areas. Thus, some 36,200 jobs or 9 per cent of the total employment decline can be attributed to movement to Assisted Areas by London firms.

The New and Expanding Towns, supported by both the GLC and the central government in this period, have obviously been an important destination. The transfer of establishments from London to these overspill towns has been responsible for a larger loss of jobs in London than has that to the Assisted Areas, totalling some 26,400 in all. Eighty per cent of this job loss to overspill towns was due to the movement of establishments to new locations, with only a limited movement to existing plants. On the other hand, the creation of branches originating from London parent plants in these towns has been associated with a small net gain in employment at the parent plant. Overall then, movement to the London overspill towns accounted for the loss of only 26,000 jobs or 7 per cent of the decline in manufacturing employment in this period.

The remaining 'unplanned' movement from London, primarily to locations within the South-East and East Anglia, accounted for 43,100 or 11 per cent of the total industrial decline – a somewhat higher proportion than movement to either the Assisted Areas or the overspill towns. This 11 per cent included the loss of about 48,600 jobs from transfers to these locations, half of which were to existing plants – a higher proportion than in either of the other two categories of location. This relatively large job loss was to some extent offset by the increase in employment of 5,500 jobs at the London parent plants of the new branches created at these remaining locations.

The analysis of employment changes at branch units and parent plants suggests that the shorter-distance branch moves are essentially extensions of the activities of the parent plant and facilitate its continued expansion, whereas the branch moves to the peripheral regions are more likely to involve whole sections of economic activity and are more self-contained and generally much larger developments than their short distance counterparts.

2.6 Complete closures

The loss of employment arising from complete factory closures in Greater London, unconnected with any significant movement elsewhere, amounted to some 183,000, whereas the openings of new manufacturing enterprises created some 9,900 new jobs. In addition a further 3,000 jobs were created by transfers originating elsewhere and new branches. Therefore, the net balance of employment from new openings and complete closures of manufacturing establishments employing over twenty people accounted for a loss of 170,300 or 44 per cent of the total decline in the nine year period.

This net deficit between openings and complete closures forms the largest single component in London's industrial decline. Unfortunately, no statistics are available for closures either for other parts of the South-East region or for earlier periods in Greater London, against which a comparison of this level of factory closures could be made, but there can be little doubt that the volume of these closures was very high between 1966 and 1974. It is also noticeable that the level of transfers and branch openings was extremely low, for London, with 55 per cent of the region's manufacturing employment in 1966, had only 6 per cent of the recorded employment generated by intersubdivisional industrial movement in the South-East in this period.[4] In contrast, London had over 40 per cent of the region's jobs created by recorded enterprises new to manufacturing. This suggests that London is still an important seedbed for new industrial growth.

There are two residual elements in this examination of the composition of this decline. First, as mentioned above, the Department of Industry's data on openings and closures only record establishments employing twenty people or more. Those unrecorded small establishments below this limit are estimated to account for only about 7 per cent of all manufacturing employment in London. Assuming that they account for a similar proportion of the decline in manufacturing employment, then the net decline in this size group would have been about 26,000 jobs.

The second element in the residual is the net loss of some 88,500 jobs (23 per cent of the total), in which three components may be distinguished:

(a) net shrinkage of employment at plants remaining in London throughout the study period and not associated with Industrial movement;

[4]It should be noted, however, that the register only records openings employing twenty or more in London, whereas in the rest of the South-East the lower limit is eleven or more. Therefore, the London percentages given here under-represent somewhat the real comparison with the rest of the region.

b) net employment change at plants that closed during this period but whose employment rundown exceeded two years; and

c) movement of production by multiplant companies from their London establishments to existing plants elsewhere, without involving either a London closure or the establishment of a new branch in this period.

While this residual shrinkage is clearly an important component in London's industrial decline, it is of less significance than either industrial movement or net loss through openings and complete closures. The composition of the industrial decline in Greater London is summarised in Table 2.3.

2.7 Inner and outer London

To examine the incidence of decline *within* Greater London an analysis has been undertaken of inner and outer London, based on the GLC definition of group A and B boroughs (see Figure 2.1). The analysis is the same as that carried out for Greater London as a whole, but unfortunately no figures are available of the net decline in manufacturing employment in these areas. The only yardstick

Table 2.3 The composition of industrial decline in Greater London, 1966–74.

Type of decline	Employment loss	% of total employment decline
Decline due to movement to assisted areas	36,200	9
Decline due to movement to overspill towns	26,000	7
Decline due to remaining 'unplanned' movement	43,100	11
Net decline due to difference between openings and *complete* closures unassociated with movement	170,300	44
Estimated decline in firms employing under 20 people	26,000	7
Residual shrinkage	88,500	23
Total decline in manufacturing employment	390,100	101

against which the recorded loss of employment can be measure
therefore, is the 1966 manufacturing employment derived from tl
Census of Population. It will also be noted that no calculation h
been made of the decline in employment in firms employing le
than twenty workers or of the residual shrinkage. The percentag
given in this section are the proportions of the total job loss arisii
from known closures and from branch openings outside Londo
They are not comparable with the percentages given for Great
London as a whole. The results of this analysis are given in Tab
2.4.

A common assumption regarding the decline of manufacturing
London is that it is the inner city that has borne the brunt of tl
decline. A comparison of these tables shows that the decline in inn
London attributable to factory closures and to loss of employme
due to branch openings elsewhere is only marginally greater tha
that for the outer area (22 per cent as against 21 per cent of the 19
manufacturing employment). However, if Greenwich is exclude
from the outer boroughs group and included in the inner area, tl
figures are 24 per cent for inner London and 20 per cent for out
London. The point remains that the difference between inner ar
outer London is not great. The industrial decline is clearly a featui

**Table 2.4 The composition of industrial decline in inner and out
London, 1966–74.**

Type of loss	Inner London		Outer Londo	
	Jobs lost	%	Jobs lost	%
Loss due to movement to assisted areas	11,300	9	24,900	1
Loss due to movement to overspill towns	14,400	11	11,600	
Loss due to other 'unplanned' movement	20,200	15	22,900	1
Net loss due to difference between openings and complete closures	88,200	66	82,100	5
Total estimated gross employment loss from industrial movement and closures of factories employing over 20 people (as % of 1966 employment)	134,100	100 (22)	141,500	10 (2

f the whole conurbation and is not confined to the inner city. These
verall rates disguise differences in the nature of the decline in the
wo areas. A larger proportion of the decline in inner London can be
ttributed to the difference between openings and complete clos-
res of manufacturing establishments than is the case in outer
ondon (66 per cent as against 58 per cent). The role of industrial
iovement in inner London's decline is correspondingly smaller,
ccounting for only 34 per cent, with most of that being shorter
istance movement either to London overspill towns (11 per cent)
r to other locations primarily in the South-East and East Anglia
15 per cent). In outer London, on the other hand, industrial
iovement is much more important, accounting for 42 per cent of
he total job loss. In so far as firms move to expand this is an
ndication, perhaps, of the more dynamic nature of manufacturing
n the outer areas. It is interesting that for outer London firms the
;reatest job loss is attributable to moves to the Assisted Areas,
ather than to any other category of location.

An examination was made of the incidence of job loss associated
vith factory closures for each of the London boroughs, and this has
)een measured against the 1966 census data on employees in emp-
oyment by area of workplace, as the only available datum against
vhich to measure the impact of these closures. This is presented in
Table 2.5.

The average loss for all the boroughs was 22 per cent of the 1966
nanufacturing employment. Not unexpectedly, the areas of south-
:ast London have been the worst hit (Greenwich, Southwark, Lam-
)eth, Bexley, and Lewisham), with the East End of London also
:aring badly (Newham, Tower Hamlets, Hackney, and Islington).
Other boroughs that have suffered particularly heavy incidences of
'actory closures are Merton and Hounslow. It is important to
emphasise that these figures are not *net* losses of manufacturing
employment in these boroughs. They do not take account of closures in plants employing less than twenty people, of transfers of
plants between boroughs, of net employment changes at establishments remaining throughout the period, or of new openings.

2.8 Size distribution of factory closures

There is one final aspect of the incidence of factory closures that is
worth investigation, and that is the size distribution of these clos-

Table 2.5 Factory closures and manufacturing employment: a analysis by London borough, 1966–74.

Borough	Estimated employment loss accounted for by closures (no.)	Estimated employment loss as % of manufacturing employment, 1966 (Census of Population)
Inner London		
City	9,200	15
Camden	10,700	23
Hackney	16,600	31
Hammersmith	5,700	22
Haringey	6,800	20
Islington	15,100	25
Kensington and Chelsea	1,600	19
Lambeth	7,100	28
Lewisham	5,000	25
Newham	12,100	30
Southwark	19,300	38
Tower Hamlets	14,400	26
Wandsworth	4,700	17
Westminster	10,000	10
Outer London		
Barking	5,800	10
Barnet	4,500	15
Bexley	5,900	25
Brent	16,400	24
Bromley	5,200	22
Croydon	8,300	21
Ealing	16,500	22
Enfield	10,500	19
Greenwich	14,100	43
Harrow	1,700	10
Havering	4,100	19
Hillingdon	9,500	22
Hounslow	13,500	28
Kingston	2,900	13
Merton	8,700	29
Redbridge	2,500	11
Richmond	2,400	17
Sutton	800	7
Waltham Forest	8,700	25

**able 2.6 Size distribution of manufacturing establishments em-
ploying twenty-five or more persons compared with the
size of plant closures, 1966–74.**

ize roup	% of all establishments in 1968	% of all establishment closures, 1966–74	% of all employment in 1968	% of employment loss from closures, 1966–74
ner London:				
25–99	72	74	26	35
100–499	23	23	35	41
500+	5	3	39	24
)uter London:				
25–99	56	61	12	19
100–499	35	32	34	39
500+	9	6	54	41

res. Table 2.6 shows the incidence of closures by size for inner and
)uter London, compared with the size distribution of establish-
nents in existence in 1968 (the nearest date available to the base
ear for this study).

As expected, the proportion of smaller plants is greater in inner
London than in outer London. In terms of employment loss through
closure in these smaller plants, the proportion in both areas of
London is higher than expected from the proportion of employment
in establishments in this size range. It cannot be concluded from this
that Greater London is of declining importance as a location for
small firms, for it may be that the rates of both closures and
openings of small establishments are greater nationally than for
larger establishments. In any case the closures give only a partial
view of the changes in employment in the small firm sector.

At the other extreme, closures among the large establishments
are less than expected from the proportion of establishments in that
size range in both inner and outer London, suggesting less
susceptibility to closure, possibly because of the greater capital
investment in these larger plants. Yet, particularly in outer London,
the large closures that do take place still account for a significant
part of all employment loss.

2.9 The causes of the high incidence of factory closures

Direct evidence from the firms themselves that could explain the high level of factory closures in London is at present limited to those companies that moved to new locations. Two surveys have examined the 'push' factors causing firms to move from London. The earlier of these was the Inquiry into Location Attitudes Group (ILAG) survey, which included 159 establishments that had a London origin and opened at their new locations elsewhere in the United Kingdom between 1964 and 1967 (Expenditure Committee, 1973). The other was a survey of fifty-three firms that relocated from London to one of the New or Expanding Towns (NETs) in the South-East or East Anglia between 1970 and 1973 (Department of Industry, 1976). The latter survey covered almost all the firms known to have moved to these locations in this period. These were predominantly small firms, for only two of the fifty-three firms surveyed employed over 200 people at their London location. The ILAG survey was a comprehensive survey covering a wide range of sizes of establishment, as well as all types of destination.

The relative findings of these surveys are summarised in Tables 2.7 and 2.8.

In both surveys about three-quarters of all moves were primarily motivated by the need to expand output. This expansion of output was clearly not possible at the London location in many cases.

The main factor inhibiting this expansion was the fact that the site was already fully occupied. Thus, in the ILAG survey 63 per cent of firms were experiencing some degree of site congestion, while in the NETs survey 47 per cent mentioned this factor. This congestion was further reinforced in the NETs sample by the old inefficient nature of the existing premises; 87 per cent of these firms considered their premises inadequate. This inadequacy was reflected in their having to operate from a number of separate buildings (26 per cent) or in multistorey buildings (36 per cent), which imposed severe restraints on the efficient layout of plant as well as considerable material-handling difficulties. Other congestion factors mentioned by firms were site access problems for heavy vehicles (17 per cent, NETs survey) and increasing traffic congestion in the neighbourhood (22 per cent, ILAG survey).

The termination of the leases on their London premises also was a factor for a number of firms in their relocation decision. In the able 2.7 ILAG survey of 159 new establishments with a London origin, 1964–67 (% of all cases).[a]

ctors causing firms to seek ternative or additional emises	Major factor	Minor factor	Played no part
xpansion of output	72	11	17
eorganisation of production space	41	18	42
te congestion	55	8	38
raffic congestion	8	14	77
nd of lease	9	2	89
ocal planning:			
Premises to be demolished	11	4	85
Refused planning permission	6	1	92
)C control:			
Refused IDC	3	0	97
Expected refusal if applied	5	3	92
abour shortages:			
Male	25	13	62
Female	35	7	58
Skilled	16	10	74

Percentage of all cases citing factor in question. On average, firms cited about ree factors each. Those factors which received very few responses have been mitted from this table.

LAG survey only some 11 per cent were influenced by this factor, ut the NETs survey with 32 per cent suggests its importance as a actor for the smaller firm, which is nore likely to lease than to own s premises. In almost half the latter cases there was no prospect of enewal, and even where renewal was possible firms faced the rospect of having to pay significantly higher rents. Therefore, they ought cheaper premises elsewhere. At the end of 1976 rental levels

able 2.8 New and Expanding Towns survey of fifty-three firms' relocation from London, 1970–75.

Factors causing firms to relocate	% of all cases
Expansion of output	76
Inadequacy of existing premises	87
Site congestion	47
Lease difficulties	32
Local planning problems	41
Labour shortages	23

for modern factory units in the New and Expanding Towns range from about 90p to £1.50 per sq. ft. In London, on the other hand comparable modern premises with room for further expansion were difficult to find, but even for unmodernised interwar premises on the Park Royal estate rentals ranged between £1.50 and £1.75 per sq. ft. In these circumstances it is not surprising that almost all those interviewed in the NETs survey (98 per cent) maintained that the most important factor attracting them to the New and Expanding Towns was the availability of suitable premises at a reasonable price.

Local planning difficulties also were instrumental in causing some firms to relocate. The proposed demolition of factories, usually for housing redevelopment or road improvement schemes, affected some 15 per cent of those in the ILAG survey and 23 per cent in the NETs survey. In addition a further 5 per cent in the NETs survey were in non-conforming premises, although not faced with an immediate compulsory purchase order. Even where redevelopment by the local authority was not contemplated a small proportion of firms still had their planning applications for development on their London sites refused (7 per cent, ILAG survey; 11 per cent, NETs survey).

The role of the central government's Industrial Development Certificate (IDC) control as a factor in causing firms to relocate seems to have been only a minor one and of diminishing importance. In the ILAG survey only 3 per cent of respondents said that the refusal of an IDC in their home area was a factor in their move out of London, while a further 8 per cent claimed that the expected refusal of an IDC was a factor. In the NETs survey none of the firms interviewed had been influenced at all by the IDC control. This could be partly a reflection of the easing of the control in the 1970s compared with the mid-1960s, as well as of the greater ease that the small firm has in presenting a convincing case for a given location.

Shortages of labour figured prominently in the ILAG survey in causing firms to locate elsewhere. Female labour was in most acute shortage at that time (a factor for 42 per cent of those interviewed), while male shortages (38 per cent) and shortages of particular skills (26 per cent) were also important. In the NETs survey, however, labour shortages were only mentioned by 23 per cent of those interviewed as influencing their relocation decision. Once again this difference may reflect the less critical nature of labour shortages for the smaller firm, or the changing labour supply situation between the early 1960s and early 1970s may be the explanation.

The picture that emerges from these two surveys is one of predominantly expanding firms faced with severe site and premises constraints, as well as varying degrees of labour shortage. To these difficulties were added traffic congestion and local planning difficulties. It was varying combinations of these factors that caused firms to abandon the idea of a London development and to establish a plant elsewhere.

Others have claimed that apart from these environmental and planning factors the changing ownership pattern of British industry has influenced the decline of manufacturing in the main cities (Keeble, Chapter 5; Goddard and Spence, 1976). While there is little doubt that the concentration of ownership in the last twenty years or so has been a major feature of the manufacturing sector (Prais, 1976) and that this has been accompanied by a gradual increase in productivity (Department of Employment, 1976a), which may have encouraged some plant closures in these large organisations, there is no direct evidence that the concentration of ownership and the high factory closure rate in London are causally related. This remains a subject for further investigation. Just how influential are the environmental and planning factors identified above in causing complete closures or the transfer of production to existing plants outside London is also the subject of studies now under way in the Department of Industry.

2.10 Conclusions

The rate of decline of manufacturing employment in Greater London in the period 1966–74 has been considerably greater than the rate of population decline in the same period and has undoubtedly led to major changes in the economic structure of London over a relatively short time. This decline has been independent of national trends and of London's industrial structure and must be the result of factors that adversely affect all London-based industry.

The cause of the decline is primarily the result not of the movement of manufacturing industry from London, which accounts for only 27 per cent of the total decline, but of the high rate of factory closures unconnected with industrial movement (44 per cent). The shrinkage of employment at plants remaining in the capital (and shrinkage at closed plants prior to two years before closure) comprised some 23 per cent of the total decline. Loss of manufacturing employment in London arising from movement has been due more to unplanned movement (11 per cent of the total decline) than to movement to the Assisted Areas (9 per cent) or to the London overspill towns (7 per cent). A large part of the total movement (41 per cent) was by multiplant companies closing in London and transferring production to existing plants elsewhere.

This decline has occurred throught the conurbation, with inner London experiencing only a slightly higher share of the decline than outer London. In inner London complete closures unconnected with movement have been of greater importance than in outer London. In outer London it has been movement, particularly to the Assisted Areas, that has been more significant in that area's industrial decline (although industrial movement still accounted for a smaller proportion of the total than complete closures). The areas of London that have borne the brunt of the industrial closures are south-east London and the East End, but other boroughs having a high incidence of closures are Merton and Hounslow. The employment loss from factory closures has been disproportionately high among smaller plants and to a lesser extent among the medium-sized plants. However, among the larger plants there have been fewer closures than expected.

Evidence on the reasons for the high level of factory closures in London is confined to firms moving from London rather than those closing completely or transferring production to existing plants elsewhere. Evidence presented from two surveys on industrial movement has indicated that most of the firms covered wanted to expand or reorganise their production more efficiently and were prevented from doing so in London by site congestion, inefficient old premises, and labour shortages. Other contributory factors causing them to move were local planning difficulties and traffic congestion. Further work is necessary not only to examine the extent to which these factors have affected the complete factory closures and those transferring to existing plants, but also to see whether yet other factors are significant in accounting for these – the major components of London's manufacturing decline.

3 Economic Decline in South-east London

Peter Gripaios

3.1 Introduction

Much concern has been expressed in recent years regarding the problems of the core areas of cities. These problems include a lack of employment opportunities, deprivation, and increasing local-government indebtedness.

In London the area most affected includes not only the core but also most of the area to the east of it both north and south of the river. This chapter relates to a substantial part of this area in that it examines the economic decline of the inner part of south-east London – an area covered by the three London Boroughs of Greenwich, Lewisham, and Southwark. In some parts of the chapter, because of data non-availability, the area is defined as the six employment-exchange areas of Borough, Bermondsey, Camberwell, Deptford, Lewisham, and Southwark or as the south-east London postal districts. The three alternative areas do not differ significantly from one another.

The first half of the chapter deals with the indicators of economic decline – changes in employment and changes in the structure of industry. The second half examines the reasons for this economic decline and looks briefly at the policy implications.

3.2 Economic decline

Economic decline will be analysed in two ways in this section. First the data on employment will be examined, then the data on industry.

3.2.1. Employment

Employment trends

In 1971 – the latest date for which Census of Population data are available – the resident south-east London workforce amounted to more than 380,000 – greater than that of the whole of Tyneside. More than 300,000 were employed in the area itself. Of these the majority (62.5 per cent) were employed in service activities, the most important of the latter being the distributive trades and professional and scientific services. Manufacturing industries employed 25 per cent of the total workforce, the figures ranging from 22.3 per cent in Greenwich to 27.3 per cent in Southwark. The largest manufacturing activity was 'Engineering and electrical goods' with 20,300 workers. Also important were 'Food, drink, and tobacco' and 'Paper, printing, and publishing'. These three industries taken together accounted for 62 per cent of the manufacturing employment and over 15 per cent of the total employment in the area.

The industrial structure in 1971 contrasted with that in 1961 is shown in Table 3.1. The changes in industrial structure were associated with marked employment shifts. Total employment fell from 366,000 in 1961 to around 308,000 in 1971, mainly as a result of a sharp decline in manufacturing employment. In fact, of the 58,000 jobs lost in the decade, 52,000 were in the manufacturing sector. It is important to notice, however, that service industry decline became important after 1966, accounting for 24 per cent of the loss of jobs from 1966 to 1971.

The significance of such changes is emphasised by comparing south-east London with Greater London and England and Wales (Table 3.2). Clearly, south-east London compares unfavourably with both the other areas. The generality of the problem in inner London is indicated, however, by the fact that the rate of decline in

Table 3.1 Percentage employed by sector in south-east London, 1961–71

Sector	1961	1971
Manufacturing	35.2	25.0
Construction	11.5	12.5
Services	53.3	62.5

Source: Census of Population.

Table 3.2 Percentage changes in employment, 1966–71

Area	Manufacturing	Construction	Services	Total
South-east London	−25.2	−21.8	−6.5	−12.5
Greater London	−14.6	−16.1	1.2	− 5.5
England and Wales	− 3.5	−11.3	2.0	− 1.6

Source: Census of Population.

the conurbation as a whole was markedly greater than that in England and Wales. In both south-east London and Greater London the decline in the number of jobs accelerated between 1961 and 1971. In south-east London employment in manufacturing declined by 40.3 per cent in the decade, with a 25.2 per cent decline in the period 1966–71.

The poor performance of south-east London is highlighted by examining changes by industry at the Order level of the Standard Industrial Classification (SIC). Unfortunately, these could only be compared for the period 1961–66 owing to the revision of the SIC in 1968, but this comparison is given in Table 3.3. The figures show a significant decline in south-east London in nearly all industries. Employment increased in only five industries: 'Construction', 'Professional and scientific services', 'Miscellaneous services', and 'Distributive trades', and of course none of these are manufacturing industries. This general decline cannot be attributed to the trade cycle, as comparison with England and Wales shows that in all but three Orders ('Textiles', 'Distributive trades', and 'Professional and scientific services') south-east London compares very unfavourably. Crude estimates of employment change since 1966 are consistent with these earlier data.

Unemployment

The trends in employment have been reflected in the unemployment rate of the area, as is indicated by Table 3.4. The table shows that the 1971 unemployment rate in south-east London was much higher than that for earlier years. This is partly explained by the trade cycle, but not completely; for whereas in 1961 unemployment rates were lower in south-east London than in England and Wales, in 1971 they were significantly higher.

Table 3.3 Percentage change in employment by SIC (1953), 1961–66

SIC Order	South-east London	England and Wales
3 Food, drink, etc.	− 7.7	+ 5.0
4 Chemical and allied industries	−31.8	− 0.6
5 Metal manufacture	−11.8	− 4.8
6 Engineering and electrical goods	−23.3	+ 7.6
7 Shipbuilding, etc.	−36.8	−24.3
8 Vehicles	−21.7	− 4.7
9 Other metal goods	−15.5	+ 6.4
10 Textiles	− 9.1	− 9.2
11 Leather, etc.	−18.5	− 1.8
12 Clothing and footwear	−22.2	− 6.4
13 Bricks, etc.	−28.3	+ 2.0
14 Timber, furniture	−40.0	− 1.4
15 Paper, printing, etc.	−13.3	+ 1.6
16 Other manufacturing	−27.0	+12.3
17 Construction	+15.7	+17.7
18 Public utilities	−17.1	+ 8.3
19 Transport, etc.	−11.1	− 3.1
20 Distributive trades	+ 6.0	+ 2.2
21 Insurance, banking, finance	− 3.2	+15.1
22 Professional and scientific services	+16.9	+17.4
23 Miscellaneous services	+12.5	+14.9
24 Public administration, etc.	+ 0.7	− 1.3

Source: Census of Population.

It should be pointed out that high rates of unemployment in parts of Greater London are especially significant because of the large number of people who work in the conurbation. Thus, even a relatively low unemployment rate may mean a large absolute number of unemployed. An examination of the absolute numbers unemployed in south-east London does reveal a disturbing trend. There were 20,700 unemployed persons in 1971 compared with 10,680 in 1961 and 11,180 in 1966.

Table 3.4 Unemployment rates in south-east London, 1961–71 (total out of employment, including sick, as a percentage of the total economically active)

Sector	1961	1966	1971
Males	2.7	2.7	6.0
Females	2.0	2.7	4.7
All unemployed	2.4	2.7	5.4

Source: Census of Population.

Activity rates

The economic activity rate of an area is indicative of its employment opportunities and/or the characteristics of its labour force. It is defined as the

$$\frac{\text{economically active population}}{\text{population aged } 15+}$$

Table 3.5 Economic activity rates for south-east London, 1961–71

Sector	1961	1966	1971
Males	88.0	85.9	83.3
Females	47.0	50.1	50.2
All	66.4	67.0	65.8

Source: Census of Population.

Activity rates for south-east London are presented in Table 3.5. It can be seen that, although there was a slight improvement in the female activity rate, this did not compensate for a continued and significant decline in the male rate. Increasing female and declining male activity rates are doubtless a reflection of the decreasing importance of the manufacturing trades and of more advanced processes requiring less heavy manual labour and a lower level of labour skills.

Residence and workplace

The analysis of data on residence and workplace for the years 1966 and 1971 also indicates declining employment opportunities in the south-east London area. As Table 3.6 shows, the percentage of the

Table 3.6 Percentage of the resident labour force living and working in the same borough, 1966–71

Borough	1966	1971
Greenwich	52.7	48.5
Lewisham	36.7	37.2
Southwark	48.3	46.3

Source: Census of Population.

resident workforce working locally declined in two of the three boroughs during 1966–71, while over the same period the percentage of local jobs held by local residents declined in all three boroughs. Thus, there appears to have been an increasingly poor fit of workers to jobs on offer.

The conclusion that arises from the analysis of the employment data is that there has been a considerable loss of jobs in south-east London, particularly in manufacturing but also, since 1966, in services. This has caused employment problems as indicated by falling activity rates, higher unemployment, and an increasingly poor fit of workers to jobs.

3.2.2 Industry

Three sources of data were used to analyse the loss of industry in south-east London. First, the Department of Industry (DI) provided data on openings and closures of manufacturing establishments with more than twenty employees in the period 1966–74. Second, a survey was made of firms with an establishment address in south-east London postal districts, listed in the *Kompass* directory in any of the years 1968, 1971, and 1974. Finally, the Department of Employment (DE) provided data on closures of establishments of more than ten employees in all industries for the period 1970–75.[1] This section summarises the analysis, full details of which have been published elsewhere (Gripaios, 1977a, 1977b).

The stock of establishments

All three sources of industry data indicate a significant fall in the total number of establishments in the south-east London area. The DI data show a net loss (closures – openings) of 211 manufacturing establishments with twenty or more employees in the period 1966–74. The number of establishments listed in *Kompass* declined from 462 in 1968 to 370 in 1974. Finally, the DE data show a loss of 359 establishments with ten or more employees in the period 1970–75.

The survey data indicated that the percentage loss of establishments was greater the more central the location. The south-east London area was split into eleven subareas ranked by distance from Westminster and by the percentage loss of establishments in each

[1]Roger Fox at Thames Polytechnic helped in the analysis of these data.

subarea. It was found that the inverse relationship between the distance from the centre and the percentage loss of establishments was high enough to be statistically significant.

It appears that most closures involved the smaller establishments, the DE data indicating that 53 per cent of closures were in establishments with ten to thirty employees and 72 per cent in those with less than fifty. There was, however, no evidence to suggest that small establishments were more likely to close than their larger counterparts, since the smaller establishments were more numerous.

The industry data confirm that manufacturing declined more than services but ascribe relatively more importance to service industry decline than the Census of Population employment data. The *Kompass* survey showed that manufacturing plants fell by 22 per cent between 1968 and 1974 while service establishments fell by only 16 per cent. In the case of DE data, 48 per cent of closures were in manufacturing and 42 per cent in services. As the size distribution of firms was similar in each sector the difference did not stem from this latter factor.

The DE data showed that there were establishment closures in virtually all industry Orders, indicating the same sort of general decline suggested by the employment data. Regarding individual industry Orders, it is difficult to estimate whether particular industries declined more than would have been expected given the industrial distribution of establishments in the study area, as the latter data could not be provided by the Department of Employment. A comparison of closures by industry with 1971 Census of Population employment data, however, indicates that the number of closures per industry Order was proportional to 1971 employment in those Orders. The Spearman rank correlation coefficient between 1971 employment and the number of closures in each industry was 0.7, which was statistically significant at the 0.5 per cent level.

Closures and openings

It is clear that there have been very few plant openings and many plant closures in south-east London since 1966. The actual numbers are given in Table 3.7.

All three sets of data indicate that with regard to closures, the most important factor was plant deaths rather than relocations. Deaths as a percentage of plant closures were 69, 61, and 74 per

Table 3.7 Openings and closures in south-east London, 1966–74

	DI data 1966–74	Survey data 1968–74
Openings	20	69
Closures	231	161

Sources: Department of Industry (unpublished); and *Kompass* survey.

cent in the case of the DI, *Kompass* survey, and DE data respectively.

The DE data suggest that the size of firms affects the type of closure. Deaths as a percentage of closures varied from 78 per cent in establishments of less than fifty employees to 55 per cent in larger ones. Moreover, a χ^2 test showed that this difference was statistically significant; that is, the larger the firm the more likely it was to move than to die.

In no industry Order were deaths less than 40 per cent of closures, indicating that the locational pressures on firms were general and not specific to one industry (DE data). In terms of sectors, deaths accounted for 68 per cent of closures in manufacturing, 85 per cent in construction, and 79 per cent in services. The service and construction establishment were therefore more likely to die than their manufacturing counterparts – a difference found to be statistically significant.

The pattern of movement

The direction of firm movements in the case of both immigrant and emigrant firms was almost invariably either outward or orbital in character. Of the 39 immigrant firms in the survey, 17 came from central London, 21 from the rest of Greater London and 1 from the rest of the south-east region. Of the 63 survey firms that moved out of the area, 4 moved to central London, 31 to the rest of Greater London, and 28 to the south-east region and beyond.

In the case of the DE data, moves within inner London accounted for 48 per cent of all outward moves. Of the rest, 6.5 per cent were to outer London, 15.2 per cent to the outer metropolitan area, and 16.3 per cent to the rest of the South-East region. The evidence suggests that decentralisation policy has had little direct influence on firm movements as only 2 per cent of moves were to new towns and only 3 per cent to development areas. The DE data suggest that small firms were more likely to move locally than large ones, in that 54 per cent of establishments with less than fifty employees moved within inner London compared with 36 per cent of larger ones. Rather surprisingly, the sectoral classification of relocating firms did not appear to influence destination.

The industry data thus confirm the general pattern of economic decline in the south-east London area showed by the employment data.

3.3 The reasons for decline

A number of influences have operated simultaneously in the London labour market, and as a result it is very difficult to determine which have contributed most to economic decline in south-east London. Some of the more likely influences are discussed below.

3.3.1 The supply of labour

Firms moving from London have often mentioned labour supply difficulties in the capital as one of the reasons for leaving (Keeble, 1968; South-East Joint Planning Team, 1971), and it does therefore seem likely that the falling supply of labour may have been an important influence. The inner London labour supply has fallen as population has decentralised to the suburbs and to new and to expanding towns. Part of this decentralisation can be attributed to government policy, but it has also reflected the desire of London residents for better living and working conditions.

However, an alternative explanation of population decentralisation is that falling demand for labour in the capital as a result of firm closures has forced the labour force to move to the jobs. The high deathrate of London plants suggests that, while the falling supply of labour has doubtless been a factor, the falling demand for labour must also have been important (Dennis, Chapter 2; Gripaios, 1977a, 1977b).

3.3.2 Structural influences

One possible reason for the falling demand for labour in south-east London is that the area may have an industrial structure in which declining trades are strongly represented. However, the general decline across all industries as indicated by the data on both employment and the stock of establishments suggests that this is far from the case.

That structural influences have been insignificant was confirmed by a shift-share analysis that compared south-east London with England and Wales for the period 1961–66, it being impossible to compare the figures for 1971 owing to the revision of the SIC in 1968. The analysis showed that the area had a relatively advantageous industrial structure, which mitigated against the fact that nearly all industries performed badly there compared with England and Wales (Gripaios, 1977a).

3.3.3   Locational influences

Locational influences have contributed to the decentralisation of manufacturing industry in many large cities, as studies of New York (Hoover and Vernon, 1959; Lichtenberg, 1960; Leone, 1971), Chicago (Moses and Williamson, 1967), Sydney (Logan, 1966), and Glasgow (Firn and Hughes, 1973) have shown. In particular, improvements in transportation and telecommunications have enabled firms to derive economies of scale from the building of large single-storey assembly-line plants away from the inner areas of cities and have enabled such firms to differentiate such production activities from those requiring face-to-face contacts. Thus, production activities have been decentralised, and only head offices have remained in the inner city.

The south-east London data are consistent with the view that changes in cost conditions must have been an influence in the area; for as shown above, decline has been concentrated in the manufacturing sector, the movement of firms has been outward, and decline worsens the more central the location (Gripaios, 1977a).

3.4   The decline of the docks

The London docks have long been in decline due to obsolescence resulting from changes in the bulk handling of general cargo traffic (containerisation) and the trend towards increasing ship size. The south-east London data indicate that this decline of the docks has resulted in many firm closures. The Census of Population shows that in the two boroughs with extensive riverside boundaries, namely, Greenwich and Southwark, employment declined by around 20 per cent in the period 1961–71, while in Lewisham it declined by only 1 per cent. As the industrial structure of all three boroughs is similar and Lewisham is the middle borough in terms of centrality, this suggests that the decline of the docks has been influential. Similarly, the survey data show that in central and riverside postal districts the number of establishments fell by 24.9 per cent, whereas in outer districts it fell by only 6.7 per cent (Gripaios, 1977a).

3.5 Merger and rationalisation

Increasing concentration in British industry has probably closed many south-east London establishments. Merger can lead to surplus capacity and rationalisation. If firms have plants in London and elsewhere, there is the incentive to close the London plant to capitalise on high site values in the capital and to utilise cheaper labour. The closure of the large AEI plant in Woolwich is a well-documented example (Daniels, 1972; see also Massey and Meegan, Chapter 4). A recent study by Southwark Trades Council and Roberts (1976) has shown that many Southwark closures have resulted from rationalisation.

3.6 Regional and urban policy

Both regional and urban policy must have influenced industrial decline in London. Industrial Development Certificate (IDC) controls have hindered expansion in London, while the payment of capital and labour subsidies has encouraged firms to move to Development Areas, and overspill policy has encouraged firms to move to New and Expanding Towns. An early study by Keeble (1968) has shown that many firms moved from north-west London to New and overspill towns in the period before 1964, while more recently a Department of Industry White Paper (1975) has shown a considerable movement of firms from inner London to Development Areas.

The south-east London evidence suggests, however, that neither regional nor overspill policy can have been of much direct influence in recent years, since only 5 per cent of establishments relocating since 1970 moved to Development Areas or New Towns (Gripaios,

1977b). The high deathrate among London plants may indicate considerable indirect influence, however, for the payment of capital and labour subsidies to firms elsewhere may have given such firms an absolute cost advantage over their London counterparts. There may also have been long run effects of policy-induced firm movements in earlier periods (see section 3.7), while the policy propaganda may have made businessmen increasingly aware of the (alleged) disadvantages of a London location. Evidence of this may be the fact that the greatest loss of inner London jobs has coincided with the period during which regional policy has been most 'actively' applied (Moore and Rhodes, 1973).

The compulsory purchase of sites as part of local-authority redevelopment schemes may also have caused many firm deaths where firms did not wish to move to other sites. A recent report by the London Borough of Wandsworth (1976), for example, has indicated that redevelopment schemes associated with the provision of council housing displaced 250 firms, of which only 13 relocated, in the period 1966–76 (Gripaios, 1977a).

3.7 Long run effects

The high deathrate of south-east London firms and the fact that service industry is also now beginning to close may be the results of negative multiplier effects arising from past decentralisation. The movement of manufacturing firms in the 1960s may have affected the viability of remaining firms through reduced interindustry and consumption demands for the products and services of the latter. There is evidence to suggest that real income levels (and therefore consumption) do fall in an area following the exodus of a large employer (Daniels 1972); so, this may have been the case.

3.8 The policy implications

The existence of severe employment problems in inner areas like south-east London suggests that there are grounds for rethinking the present spatial employment policy of decentralisation. Given the changes in the relative profitability of an inner city location, some dispersal of economic activity would have occurred anyway; but the particular policy adopted in the United Kingdom has increased the speed and type of response to these changes, thereby magnifying the effects on remaining inner-city residents and firms. Even so, it is doubtful whether a complete policy reversal of encouraging population and industry to move back to the inner cities is called for. The south-east London evidence suggests that industrial decline has been so extensive in the inner cities as to be irreversible, at least given the resources that could be provided by a slowly growing national economy. It is the competitiveness of the latter that must be the primary consideration for some time, and this would hardly be improved by concentrating production at uneconomic sites. The best way to help the inner cities now would be to change the emphasis of decentralisation policy from the encouragement of relatively long-distance movement to movement to the outer cities. In this way the outer cities could develop as the inner cities decline. Industrial expansion in the suburbs could in the first instance be facilitated by, for example, the relaxation of green belt controls, while the relaxation of rigidities in the markets for labour and land would encourage the redevelopment of the inner city.

4 Industrial Restructuring versus the Cities

Doreen Massey and Richard Meegan

4.1 Introduction and methodology

4.1.1 The industrial location project

The decline of manufacturing in the cities has been the subject of much recent research. One unfortunate side effect of this concern, however, has been the tendency for the problem to be defined in spatial terms, and consequently for the causes of the problem to be sought within the same spatial area. This tendency to study the working of the city in economic and spatial isolation from the rest of the national economy has often seen emphasis being placed, for example, on the assessment of the influence of such factors as the built environment of the inner city areas (congestion, dereliction, site availability, etc.) or the personal characteristics of their residents (e.g. relating unemployment to age, race, or skill). The outcome of such research is often to blur and confuse the issue of causality.

The present decline in manufacturing in the cities is occurring at a time when fundamental structural changes are taking place at the level of the economy as a whole (Treasury, 1976; Chisholm, 1976). It is part of the wider phenomenon of contraction and change in the manufacturing base of the UK economy. The argument of this chapter is that it is only in this wider context that the specific problems of manufacturing in city areas can be properly understood. The aim is therefore to demonstrate the link between locational change and developments at the level of both the national and international economy.

The chapter draws on research the broad purpose of which was to examine the locational implications of financial restructuring in British manufacturing since the mid-1960s (see Massey and Meegan, 1979). This interest was focused down in the research project into a study of the spatial repercussions of the intervention of the Industrial Reorganisation Corporation (IRC) into the electrical, electronics, and aerospace equipment sectors. The IRC was established by the Labour government in 1966 'for the purpose of promoting industrial efficiency and profitability and assisting the economy of the United Kingdom or any part of the United Kingdom' (Industrial Reorganisation Corporation Act, 1966). Its intervention, before it was abolished in 1971, took the form of encouraging mergers, intrasectoral reorganisation, and investment.[1] It should be stressed, however, that the fundamental concern of the research was with the processes of restructuring themselves rather than with their specific attribution to intervention by the IRC. The purpose of the present chapter is to draw out the implications of the results of this research for the major cities significantly represented in the survey.

The form of explanation adopted reflected the theoretical concerns and comprised four discrete stages.[2] The first step involved an examination of the major characteristics of the overall economic situation within which restructuring was operating. These characteristics were analysed as being, first, the declining profitability and, second, the worsening international competitive position of British manufacturing industry. The second stage of the research was concerned with the precise ways in which these general economic forces operated at the level of specific cases, and therefore with the ways in which they presented pressures towards financial restructuring. As a result of this analysis it was possible to develop a broad classification of the causes of financial restructuring, which was directly related to macroeconomic conditions. The next step was to assess the implications for production reorganisation of each such category of restructuring. The question to be answered at this stage was therefore: what changes in the organisation of production and the use of labour are allowed by the financial restructuring? The identification of the locational implications of these changes formed the

[1]These various forms of intervention will be referred to collectively under the general heading of 'financial restructuring'.

[2]This is a simplified version of the structure of explanation employed in the project. For a more detailed discussion see Massey and Meegan, 1979.

fourth and final step in the research. With the completion of this stage it was thus possible to relate the spatial incidence of employment changes identified in the empirical research back through the production reorganisation to the forms of restructuring themselves and their specific relation to changes in the national economy.

The survey examined the interests of twenty-five firms in the following Minimum List Headings (MLH) of the 1968 Standard Industrial Classification (SIC):

Order 8: Instrument engineering
MLH 354: Scientific and industrial instruments and systems
Order 9: Electrical engineering
MLH 361: Electrical machinery
MLH 362: Insulated wires and cables
MLH 363: Telegraph and telephone apparatus and equipment
MLH 364: Radio and electronic components
MLH 365: Broadcast receiving and sound-reproducing equipment
MLH 366: Electronic computers
MLH 367: Radio, radar, and electronic capital goods
MLH 368: Electrical appliances primarily for domestic use
MLH 369: Other electrical goods

Order 11: Vehicles
MLH 383: Aerospace equipment manufacturing and repairing

The electrical engineering sector produces both consumer goods and capital goods, includes major suppliers to the public sector, and encompasses some of the country's major exporters. The sector is important not just for the stage that it has reached in its own technological development (with, for example, the transition from electrical to electronic components) but also for its potential contribution to technological changes in other manufacturing sectors. Although the sector is still predominantly based in the South-East, some of its industries, especially in electronics, are exhibiting an increased degree of mobility and are accordingly important in terms of regional policy. In 1966 there were 1,911,000 people employed in the sector, representing about 14 per cent of the total workforce in all manufacturing industries (Department of Employment, 1975b). According to the Census of Production the sector accounted in 1968 for 10 per cent of the net output of all manufacturing industries. At the time of IRC intervention the survey firms employed 226,000 people in the sector – approximately 19 per cent of total employment in these industries.[3]

The restructuring processes analysed resulted in an overall net employment loss of 36,016 jobs in the survey firms – a decline of 16 per cent.[4] In terms of its geographical distribution this overall change was dominated by three regions (the South-East, the North-West, and the West Midlands), which experienced major declines in employment in both absolute and percentage terms.[5] Together they accounted for 94 per cent of the net overall loss (34,016 out of 36,016). Further disaggregation of the data, however, showed that 89 per cent of the losses suffered by these regions could be explained by the significant declines that occurred in the four major cities located within them, namely, Greater London, Liverpool, Manchester, and Birmingham.[6] These four cities together lost 30,315 jobs in the sector or 84 per cent of the overall net decline in the survey firms' employment. The seriousness of this decline for the cities was emphasised by the fact that at the beginning of the period they only accounted for some 32 per cent of survey employment in the sector.

[3]The total figure does not relate to a single point in time since the individual cases of intervention took place over a period of four years. The percentage is therefore a 'rule of thumb' measure derived by comparing the survey total with total national employment in the sector at the beginning of the period (1966).

[4]Between 1966 and 1972. Although the IRC was most active in the sector in 1968 and 1969 and was abolished early in 1971, evidence was found of postmerger rationalisation, following its intervention, as late as 1972. Indeed, there was one case identified that involved the opening of a new plant in 1976 as a direct result of the production reorganisation following an IRC-sponsored merger six years before.

[5]The implications of this regional breakdown of employment change, particularly for development and non-development areas, is discussed in greater detail in Massey and Meegan, 1979.

[6]The geographical areas used were:
   Birmingham: Birmingham City Borough
   Liverpool: Liverpool City Borough (including Netherton)
   London: Greater London Council area
   Manchester: Manchester County Borough
Newcastle was the only other city for which survey observations were recorded. Unlike the other cities, however, these observations were confined to one plant and one specific product group. Because of the limited nature of the results for Newcastle, this chapter will concentrate on the changes experienced by the four cities already mentioned.

The problem addressed by this chapter is therefore that of explaining this net loss of 30,315 jobs by direct reference to the economy level pressures operating on the sector at the time. The approach will therefore be to suggest ways in which these various pressures moulded the form taken by inter- and intrasectoral restructuring and helped to shape its differential spatial impact – and hence its specific consequences for the cities. This will be done in section 4.2. Before going on to this, however, it is necessary to describe briefly the classification of employment change used in the analysis.

4.1.2. A typology of employment changes

The employment changes identified can be divided into four categories: absolute loss, locational loss, absolute gain, and locational gain. An *absolute* change is one that occurs at the level of the economy as a whole, where new jobs are created or jobs disappear altogether. A *locational* change is one that results from the locational transfer of production, the loss or gain thus being specific to a particular geographical area within the nation. The point of this categorisation is to enable a distinction to be made between employment changes due to job mobility and those due to differential growth and decline. This distinction is of obvious importance in any consideration of the potential effects of spatial policies.

Locational change needs to be more precisely defined, however. At any given level of spatial disaggregation the total number of jobs lost through locational shift will equal the number gained. Such figures refer to jobs that are neither gained nor lost to the economy as a whole but that change location. Locational shifts, however, are rarely symmetrical. The figures given here under 'locational shift' represent the employment that actually arrived at the recipient location. This number is far smaller than the loss recorded at the original factories. Job movement, in other words, has frequently been either part of a process of overall cutbacks or the occasion for cutback. In the first case overall cuts in capacity often entail concentrating the work of smaller factories on a reduced number of larger ones. Such moves are frequently announced as transfers, and indeed some production may well be moved. They do not, however, represent a transfer of all jobs at the previous location. In the second case locational shift may be the occasion for major changes in production technology, again leading to a reduced workforce in the recipient region. The locational shift may be brought about because the nature of the technological change demands either new fixed capital or a new workforce. In the first case it may be necessary, in the second prudent, to move, thus reducing conflict with trade unions. The figures for the number of jobs lost in the origin region, but never recreated in the recipient region, are included under the category of 'absolute loss'. Such jobs were lost to the economy as a whole. They are separately accounted for in the tables, however, by a disaggregation of absolute loss into *in situ* and *in transit* losses. *In situ* losses are straightforward losses in which no locational transfer of employment or production is involved. *In transit* losses are just as absolute, but they take place in the context of a locational change. The classification of *in transit* losses as part of absolute losses is important, since, while a particular area may appear to be losing considerable numbers of jobs through locational shifts, only a small proportion of this employment loss may subsequently benefit another locality.

4.2 The forms of restructuring and their employment implications for the cities

4.2.1 Introduction

Three different groups of stimuli for the financial restructuring were identified:[7]

> group 1: restructuring in the face of overcapacity and high costs
> group 2: restructuring to achieve scale advantages
> group 3: restructuring for reasons of market standing

The inclusion of major multidivisional firms (e.g. AEI, English Electric, and GEC) made the analysis more complex, however, in that it necessitated a differentiation between those divisions which acted as stimuli to the subsequent reorganisation and those which did not. The fact that certain divisions were not important stimuli for restructuring, however, does not mean that they can be assumed to be unaffected by it. The merger of multidivisional firms including

[7]The group titles relate specifically to the forms of restructuring identified in the survey and do not constitute absolute types that can be expected to occur in every instance of restructuring. Thus 'restructuring in the face of overcapacity and high costs' will not always produce the particular forms discussed in this chapter.

both stimulant and non-stimulant sectors alters the situation of the latter, which can be affected both by the indirect impact of the reorganisation of the stimulant sectors (with, say, a shifting of emphasis within the newly merged firm) and by their own independent organisational integration. Moreover, such sectors are also subject to economy level pressures (albeit not requiring financial restructuring). Non-stimulant sectors can therefore be regarded as responding to the *fact* of the merger rather than, as in the case of the stimulant sectors, to the reasons for it. To accommodate them in the analysis a separate 'secondary' classification was therefore required. The non-stimulant cases are dealt with, in this chapter, under the broad heading of 'non-stimulant sectors' (section 4.25).

The detailed impact of the three forms of restructuring on stimulant sectors are best examined by taking each group in turn.

4.2.2   Group 1:   Restructuring in the face of overcapacity and high costs

This group included product groups within the following industries:

(a) heavy electrical machinery, particularly turbine generators, switchgear and transformers (part MLH 361)
(b) supertension cables (part MLH 362); and
(c) aerospace equipment (part MLH 383)

The circumstances of the individual product groups were different, but they all shared the same problems of excess capacity and the need to cut costs and were all suffering from a pronounced deterioration in their competitive position. The power-engineering industry in its domestic market had to contend with a major downward revision of demand from its main customer (the Central Electricity Generating Board).[8] The potential for raising exports to counteract this shift was heavily constrained by increasing competition in overseas markets, particularly as a result of the ending of Commonwealth preference. The industry had therefore lost hitherto secure markets at home and abroad and faced increasingly severe competition in those that remained. For supertension cables, again the basic problem was a decline in domestic demand for which exports were unable to compensate. Exports to non-Commonwealth Third

---

[8]This was not an *ad hoc* phenomenon. It occurred in the context of a general decline in the rate of growth of demand for electrical energy – a situation exacerbated by the onset of recession in industrial activity.

World countries did increase, but margins were low, and competition, especially from Japan, was particularly severe. The problem of overcapacity was made even more acute by the industry's high degree of capital intensity. The aerospace equipment industry was also suffering from increasingly severe competition from abroad (especially from the United States) as a result of the ending of the Korean War, defence cancellations at home (TSR2, 1154, and 681), and the eventual collapse of the sellers' market that had followed the Second World War. The failure of Rolls-Royce served to intensify the industry's problems. There were thus two particularly dominant pressures for financial restructuring at work in group 1:

(a) a problem of over-capacity; and
(b) a need to cut production costs in the context of increasing international competition and a general slackening of the rate of growth of markets.

Financial restructuring was needed in this situation to enable co-ordinated capacity cutting and to facilitate the reallocation of capital into other more profitable areas of production. The financial restructuring itself allowed a number of responses in terms of actual production reorganisation. The reaction to the problem of excess capacity involved straight cutbacks in production, characterised by factory closures and major redundancies. The need to cut production costs and increase relative profitability resulted in an attempt by the firms concerned to increase individual labour productivity and to reduce aggregate labour costs. This was attempted in a number of ways:

(a) by the selection for closure of the most labour-intensive plants;
(b) by intensification, i.e. reducing the labour force in any given production process without any change in output or production techniques;
(c) by partial standardisation, which in turn allowed some automated methods in production and cuts in labour costs, with the ensuing requirement overall for less-skilled labour;
(d) by the introduction of numerically-controlled machine tools in production processes where full automation was not possible (usually small-batch processes), which allowed an overall reduction in the labour required and a dichotomisation of the skills of the remaining labour force; and finally,

(e) by a shift to mass production techniques where this was possible, enabling large reductions in the workforce and a change in
the type of labour from craft to semiskilled.

These measures all featured in the reorganisation of production
in the industries in group 1. How did they make themselves felt in
the cities? Table 4.1 shows the overall employment changes in
group 1 in the four conurbations. It is clear from the table that the
restructuring in group 1 had a particularly severe impact on the four
cities. Together they lost some 21,084 jobs as a result of the processes at work in this group. This amounted to 70 per cent of the cities'
total net loss of survey employment during the period under study.

The 'typology' of this overall employment change is particularly
revealing. Nearly three-quarters of the jobs lost to the cities in this
group were not linked in any way to the transfer elsewhere of either
capital equipment or jobs (15,528 *in situ* absolute loss). This is not
surprising, however; for as argued above, the pressures for capacity
cutting and cost reduction, and the nature of technological change
in this group of industries, meant that employment change was
dominated by absolute cutbacks in employment – losses both to
individual locations and to the economy as a whole. Furthermore, of
those jobs actually linked to some locational transfer, the vast
majority (89 per cent) disappeared *in transit* (i.e. *in transit* absolute
loss expressed as a percentage of total *in transit* and locational loss –

Table 4.1 Employment change in group 1 in the four cities

Category of employment change	No.
Employment loss:	
Absolute loss:	
in situ	(15,528)
in transit[a]	(4,980)
Locational loss[b]	(606)
Total loss	(21,114)
Employment gain:	
Absolute gain	0
Locational gain[b]	30
Total gain	30
Net gain (loss)	(21,084)

[a] Figure includes 1,750 jobs linked to transfers of production within or between
cities.
[b] Figure excludes 330 jobs transferred within or between cities.

4,980 out of 5,586). Even in such cases of transfer, then, the loss to the cities was not matched by corresponding gains elsewhere, potential job mobility being constrained by the overriding need for absolute cutbacks in both capacity and employment. Third, the cities themselves did not experience any significant gains from the locational shifts of jobs occurring in the country as a whole. In return for their locational loss of some 606 jobs, the cities received 30. Finally, there were no new jobs created in the cities as a result of the restructuring in group 1 (absolute gains were zero). The consequences for the cities of restructuring in the group 1 industries were therefore especially traumatic. There are three major threads in the explanation for this:

1. *The group 1 industries were heavily represented in the cities*   At the time of IRC intervention the survey plants located in the cities accounted for approximately 44 per cent of employment in the dominant group 1 industries (MLHs 361, 369, and 383);[9] yet, their share of total employment in the survey only amounted to 32 per cent. Therefore, even had the impact of the production reorganisation in group 1 been in proportion to employment, the cities could be expected to have been significantly affected.

2. *The plants in group 1 industries located in the cities were particularly susceptible to the processes of restructuring*   In fact, however, the cities experienced higher-than-proportionate employment losses as a result of the restructuring in group 1; approximately 88 per cent of the total net national employment loss in group 1 occurred there (21,084 out of a total net national decline in group 1 of 24,013). This was largely explained by the fact that the choice of plants for closure (the first of the five measures listed above) was based primarily on considerations of labour productivity. The overriding pressure in the production reorganisation in group 1 was the need to cut labour costs. The plants chosen for closure therefore had to be those which were relatively labour-intensive, and these factories were predominantly located in the older industrial areas of the cities.

[9]These industries do not correspond exactly to group 1. Indeed, it is important to stress again that the group classification was based on an examination of national economic pressures for restructuring. These did not follow any precise sectoral breakdown. In particular, parts of MLH 361 fall into group 3, and parts of MLH 354 could be included here under group 1. It was not possible to tabulate the initial distribution of the survey firms' employment by group.

3. *The cities did not gain from the locational shifts of production that occurred in the restructuring in group 1*   The cities were the origin of the bulk of the jobs that actually shifted location in the restructuring in group 1. Nationally, there was a locational shift of some 966 jobs in group 1, and 936 of these had their origins in the conurbations. Of these 936 jobs, 330 were transferred either within or between individual cities, while the remaining 606 jobs shifted to locations outside them. At first sight this locational shift appears relatively small, but it must be remembered that it in fact represents only one (and the smaller) component of the process of job movement. In forms of restructuring in which retrenchment is the dominant feature, job relocation is inevitably linked to high *in transit* absolute loss. In group 1 locational loss and *in transit* absolute loss accounted for approximately 26 per cent of total employment decline in the cities (5,586 out of 21,114).

Even in those cases where the cities retained some employment in the geographical reorganisation of production, employment losses far outweighed any gain. Part of the restructuring in group 1, for example, involved the redistribution of 150 jobs previously carried on in London between factories in Birmingham, Manchester, and Newcastle. The gain to these locations, however, has to be balanced against the disappearance of 1,850 jobs at the original sites in London. The same phenomenon also occurred at an intracity level. Economies of scale were frequently achieved by the closure of small and outlying factories, with the 'drawing in' on major locations thus allowing savings primarily on service labour costs.

The cities were also affected by the concentration of production at a number of major plants in such medium-sized towns as Bradford, Lincoln, Stafford, and Rugby. The first three locations, for example, gained 376 jobs as a result of the restructuring of the group 1 industries in the four cities, while the last site was the only major factory to experience an absolute gain of employment in group 1. The process of restructuring in group 1 thus involved the (albeit limited) strengthening of the position of certain favoured locations, and few of these were in the cities.

Locational transfer was also linked to changes in production techniques. One important case of production transfer in this group followed the introduction of product standardisation, which allowed the use of mass production methods (involving an *in transit* absolute loss of 300 jobs and a locational transfer of 100 jobs). This change meant not only that new plant and equipment were needed but also, and perhaps more importantly, that the production process in question was effectively freed from its existing ties to the cities as a result of the changed skill requirements of the labour force. The location that benefited from this particular transfer was in a Development Area – a site that now combined the attraction of government assistance with a newly suitable and readily available labour force (predominantly unskilled workers). Such developments clearly have serious portents for the inner cities.

4.2.3 Group 2: Restructuring to achieve scale advantages

The cases in this group were primarily in the following sectors:

(a) industrial systems, process control, etc. (MLH 354);
(b) electronic computers (MLH 366); and
(c) radio, radar, and electronic capital goods (MLH 367).

Pressures for restructuring in this group operated at two distinct levels: at the level of the economy as a whole, and at the level of the individual firms involved. In the first case government intervention was designed to facilitate the increased *application* of the products of these capital goods industries to improve the productivity of *other* manufacturing sectors. There was therefore general pressure at the level of the economy for both an increase in, and a cheapening of, the output of the group 2 industries. At the same time there was growing pressure at the level of the individual electronics firms for an increased scale of resources to keep up with the rapid rate of technological innovation that was for them the dominant aspect of international competition. An integral feature of the financial restructuring in group 2 was thus the need to increase the absolute amount of financial resources at the disposal of individual firms. This was necessary to enable a reduction in the proportion of funds devoted to research and development (R and D), the financing of the high absolute costs of development of new products, and the self-financing of large investment programmes (to overcome the problem of raising capital for long-term high-risk projects). The pressures for restructuring in group 2 were therefore:

(a) to increase the output of these industries;
(b) to cheapen the production of that output; and
(c) to keep up with the rapid rate of technological innovation.

The subsequent reorganisation of production responded to these pressures in a number of ways:

1. The need to cheapen output led to increased efforts to reduce the labour content of the products, with the introduction where possible of numerically controlled machine tools and mass production techniques. This is a long term process and not one produced just as a result of restructuring. (With each new generation of computer, for example, it is estimated that the direct labour content is reduced by one-tenth (interview with survey firm).) Moreover, the potential for the introduction of automated techniques varies between and within industries and product groups. Mass production, for example, is not feasible in the manufacture of industrial and scientific instruments, which is still heavily dependent on small-batch production processes. In those cases where automated techniques were introduced, however, there was a significant reduction in the overall size of the labour force.

2. This enabled a reduction in the level of skill required of the production workforce and produced a growing dichotomisation of skills in the labour force, between production (predominantly semiskilled assembly work) on the one hand and R and D and control functions on the other.

3. The need for increased output meant that major new capital investment was required.

4. The consolidation of research and development facilities into a smaller number of larger groupings was generally necessary if the rate of technological innovation was to be maintained.

How did the reorganisation in group 2 affect the cities? Table 4.2 shows the overall employment changes that occurred in this group. Together the cities lost some 1,466 jobs as a result of the restructuring in this group – 5 per cent of the cities' total net loss of employment during the period. This small proportion nevertheless represented 42 per cent of the total national employment decline in group 2. The significance of this loss is emphasised even more by the fact that, at the time of IRC intervention, the cities only accounted for 18 per cent of total national employment in MLHs 354, 364, 366, and 367 in the survey.

The explanation for this performance, as in group 1, is to be found in the economic pressures that created the need for restructuring. The overall process of output cheapening (including within this the

Table 4.2 Employment change in group 2 in the four cities

Category of employment change	No.
Employment loss:	
Absolute loss:	
in situ	(1,350)
in transit [a]	(136)
Locational loss [b]	(0)
Total loss	(1,486)
Employment gain:	
Absolute gain	0
Locational gain	20
Total gain	20
Net gain (loss)	(1,466)

[a] Figure includes 130 jobs linked to a transfer of production between two cities.
[b] Figure does not include a transfer of production between cities of thirteen jobs.

impact of long-term technological change) was particularly important for the cities. The 1,486 absolute loss of jobs in group 2
occurred in MLH 366, and the factories affected were relatively
labour intensive, mainly producing electromechanical equipment.
The increasing pressure for savings in labour costs within the industry and the concomitant move towards more automated production
techniques rendered such plants obsolete. This orientation meant
that the plants were particularly susceptible to the increasing pressure for labour cuts in the production workforce.

This is only part of the explanation for the effects of group 2
restructuring on the cities, however. Nationally, group 2 was
responsible for 90 per cent of the absolute gains in the survey (1,750
out of 1,970). The cities did not benefit from any of these developments. This is partly explained of course by the fact that the initial
distribution of employment in the group 2 industries was biased
against the cities. As already stated, the cities only accounted for
about 18 per cent of this employment. Any 'incremental growth'
(i.e. additions to existing facilities on site) in these industries was
therefore unlikely significantly to benefit the cities. Yet, even where
major new developments occurred they were not sited in the conurbations. In the cases examined in the survey these new investments
took the form of 'greenfield developments' in locations outside the
cities, particularly in the Development Areas.

4.2.4   Group 3:   Restructuring for reasons of market standing

This group can be quickly dealt with. The mergers that it covered came from a range of product groupings, as follows:

(a) military manpacks and nucleonics (part MLH 354);
(b) medium-sized electrical machines (part MLH 361); and
(c) computer software (part MLH 366).

The financial restructuring in this group was aimed essentially at increasing the market standing of the firms involved through sheer size and, for example, market share. The achievement of this did not require any major reorganisation of production, and there were therefore no major effects on the spatial distribution of employment. Some changes in production did occur, however, usually as a result of organisational integration after the mergers (with, say, the elimination of duplicated research facilities). Moves of this type accounted for a net loss of 200 jobs to the cities.

4.2.5   'Non-stimulant' sectors

In mergers involving multidivisional firms, the framework for analysing stimulant sectors was extended to non-stimulant sectors.[10] The effects of the reorganisation of these latter sectors were particularly significant for the cities, accounting for about 25 per cent of their total net loss of employment (7,565 jobs). These losses occurred in three industries (MLHs 354, 363, and 367); and although the reasons behind them differed in individual cases, the *forms* that they took had much in common with those displayed by groups 1 and 2. All involved closures of old labour-intensive plants in inner city locations, and the telecommunications case in particular provided a further example of the way in which technological changes within an industry can influence the spatial distribution of its activities.[11]

[10]For a detailed discussion of the role of 'non-stimulant' sectors in the restructuring, see Massey and Meegan, 1979.
[11]For a detailed discussion of the telecommunications reorganisation, see Massey and Meegan, 1979.

4.3 Employment change in the cities

This section will attempt to draw together the employment implications of the forms of restructuring discussed in section 4.2 to show how they shaped the overall performance of the cities in the survey. This perspective is best provided by a breakdown of the overall employment change into its different components.

The complete breakdown of *employment loss* in the four cities is given in Table 4.3. It is immediately clear from this table that the majority of jobs lost to the inner cities (58 per cent) resulted from either closures or capacity cuts *in which no locational change was involved*. This is an important finding, for it contradicts the widely held view that the inner cities are losing employment predominantly because of job relocation – usually, so the argument proceeds, to the Assisted Areas and as a result of the various government incentives. The great majority of the employment lost in the inner cities in the survey (89 per cent) comprised jobs lost to the economy as a whole, and such losses are in no sense locationally divertible by regional policy measures. Locational losses (in other words, employment actually lost to the inner cities and gained by another location[12]) formed a relatively insignificant component of decline in the cities. Excluding jobs transferred either within or between the four cities in the survey, this category comprised only 3,252 jobs or 11 per cent of total job loss.

It is nevertheless the case that, of the jobs that did shift location,

Table 4.3 Employment losses in the four cities

Job loss	No.	%
Absolute loss:		
In situ	17,478	57
In transit	9,635	32
Total absolute loss	27,113	89
Locational loss [a]	3,252	11
Total loss	30,365	100

[a] Excluding 373 jobs transferred within or between cities.

[12]Only *numbers* of jobs are of concern here; the *type* of employment may also change *in transit* (see later).

62 per cent (2,012) went to the Developing Areas. The argument is therefore not that the cities do not lose employment to locations in Assisted Areas, but rather that the numerical significance of this loss can be much exaggerated. Moreover, the policy significance even of the employment relocated to Assisted Areas is further reduced by the fact that only 3 per cent (sixty) of these gains to such areas were in city locations.[13] In other words, it is entirely possible that restructuring could have led to a city-non-city move even in the absence of regional policy. The argument is further strengthened when Liverpool's performance in the survey is examined. As Table 4.4. demonstrates, that city's status as a Development Area certainly did not accord it any immunity. The processes examined in this chapter would have resulted in serious employment losses in the inner cities with or without the existence elsewhere of Development Areas.[14]

The *employment gains* to the cities as a result of locational shifts of production were negligible. In the survey as a whole there were 4,495 jobs identified as locational transfers. Of these, 3,625 had their origins in plants in the four conurbations, while the remainder (870) were initially located in other parts of the country. The cities only retained 373 of the former and only received thirty of the latter. Moreover, there were *no new jobs* created in the cities as a direct result of the processes examined in this chapter (absolute gains were zero). The lack of employment gains (both locational and absolute) could of course again be argued to be a result of the

[13]These gains were all in Newcastle. This is perhaps an appropriate point for a brief comment on Newcastle's performance in the survey. As already mentioned in section 4.1, the results for Newcastle relate to one plant and followed a merger classified in group 1. The sixty locational gains were obtained at the expense of another city (London) and were offset by an absolute loss of 1,500 jobs at the Newcastle factory, giving a net decline of employment of 22 per cent. As in the other cities, there were no absolute gains of employment. Thus, although its net loss of employment was greater than the national net decline of 16 per cent, Newcastle did fare relatively well in comparison with the other cities in the survey (cf. Table 4.4). From the evidence that is available, however, it is difficult to assess whether this performance was significantly influenced by Newcastle's location in a Development Area. Any judgement on this question is complicated by the fact that the plant involved in the production reorganisation formed the 'homeland' of the firm in question. The rationalisation measure could therefore be interpreted as forming a retreat to the home base in a general period of contraction, which would have happened with or without Development Area status. The regrouping certainly appears to have been only a temporary reprieve from the rationalisation pressures in group 1; at the time of writing the plant faces substantial redundancies and possible closure.

[14]Of course it could be argued that the processes themselves were enabled by the very existence of regional policy. This point will be returned to in section 4.4.

Table 4.4 Net change in employment in the four cities (no. of jobs)

City	Total employment at time of IRC intervention		Absolute loss		Locational loss		Locational gain		Absolute gain		Result	Difference (loss)	% change (loss)
Birmingham	11,950	−	3,020	−	0	+	40	+	0	=	8,970	(2,980)	(25)
Greater London	26,473	−	10,228	−	2,563[a]	+	20[a]	+	0	=	13,702	(12,771)	(48)
Liverpool	11,350	−	4,910	−	250	+	0	+	0	=	6,190	(5,160)	(45)
Manchester	22,740	−	8,955	−	542[b]	+	93[b]	+	0	=	13,336	(9,404)	(41)
Total	72,513	−	27,113	−	3,252[c]	+	50[c]	+	0	=	42,198	(30,315)	(42)

[a] Excludes thirty jobs transferred within London but includes 103 jobs transferred to other cities.
[b] Excludes 240 jobs transferred within Manchester.
[c] Total column does not add as it excludes all jobs transferred within and between cities.

Table 4.5 The components of employment changes

Components of employment change	All survey firms (no.)	(% of inititial employment	Cities (no.)	(% of initial employment)
Absolute loss:				
in situ	(26,741)	(12)	(17,478)	(24)
in transit	(11,245)	(5)	(9,635)	(13)
Total absolute loss	(37,986)	(17)	(27,113)	(37)
Locational loss	(0)	(0)	(3,252)	(4)
Absolute gain	1,970	1	0	0
Locational gain	0	0	50	0
Net change	(36,016)	(16)	(30,315)	(42)

diversionary impact of regional policy; but once again it should be pointed out not only that Liverpool (which is in a Development Area) performed in the same manner as the cities in the non-assisted parts of the country, but also that, conversely, of the mobile employment identified in the survey only 10 per cent (433 out of 4,495)[15] went to cities at all.

Table 4.5 illustrates the impact of the employment changes on the four cities. The proportionate change, expressed as a percentage of intitial employment, was significantly greater for the cities than for the aggregate national total in every component of employment loss. The gains were negligible.

The discussion of the employment changes has so far been conducted solely in terms of the numbers of jobs gained or lost. The restructuring, however, also had profound implications for the *type of labour* demanded, both in the sector as a whole and in the cities in particular.

The first point to be noted is that in absolute terms the bulk of the losses in the cities was of relatively skilled jobs. The broad occupational distribution of employees within the sector (as a whole, and not just the survey firms) is given in Table 4.6. May 1970 is the earliest date for such a disaggregation using the 1968 SIC. The table therefore already reflects some of the changes brought about by the processes discussed in this chapter.[16] It is nevertheless indicative.

It is clear from the table that the reorganisation of production in the group 1 industries was bound to have a particularly significant

[15]Figure includes results for Newcastle.
[16]If anything, this means that it will underestimate the levels of skill at MLH level.

Table 4.6 Percentage distribution of employees (male and female)ᵃ by broad occupational category and industry, May 1970

MLH	Administrative technical, and clerical		Skilled operatives		Semiskilled		Other		Total	
354	36.6	(31.4)	24.6	(6.4)	26.7	(58.0)	12.1	(38.4)	100.0	(33.2)
361	34.9	(26.7)	26.9	(2.7)	24.5	(50.3)	13.8	(22.9)	100.1	(26.0)
362	30.9	(32.4)	8.5	(3.1)	42.6	(36.8)	18.0	(14.7)	100.0	(30.6)
363	29.7	(28.6)	12.4	(3.0)	51.0	(66.2)	6.9	(8.8)	100.0	(44.3)
364	32.1	(29.8)	11.9	(5.3)	47.0	(77.4)	9.0	(28.6)	100.0	(50.8)
365	25.7	(37.7)	10.5	(15.3)	53.8	(79.9)	10.1	(20.9)	100.1	(57.0)
366	64.2	(22.3)	14.0	(5.1)	15.8	(68.3)	6.0	(25.5)	100.0	(27.6)
367	57.9	(24.1)	18.6	(6.2)	15.4	(75.0)	8.1	(41.3)	100.0	(29.4)
368	31.2	(38.6)	11.3	(2.1)	37.5	(56.0)	20.0	(23.3)	100.0	(28.1)
369	27.4	(35.6)	15.3	(2.9)	43.8	(71.4)	13.5	(27.2)	100.0	(46.1)
383	44.6	(20.2)	33.8	(0.5)	11.0	(19.4)	10.6	(20.1)	100.0	(13.6)

ᵃFigures in brackets refer to the percentage of the category accounted for by females only.
Source: Derived from British Labour Statistics, 1970, table 100.

impact on male skilled labour. MLHs 361 and 383 have the highest percentage of skilled workers and the lowest share of female employees. For MLH 362 the official statistics give a different picture, with 61 per cent of the total workforce being unskilled or semiskilled. This initial assessment must be qualified, however. The survey results for MLH 362 related to the rationalisation of the supertension cable industry only. In a detailed interview with the company involved in the major closure of this sector the problems of skill classification became fully apparent. Thus, hourly paid workers in the industry are divisible into two categories: process workers (primarily semiskilled, working the machines) and skilled workers (mechanical and electrical maintenance workers). The second category (skilled) is small in relation to the semiskilled category. However, the semiskilled category is itself divided into eight grades, with workers in the top two grades having a very high degree of specialised skill and training. The skill, however, is acquired on the job in the grades, even when new employment is found, is likely to cable industry. On the general job market that they now face these workers are effectively unskilled or semiskilled. Since basic pay was negotiated nationally in line with these eight grades (with individual companies having their own incentive schemes), the loss of the top job in the grades, even when new employment is found, is likely to mean both a decline in the degree of skill used and a fall in income. The workers occupying these jobs were mostly male.

The employment losses occurring in the conurbations as a result of the restructuring in group 2 also had implications for the skill levels of the workforce involved. The losses in this group took place in the older electromechanical factories, which employed more traditional engineering craft skills. Moreover, the restructuring was itself part of an overall trend towards a further dichotomisation of skills within the group 2 industries, and this too has its implications for the cities. The workforce in these industries is increasingly coming to be divided between highly qualified scientific and technical staff and semiskilled (predominantly female) assembly workers. This dichotomisation of skill within the labour force has some tendency to be reflected within the spatial pattern of the industry. On the one hand, there is a growing concentration of skilled and qualified workers predominantly in the outer South-East region; on the other hand, semiskilled production increasingly favours non-urban locations within the Development Areas.

The general conclusion must therefore be that, as far as the processes that this chapter is studying are concerned, the bulk of the losses are of relatively skilled jobs. Moreover, most of these losses are absolute (see Table 4.3).

At this point it is worth clarifying the implications of this conclusion and distinguishing it from other apparently similar ones. In particular, Lomas (1974) in his study of London has assessed 'the degree of permanence of these manufacturing losses'. He has noted the frequency and importance of the following factors as determinants of the loss of employment:

the closure of the plant or unit
the transfer of production to other centres, including overspill
a compulsory purchase order
a reorganisation of production methods
economic difficulties and changes
takeovers and mergers.

Examination of the relative importance of these factors in the inner ring north and the inner ring south indicates that the first three factors dominate. He has concluded: 'The first three factors in particular . . . would suggest that the losses would be irreversible . . . . The loss of the majority of jobs therefore is permanent.' The classification of employment change used in this chapter should be distinguished from that of Lomas in that, whereas he has looked at the *causes* of loss and at the permanence of loss *to the cities*, this chapter is examining the relationship between the loss (or gain) to the inner city and the loss (or gain) *to the economy as a whole*. For present purposes then, 'the transfer of production to other centres' is a locational loss (production/employment was not lost to the economy as a whole). For Lomas it is a permanent loss because it is irreversible for the inner city. This is not to oppose the present conclusions to Lomas's; it is merely to distinguish them. The implications of Lomas's categories bear on the degree of possibility in the future of recovering for the cities some of the actual jobs lost in the past (although here some doubt must surely be thrown on the categorisation of 'the reorganisation of production methods' and 'takeovers and mergers' as processes whose employment implications are potentially reversible). The implications of the categories used in this chapter bear on the nature of the macroeconomic process that 'produced' the change at the level of the city. The present classification is also concerned with categories of employment change *in general*, rather than with specific jobs. Thus, in the terms of this chapter, the number of jobs relocated out of the inner

Table 4.7   Employment change in Greater London by skill category (males only), 1966–71

Skill category	%, 1966	Numerical change, 1966–71	% change, 1966–71	%, [a] 1971
Skilled	34.1	−106,540	−11.4	31.7
Semiskilled	14.3	− 47,700	−12.4	13.1
Unskilled	8.1	− 31,100	−14.0	7.3

[a] The percentages are of the total of active and retired males.
Source: Lomas (1974).

cities may indicate, *as a category*, the degree of possibility to which changed policies of industrial location may enable the retention of such employment for the inner city.

This latter point is worth a further comment in view of the fact that most concern is usually expressed over the unemployment of unskilled workers. Certainly, as Lomas has pointed out, the largest group among the unemployed is labourers. A distinction should be made, however, between the loss of jobs and unemployment. The figures given in this chapter concern loss of jobs. Thus, for the period 1966–71 and for London only, Lomas has given the figures in Table 4.7. Although the absolute loss of skilled male jobs was larger (as the evidence of the present study agrees), the *percentage* loss was higher in the less skilled categories. This, together with the difficulty of skill categorisation, and with the fact that higher-skilled workers are supposedly more mobile both locationally and occupationally, may account for the worse unemployment figures for unskilled male workers. Lomas (1974) has also pointed out that unemployment figures are sometimes ambiguous in that they may describe the future expectations of workers rather than their previous employment. Lomas has made this point in relation to the manufacturing/service division; but as the evidence from the super-tension cable industry, cited above, indicates, it may apply also to the distinction between skilled and unskilled.

The second major conclusion from the present examination of skill categories concerns the nature of the change in the demand for skills brought about by technological change and increasing capital intensity. There appears to be some division of opinion on this matter. Thus, Falk and Martinos (1975) have written that 'rising levels of mechanisation do away with the need for unskilled labour' (p. 4) and, talking of the kind of large firms that should be retained in cities, recommended 'labour intensive . . . industries that would create high unemployment for unskilled and semi-skilled workers if they moved out of the inner city areas' (p. 16). Although the process will evidently vary both with different industries and with the level of automation being considered, the evidence of the present study indicates that increased mechanisation, standardisation, and technological advance lead to a *relative* decline in the demand for skilled labour. Some distinctions can be made – for instance, between trends towards the standardisation and mass production of specified commodities and major technological shifts such as that from electrical to electronic – but the overall movement in each case is in the same direction.

The results in this chapter therefore agree with the findings of the recent report of the Department of Employment's Unit for Manpower Studies, *The Changing Structure of the Labour Force* (Department of Employment, 1975a). In an attempt to explain the fall of some 990,000 in skilled and semiskilled manual workers in Great Britain over the period 1961–71, the unit has isolated two major contributory factors: 'technical changes leading to changes in the occupational skills required by an industry (the occupational effect) and changes in the relative size of industries (the industry effect)' (p. 27). The unit has then proceeded to demonstrate that, in the case of skilled and semiskilled manual occupations, the overall shift away from employment in production industries (the industry effect) 'has been reinforced by an occupation effect which in itself would have induced a significant reduction in numbers *had the structure of industry remained unchanged*' (p. 28, present authors' italics). In the specific case of inner cities it does seem true that the major losses are occurring in skilled and semiskilled jobs; and the bulk of the losses in MLHs 361 and 362 should be classified as 'industry effects', with some of the losses in MLH 361 and the main part of those in MLH 363 being due to the 'occupational effect'.

This conclusion is interesting in that the factor of labour skill is frequently mentioned in the context of industrial migration from the cities. None of the evidence unearthed by the present study, however, suggests that firms have moved out of the cities in search of a *more* skilled manual labour force.

4.4 Conclusions

A major aim of this chapter has been to reformulate the 'problem of the city' in such a way that it can be related to an analysis of the changing structure of the national economy.[17] It is clear that the repercussions of the processes of restructuring outlined in this chapter have had considerable implications for the cities and, further, that it is only at this level of analysis that the employment changes identified could have been adequately accounted for. It is also clear that such a form of analysis may lead to rather distinctive policy conclusions.

First, while the focus of *interest* in this chapter has remained at the level of the city, the nature of the definition of the problem has meant that its causes have not also had to be located within the same confines. One result of this is that to a considerable extent such an approach shifts the locus of 'blame' away from local authorities. This is not to deny that the processes of planning and of development control have any negative impact at all; rather, it is to stress that that impact operates within the context of circumstances determined at, for instance, the level of the economy as a whole.

In another way too the results of this research lead to the argument that it is incorrect to interpret the present problems of the cities as in some way the 'fault' of state policies, referring in this case to regional policy. It is a common proposition that the existence of regional policies has been significantly responsible for the decline of manufacturing employment in major cities. A number of points on this have already been made in section 4.3. The major consideration is of course that a large part of the decline identified consisted of *absolute* loss. Such job losses are in no way divertible by spatial policies; nor are the reasons for the cutbacks likely to be influenced by such policies. These reasons have been discussed in section 4.2; it should be noted here, however, that the losses did *not* result from company failure – a possibility that might in turn be attributable at least in part to detrimental locational conditions. On the contrary, it must be stressed that the closures, the redundancies, and the cutbacks that occurred indicate not failure but the only possibility for 'success'. Such action was necessary in order to increase the firms' profitability and international competitiveness.

[17]It should be emphasised that this is a study of only one branch (although a major one) of that economy. In particular, the possibility of employment growth in the service industries has not been considered in this chapter.

The remaining loss (11 per cent gross) did, however, as recorded in section 4.3 occur through, or as part of, a locational change. Two questions arise here: the first is whether regional policies form part of the stimulus to, or critically enable, the processes involved in the locational change; the second is, given that some locational change may occur, whether the existence of regional policies influence the 'destination' of these changes. Falk and Martinos (1975), who have discussed the importance of factors such as those considered here, have argued that the system of regional incentives has not merely influenced subsequent locational choices, but also made possible the processes themselves; regional assistance 'has made mergers and the subsequent rationalisation of plants easier, and has encouraged concentration and the substitution of capital for labour' (p. 14). One of the implications of this argument is that regional policy is, at least to some extent, part and parcel of overall national economic policy. In other words, it is part of the same strategy as the IRC. This is an important point and one for which there is considerable evidence. However, if regional policy is not simply regional policy but is part of the attempt to increase the productivity of industry, and if it is thereby reinforcing employment problems in inner cities, that does not mean that regional policy can simply be abandoned. Alternative, and at least equally effective, means that increase competitiveness without producing such problematical spatial repercussions have to be found.

The relationship between inner city problems and regional policies is anyway more complex than that. In the first place, mergers, rationalisations, and the concentration and reorganisation of capacity rarely demand investment in brand new plant. This will usually only be necessary when other changes (e.g. in production techniques) are implemented at the same time. In most cases, therefore, regional incentives on capital investment will be (mainly) inoperative; and on the other hand, Industrial Development Certificates will be unnecessary since existing capacity will be used. Thus, much of the locational loss of employment to the cities resulting from the processes studied here may have produced relative gains elsewhere, but it has done so within existing plant and within the medium-sized towns of the non-assisted areas of England (see on this, for example, Eversley's Introduction to this book). Indeed, a few cases were found where closures occurred in an inner city (Liverpool) in a Development Area, with the transfer of part of the production and job opportunities to non-assisted areas. These

Table 4.8 Effect of inner-city plant closures on employment in plants in development areas (no. employed in receiving plant)

Development area		At time of merger	One year after merger
Wales		480	603
North:	plant 1	1,500 ⎫	1,802 ⎫
	plant 2	5,400 ⎬ 7,340	4,450 ⎬ 6,577
	plant 3	440 ⎭	325 ⎭
Scotland:	plant 1	1,140 ⎫ 2,100	923 ⎫ 2,063
	plant 2	960 ⎭	1,140 ⎭
Total		9,920	9,243

aspects of mergers and subsequent rationalisation, then, are not themselves frequently influenced by the incentives (or disincentives) that are available as part of regional policy.

As the analysis in section 4.3 has shown, however, this does leave 62 per cent of the net locational loss to the cities, which was involved in locational moves to the Assisted Areas. The nature of these moves should therefore be examined in more detail. In the first place, and at a simple numerical level, it should be pointed out that it was the locational losses in this category that were responsible for the greater part of absolute losses *in transit*. The number of new jobs directly created in the recipient Development Areas was only about two-thirds of the number lost in the cities.[18] The figures in Table 4.8 are for the plants, by Development Area, receiving production from the largest of the inner city closures.

These employment figures of course cover all the employment in the receiving plants, not just that transferred; and moreover, other changes and reorganisations in the sector were going on at the same time. The numbers nevertheless indicate that a massive loss to the cities, and an apparent transfer of work, did not mean a corresponding gain to the Assisted Areas. Moreover, since the second date, and as a result both of increasing efficiency (increasing the capital–labour ratio) and of reduced orders, employment at all the

---

[18]It should be pointed out that it was this category of changes that was most dominated by a few large moves, and the figures should be treated accordingly. On the other hand, evidence from other sources (e.g. Keeble, 1971; Firn, 1975) indicates that one would *expect* this category to be the one most dominated by a few large moves by a few large firms.

plants has been further reduced, and one of them has been closed. The conclusion must be that, if the *processes* involved are going to continue even (if they could do so) without a change in location, they will anyway involve considerable losses of employment in the inner cities.

Part of the argument is, however, that the processes themselves are enabled or encouraged by regional policy, particularly by the incentives available. While not disagreeing with this position, it is also necessary to ask whether the locational attractions may be characteristics of Development Areas *other than* the availability there of regional policy incentives. In other words, to what extent is movement to a depressed area an integral part of the economic process? One such frequently quoted attraction is space availability, including both absolute availability and price. There was one 'location factor' for which some evidence on this score was found. This was the labour factor. It should be stressed again that in terms of actual location shifts these results refer to only a small number of cases, but for the purposes of this argument evidence from the absolute gains in employment that benefited the Assisted Areas can also be used. The main result of the analysis is that the jobs created in the Development Areas were almost entirely semiskilled. That is, they demanded less skill than the employment lost in the cities in these industries over the same period; and in the cases where an actual spatial shift was involved, this took place in a context of technological change and, consequently, of both an absolute reduction in the total number of jobs and a downward change in the nature of the skills required.

Four conclusions emerged from the study. First, and most conclusively, none of the evidence that is available suggests that in this situation firms will move out of industrial cities in search of a *more* skilled labour force. Second, even had it been possible for the restructuring processes to have occurred *without* locational change, there would nevertheless have been a considerable downward shift in the balance of labour skills demanded in the major industrial cities studied. Third, given the direction of change in production–skill requirements indicated by the study, it may be that the balance of location factors is changing to release such industries from their previous requirement for highly skilled labour. This in turn may loosen their existing spatial ties to the major established industrial cities. This of course, while indicating a shift away from metropolitan areas, does not necessarily imply growth in assisted regions. The fourth, and very tentative, indication of the results was that, given this changing demand for labour, more emphasis could now be placed in the location decision on the locationally differentiated characteristics of *less*-skilled labour. There are of course reserves of unemployed unskilled and semiskilled labour in the cities. The indications were, however, that such labour was regarded as probably more expensive and potentially more militant. In contrast, the labour of small towns in Development Areas was cheaper and, because of its pressing need for employment, less demanding.[19]

Although this chapter has considered only one major sector of industry, Harris and Taylor (1976) have argued that the restructuring of the labour force is an economy level phenomenon. Under such circumstances it seems that the problem of the cities cannot be approached by setting them up as yet more areas with incentives of the regional policy type. The question is one of national level planning, not one of increasing the number of competing incentives for any given piece of new capital investment. Moreover, regional policy incentives as they stand at present would be inoperative at the level of detail required to attack the problems of the inner cities. In order adequately to counter the present population–employment imbalance within these areas, it would be necessary for a policy to be able to specify or to influence the kind of industries attracted and, further, to operate at a fairly precise spatial level. That is, it would be necessary to be able to distinguish between location policies for the inner city and location policies for outer regional areas. General incentive policies are rarely able to achieve such precision.

The major concern of this chapter has been to relate the employment changes at present going on in the cities to economic processes at national and international levels. Although any individual case was the result of a complex of causes, the dominant processes affecting the four cities under study were clearly responses to the problems of overcapacity and to relative technological shifts in favour of cheaper (and in all the cases studied, less labour-intensive) production processes. Frequently, the major companies involved were seeking to change the balance of their home production away from the heavy electrical part of the sector. Cuts in

[19]The Development Areas were not the only parts of the country apparently benefiting from such changes in labour requirements. Tourist areas where 'new' labour could be brought into the labour force were also increasingly feasible (see Massey, 1977).

capacity thus added to the viability of the firm as a whole in international competition in its other products. These specific processes were found to be important partly *because* the study was of the IRC, whose activity was focused on such cases, but it should be noted that their effect was proportionately more important on the cities than on the nation as a whole. It should be argued that, as a general form, such restructuring and reorganisation of major sectors and of particular product groups is a necessary process in the development of the UK economy. It is therefore not possible to consider policy options that rule out the operation of the economic processes themselves. If there is a contradiction at the heart of this process of decline, the research outlined above indicates that it is not between inner cities and policy-aided Development Areas, but between the cities and the demands of profitability and international competitiveness.

5 Industrial Decline in the Inner City and Conurbation

David Keeble

5.1 Abstract[1]

This review considers the components of, reasons for, and some policy implications relating to, rapid recent manufacturing decline in Britain's conurbations and their inner city areas. Although complete factory closures are very important in short term decline, industrial migration, it is argued, has been of major long-term significance. Stress is also placed on the role of larger multiplant corporations in closing inner city and conurbation factories. Closures and migration are viewed as a response both to organisational differences in conurbation industry, as crudely measured by plant size, and to an increasingly unattractive conurbation operating environment. Key factors in the latter are cost, the age and character of premises, changing residential preferences on the part of industrialists and workers, and, to a lesser degree, central and local government policies. It is argued that a major shift in industrial incentives and controls designed to steer mobile industry into inner city areas is undesirable; rather, policy emphasis should be on local government aid to existing firms and on the provision of cheap and suitable modern factories.

5.2 Introduction

Since the early 1960s all Britain's major cities have experienced massive industrial decline, measured by numbers of firms and jobs,

[1]First published in *Transactions of the Institute of British Geographers*, new series, vol. 3, no. 1 (1978).

particularly in their inner areas. Thus, Greater London, for example, appears to have lost no less than 560,000 manufacturing jobs or 40 per cent of its base year total between 1961 and 1975, while losses in Greater Manchester between 1959 and 1971 were of the order of 107,000 jobs or 18 per cent (Reeve, 1974, table 3.1). Clydeside's manufacturing employment declined over the same period by 64,000 jobs or 14 per cent. The concentration of decline in inner as compared with suburban conurbation areas is strongly suggested by various evidence. Thus, the City of Manchester – the inner core of Greater Manchester – lost nearly 50,000 manufacturing jobs in 1961–71 at an annual rate (3 per cent) that was nearly three times that of the rest of the conurbation, while Martin and Seaman (1975) have reported a 1954–68 decline of larger factories, employing over 100 workers, of 44 per cent in inner London but only 17 per cent in outer London. Admittedly, a recent Department of Industry study (Dennis, Chapter 2) argues that industrial employment decline rates have been fairly similar in the latter two areas, but this study does run counter to most other evidence.

Rapid industrial decline in conurbation and inner-city areas raises many questions. This chapter considers briefly three key questions: namely, what is the nature of decline, what are the probable reasons for it, and what are the possible policy implications that arise? A few initial comments are, however, appropriate. First, the chapter is concerned solely with manufacturing industry, on the grounds that the recent decline in the levels of the service industry is both much less dramatic and easier to explain. For example, Table 5.1 reveals that, in contrast to rapid manufacturing decline, higher-order 'basic' service employment has still been growing in both Manchester and London in recent years, while even lower-order 'non-basic' services have not been declining at anything like the rate of volume of manufacturing. The moderate decline of 'non-basic' services is also of course readily attributable to the preceding and current population decline in these cities, since almost by definition the level of such 'personal' services as retailing, entertainment, and local transport is heavily geared to local population levels.

Second, industrial decline in conurbation and inner-city areas must be seen as an integral part of the remarkable wider national trend towards industrial *dispersion*, at all geographic scales – national, regional, and local (Keeble, 1976, pp. 25–9, 286–8). Dispersion, in the sense of the relative and absolute decline of

Table 5.1 Employment change in Greater London and Greater Manchester by sector of economic activity, 1971–75

Sector	Greater London			Greater Manchester		
	1971 (thousands)	Change, 1971–75 (thousands)	(%)	1967 (thousands)	Change, 1967–72 (thousands)	(%)
Manufacturing	1,049.3	−213.4	−20.3	596.6	−93.8	−15.7
Non-basic services[a]	1,440.8	−42.8	−3.0	363.5	−27.0	−7.4
Basic services[b]	1,246.4	+121.1	+9.7	228.5	+38.7	+16.9

[a] Defined as Orders 21, 22, 23, and 26 of the SIC ('Gas, electricity, and water', 'Transport and communication', 'Distributive trades', and 'Miscellaneous services').
[b] Defined as Orders 24, 25, and 27 of the SIC ('Insurance, banking, finance, and business services', 'Professional and scientific services', and 'Public administration and defence').
Sources: London – Unpublished Department of Employment statistics; Manchester – Greater Manchester Council (1975, pp. 91–2).

manufacturing industry in larger industrial centres and its relative and absolute growth in smaller ones, is clearly illustrated for recent regional scale change by Table 5.2. This shows that between 1965 and 1975 the four largest industrial regions of the United Kingdom all recorded massive manufacturing–employment decline, whereas the only three regions exhibiting growth were among the four

Table 5.2 Regional manufacturing employment change in the United Kingdom, 1965–75

Region	1965 (thousands)	(% of U.K.)	1975 (thousands)	(% of U.K.)	Change, 1965–75 (thousands)	(%)
East Anglia	167	2.0	198	2.6	+31	+18.6
Wales	311	3.6	317	4.2	+6	+2.0
South-West	422	4.9	427	5.7	+5	+1.2
North	459	5.4	454	6.1	−5	−1.1
East Midlands	620	7.2	593	7.9	−27	−4.4
Northern Ireland	171	2.0	154	2.1	−17	−9.9
Scotland	725	8.5	637	8.5	−88	−12.1
West Midlands	1,185	13.8	1,021	13.6	−164	−13.8
Yorkshire and Humberside	860	10.1	733	9.8	−127	−14.8
North-West	1,252	14.6	1,042	13.9	−210	−16.8
South-East	2,389	27.9	1,913	25.5	−476	−19.9
United Kingdom	8,561	100.0	7,489	100.1	−1,072	−12.5

Source: Department of Employment Gazette (August 1976).

smallest industrially in 1965. The inverse relationship between 1965 size and the subsequent rate of manufacturing employment change of the eleven regions in fact yields the very high Spearman's rank correlation coefficient of -0.90, significant, ignoring the problems of spatial autocorrelation, at the 0.01 probability level. If Northern Ireland, the only but easily explicable anomaly, is excluded, the inverse correlation for the regions of Great Britain is almost perfect.

An exactly similar dispersion trend is also evident at the more detailed subregional and local scales. Thus, out of the 61 subregions into which Britain was until recently divided for statistical purposes, no less than 17 (or 85 per cent) of the 20 largest (100,000 manufacturing workers or more) in 1971 had recorded manufacturing employment *decline* by 1973, whereas 16 (or 80 per cent) of the 20 smallest subregions in 1971 (38,000 manufacturing workers or less) exhibited subsequent manufacturing *growth* (Keeble, 1977). Marked recent local dispersion, e.g. within the South-East and East Anglia, is documented in Keeble (1976, pp. 269–73). Similar trends appear to characterise other advanced industrial countries, such as the United States, Sweden and France. At all geographic scales the balance of manufacturing activity measured by employment is shifting from large to small centres, presumably as a response to powerful 'natural' forces, and conurbations and inner cities are inevitably losing industry as a result.

The last initial comment is simply to stress how fragmentary and impressionistic is much of the available evidence on inner-city manufacturing decline and how little detailed research has yet been completed on it. The views and arguments presented here must therefore be subject to qualification and modification as more reliable information becomes available.

5.3 The nature of decline

Recent Department of Industry research (Dennis, Chapter 2) on Greater London has established that the largest single component of manufacturing decline in the capital since the late 1960s or earlier has been the complete closure or 'death' of previously existing factories. Thus, between 1966 and 1974 Greater London lost 390,000 manufacturing jobs, no less than 183,000 or 47 per cent of which were in larger factories (employing over twenty workers) that apparently closed down completely without any transference of production elsewhere. Only 10,000 jobs were gained through industrial births or the opening of entirely new factories. Net losses of jobs through the migration of manufacturing firms in and, primarily, out of London totalled 102,000 or 26 per cent. In inner London (the group A boroughs of the Greater London Council), large firm closures were relatively even more important than net migration, with 94,000 jobs lost through closures but only 46,000 or less than half the closure total, lost through net migration. An even more striking picture is evident in Glasgow, where Firn (1976) has established that at least 80 per cent of manufacturing job losses between 1958 and 1968 were due to plant closure (allowing for offsetting growth in entirely new firms) with only one-fifth or so losses a result of net emigration;[2] interestingly, substantial *in situ* growth and contraction in existing plants which operated in Glasgow throughout the decade more or less exactly balanced, with no net change as a result. A dominance of closures has also been reported by the inner area consultants studying Small Heath, Birmingham (Department of the Environment, 1977a, pp. 22–3).

At first sight one important possible implication of these findings may be that drastic conurbation and inner-city industrial decline reflects primarily the currently uncompetitive nature of the particular *firms* and *industries* historically concentrated there, rather than a conscious comparative assessment by firms of the *locational disadvantages* of these areas relative to others. This view certainly has received considerable support from Firn (1976), who has stressed that in the Glasgow case industry in the core city is 'comprised mainly of small indigenous plants in declining or static industrial sectors' and that closure rates by size of plant suggest that there has been a disproportionate loss of *medium-sized* establishments, many of which seem to have been 'old-established heavy engineering firms, finally succumbing to the competitive pressures of modern industry'. Firn has thus pointed to the possibility of explaining inner city decline in terms of 'the natural result of urban industrial dendrochronology'.

This kind of explanation, stemming directly from the findings on the components of change noted above, may well have considerable validity, particularly in the Clydeside case; but at least three comments or qualifications about the component findings are perhaps

[2]Although Firn has quoted 80 per cent for closures net of births in his 1976 paper, his earlier report (Firn and Hughes, 1974), referenced in his 1976 paper, gives 91 per cent and 8 per cent as the net closure and migration proportions respectively.

necessary. First, any simple link between a very high closure rate and an industry-oriented explanation for decline is not readily apparent in cases such as Birmingham or London, the latter being of course the greatest single industrial-decline centre of Britain today. Thus, analysis at the very detailed Minimum List Heading level of the Standard Industrial Classification (SIC) reveals that in 1959 Greater London's industrial structure was more favourable, in terms of bias towards industries whose employment subsequently expanded rather than declined nationally, than that of all but five of the United Kingdom's other sixty-one official subregions. The West Midlands conurbation – another industrial-decline centre – had the second most favourable structure in the whole country (Keeble, 1976, pp. 98–101). That London's industrial decline is not primarily due to industrial structure is also one of the main conclusions of the Department of Industry's research (Dennis, Chapter 2) and of Gripaios's study (1977a, p. 2) of closures in inner south-east London.

Second, it can be argued that, taking a longer perspective than a period of only eight or ten years, industrial migration is an even more significant component of conurbation and inner-city decline than at first sight appears. This is so for at least two reasons. One is that mobile firms are exceptional and atypical of urban industry generally in being characterised by above average growth of both output and employment. Movement is in fact usually prompted by growth. However, this well-documented characteristic (Keeble, 1976, pp. 127–9) means that continuous net emigration over several decades, as experienced by, for example, London and Birmingham, removes precisely those firms which could by expansion offset natural decline in other local firms whose products are no longer in demand or whose managers are unable to adapt to changed circumstances. The long term magnitude of 'lost' employment through growth firm emigration is illustrated by the Department of Industry's estimate of 330,000 jobs in moves to other parts of the United Kingdom from Greater London between 1945 and 1965 (Howard, 1968), although this is admittedly an extreme case.

The other reason for arguing for a greater long-term impact is that migration is industry- as well as growth-specific, and it so happens that several of the country's most mobile industries are also characterised by relatively high intraindustry linkages. Classic examples here are the electrical and mechanical engineering industries, which not only have dominated industrial migration flows in postwar Britain (Keeble, 1975) but also exhibit an unusually high level of industrial linkage, with substantial flows of semifinished goods and components between different engineering firms (Lever, 1972). Survey research has shown, however, that in both the inner and suburban city small engineering firms may be acutely dependent upon larger local engineering concerns for their viability (Martin, 1957; Keeble, 1969). The same may also be true for firms in the clothing and textile industries, which are also characterised by unusually high migration and, in cities such as London or Manchester, linkage rates. So, migration out of the city of larger firms in these industries could exert a particularly strong negative multiplier effect, with a chain reaction of decline or closure among the small firms left behind. Some part of observed closures, particularly of small firms, may therefore in fact be a direct result of industrial emigration. This argument, and the view that migration has major long-term significance for inner-city industrial decline, has also recently been advanced by Gripaios (1977a) on the basis of research in inner south-east London.

A third point concerns the nature of the dominant component in inner-city manufacturing decline – the complete closure of existing factories. Evidence here is particularly fragmentary, but there are indications that a key factor in a high rate of job loss through closures is the locational decision-making of larger multiplant firms, which close down their inner city or conurbation factories after locational evaluation against other currently or potentially more profitable non-conurbation plants. In other words, closures as well as migration may reflect the conscious locational evaluation of operating conditions and prospects in the conurbations and inner cities as compared with other areas. The evidence for this suggestion involves studies both of the relative importance of multiplant companies in the conurbations and of actual closures in particular instances. Two recent studies suggest, for example, that the relative importance of multiplant factories for manufacturing employment is significantly greater in the conurbations than in other areas. Thus, Firn (1975, p. 408) has shown that no less than 64 per cent of 1973 manufacturing employment in the Glasgow region was in factories controlled by multiplant organisations with headquarters or parent establishments located outside Scotland, whereas outside Glasgow the proportion was only 52 per cent, with values as low as 45 per cent on Tayside and in the Highlands. Second, McDermott (1977, pp. 95–6) has shown for a representative sample of electronics-

Table 5.3 Multiplant factories and employment in electronics engineering, London and the OMA

	Greater London	OMA	
Firms			*No. of firms sampled*
% single-plant	67	79	London 39
% multiplant	33	21	OMA 43
Employment			*Total employment*
% single-plant	17	45	London 20,859
% multiplant	83	55	OMA 11,816

Source: McDermott (1977), pp. 95–6, unpublished sample data.

engineering firms that, whereas single-plant companies are proportionately much more numerous than multiplant companies in Greater London, it is the latter that dominate employment, with 83 per cent of the 1974 total in the London firms sampled (Table 5.3)[3]. In contrast, multiplant firms in the surrounding outer metropolitan area (OMA) of south-east England, although still more important for employment than single-plant companies, were responsible for only 55 per cent of jobs in sampled OMA electronics concerns. Both these studies thus agree that conurbation industrial employment appears to be significantly more dependent on factories operated by multiplant firms than is the case with employment in other areas.

Evidence for the view that, in turn, a high proportion of job losses through closures in inner-city or conurbation areas is in factory closures by larger multiplant companies is more debatable. However, in addition to the anecdotal evidence provided by such much publicised cases as the Woolwich AEI and Greenford Rockware factory closures (Keeble, 1976, pp. 123–4), this argument is supported by the findings of Community Development Project (CDP) studies and inner area researchers. Thus, the CDP review (1976, p. 25) of industrial decline in the five urban and inner-city project areas of North Shields, Benwell (Newcastle upon Tyne), Batley (West Yorkshire), Saltley (Birmingham), and Canning Town (Lon-

---

[3] In this very new industry, however, inner London firms were dominantly small single-plant concerns; nearly all the multiplant companies were located in outer London (McDermott, 1978).

don) claims that large multiplant firms are the key agents in recent local manufacturing decline: 'a relatively small number of companies are responsible for cutting these jobs. They are often established firms, frequently the subsidiaries of major corporations pursuing rationalisation policies. In some areas less than half a dozen firms have been responsible for three-quarters of local job losses.' The latter areas are in fact Canning Town and Saltley, where national firms such as Tate and Lyle, Unilever, and British Leyland have played an especially important role in local factory closures and job losses. This role is documented in some detail in a CDP report on Canning Town (Community Development Project, 1975a).

The CDP reports are clearly arguing from a particular political viewpoint, and their interpretation and policy prescriptions concerning industrial decline are debatable; but their analytical findings do support the view that locational evaluation by multiplant firms is a very important aspect of inner city closures. So too does at least one Inner Area Study by the Department of the Environment, namely, that dealing with Small Heath, Birmingham; for one of the 'three crucial points' arising from the consultant's analysis of manufacturing job loss was that 'much the largest part of this loss has been due to the death of large establishments, which have closed because of trading changes; the loss of jobs in small firms has been less important in aggregate terms' (Department of the Environment, 1977a, p. 23). This also appears to be true for manufacturing and service firm closures, excluding closures associated with migration, in inner south-east London, on the basis of data presented by Gripaios (1977a, table 2). Although detailed figures are not provided, a crude but conservative estimate based on closures by five establishment-size groupings suggests that approximately 70 per cent of total job losses through closures were in larger establishments employing over 100 workers. Exactly the same conclusion, that 'the inner city is losing manufacturing . . . because it has suffered from relatively large closures', has also been arrived at by Cameron (1977a, p. 217) for Glasgow. So, in Birmingham, London, and Clydeside the evidence indicates that the single most important element in inner-city employment decline through closures is the loss of relatively large factories, and this in turn could well reflect locational evaluation by multiplant firms of their operating costs and future potential compared with company factories elsewhere.

5.4 The reasons for decline

Analysis of the nature and components of manufacturing decline in
inner city areas leads on to the consideration of the possible reasons
for a rate of decline that is far greater than could be expected on
national trends or as a result of industrial structure. In this context
the argument advanced above concerning multiplant firms is important; for if correct, it could imply that the forces that are responsible
are chiefly of a locational, rather than an historical, nature. Put
another way, industrial emigration to areas perceived as possessing
a better environment for growth and profitable operation, *plus*
closures as part of conscious multiplant locational evaluation, may
be more important factors in most conurbations than deaths reflecting simply an historic concentration of now relict aging firms characterised by outmoded organisational and technological methods or
inadequate entrepreneurship.

Of course, as noted earlier, this is not to say that the latter may not
have played a significant part in decline, particularly in certain
conurbations. *Organisational* differences between firms in the same
industry but located in different areas may well be a hitherto
under-rated factor in industrial location shifts, as McDermott
(1977) has argued. Intriguingly, this view is supported to some
degree by the aggregate statistics for Britain's seven major conurbations, recorded in Table 5.4. The latter shows average factory size,
for all establishments employing more than ten workers, in each
conurbation in 1972, together with the rates of change in aggregate
manufacturing employment over the most recent twelve-year
period for which figures are available, namely, 1959–71. Using a
rank rather than product-moment correlation test because of the
small sample involved, the two sets of data yield a Spearman's r_s
coefficient of 0.93, significant at the 0.01 probability level. In other
words, the smaller its average factory size (a classic indicator of the
way a firm is organised and operates), the greater is an area's rate
of manufacturing decline. Of course this very simple test is open to
all manner of criticisms, notably that the data make no allowance
for variation between conurbations in industrial structure or government industrial-location policy and that figures for factory size
at the *end* of a period are by inference related causally to *preceding*
employment change. In some defence, however, it may be argued
that it is unlikely that 1959 data for factory size, were they available
(which they are not), would radically alter the relative rankings in

Table 5.4   Factory size and manufacturing employment change in Britain's conurbations, 1972 and 1959–71

Conurbation	A		B	
	Mean factory size, 1972 (no. of employees)^a	Rank	Change in manufacturing employment 1959–71(%)	Rank
London	85	1	−23.4	1
West Yorkshire	104	2	−15.9	3
Manchester	116	3	−17.9	2
West Midlands	128	4	−8.6	5
Clydeside	150	5	−13.9	4
Merseyside	177	6	+0.2	6
Tyneside	184	7	+1.3	7

^{a} The data exclude employment in establishments of ten employees or less. While inclusion of the latter would obviously deflate the mean values, it can be argued that it is unlikely that this would alter the relative rankings shown.
Sources: Column A – Business Statistics Office (1975), *Business Monitor*, PA1003; column B – unpublished Department of Employment statistics.

column A, with the possible exception of Merseyside. It may further be argued that *within* the two sets of assisted area conurbations as scheduled during this perod (Clydeside, Merseyside, and Tyneside) and non-assisted area conurbations (the remainder), taken separately, the relationship holds even better than for all seven conurbations considered together. The industrial structure qualification is obviously a very important one. Nevertheless, Table 5.4 provides at least some *prima facie* evidence for the view that *within* the set of declining conurbations the rates of industrial decline may partly reflect differences in industrial organisation as crudely represented by establishment size.

If decline is even more a response to conscious locational evaluation, however, which aspects of the inner city environment are most comparatively disadvantageous for long-term efficient manufacturing? Again, the evidence here is fragmentary and sometimes impressionistic; but as a thesis supported by much of the available evidence, it will be argued that three interlinked aspects of this environment may well be of key significance: the nature and value of industrial premises and sites; deterioration, both absolute and relative, in the inner-city residential environment; and local and central government planning. These 'compulsive' factors, are, moreover, strengthened by certain 'permissive' influences that, while not directly compelling locational shift, render such shift more likely, *given* a balance of locational advantage in favour of non-conurbation areas.

One very important 'permissive' factor is the substantial improvement in road, and to a lesser extent rail, communications that has taken place in Britain over recent decades (Keeble, 1976, pp. 55–9). The relative decline in distance costs for movements of supplies, finished products, and high level staff is a consequent long-term trend that has conferred greater locational freedom and flexibility on firms in most modern industries. Again, technological change in certain industries has reduced traditional ties to particular locations, as, for example, with production processes hitherto dependent upon especially skilled conurbation or inner-city labour. National growth in the average size of firms may have led to the increased internalisation of linkages and processes that in small firms have traditionally been bought-in externally and hence may have tied them to a particular inner-city location. Large firms certainly seem able to stretch intracompany links between different plants over greater distances than small firms whose linkages are with external organisations (Lever, 1974). These and other 'permissive' factors have almost certainly widened the range of locational choice for many modern firms, particularly larger firms.

The first 'compulsive' factor suggested by many different studies is the nature and cost of industrial premises and sites. The relatively very high cost of industrial land and premises in inner-city and conurbation areas has of course been recognised as a major agglomeration diseconomy ever since Alfred Weber's discussion of this factor in 1909. The extent of the cost differential with other non-conurbation areas is evident from figures for London collected by Vallis (1972) and listed in Table 5.5.

As these show, in the 1950s and early 1960s industrial land prices in London were very much greater than those in the rest of the South-East, and the differential, although narrowing, was still very substantial in the later 1960s. Within London there was a substantial cost-of-premises differential in the earlier period between the inner city – e.g. the EC, WC, W1, and SW1 postal areas – and the other more suburban zones, although again some narrowing had occurred by the later 1960s, with a marked relative decline in the west-central area. It must also be stressed that these figures of course relate to existing factory stock and therefore make no allow-

Table 5.5 Industrial land and building prices in London and south-east England

Median industrial land prices (£1,000 per acre)			
	GLC area	Rest of South-East	All England
1946–63	26.1	1.4	4.2
1964–69	50.0	20.0	11.9

Median industrial building values (£ per sq.ft) within Greater London						
	EC	WC, SW1, W1	SE	N, E	W, NW, Middlesex	SW
1946–63	2.4	3.2	1.4	1.9	2.0	2.2
1964–69	4.8	4.3	2.8	3.8	4.6	4.5

Source: Vallis (1972), p. 1406.

ance for the poorer quality of inner city factories as compared with more recently constructed premises on suburban industrial estates.

Traditionally, a marked factory or land-cost gradient has of course been taken as reflecting buoyant demand from industrial users. In the absence of such demand today, any maintenance of high asking prices for industrial land or premises in inner city areas seems clearly to reflect unrealistic expectations on the part of owners, together with time lags in market adjustment and, possibly, an artificial inflation of local authority valuations because of the paucity of actual transactions (Edwards, 1977, p. 206). However, it can be argued that historically high prices have been an important factor in recent locational shifts, especially during and since the 1960s, for various reasons. One is that modern growth industry is becoming increasingly space-intensive rather than labour-intensive. Thus, for example, Department of Industry figures show that between 1960 and 1969 the area of new factory floorspace actually constructed in Great Britain, relative to the workforce to be employed, rose steadily year by year, from 60 m² per worker employed in the new factory to 70 m² (Keeble, 1976, p. 75). This trend must increase the relative significance of high land costs as a factor in long-term locational planning by conurbation firms, all else being equal.

Another reason is that high-value conurbation sites may well represent a major item in the asset balances of multiplant firms; and the striking decline in such firms' profit levels that occurred in the 1960s and early 1970s (Treasury, 1976, p. 3) may well have encouraged, if not forced, many such firms to disinvest themselves of conurbation sites in order both to provide much-needed capital for new plant and machinery and to avoid the activities of asset strippers (Keeble, 1976, p. 124). This is most likely to be true of multiplant firms in London, Birmingham, and Manchester, rather than the development area conurbations of Merseyside, Tyneside, and Clydeside where substantial government investment grants have been available as a source of finance for development. Interestingly, McDermott's findings (1977, p. 158) on sources of investment capital in 1969–74 for London and Scottish electronics firms pinpoint just such a difference. In each case corporate finance provided the greatest single share (43 per cent and 52 per cent respectively); but London firms were significantly more dependent on internally generated funds (16 per cent and 7 per cent respectively), whereas Scottish firms relied relatively heavily on government grants (23 per cent compared with London's 2 per cent). These findings support the view that there may well be an important difference in the impact of high land values on multiplant firms in assisted area and non-assisted area conurbations.

Closely related to land and building values, if not more important, is the factor of inadequate, outdated, and deteriorating conurbation factory buildings. The fact that so many conurbation, and especially inner-city, industrial premises are fifty or more years old, are multistoreyed, cramped, and very poorly designed for modern production requirements, lack any room for expansion, and suffer from very poor access via congested inner-urban roads is singled out in almost all surveys of industrial emigration as *the* primary reason for locational shift (Economy Group, South-East Joint Planning Team, 1976, p. 36). Again, multiplant firms in inner city areas are clearly subject to exactly the same disadvantages. In both cases the transfer of production, either explicitly or implicitly, to another location almost always represents a more efficient and significantly cheaper long-run solution than attempts to redevelop existing buildings and sites while maintaining production and output in them. Thus, for housing Stone (1970, p. 168) has shown that site clearance, development, and service costs are 50 per cent greater on redeveloped than virgin sites; with the extra cost of output dislocation in the industrial case, this differential is probably even greater for manufacturing.

The second 'compulsive' factor that, it may be argued, helps to explain conurbation industrial decline is the impact on entrepreneurs, managers, and workers of deterioration, both relative and absolute, in the urban residential environment. In this context industrial decline may be viewed as directly related to population decline, the latter having of course been proceeding in Britain's inner cities and conurbations for a considerably longer period than manufacturing decline. By far the dominant component in population decline is net emigration, most typically to areas surrounding the conurbation concerned (e.g. South-East Joint Planning Team, 1976, p. 15) – a trend that appears to have intensified markedly in recent years (Champion, 1976, pp. 412–14). Net emigration is, however, to some if not a considerable degree selective – selective of younger families (Hall, 1975) and of skilled workers (South-East Joint Planning Team, 1976, pp. 35–7), from whose ranks are drawn many industrial entrepreneurs.

The reasons for the emigration of such households and individuals are varied and of course include relatively high conurbation housing costs; but taking a long term view it can be argued that increased emigration primarily reflects the deterioration over the last two or three decades in conurbation residential environments, relative to other areas. At least three factors are involved here. One is of course the aging of the existing conurbation housing stock. In inner Liverpool, for example, nearly three-quarters of available housing was originally constructed before 1914, much of it before 1891 (Department of the Environment, 1977a, p. 5). Increasing age inevitably means increasing maintenance costs, if not increasing dilapidation. Second, increasing household incomes over time have meant increasing expectations and demand for better-quality private housing of a type that is not readily available in inner-city or conurbation areas. In particular, increasing incomes have generated disproportionately increasing demands for residential *space* – for larger houses with more rooms, gardens, and garages. Put another way, the consumption of residential space appears to have a high income elasticity of demand. In this context inner city areas and conurbations cannot hope to compete with other areas, given the high cost of both existing land and redevelopment. A third factor is the deterioration in local residential environments because of increasing traffic and traffic congestion. For all these reasons it can be argued that, from the viewpoint of residential living conditions, Britain's conurbations are increasingly being regarded by middle- if not higher-income households as much less desirable locations than non-conurbation areas – a conclusion fully supported by studies of people's 'mental maps' of residential preference (Gould and White, 1968).

The difficulty in arguing that industrial decline reflects population migration resulting from the deterioration of the urban residential environment is of course to establish the exact links between the movement of people and industrial losses. There is, however, considerable survey evidence of the impact of residential amenity considerations on industrialists moving their firms from conurbation areas (Keeble, 1976, pp. 83–5), particularly when it is borne in mind that industrialists are frequently reluctant to admit the importance of such considerations because of their apparently economically-irrational nature. This survey evidence is, moreover, corroborated by statistical modelling tests, both of industrial migration flows and of aggregate manufacturing change during the 1960s and early 1970s, at the UK subregional level (Keeble, 1976, pp. 114, 145). Moreover, it seems probable, although it is so far unresearched, that firm birthrates in non-conurbation areas such as East Anglia, outer south-east England, or the Edinburgh region are higher, relative to these areas' existing industrial base, than in the conurbations, because of a relative concentration of potential entrepreneurs attracted by the residential environment. Links with multiplant locational evaluation are more difficult to establish, although the residential preferences of senior executives and skilled staff could well be one important factor in such evaluation. There is certainly considerable case-study and statistical evidence that this is so for industries, such as capital-goods electronics, that are dependent upon a high level of research and development activity (Keeble, 1976, pp. 198–9).

The third 'compulsive' factor suggested (central- and local-government planning policies) is in some ways the most difficult and controversial topic to evaluate of the three. On the one hand, as the review of the South-East Strategic Plan points out (South-East Joint Planning Team, 1976, p. 37), regional policy and local planning controls in conurbations such as London are viewed by many local industrialists as a, if not *the*, fundamental constraint on *in situ* modernisation and growth and hence as a major factor behind the problems associated with outdated and inadequate premises, already discussed. Local planning policy has been particularly heavily criticised by commentators such as Darley and Saunders (1976, p. 213), who have claimed that 'by the end of 1969 between 21 per cent and 31 per cent of the 1500 firms displaced by five of Birmingham's "first phase" redevelopment schemes had gone out of business' and, even more dramatically, that 'Liverpool Corporation admits that an estimated 80 per cent of jobs in their redevelopment areas have been lost'.

On the other hand, detailed analytical studies in, for example, London and Glasgow conclude in contrast that both regional policy, operating through Industrial Development Certificate (IDC) control, and local planning in the form of inner-city Comprehensive Development Area (CDA) renewal, cannot be blamed directly for more than a limited impact upon decline. Thus, the Economy Group, South-East Joint Planning Team (1976, pp. 42, 80–1), found that only 6 per cent of all IDC applications in London in 1970–74 (84 out of 1,421), covering only 12 per cent of total floorspace in all applications (4.2 out of 35.6 million sq.ft), were actually refused; and it further found that a special survey of very large, mainly multiplant, manufacturing firms in the South-East indicated that 'the negative element of regional policy, namely the refusal of an IDC for expansion within the region, did not appear to be a problem to firms. The overall view of firms was that IDC controls were sensibly applied but had only a limited effect in influencing companies' decision-making'. In similar vein, McKean (1975, pp. 6–7) has found that Glasgow inner-city CDA, where the wholesale demolition of premises was carried out in the 1960s, recorded a gross closure rate of factories (31.7 per cent over 1958–68) that was only marginally higher than that in the rest of Glasgow's inner-city zone (28.3 per cent); and he has written that this similarity 'verifies the conclusion that the liquidation etc. in the CDA is more the outcome of economic pressures on a weak industrial structure than the result of urban renewal'. Only with emigration did urban renewal have an obvious impact, with the emigration rate for the CDA (54.5 per cent) being substantially higher than that for the remaining inner-city zone (18.7 per cent). However, 85 per cent of the CDA moves simply relocated elsewhere in the City of Glasgow, so that net losses to Glasgow as a whole were very small.

These findings support the view that central- and local-government planning policies are only a minor factor in inner-city and conurbation industrial decline; but the situation is, however, almost certainly more complex than these studies suggest. For example, in addition to the point, acknowledged by the Economy Group, that IDC refusals do not measure the extent to which London or Birmingham companies have been deterred even from applying for IDCs because of their impression or advice that permission is very difficult to obtain, there is the possible impact of assisted area *incentives*. These incentives – until 1977 both the regional employment premiums (REPs) and regional development grants – could have had at least two possible negative effects upon firms in London and Birmingham. First, multiplants firms in these centres could well have been encouraged by the availability of such incentives, which have been considerable since 1966, to expand production in existing Assisted Area plants, but to run down or even close factories in the two non-assisted conurbations. This hypothesis is supported, indirectly at least, by Atkin's (1973) study of changes in employment over 1966–71 in Assisted Area branches and non-Assisted Area parent factories, with its finding that the former, although declining, lost employment at a significantly lower rate than the latter, many of which must have been in London or Birmingham. Second, assisted area incentives, especially REPs, have of course been designed quite deliberately to improve the efficiency and competitiveness of factories in the assisted regions. It may therefore be hypothesised that such incentives may well have enabled Assisted Area plants to capture sales and markets previously served by plants in London, Birmingham, or Manchester, thus leading to declining employment or even the closure of these factories. Even the CDA findings can be qualified, for example, by the fact that they ignore the question of the impact of inner city renewal on firm *births*, which may well have been substantially reduced by such a process. There are thus grounds for arguing that central and local government policies may have had a significant further effect on inner-city and conurbation industrial decline, notably in the case of non-assisted conurbations such as London and Birmingham.

5.5 Policy implications

As so often is the case, policy development for inner city decline appears currently to be taking place in advance of a comprehensive rigorous evaluation of the nature and extent of the decline and the problems that it may be posing. Although imaginative, central and local government partnership schemes and the channelling of money to construction and urban aid projects in selected areas, as announced by the Secretary of State for the Environment in April 1977, may exert little influence on decline, especially of industrial employment, if the nature of and reasons for decline are not more clearly established than at present. In this connection it is of note that the Secretary of State's announcement of the new policy singled out three areas of industrial promotion activity, designed to reflect 'our immediate priority . . . to strengthen the economies of these areas'. Thus:

> . . . subject only to priority for regional policy, suitable firms will be encouraged to establish themselves in the inner areas of major cities. We shall introduce legislation to enhance the powers of local authorities with serious inner-area problems to enable them to assist industry and to designate industrial improvement areas. We shall encourage local authorities to give more consideration to the needs of industry, particularly of small firms, in their planning policies.

The questions arise, of course: are these policy initiatives appropriate in the light of present knowledge of industrial decline, and do they fit with the policy implications that may be drawn from the previous discussion?

As far as the latter is concerned, three points stand out. First, the fact that manufacturing decline is so obviously part of much wider trends in industrial location in advanced economies, as well as being subject to such fundamental considerations as people's basic preferences for different residential environments, suggests that the reversal of decline is very unlikely, at least in the short or medium term. More important, it may well also be undesirable in terms of national industrial efficiency. After all it has been suggested earlier that probably the most important single factor in inner city and conurbation industrial decline is the powerful constraints on efficiency and growth imposed by the local environment, especially outdated and expensive sites and buildings. If this is the case, then, along with Gripaios (1977c) and Cameron (1977a), it can be argued that a major effort to steer mobile industry back into inner city areas, whether by coercion or by substantial grants, is not the priority for the 1980s. Rather, national industrial efficiency and 'our desperately low rate of economic growth require[s] us to locate manufacturing jobs where costs of production are minimized' (Cameron, 1977a, p. 217). Of course, this does not rule out a shift in central government aid to inner city local authorities on the grounds of greater social need than, for example, many non-conurbation areas within the present assisted regions (Keeble, 1977); but it does suggest that, from a national viewpoint, direct controls and financial incentives to mobile firms along traditional regional policy lines are not the right approach to inner city economic assistance.

The second suggestion follows from the first. If mobile firms are not to be steered back into inner city or conurbation areas, an economic priority in these areas should be assistance to *existing* firms, channelled through local authorities and specially appointed industrial development officers. The significance of the latter for local industrial expansion in non-conurbation areas has been established by Camina (1974), whose survey of a large sample of local authorities in England and Wales reveals that authorities actively seeking new industry attracted significantly larger numbers of firms than relatively passive authorities and that in industrial promotion the appointment of a full-time development officer with the full and positive backing of the council was of crucial significance for success. This conclusion is supported, in the different context of inner city assistance to existing industry, by anecdotal evidence from certain London boroughs such as Greenwich. The latter's employment development officer, appointed only in 1973, has claimed that since that date the efforts of his department have been associated with the creation of over 6,000 new jobs and the rehabilitation of 1½ million sq. ft of industrial space (Foy, 1977), much of it for use by new small firms.

Greenwich's apparent stress on the role of new small firms in inner city regeneration is certainly an interesting one and has been supported by other commentators, such as Darley and Saunders (1976). Indeed, the latter have gone so far as to advocate the setting up of a new central-government body COSURBA (Council for Small Industries in Urban Areas), to parallel the long-established promotional and advisory activities of COSIRA (Council for Small Industries in Rural Areas). This is certainly a suggestion well worth consideration; but if the logic of the preceding argument is correct, the most important short-term target for local authority activity in both inner and outer conurbation areas is not small firms, with their limited employment potential and probable high deathrate, but existing medium-sized and multiplant firms. The identification of their needs and problems, and of the extent to which local government can help provide the right local environment for their continued operation, must be a priority for the inner city and suburban local authorities. The stress on this kind of action in the Secretary of State's 1977 statement thus appears to be entirely appropriate.

The third and last obvious implication of the preceding analysis is that inner city local authorities must involve themselves much more actively in the local provision of modern and reasonably-priced industrial premises. This point is of course already recognised by central government, with the reference to industrial improvement areas in the Secretary of State's announcement and the provision of funds (£100 million from May 1977 over two years) for construction projects in specific inner city areas. These funds are being supplemented by local authority grants. Some conurbation authorities have of course experience in factory building and leasing, because of the need to rehouse firms displaced by comprehensive development schemes. An example is Glasgow City Council, with its successful high-density Clydeway industrial centre at Anderston, close to the city centre. The latter, built in 1969 as a complex of flatted factories, now houses firms employing 1,500 workers. Part of its success may be due to subsidised rents – a very important consideration for small to medium-sized firms (Franklin and Stafford, 1977, p. 212). Other authorities, e.g. Liverpool, are now actively building advanced factories in their inner cities.

However, shortage of funds, even with increasing central government aid, suggests that an alternative but equally effective method of providing modern factories in inner city areas may be through partnership schemes between local councils and private builders. Two examples in London may be cited. In Woolwich the former AEI industrial complex has been redeveloped for small and medium-sized firms by a partnership between the Westminster Bunting Ltd development company and the Co-op Insurance Society. The Borough of Greenwich has provided full backing for this scheme, which now houses firms employing 5,000 workers in both converted flatted factories and entirely new buildings. The variety of buildings provided enables small but growing firms to move easily to larger premises as their needs expand. The borough has also helped towards the provision of central canteen facilities on the estate (Franklin and Stafford, 1977, p. 213; Foy, 1977). An even more interesting example is the direct partnership scheme, of the type envisaged under the 1975 Community Land Act, between the Borough of Newham and two private companies: Landware Group Holdings and Fairview Estates. Having assembled an industrial site at Leyton Road, Newham, the borough signed an agreement in 1977 with the two private companies for the construction of an industrial estate of some fifteen factory units, ranging in size from 900 to 4,800 sq. ft and totalling in all 33,000 sq. ft of floorspace, excluding offices. Fairview has provided finance and is responsible for construction by March 1978, while the estate will be managed by

Landware. This type of development, actively pursued throughout the inner city, could have some impact in slowing decline in London, especially if, as Greenwich's employment development officer has claimed, 'London and the south east are bubbling over with entrepreneurs who really need little encouragement to get started. We can give, and are now giving, that encouragement' (Foy, 1977). In stressing local authority action to aid local industry, the government's approach to economic assistance in inner city areas thus seems, on present evidence, reasonably appropriate and realistic.

II The Conurbations and Regional Policy

6 Comparative Views from the North-East and Other Northern Regions of Britain

Alan R. Townsend

6.1 Introduction

With investment limited, how far, how formally, and in which directions should government policy towards different regions be redefined towards a spatially more selective approach? National unemployment levels may continue to be high to the end of the 1970s at least. In the short term and for the ensuing period, most people hold that regional and local authority planning should maximise personal equity in terms of access to jobs and simultaneously encourage all opportunities of productive investment. Yet, parts of regional policy and of the programme of new towns and overspill (whether from London or, say, Glasgow) now appear outdated. They were conceived in a different economic and demographic climate, and Chisholm (1976) has argued that the basic premises of regional policy have changed.

The current national recession has a searching and complex impact on employment levels – both those of different sectors of the economy and those of different regions and labour markets. This has accentuated the effect of deep-seated trends within London itself. The rates of unemployment in inner London, if calculated, have been higher than in parts of the official 'Assisted Areas'. Are the Assisted Areas to lose some of their status? Certainly, it is no cause for satisfaction in the Developing Areas or Ulster that unemployment rates in other parts of the country have tended, until the autumn of 1976, to rise or 'level' upwards' towards their own higher rates.

What are the connections between the problems of the 'inner city' of London and the problems of the assisted areas?

1. There may be similarities of experience between the metropolitan counties, Greater Glasgow, and the Greater London Council (GLC) area. Five of the six metropolitan counties lie in English assisted areas, Merseyside and Tyne and Wear lying in 'special development areas' and Greater Manchester, West Yorkshire, and South Yorkshire in 'intermediate areas'. For instance, the North-East has the greatest provision *per capita* of government Skillcentres, while the GLC, the West Midlands, and the Inner Area Studies are stressing the need for training provision.

2. There may be an emerging political situation of competition for mobile employment between the metropolitan areas and the rest of the country: 'There is a lobby of increasing strength to have regional economic intervention entirely or in part superseded by preferential economic policy operated in the context of inner-city areas vis-a-vis other areas' (Rose, 1976).

3. There is also the view that regional policy is directly in conflict with, and the main cause of, unemployment in the GLC area and the West Midlands conurbation, as the two areas have indeed been the main source of manufacturing jobs transferred to the 'assisted areas' (normally through the establishment of branches).

4. There has even been the view that the 'regional problem' has been solved, based on the unemployment trends mentioned above, the better prospects of the coalmining industry, and perhaps a somewhat distant view of the benefits of North Sea oil.

5. There appears to be no active conflict over the actual dispersal of offices from London to the Assisted Areas. Very few, apart from particular civil service offices, ever transfer as far as the Assisted Areas, and there is increasing trade union opposition to the present programme in the civil service. The absence of office (and research) occupations is one of the most marked feature of the Development Areas; if regional policy were to achieve a greater measure of success for inducements to attract offices, as suggested by Manners (1976), there would be a fresh area of conflict with the GLC.

The analysis of trends themselves indicates that there is no clear path to a new order of priorities, but for the purposes of presentation this chapter is framed around the logical heads resulting from the question: is 'the inner-city employment problem' a straightforward matter of competition by 'generously defined' Assisted Areas for the manufacturing resources of the GLC? The Assisted Areas considered in the analysis comprise the large and continuous territory made up of Scotland and the economic-planning regions of the North, the North-West, and Yorkshire and Humberside. Section 6.2 departs from the main analysis with a theoretical contribution suggesting that the most *common* characteristics of workplaces around city centres are not only manufacturing decentralisation but also the concentration there of a wide set of 'non-personal services' in which national employment also happens to have been in decline.

6.2 Similarities between the metropolitan conurbations?

It is necessary at the outset to recognise major planning differences that are evident on the ground in the situation of Assisted Areas:
1. Decentralisation has occurred predominantly through the attraction of new firms to the periphery of the area rather than through the outward movement of local firms. The mixture varies, but one example is the postwar New Town of East Kilbride; although the great majority of firms is from Glasgow, the great majority of jobs is from England or abroad.
2. Early government industrial estates, like the major ones of 1936 – Hillington (Glasgow) and Team Valley (Gateshead) – appear to lie in the nearest open land that was available at that date. The provision of 'second-generation' New Towns for Liverpool, Glasgow, and Tyneside has been among the factors extending the distance of industrial sites from the conurbation cores. Such was the town-planning orthodoxy of the early 1960s that the location of Ford's Halewood site was criticised for being too *near* Liverpool, i.e. for disrupting planned overspill.
3. The metropolitan counties vary in their success in taking New Towns and Expanded Towns within their boundaries. The economic reports of survey of both Greater Manchester Council (1975) and Merseyside County Council (1975b) refer to the competitive growth of Skelmersdale, Warrington, and Runcorn new towns and of Ellesmere Port (none of which lies in either county's territory). Even Strathclyde finds itself with a legacy of

overspill plans to the Lothians (Livingston new town) and other regions of Scotland. Although new towns and inner areas are not 'opposite poles' in every regard, it will be of interest to compare metropolitan counties' draft policies for industrial land at the end of this section.

4. The dependence on council housing is greater in Scotland and the poorer northern cities, and it is notable that the pressure for land in the former county boroughs led (a) to the forced movement of population to major estates bordering city limits, (b) to the comparative neglect of space for industry in or near these estates, and (c) to associated indications of social deprivation in these *outer* areas.

American literature on the decentralisation of employment tends to talk in terms of four main sectors: manufacturing, offices, wholesaling, and retailing. Urban geographers' theoretical constructions of the urban land-use pattern are often no more refined. It is contended here that these analyses neglect both the overall size and the diversity of the service sector, which are most significant in the inner city where there is a variety of 'city-serving' services.

The central metropolitan districts are 'more open' to changes in the 'service economy' than to changes in manufacturing (although Birmingham and Sheffield retain their distinctive basis as 'manufacturing cities', and *some* services will be dependent for their existence on local manufacturing in all cases). There is patently need for refinement (a) locationally and (b) in the analysis of service employment trends by Minimum List Headings (MLHs) – subdivisions of Order totals of the Standard Industrial Classification (SIC).

In the first place: 'Whereas the C.B.D. core has been the object of much specific research, the central regional surrounding it (henceforth termed the CBD *frame*) has received very little attention. In fact the concept of CBD frame as a region is presented here for the first time' (Horwood and Boyce, 1959, pp. 15–16). In their well-known study Horwood and Boyce have pointed out that the seminal models of Park and Burgess predated the shift to motor transport, and in a schematic diagram they have demonstrated their concept of a variety of land uses surrounding the central business district (CBD): transport terminals, wholesaling with stocks, car sales and service, warehousing, as well as 'multifamily residence' and light manufacturing. The employment of the area is patently the most accessible to many inner area residents. Although not necessarily indicating a continuous area surrounding the CBD on all sides, the model is applicable to Newcastle upon Tyne and inner Glasgow and is particularly susceptible of testing in Teesside because two CBDs survive there, namely, Stockton and Middlesbrough.

Second, surveys of Teesside survey and plan (Wilson *et al*, 1969) allowed a comprehensive approach to the location of workplaces in MLHs of the service sector and their aggregation into four summary groups for spatial-planning purposes: 'Retailing', 'central services', 'non-personal services', and 'health and education'. The non-personal services comprised activities where there was no direct contact with the public at the main employment point (e.g. a bus garage); otherwise they would bid for more central sites in serving the area. The employment survey of 1966 established the locations of 30,300 jobs of this group (of which 26,300 were male) out of an estimated total in the survey area of 37,400 (19 per cent of all employment). The group accounted for 19 per cent of surveyed employment in the CBD of Middlesbrough and 16 per cent in that of Stockton, but for 40 per cent or more of employment in six of the survey's fifty-eight zones; these lay directly around *and between* the two town centres. The CBD frame appears conceptually to be eminently relevant.

The *general* suggestion from this static analysis is a need for refinement in assessing the locational supply of blue collar male service jobs. Large parts of the sector are liable to low pay, to the structural reduction of employment, and/or to decentralisation from their characteristic locations around the CBD frame. In terms of the structural reduction of employment it is necessary to think, for example, of the location of activities like the famous old locomotive depots of each British city. It is insufficient to generalise about 'wholesaling', 'transport jobs', or even 'dockland'. What emerges is that dominant locational and employment characteristics are shared by about twenty MLHs as varied as laundries and road haulage and, therefore, that much inner-city employment requires disaggregation for the purposes of grasping a 'humdrum' inventory of:

(a) 'depot' functions (e.g. the manual staff of GPO engineering departments, local-authority maintenance and cleaning departments, and television rental companies);
(b) 'repair' functions (e.g. furniture, shoes, dry-cleaning, and cars); and
(c) 'supply' functions (e.g. wholesalers and dealers).

The pattern is not necessarily breaking up in all British conurbations, but it has long been dominant (albeit neglected in favour of academic attention to shops and offices; it should also be associated with 'local' manufactures like soft drinks, bakeries, and some surviving breweries).

The *specific* suggestion from this analysis is that, while the age structure of inner city manufacturing may *tend* to give similar trends in different cities, the more systematic disposition of these non-personal service activities in different cities may well account for a large part of the common employment trends experienced in different inner areas. The performance of the 'growth services' until *now* (education, health, finance, etc.) may have masked the overall picture for the service sector, but there are cities where that sector has contributed heavily to decline. Most notable is of course Liverpool, but it is also relevant that Newcastle's decline in insured population, from 180,600 in 1966 to 157,400 in 1971, is only *half* accounted for by the loss of 6,500 manufacturing jobs.

The Teesside analysis is for one date only, and the area is unusual in having land for *ongoing* development in service industry between its two CBDs. Glasgow's Dixon Blazes site (near the Gorbals) is another case where property developers have attracted new building in warehousing, etc. The trends are not all one way.

The non-personal services are, however, as a *whole* in decline and have been identified as such in a fairly similar grouping for London. It is striking how many categories of the non-personal services group have started to decline nationally since 1966 – and indeed have been distinguished by Stone (1975) from the growth services in his comparisons of GLC and national performance. From 1966 to 1974 the following MLHs showed a national decline of more than 20,000: 601, 602, 701, 702, 705, 706, 831, 892, 893, and 894. If, as is generally the case, these sectors were declining at the national rate or faster in the GLC area, it is likely, from their urban location, that they were contributing systematically to the inner-area employment decline of the major provincial cities (albeit of simpler spatial structure).

A diffusion of planning ideology from London coincides with some recognition of inner area problems in the current reports of survey (for their structure plans) of the metropolitan counties. The level of commitment and of district council implementation varies; but it is possible to see a turnaround of *thought* since, for instance, the general acclaim accorded to the 1963 government's 'growth area' policies, presented in their White Papers for Central Scotland (Scottish Development Department, 1963) and north-east England (Board of Trade, 1963).

'In practice, it is uncertain how far a Growth Area policy was actively pursued in the nineteen-sixties' (West Central Scotland Plan, 1974, p. 367), but one major result was the establishment of Washington new town within the North-East growth zone, which extended from Tyneside to Teesside *inclusive*. (The belt of the A1 adjacent to the town was already one of decentralised growth in the service industry). By 1966 Teesside survey and plan (Wilson *et al*, 1969) had already rejected the 'strategy' of a New Town solution for a northern conurbation's problems; a New Town at Stokesley (now in the County of North Yorkshire) was excluded first because:

> . . . there is not sufficient employment growth potential on Teesside to sustain a self-contained new town particularly as the number of firms likely to be displaced and who would wish to relocate in new premises is very small. Much of the expected growth in manufacturing or office employment necessary for the future prosperity of Teesside will take place within the existing built-up area. (Wilson and Womersley *et al.*, 1969, p. 76)

The consultants for the Tyne and Wear plan (Voorhees *et al.*, 1973) have weighed up the merits of concentrating growth on the existing fabric of the area compared with those of dispersal but concluded:

> It is important to note that by 'centralised strategy' we do not mean the grouping of development tightly against the periphery of the existing built-up areas of Tyneside and Wearside: in fact, we recommend very substantial development around Killingworth and to the north, and around Washington and southward. (p. i)

Washington had not been planned as a self-contained town, but the scale of public and private investment *now* stand in marked contrast to surrounding social and economic provision (for analysis see Hudson *et al.*, 1976).

The report of survey of the Tyne and Wear County Council (1976) presents a change of policy in so far as it puts a choice between the old inner industrial areas and the outer peripheral areas as the second key issue of the report. After presenting the basic choice a supplementary paragraph mentions 'a balanced provision for the inner and outer areas with a three level industrial land policy'. The three levels are: large greenfield sites to secure employment growth from mobile industry; medium-sized sites within convenient travel-to-work distance of inner areas; and:

... the development and improvement of the best sites possible in the inner areas, together with the improvement of existing vacant buildings and environmental and access improvements, in order to retain existing employment, provide for its expansion, and to attract new employment. This could be co-ordinated through industrial general improvement areas wherever possible and would aim to make the maximum use of existing land and buildings in the inner urban areas. The Department of Industry could be encouraged to provide more advance factories on inner sites as opposed to their emphasis on 'greenfield' sites in the past with any necessary co-operation from Local Authorities in making suitable sites available. (pp. 212–13)

This echoes the heavy stress on site development in Strathclyde documents. The spatial issues are perhaps not so sharp as in Strathclyde, where the rejection of Stonehouse new town (accepted by the government in May 1976) is accompanied in the regional report of the Strathclyde Regional Council (1976a) by proposals to reduce many peripheral housing schemes. It is seen as advisable and possible for the first time to halve the overspill of population from Glasgow itself. On the other hand:

There is some indication, although the evidence presented is by no means conclusive, that the New Towns have been highly favoured by the discriminatory use of resources. Their growth has therefore been at the expense of the old areas which are in need of renewal, and the evidence of socio-economic structures shows that the New Towns have not really catered for the disadvantaged groups from those urban areas. This has accentuated a high concentration of deprivation in these areas which have been recognised in the Regional Report and are specified in the Areas for Priority Treatment Report as areas requiring the discriminatory use of resources in the future. (Strathclyde Regional Council, 1976b, p. 80)

Manchester's situation appears to be more complex, partly because of the varied prosperity of surrounding 'cotton towns', but the Liverpool Inner Area Study notes that new approaches are beginning to gain recognition; Merseyside's proposed strategy would 'concentrate investment and development within the urban county and particularly in those areas with the most acute problems ... restricting development on the edge of the built-up areas to a minimum' (Merseyside County Council, 1975a).

In all this there are two major notes of qualification. First, the *overall* growth of an area should not be jeopardised by the firm restriction of all peripheral growth. There is, philosophically almost, a problem in proving that a new town has not through its own attractions increased the flow of incoming firms to a needy subregion. The Liverpool Inner Area Study (Wilson and Womersley, 1976) reports that:

> The inner area is not a suitable location for many types of large scale industry and only partially so for certain other types of industrial, commercial and housing development. Economic development on Merseyside as a whole has to include a measure of resources continuing to be invested in the outer areas.

Second, some of the proposed gains in efficiency from the planning of new growth areas have proved illusory, as predicted by Cameron and Reid (1966). The philosophy of concentrating new public investment at particular places now seems particularly unconvincing, while the expected linkages between new factories have been rare throughout: 'The answer, briefly, is that Central Scotland is probably much too small and well-developed for the growth area policy to have much effect in inducing firms to grow faster because of technical or external economies'.

The general picture, then, from the areas described is that the inner areas' problems are severe enough to contribute a major argument against new areas of physical growth and that they themselves deserve fresh efforts of site development in the possible hope of gaining from commercial growth and development area policy. There are, however, severe policy dilemmas (as well as direct political problems) inherent in the allocation of industrial land within conurbations.

6.3 Do all the Assisted Areas require assistance?

A link between the problems of the GLC area and the inner city situations already mentioned lies through government regional policy. This has evolved into a complex set of provisions, particularly since 1958. The areas of Merseyside, Clydeside, and Tyne and Wear appear from the above to deserve detailed internal attention as subregional 'functional' units within their wider respective assisted areas. In fact, with somewhat wider boundaries they do constitute the main populations of the special development areas now. With the recognition of Merseyside in 1949 they constituted, with South Wales, the larger part of the main development areas from 1945 to 1960. Should there be a return to a policy of such selectivity or of more?

Regional averages are a misleading indication of the overall position, and residents themselves rarely have experience extending beyond one subregion, as demonstrated by Townsend and Taylor (1975). Economic arguments, especially in the financial assistance of indigenous industry, tend to argue for broadly defined areas, but the more pressing policy situation tends to argue for the *attraction* of new industry to the worst-hit areas. This chapter focuses on the latter question.

A legislator working now from a clean sheet might well adopt the strict philosophy of the Local Employment Act 1960, which defined development districts anywhere in the country by reference to quoted local unemployment rates. This carried with it administrative problems and geographical anomalies (not least the missing recognition of inner city areas), but it did introduce assistance to the South-West and small parts of the South-East and East Anglia according to equal 'merit'. Today, there is an increasing variety of data for the new counties (and Scottish regions). For instance, the New Earnings Survey shows that the average gross weekly earnings of full time men (aged 21 and over) were above the level of Great Britain in Strathclyde and Cleveland in April 1975, but with 11.4 per cent of males (73,443) unemployed in Strathclyde in February 1977 the level of unemployment still cannot be ignored. The figures of Table 6.1 show the unemployment figures for that date for the larger towns in the Assisted Areas and for Greater London.

The persistently better performance of Leeds, Sheffield, Manchester, and Edinburgh is enough to sustain a subregional approach. Indeed, the position has been reached in this depression where many smaller labour markets in Assisted Areas have established unemployment levels below the national average. In Scotland four (but only four) of the new administrative regions showed better figures than Great Britain: Shetland, 4.8 per cent; Orkney, 4.3 per cent; Grampian, 4.6 per cent; and Borders, 4.5 per cent. Freestanding service centres have a good employment record in many regions, and they provide the main feature of the list of travel-to-work areas with unemployment below the Great Britain average in the Northern region: Carlisle, Cramlington, Darlington, Durham, Furness, Hexham, Kendal, Morpeth, Penrith – a list that includes all the freestanding market towns of the region.

There remain of course freestanding labour markets with high

Table 6.1 Unemployment levels in travel-to-work areas with more than 10,000 unemployed, 1976–77

Region/City	February 1977						February 1976
	Males		Females		Total		Total
	No.	*%*	*No.*	*%*	*No.*	*%*	*%*
Scotland:	*126,549*	9.8	*53,023*	6.0	*179,572*	8.3	6.7
Glasgow City	38,950	12.4	11,565	5.2	50,515	9.4	7.6
North Lanarkshire	11,606	10.7	7,566	10.7	19,172	10.7	8.9
Edinburgh	13,611	8.8	4,177	3.5	17,788	6.5	5.1
North:	*77,204*	9.3	*28,663*	5.7	*105,867*	7.9	7.0
Tyneside	26,608	10.4	8,287	5.1	34,895	8.3	7.3
Teesside	11,819	8.4	4,625	5.7	16,444	7.4	6.5
Wearside	10,086	13.5	3,745	7.8	13,831	11.3	10.2
North-West:	*148,675*	8.8	*50,350*	4.5	*199,025*	7.1	6.7
Liverpool	51,992	13.3	18,710	7.4	70,702	11.0	10.5
Manchester	32,751	7.8	7,794	2.8	40,545	5.8	5.3
Yorkshire and Humberside:	*85,489*	6.8	*28,033*	3.5	*113,522*	5.5	5.4
Leeds	13,954	7.5	3,800	3.0	17,754	5.7	5.4
Hull	11,018	9.8	2,840	4.2	13,858	7.7	7.7
Sheffield	9,115	5.2	3,021	2.8	12,136	4.3	4.1
Bradford	8,205	8.4	2,464	3.6	10,669	6.4	6.3
Greater London	*127,317*	5.5	*35,324*	2.3	*162,641*	4.2	3.7
Great Britain	—	7.3	—	3.8	—	5.9	5.4

Source: Regional Office monthly summaries, Department of Employment.

unemployment. The fact, however, that Durham and Darlington lie below the national average provides an example of a recognisably improved situation in medium-sized labour markets. The two towns have benefited from the strong regional policy orientation towards mining decline in the 1960s and from the availability of sites (if not always in the immediate area of redundancy) in an area of relatively lower density of land use. The report of survey of Durham County Council (1976) is dealing now palpably with a problem of different scale from the problems of the adjoining more urban Counties of Cleveland and Tyne and Wear, where the problems have proved more intractable.

The future policy emphasis should surely lie on metropolitan areas such as Tyneside, and their worst-hit subareas, and on vulnerable points in the urban system like Hartlepool. It must be noted that conventional travel-to-work areas will not provide sufficient disaggregation to indicate the narrower areas of travel of the lower skill groups of inner areas and that their needs must be specially analysed. Together, however, these types of area provide the basis of a selective approach within the urban system.

Some return to a more selective approach may of course be in government minds and is required by the expectation of continued unemployment and the low starting level of investment from the present time; but there do seem to be some undesirable results from the 'blanket approach' of 1966 of creating regional-sized development areas, which have been unfavourable to the more built-up and environmentally less-attractive areas. Strathclyde, with 50 per cent of the Scottish population, was receiving 58 per cent of firms moving to Scotland and 66 per cent of resulting jobs in 1963, but the figures had dropped to 35 and 38 per cent respectively by 1973. Their answer (Strathclyde Regional Council, 1976a) and that of the Northern Region Strategy Team (1977) is to propose an increase in the differential in financial inducements between Special Development Areas and Development Areas. However much policy steers away from 'greenfield areas' towards metropolitan areas, it is clear that Merseyside, Clydeside, and Tyneside ought to share significantly in the national renewal of factory investment.

6.4 The continued needs of the regional economies

There has often been cause to lose sight of the ultimate objective of regional self-sustaining growth within the national framework; but the West Central Scotland Plan (1974) and the Northern Region Strategy Team (1977) have laid stress on possible greater efforts towards indigenous growth, whose marked absence hitherto may have deep historical causes in both areas' industrial and occupational structure. The strategy team still recommends the maintenance of current policy towards mobile manufacturing industry well into the 1980s and recognises that the present picture would be even worse without the past operation of regional policy, which introduced 35,000 jobs in the period 1966–71. This growth had tailed off by 1974–75, and a different source must be found for the *relative* improvement of this and other 'peripheral regions' unemployment rates at the same time.

In examining *Causes of the Recent Improvement in the Rate of Unemployment in the Northern Region Relative to Great Britain* the Northern Region Strategy Team (1976) has attributed the difference to lower-than-normal job losses in coalmining, to a greater increase in public sector employment than in Great Britain as a whole, and to a relatively greater increase in consumer spending due to national flat-rate pay policy. North Sea oil is normally credited with generating only 2,000 jobs in the North-East (about the same as in Strathclyde), compared with 13,000 specifically new jobs in Scotland as a whole (Strathclyde Regional Council, 1976c). Table 6.1 shows that by February 1977 a greater difference in regional unemployment rates was beginning to reassert itself.

The longer term pattern, as demonstrated by Table 6.2 for the regional gross domestic product (GDP), has been of little proportionate gain for peripheral regions relative to the UK average. There has been some 'convergence' in that the GDPs of Scotland and the North have moved nearer the national average, but Yorkshire and Humberside's has fallen towards their level. It is necess-

Table 6.2 Regional GDPs: factor cost at current prices, 1966–74

Region	1966	1972	1973	1974
United Kingdom	100.0	100.0	100.0	100.0
Northern Ireland	67.9	72.2	74.0	74.0
Scotland	89.1	90.9	92.8	93.4
North	84.1	87.8	88.8	90.1
North-West	95.7	96.2	95.9	94.5
Yorkshire and Humberside	96.7	91.9	91.5	93.0
South-East	114.7	116.2	115.8	116.6

Source: Central Statistical Office, *Economic Trends* (February 1976)

ary, however, to consider that the development areas and their inner areas face a *worse* relative and absolute future position than at present. This is partly because of the weakening of regional policy through lack of investment, the secular decline of national manufacturing employment and its effects on Industrial Development Certificate (IDC) policy, and perhaps an increasing diversion of projects abroad. It is more particularly because long-awaited redundancies in shipbuilding, steel, and heavy engineering may create a situation as difficult as that created by coalmining redundancy in the 1960s – only this time frequently in inner riverside areas.

The traditional geography textbook, with its roots in the specialist locations of 1900, is almost a guide to today's vulnerable locations. In an era of slow population growth and higher unemployment not all towns can be protected from declining population (Chisholm, 1976). However, vulnerability is apparently not so common in the non-Assisted Areas, and the experience of the Assisted Areas is for the apparent solution of one problem to be soon followed by the emergence of another.

6.5 Sources of growth for the Assisted Areas

Do the Assisted Areas really depend on the long distance 'movement' of industry, bearing in mind that there is a fall-off with distance in this supply of moves within the United Kingdom, i.e. a fall-off relative to different Development Areas' needs (Townsend and Gault, 1972)?

How much growth originates in individual assisted areas? The Industry Act 1972 increased the provision for assistance to firms already in them, and this was relevant to job retention and development in 'intermediate areas' such as Yorkshire and Humberside. The assessment of indigenous openings within subregions is complicated but was consolidated for the preceding period, 1966–71, by the Department of Industry's Record of Openings (unpublished but supplied by the department). This new source of data is of great interest in suggesting that between one-third and two-thirds of employment growth at new factories in the larger assisted subregions may be attributed to indigenous origins. Where employment data are available they show how indigenous openings account for 13,000 out of 35,000 jobs established in the North by 1971 and about 24,000 of the 40,000 established in Scotland. This is of course before counting the number of service employment jobs *sustained* and expanded in consequence.

The most striking feature is that Greater London, the West Midlands, and West Yorkshire were virtually self-sufficient for more than 90 per cent of their openings. The Manchester area too was also still largely self-sufficient in this period and not importing large plant like the industrial North-East. Some Assisted Areas were in fact still exploring moves in this period.

How much, then, have the assisted areas assisted each other? Data for the period 1945–65 (Howard, 1968) do show significant past movements of factories out of east-central Scotland, south-east Lancashire, north-east Cheshire, and the West Riding to surrounding areas including Clydeside, Tyneside, and Merseyside. In nearly all cases, however, these were only supplementary, at the destination, to more major movements from the South-East and West Midlands. So far as can be told from comparison with data for the period 1966–71, nearly all these provincial sources of movement had fallen off in importance by then. The Manchester area may not perhaps have done so, but others certainly had; the 'West Riding textile' zone exported 34,000 jobs over the period 1945–65, whereas the similar 'West Yorkshire' area had exported only 3,500 by the end of the period 1966–71. Leeds itself as well as Greater Manchester is now campaigning to attract industry. The conclusions must be that the national industrial decline in employment levels has brought about a southward spread of industrial weakness and that very few Assisted Areas are any longer significant potential sources of mobile industry.

It is now possible to look at the *extent of dependency on the metropolis and the Midlands*. Table 6.3 represents two summary matrices at the level of economic-planning regions, with the heavy proviso that transferred employment would often not have materialised at the point of origin because of labour shortage. The South-East was the source of 47 per cent of all *inter-regional* movement, measured in terms of employment provided in the period 1945–65, and was followed in importance by the West Midlands region with a contribution of 20 per cent. Because of differences in accessibility the relative contribution varied in the four destination regions considered.

In the more recent period, 1966–71, only the Northern region was *definitely* growing at the same rate as the average for the long period 1945–65. Unless its new foreign and West Midlands firms

Table 6.3 Movement of manufacturing industry between selected economic-planning regions, 1945–65 and 1966–71[a]: (1) number of surviving cases, (2) employment in thousands (for 1966 and 1971 where available)

Region of origin	Scotland		North		North-West		Yorkshire and Humberside		All regions of destination[b]	
	(1)	(2)	(1)	(2)	(1)	(2)	(1)	(2)	(1)	(2)
1945–65										
South-East:	97	24.5	94	35.8	86	46.7	19	3.8	732	221.0
(GLC)[b]	(65)	(13.0)	(73)	(31.0)	(54)	(26.0)	(11)	(1.0)	(515)	(144.0)
East Anglia	3	0.8	3	0.9	3	2.1	2	?	21	10.8
West Midlands	26	8.7	10	5.0	35	33.5	10	7.1	215	92.6
East Midlands	15	2.8	17	9.6	12	1.9	36	7.4	128	31.0
Other UK[b]	42	11.7	77	33.1	47	11.1	39	?	425	110.7
Abroad	76	46.2	19	5.2	32	9.5	6	2.9	258	108.5
Total[b]	259	94.7	220	89.6	215	104.8	112	31.3	1,779	574.6
1966–71										
South-East:	57	7.5	56	8.0	29	4.5	12	0.5	495	53.0
(GLC)[b]	(31)	(4.5)	(26)	(3.5)	(14)	(2.5)	(8)	(?)	(288)	(32.0)
East Anglia	4	?	4	?	0	—	2	?	17	?
West Midlands	9	1.0	11	2.0	18	6.0	1	?	121	17.0
East Midlands	7	0.5	17	4.0	5	0.5	12	1.5	74	11.0
Other UK[b]	29	?	50	?	15	1.0	5	?	189	?
Abroad	34	4.0	20	2.5	11	1.5	4	?	133	15.0
Total	140	15.5	158	22.0	78	13.5	36	?	1,029	?

Region of destination

[a] The two periods are not strictly comparable.
[b] Interregional moves only.
Sources: Figures for 1945–65 are from Board of Trade (1968), which includes similar tables for three constituent periods. Figures for 1966–71 are from the Department of

were all at a very early stage of development in 1971, Scotland was showing a much greater relative dependence on the South-East than before. The West Midlands had gained in relative importance as a source for the North-West, while the North was depending relatively more on the East Midlands.

Since 1971 not only Manchester but also Leicester has started advertising for industry. The relaxation of control limits for IDCs since 1971 has been greater outside the South-East than within it; like the greater incidence of economic difficulty in the West Midlands, this has presumably heightened the Assisted Areas' dependence on the South-East. It is important to note that the total of 53,000 jobs produced by external moves from the South-East in the 1966–71 period is almost matched by the 47,500 jobs created by openings within the overall region. It is the argument of section 6.6 that there might be transfer between these two categories (from internal to external), but it is first necessary to look sensitively at the role of the GLC area, which still contributed the majority of moves out of the South-East.

6.6 A contribution towards policy for the South-East

Greater London manufacturing employment declined from 1.43 million to 0.94 million – a loss of nearly 500,000 jobs – between 1961 and 1974. Are the assisted areas responsible? The period 1960–73 was analysed to find the address of origin, within the GLC area and elsewhere, of new projects to the North-East. However inequitable their geographical distribution within the North-East (on which see Carney, Hudson, and Taylor, 1975), the incidence of origins within the GLC area does not appear inequitable. This initially surprising result is matched by government research. A study by the Department of Industry (see Dennis, Chapter 2), covering the years 1966–74, indicates that only 27 per cent of the decline of jobs in manufacturing industry resulted from the direct movement (through transfers or branches) of firms from London and that only 9 per cent of the total reduction comprised movement to assisted areas.

The majority of 'moves' within the South-East and East Anglia are complete transfers – 609 out of 1,060 in the period 1945–65 (Howard, 1968) – but the 'peripheral areas' are only too used to receiving branches (953 out of 1,152). It seemed justified to consult

Kelly's *Manufacturers and Merchants Directory, 1975–6* to ascertain the origin of the 296 manufacturing firms 'which have located new projects in the North-East in the period between January, 1960 and December, 1973' (list supplied by the Department of Trade and Industry, Newcastle upon Tyne). This was not a comprehensive analysis, which would have delved further into changes of name, subsidiary ownership, etc.; the purpose was simply to test whether inner London addresses emerged at all, and in this connection the nearest address of a firm to central London was taken, unless it was in the very central office districts. The list was found to include a number of new openings within the North-East. In total, 47 were attributed with South-East origins, of which 19 were in the GLC area:

12 Middlesex postal addresses: Greenford 3, Brentford 2, Wembley 2, Hounslow 1, Isleworth 1, Southall 1, Sunbury on Thames 1, Uxbridge 1
7 other addresses including Croydon 2, Barking 1, Waltham 1, Chiswick Road W4 1

Unfortunately the origins of 104 firms could not be traced. It cannot be inferred that no firms came from the eastern and southern cores of higher unemployment within the former London County Council (LCC) area, nor indeed that the vacation of premises in Middlesex has not created pockets of weakness. Nevertheless, the results lay stress on outer London.

The overriding impression, however, is that the firms that are capable of sustaining long distance moves from London are those characteristically located in the interwar growth area of Middlesex. There may be some modification of planning policy for that type of area, but *unless* some of its firms can in future be induced to move *inwards*, e.g. to sites made available in docklands, it appears that there will be surprisingly little direct conflict between Development Area policy and policies to minimise the decline of manufacturing in the former LCC area. This is not to say that IDC policy may not discourage application over much of London, causing operational problems for many factories. It would be to the advantage of *both* the GLC and the Assisted Areas if the outer South-East did not interpose so many sites as an 'intervening term' in the equation. Let us look at the record of dispersal from the GLC area with reference to plant size (Table 6.4).

Although some developments are indigenous to the outer

Table 6.4 Movement of manufacturing industry from the GLC area, 1966–71

Destination	No. of moves	Employment, end 1971 (thousands)	IDC approvals [a] (million sq. ft)				
			1971	1972	1973	1974	1975
South-East:							
Outer metropolitan area	90	9.0	6.7	6.4	8.1		
Outer South-East:							
Essex	20	1.0	0.7	0.7	1.1	Change of boundaries	
Kent	28	2.0	0.6	1.0	1.8		
Sussex coast	19	1.0	0.5	0.4	0.8		
Solent	32	5.0	2.0	2.7	2.9		
Bedfordshire, Berkshire, Buckinghamshire, and Oxfordshire	10	0.5	1.3	1.5	2.6		
Total for South-East (excl. GLC area)	199	18.5	11.8	12.7	17.3	11.7	9.4
East Anglia	82	5.5	2.7	4.0	4.5	3.8	2.1
Rest of UK	206	26.5	Not applicable				

[a] In the 1972 budget the exemption level below which IDCs were not required was raised from 5,000 to 10,000 sq. ft (subsequently 12,500 sq. ft in 1976). In the same period, 1971–75, approvals in the GLC area varied between 3.5 million sq. ft (1975) and 7.5 million sq. ft (1973). Recognising the problem of aging buildings, the Department of Industry also announced in 1976 that it would consider applications for the speculative redevelopment of old sites dating from before 1918, or in certain circumstances 1939.

Source: Department of Industry, on application.

South-East (even a minority of firms in new towns), the dominant picture is the decentralisation of London firms to the rest of the South-East, including presumably many that could not, for reasons of resources, move to Assisted Areas. Greater Peterborough has now attracted twenty-eight manufacturing companies from elsewhere and Milton Keynes at least sixty. It is here suggested that *some* of the firms that can move these distances could readily move as far as Assisted Areas such as Hull or Liverpool. In fact the needs of the Assisted Areas have barely been squared with the 1964 South-East study, let alone the Strategic Plan for the South-East and its ongoing revision (South-East Joint Planning Term, 1976). Sant (1975) has shown in his time series analysis of movement since the war how the growth of London new towns has a negative influence elsewhere, although Keeble (1968) had previously shown how they in turn were recipients of only a proportion of outward moves. There is the precedent of very considerable variations in the ratio of South-East moves to long distance moves. The Board of Trade's 1968 study shows how as recently as 1965 there occurred a year in which there were 115 moves to peripheral areas from all origins compared with forty-two to the South-East and East Anglia regions.

This ratio has historically been adjustable in weak and strong periods of regional policy through IDC control; and reconsideration is now all the more necessary given the demographic need to rephase the plans of new towns, which was partly acknowledged in the figures of a ministerial statement of 5 April 1977. Strathclyde's regional report (Strathclyde Regional Council, 1976a) is alone in demanding a *strengthening* of IDC policy in the South-East. It may reasonably be contended that, with the changing climate of South-East planning, this would now be possible, if of course it took account of some internal geographical variations in prosperity. It could be presented along with a *relaxation* in south and east London.

What might be the problems in implementing such a policy during the incipient upswing of the economy? IDC policy has worked best when there has been a labour shortage. Mackay and Segal (1976) have noted that:

> There appears in the early 60's to be a strong positive association between more generous regional assistance and an increasing share of industrial building. But while regional assistance continues to rise in the late 60's the Development Area share of employment expected falls.

The contrast draws attention to the importance of I.D.C. control. In the early years more generous assistance is accompanied by more severe I.D.C. Control. The combination proves remarkably effective. In the late years the I.D.C. refusal rate falls. With I.D.C. Control relaxed the Development Area share of industrial building falls. . . . Normally when unemployment rises the refusal rate falls, the correlation tests suggest that between 1963 and 1972 over 80% of the variation in the refusal rate can be attributed to the change in unemployment levels. (pp. 3–4)

As noted by Chisholm (1976), regional policy has now faced more than a decade of higher national unemployment and may not have been rethought in the light of changed conditions. One simple point, from a regional standpoint, may be that governments may not have faced up to the need to sustain IDC policy in the South-East through a long period of unemployment. It may be argued that the IDC – the unique feature distinctive to thirty years of British regional policy – need not be lightly cast away. In the national context there is good reason to suggest that full employment will return fastest in the outer South-East, Cambridgeshire, and Northamptonshire. The last two counties showed the fastest estimated population growth in the period 1971–76 of any of England and Wales, followed by Buckinghamshire. What planning reason may there be for such rates of growth to be further fuelled by industrial expansions that could develop in the needy parts of Assisted Areas? To delay a stronger policy of IDC refusals until full employment returns in the outer South-East is to encourage later 'overheating' in these areas as the approved schemes mature. If, however, it is argued that a strengthened regional policy would draw off excess public funds, there is a counterargument that public spending *per capita* in the South-East is above the national average (1966–70 to 1973–74). Unfortunately, there is no strong argument to counter the view that a strengthened IDC policy in the South-East could draw off larger firms to the European Economic Community.

6.7 Conclusions

1. There are, at present, need and scope for greater geographical selectivity in industrial location policy, which could include relaxation in parts of London and renewed attention to parts of Assisted Areas. Regional policy has obscured problems of these areas' conurbations.

2. The inner city problems of these conurbations themselves, with their similar service–employment trends, add to the case for a continuing regional policy. The needs of the regions remain, although east Scotland has more prosperous areas than before and the incidence of mining rundown has changed.

3. Regional policy is not incompatible with GLC area development, and a relaxation of policy in the inner GLC area would have less impact on assisted areas than other areas. There is a large amount of growth within the South-East compared with the Assisted Areas; observers with a sense of the shape of 'gravity models' would easily see how the assisted areas receive only a proportion of national new openings, being on the 'outer limb' of the system.

4. The key to the situation probably lies in IDC policy in the rest of the South-East.

5. The present situation exposes a fundamental dichotomy between physical and economic planning – both in the planners' knowledge of industry, where a lack of training has become obvious, and in the inertia attached to New and Expanded Towns, which throughout the country have often created tension with more immediate areas of need.

6. As Chisholm and Oeppen (1973) have shown, the use of the most detailed industrial classifications (MLHs) has inconclusive results in relation to the subregional analysis of government policies. It was always the case in Development Areas that the locational and growth characteristics of incoming firms were best understood by considering their age, origin, and sex breakdowns rather than their exact industrial heading. The conceptual need is for statistical classification by *age groups of plant*. After forty years of regional policy the need is less for movement between the old LCC area and provincial mining towns, for example, and more for movement between the postwar growth towns of the outer South-East and the conurbations that grew strongly to 1920 upon the coal-based economy.

III The Urban Labour Market

7 Employment Trends in the Conurbations

J. T. Corkindale

7.1 Introduction[1]

This chapter does not focus specifically on the inner city; rather, it considers the broader conurbations of which they are part. Although most of the recent policy concern has been with the problems of inner city areas, for the purposes of national policy determination it is also relevant to examine the problems of these small areas in relation to broad national economic and social trends. This chapter is presented as a step towards such an examination.

7.2 Population and Employment Changes

From the industrial revolution to the middle of the present century the seven conurbations defined by the Census of Population grew in each successive decade, and for much of the nineteenth century their rates of population growth considerably exceeded those of the rest of Great Britain.[2] This has now changed, and the populations of all conurbations, with the single exception of West Yorkshire, have recently been falling. This decline may be seen as part of the general dispersal of population from more to less densely populated areas that has affected not only conurbations but other large urban areas too. The main receiving areas have been around the fringes of the

[1]This chapter was written while the author was in the Department of Employment. The paper should in no way be construed as the view of the Department of Employment or of HM Treasury. Any opinions expressed are the author's and his alone.
[2]The growth of the English conurbations up to 1951 is described in the 1951 census report on Greater London and five other conurbations.

Table 7.1 Resident labour forces of conurbations and the rest of Great Britain, 1951–71 (thousands)

Conurbation	1951	1961	1966	1971
Greater London	4,131	4,239	4,079	3,830
Central Clydeside	812	831	813	785
Merseyside	627	638	619	576
South-east Lancashire	1,237	1,231	1,204	1,151
Tyneside	371	385	383	369
West Midlands	1,111	1,197	1,225	1,170
West Yorkshire	834	852	846	820
Total	9,123	9,373 (+2.7)	9,169 (−2.2)	8,701 (−5.1)
Rest of Great Britain	13,486	14,642 (+8.6)	15,688 (+7.1)	16,321 (+4.0)

Note: Figures in parentheses are percentage increases over the previous column.
Source: Census of Population.

conurbations; more remote rural areas have been losing population. This dispersal has been going on for a long time; inner London, for example, has been losing population since the turn of the century.

Nevertheless, the conurbations still account for a major part of the population of Great Britain. In 1974 the total resident population of the seven conurbations amounted to 17.3 million, which compares with a total for Great Britain of 54.4 million. In all about a third of the population of Great Britain lives in the conurbations, which themselves comprise less than 3 per cent of the total land area.

The reduction in population of conurbations has been reflected in the size of their labour forces. During the period 1951–71 the resident labour forces of six of the conurbations stopped increasing and started falling in numbers. The exception is south-east Lancashire, whose labour force fell in each intercensal period. In contrast, the numbers of economically active persons who were resident in the rest of Great Britain rose markedly throughout the period (see Table 7.1).

Both in the conurbations and in the remainder of the country the composition of the labour force has changed radically. In the twenty years to 1971 the labour force of Great Britain rose from 22.6 million to 25 million – an increase of 10.6 per cent. This increase was comprised of a 1.9 per cent increase in the number of economi-

Table 7.2 Percentage change in the labour forces of conurbations and the rest of Great Britain: males, single females, and married females, 1951-71

Conurbation	Males	Single, widowed, and divorced females	Married females	All groups
Greater London	−13.6	−21.6	+ 37.5	− 7.3
Central Clydeside	−11.2	−32.8	+147.7	− 3.3
Merseyside	−15.0	−33.5	+ 89.6	− 8.2
South-east Lancashire	− 9.1	−32.5	+ 25.9	− 7.0
Tyneside	−10.9	−28.1	+135.7	− 0.6
West Midlands	+ 0.6	−29.4	+ 60.9	+ 5.3
West Yorkshire	− 5.4	−31.4	+ 45.1	+ 1.7
All conurbations	−10.8	−26.6	+ 49.8	− 4.6
Rest of Great Britain	+ 8.7	−17.8	+186.3	+22.0

Source: Census of Population.

cally active males (from 15.6 million to 15.9 million) and a 30 per cent increase in the number of economically active females (from 7 million to 9.1 million). Within this total the number of economically-active married females rose from 2.7 million to 5.8 million – an increase of 114 per cent. Thus, a fall in the number of economically-active single women more than offset the increase in the number of economically active males. An examination of census data shows that there are marked discrepancies between one conurbation and another and between conurbations and the remainder of the country in the rates of change of these components of the labour force (see Table 7.2).

The main explanation for the increasing importance of married women in the labour force is of course the trend in their activity rates, which has been strongly upward. Some indication of the importance of activity rate changes among married women is provided by Table 7.3. The first column of this table gives the numerical change in the female labour force over the period 1951–71. Columns 2 and 4 show what changes there would have been if only activity rates had changed but population had remained constant. Columns 3 and 5 show what changes there would have been if only demographic changes had occurred and there had been no change in activity rates. It can be seen that activity rate changes among

Table 7.3 Analysis of component of change in the female labour force: conurbations and the rest of Great Britain, 1951–71 (thousands)

Conurbation	Total change (actual) (1)	Married females		Single, widowed, and divorced females	
		Activity rate changes (2)	Demographic changes (3)	Activity rate changes (4)	Demographic changes (5)
Greater London	+ 62	+369	− 82	− 99	− 90
Central Clydeside	+ 34	+ 95	+ 1	− 45	− 24
Merseyside	− 59	+ 69	− 5	− 31	− 20
South-east Lancashire	− 71	+ 73	− 11	− 56	− 25
Tyneside	− 17	+ 50	− 1	− 16	− 6
West Midlands	+ 19	+ 93	+ 8	− 47	− 4
West Yorkshire	− 34	+ 68	− 3	− 39	− 14
Rest of Great Britain	+2,008	+1,716	+308	−530	+118

Note: The four components of columns 2–5 do not combine to give the same figure as in column 1 because of the degree of interaction between them.
Source: Derived from the Census of Population.

married women are the single most important component in all conurbations and the only one making a positive contribution to the size of their female labour forces.

There has been a distinct tendency for married-female activity rates in individual conurbations and in the rest of the country to converge. Those conurbations having the lowest rates in 1951 – Clydeside and Tyneside – have exhibited the most startling increases since. Those having the highest rates in 1951 – Greater London, south-east Lancashire, West Midlands, and West Yorkshire – have shown comparatively little increase. So, whereas at one extreme the female activity rate on Tyneside was 23 per cent lower than the British average in 1951, by 1971 it was only 3 per cent lower, while at the other extreme the rate in south-east Lancashire was 69 per cent higher than the British average in 1951 but only 15 per cent higher in 1971.

In order to analyse the changing socioeconomic structure of the labour force the seventeen socioeconomic groups (SEGs) used in the censuses of 1961, 1966, and 1971 were aggregated into eight larger groupings:

Socioeconomic grouping

Managers and professionals	(SEGs 1, 2, 3, 4, 13)
Other self-employed	(SEGs 12, 14)
Skilled manual	(SEGs 8, 9)
Other non-manual	(SEGs 5, 6)
Service, semiskilled manual, and agricultural	(SEGs 7, 10, 15)
Unskilled manual	(SEG 11)
Armed forces	(SEG 16)
Indefinite	(SEG 17)

In 1971 the most important numerically of these groupings, both in the conurbations and elsewhere, were the skilled manual workers (see Table 7.4). In comparison with the rest of the country outside the conurbations this group was under-represented in Greater London but over-represented in Clydeside, Tyneside, West Midlands, and West Yorkshire.

Greater London's socioeconomic structure differed markedly from the structures of other conurbations and had higher proportions of managers and professionals and other non-manual workers and correspondingly lower proportions of skilled manual, service, semiskilled manual, and agricultural, and unskilled manual workers. With the exception of Greater London each conurbation had a higher proportion of unskilled manual workers and a lower proportion of managers and professionals than did the rest of Great Britain.

Between 1961 and 1971 considerable structural change took place (see Table 7.5). Semiskilled and unskilled manual workers declined in numbers everywhere, while except for Merseyside and Tyneside the number of managers and professionals and other self-employed workers increased everywhere. The increase of nearly a quarter in the number of managers and professionals in Clydeside in spite of an overall reduction of 12 per cent in its male labour force is particularly striking. The number of skilled manual workers fell in each conurbation but rose marginally in the rest of the country. Of all conurbations, the one having the lowest proportion of manual workers of whatever degree of skill in 1961, namely, Greater London, experienced the most rapid reduction in their numbers in the following decade, but the main impression from Table 7.5 is of a general upgrading of the labour force.

Given that travel-to-work patterns involve commuting into the conurbations from outside, it is not surprising that the conurbations account for a higher proportion of the country's employment than

Table 7.4 Socioeconomic composition of the male labour force: conurbations and the rest of Great Britain, 1971 (%)

Socioeconomic grouping	Greater London	Central Clydeside	Merseyside	South-east Lancashire	Tyneside	West Midlands	West Yorkshire	Rest of Great Britain
Managers and professionals	19.9	13.5	13.4	16.0	12.7	14.1	15.0	17.6
Other self-employed	5.4	2.0	3.0	5.0	2.2	3.5	4.5	5.8
Skilled manual	27.3	38.5	33.0	35.5	40.4	40.9	38.1	33.8
Other non-manual	23.4	17.7	17.8	17.3	17.2	14.7	16.0	16.5
Service, semiskilled manual, and agricultural	13.4	14.2	17.9	15.1	13.8	17.2	16.7	15.6
Unskilled manual	7.2	11.9	11.9	9.0	11.2	7.5	7.9	7.3
Armed forces	0.6	0.2	0.3	0.2	0.4	0.1	0.2	2.1
Indefinite	2.6	2.1	2.6	1.9	2.1	2.0	1.6	1.4
Total[a]	100.0	100.0	100.0	100.0	100.0	100.0	100.0	100.0

[a] Percentages may not add to 100 because of rounding.
Source: Derived from the Census of Population.

Table 7.5 Percentage change in the economically active male population by socioeconomic grouping: conurbations and the rest of Great Britain, 1961–71

Socioeconomic grouping	Greater London	Central Clydeside	Merseyside	South-east Lancashire	Tyneside	West Midlands	West Yorkshire	Rest of Great Britain
Managers and professionals	+ 6.3	+21.9	− 4.3	+12.4	—	+15.5	+ 7.9	+26.7
Other self-employed	+26.1	+11.7	− 4.4	+11.2	−10.5	+16.4	+ 7.5	+24.1
Skilled manual	−23.8	−19.5	−16.7	−13.6	−13.8	−12.7	−10.5	+ 0.4
Other non-manual	−10.9	−13.4	−13.1	− 8.8	− 5.9	− 0.7	− 0.5	+14.9
Service, semiskilled manual, and agricultural	−20.7	−19.7	−14.2	−17.3	−21.6	− 6.4	−14.1	−17.1
Unskilled manual	−25.3	−14.8	−26.0	−15.6	−14.1	− 7.2	− 3.6	− 6.4
All groupings	−13.0	−12.4	−14.5	− 8.6	−11.8	− 5.4	− 6.1	+ 2.8

Source: Derived from the Census of Population.

of its labour force. In 1971 the conurbations accounted for 37.5 per cent of all employment and 34.8 per cent of all the labour force of Great Britain. Unlike the population and labour force data, which are gathered on a place-of-residence basis, the employment data published in successive censuses are recorded on a place-of-work basis. Travel-to-work patterns do of course give rise to differences between the recorded numbers of persons economically active and of persons in employment in an area. In addition the census labour-force statistics compromise both persons in employment and persons out of employment, while the employment data cover only persons in employment.

The decline of employment in the conurbations began about the same time as that of the labour force and the rates for both have been broadly similar, although the decline of employment has been slightly more rapid in central Clydeside, south-east Lancashire, and West Yorkshire and slightly less rapid in other conurbations. Outside the conurbations the increase in the labour force has been more rapid than that in employment (see Table 7.6).

Changes in the industrial distribution of employment between 1951 and 1971 were analysed by grouping the twenty-seven

Table 7.6 Percentage change in resident labour force and employment by workplace: conurbations and the rest of Great Britain, 1951–61 and 1961–71

| | 1951–61 | | 1961–71 | |
Conurbation	Labour force	Employment	Labour force	Employment
Greater London	+2.6	+4.7	− 9.6	−9.0
Central Clydeside	+2.3	n.a.	− 5.5	−8.4
Merseyside	+1.8	+2.0	− 9.7	−7.6
South-east Lancashire	−0.5	−1.0	− 6.5	−8.3
Tyneside	+3.8	+5.2	− 4.2	−2.1
West Midlands	+7.7	+9.0	− 2.3	−2.0
West Yorkshire	+2.2	+1.8	− 3.8	−5.4
Rest of Great Britain	+8.6	n.a.	+11.5	+7.9

Note: Differences between changes in employment and changes in labour force are influenced not only by commuting but also by changes in unemployment that will reduce employment without altering the labour force.
Source: Derived from the Census of Population.

industry Orders of the 1968 Standard Industrial Classification (SIC) into five industrial sectors.[3] These sectors were:

Industrial sector	*1968 SIC industry Orders*
Primary	1 and 2 ('Agriculture, forestry, and fishing' and 'Mining and quarrying').
Manufacturing	3 to 19 (all manufacturing industries).
Construction	20 ('Construction').
Public utilities, transport, and distribution	21, 22, and 23 ('Gas, electricity, water', 'Transport and communications', and 'Distributive trades').
Other services	24, 25, 26, and 27 ('Insurance, banking, finance, and business services', 'Professional and scientific services', 'Miscellaneous services', and 'Public administration and defence').

In 1971 (see Table 7.7) the most important industrial sector was manufacturing. This accounted for about a quarter of all employment in Greater London and at least one-third elsewhere. The discrepancy in this respect between Greater London and elsewhere is largely accounted for by the greater importance of employment in the other services sector in London. As may be expected, the primary sector is of somewhat greater importance outside conurbations than within them.

Between 1961 and 1971 the structure of employment changed considerably (see Table 7.8). Employment in the primary sector declined dramatically in all areas, mainly as a result of productivity improvements in agriculture and mining. The two major sectors

[3] Over the period 1951–71 there were significant changes in the SIC. The 1948 SIC, upon which the 1951 census was based, was modified in 1958, forming the basis for the industrial analysis contained in the censuses of 1961 and 1966; and the 1958 reclassifications were followed by further changes in 1968, upon which the industrial analyses of the 1971 census were based. Although this series of reclassifications mainly affect interindustry comparisons, there are cases in which they affect intersectoral comparisons. For example, in the 1958 reclassification of the SIC the 'Motor repairers and garages' subgroup of 'Vehicle industry' Order was transferred from that Order to the 'Miscellaneous services' Order. This involved a reduction in employment of about 200,000 workers in the former Order and an increase of the same number in the latter. The industrial groupings used here have been chosen in order to minimise such discontinuities, although the lack of complete standardisation should be recognised. It should also be noted that data on the industrial distribution of employees working in central Clydeside in 1951 are not available from the census of that year.

Table 7.7 Industrial composition of employment: conurbations and the rest of Great Britain, 1971 (%)

Industrial sector	Greater London	Central Clydeside	Merseyside	South-east Lancashire	Tyneside	West Midlands	West Yorkshire	Rest of Great Britain
Primary	0.2	0.6	0.2	0.6	2.4	0.2	1.3	6.6
Manufacturing	26.8	38.3	33.4	43.1	36.6	53.3	44.9	33.4
Construction	6.1	7.7	7.2	6.2	7.0	5.7	5.8	7.4
Public utilities, transport, and distribution	25.2	23.2	27.2	22.2	21.7	16.8	20.2	19.5
Other services	40.3	29.8	31.3	27.3	31.9	23.2	27.5	32.4
Total[a]	100.0	100.0	100.0	100.0	100.0	100.0	100.0	100.0

[a] Columns do not add to 100 because persons with workplaces outside Great Britain and workers who inadequately describe their industries are included in the employment totals.
Source: Census of Population.

Table 7.8 Percentage change in employment by industrial sector: conurbations and the rest of Great Britain, 1961–71

Industrial sector	Greater London	Central Clydeside	Merseyside	South-east Lancashire	Tyneside	West Midlands	West Yorkshire	Rest of Great Britain
Primary	−35.7	−57.8	−50.0	−51.1	−47.7	−62.3	−41.9	−34.3
Manufacturing	−25.1	−18.0	−9.2	−19.9	−7.3	−10.3	−15.6	+10.5
Construction	−11.0	−8.2	−4.2	+0.3	−1.5	−3.8	+3.3	+11.0
Public utilities, transport, and distribution	−12.2	−17.3	−23.5	−11.7	−14.9	−6.5	−9.9	+0.3
Other services	+7.2	+22.8	+14.2	+21.4	+26.7	+28.7	+23.9	+25.9
All sectors	−9.0	−8.4	−7.6	−8.3	−2.1	−2.0	−5.4	+7.9

Source: Derived from the Census of Population.

(manufacturing; and public utilities, transport, and distribution) declined in all conurbations and more rapidly than total employment. In contrast, the manufacturing sector expanded more rapidly than total employment in the rest of Great Britain. However, the most interesting sector is other services, which includes health, education, public administration, insurance, banking, and finance. This sector expanded in all conurbations in spite of overall employment decline. Also, in all conurbations except Greater London and Merseyside the rates of expansion were comparable with those achieved in the rest of the country.

7.3 Factor movements

It is clear that marked changes have taken place in the geographical distribution of the labour force. The major conurbations are becoming numerically less important in relation to the nation as a whole both as places of residence and as places of work. Also, trends in the industrial and occupational composition of the labour force in conurbations have to some extent diverged from national trends. These facts call for some explanation.

Brown (1972) has suggested that: (a) the biggest cause by far of the parallel movements of industry and population out of the conurbations has been the need for space; and (b) to some extent in recent years industry and commerce have moved out of conurbations partly in search of labour, but for the most part both they and their labour have moved out independently in search of land. If this view is to be accepted, it is necessary to explain, first, why congested conurbations should ever have grown up in the first place, and second, how the forces making for the agglomeration of population and employment have been replaced by others making for their dispersal.

Brown has analysed the factors affecting the long term distribution of population and employment under four headings:

(a) the disposition of the population in regard to those natural resources and features that have some relevance to their health and welfare;
(b) the aggregation or dispersion (and the forms of aggregation) of the population, again considered in its relevance to their health and welfare;

(c) the disposition of industry in relation to the natural resources and features of the country; and

(d) the disposition of industry with regard to other industry.

The gist of Brown's argument is that, with rising real incomes, factors (a) and (b) (the disposition of population) have become increasingly important, while, as a result of technological improvements particularly in transport and communications, factors (c) and (d) (the disposition of industry) have become increasingly unimportant. For the purposes of gaining an understanding of the geographical decentralisation of population and employment, it is factors (b) and (d) that require further elaboration.

The advantages of living in conurbations arise from their ability to provide a wide variety of choice in terms of different kinds of work, goods, and services. The main disadvantages stem from congestion of one form or another. Aggregations of population make land locally scarce and, *ceteris paribus*, make for smaller dwellings. The effect of land scarcity on the open space that is available for recreation is even more obvious. For people with jobs in the conurbations the alternative is to live further from work and incur heavier travel costs.

The Lambeth Inner Area Study (1975a) argues that men on low earnings choose to live in inner city areas because housing is cheap or available (for renting) or else because they cannot afford to move out or commute. On the other hand, men with high earnings tend to move out to obtain better housing conditions and can afford to commute. The implication is that emigration from the inner city tends to be selective with the more highly paid having higher rates of net emigration than the rest. Also, provided that real incomes continue to increase as they have done in most years since the war and improvements in transport and communication continue to be made, net emigration from the inner city seems likely for the foreseeable future.

The attraction of the large centres of population for industrial investors lies in the productive benefits of industrial agglomeration. These stem from the operation of economies of scale that are external to the firm, some of them connected with production and some with marketing. (In the eighteenth and nineteenth centuries the operation of external economies of scale on the production side produced a very high degree of localisation of the pottery, wool, linen and cotton textiles, cutlery, and many of the lighter metal and engineering industries.) Some of these advantages are connected with pools of specialised skills and knowledge and some with the ancillary and otherwise linked industries. The central business districts continue to function in this way for certain service industries – notably 'Insurance, banking, and finance', 'Public administration', and 'Professional and scientific services', which are among the most rapidly growing of all industries. On the marketing side the advantages of a location close to a major centre of population are obvious.

However, in general, technological progress, notably in transport and communications, is tending to weaken such ties. The growth of the motorway network, faster intercity rail links, domestic airways, the development of STD telephones, etc. have all played their part in weakening the dependence of industrial and commercial enterprises on metropolitan locations. These changes seem particularly likely to affect the location decisions of new enterprises and of established enterprises wishing to expand.

While the above is a highly plausible explanation of the process of decentralisation, it is no easy matter conclusively to confirm or refute it as a general hypothesis. There is, however, a considerable amount of factual material that is suggestive and consistent with it.

Analysing immigration and emigration in relation to the resident population of Greater London, Dugmore (1975) has been able to show that for the most part the decentralisation of the labour force has been distinctly and regularly selective. Looking at net emigration, as a proportion of the male labour force in each of five socioeconomic groupings, the rank order of outward flows was consistently professional and managerial (largest), other non-manual, skilled manual, semiskilled and service, and unskilled manual (smallest).

For the present purpose a more limited examination was made of the net emigration of economically active males from the major conurbations during the twelve months up to the 1971 census date. The results are summarised in Table 7.9 and suggest that what is true of London may also be true of the other conurbations. In general, net emigration is most marked for the non-manual groups but is low or negative for unskilled manual workers.

There are also a number of studies of the decentralisation of employment. Dennis (Chapter 2) has examined the fall in manufacturing employment in Greater London over the period 1966–74. This analysis has demonstrated that an absolute excess of

Table 7.9 Net emigration from the conurbations, 1970–71, as a proportion of the labour force in 1971 by socioeconomic groupings: economically active males (%)

Socioeconomic grouping (SEGs in brackets)	Greater London	Central Clydeside	Merseyside	South-east Lancashire	Tyneside	West Midlands	West Yorkshire
Managerial and professional (1, 2, 3, 4, 13)	1.9	2.1	1.8	1.6	3.2	2.3	1.0
Other self-employed (12, 14)	1.7	1.9	2.8	1.6	1.2	1.2	0.3
Skilled manual (8, 9)	1.4	1.1	1.5	0.4	0.9	0.8	0.3
Other non-manual (5, 6)	1.2	1.7	1.7	0.6	1.2	1.7	0.5
Service, semiskilled manual, and agricultural (7, 10, 15)	1.0	1.3	1.7	0.2	0.5	0.5	0.5
Unskilled manual (11)	0.7	0.8	0.9	—a	—	0.1	0.4
All groupings (incl. SEGs 16, 17)	1.3	1.5	1.7	0.7	1.2	1.1	0.6

a Net immigration.
Source: Census of Population (1971).

plant closures over openings was responsible for a major part of the industrial decline of London. In so far as the explanation of employment decline is in terms of plant openings and closures, this result is of course tautological. For policy purposes it is important to know whether London suffers from a rate of new openings that is lower in relation to its existing stock of plant or from a rate of closures that is higher in relation to its existing stock of plant. On which of these does London compare unfavourably with the rest of South-East region, or is it a combination of the two? In the latter case the problem presumably derives mainly from the greater difficulties of operating existing plant in London, whereas in the former case it must derive at least in part from the greater difficulties of setting up in London. A policy of making sites available on favourable terms, for example, might well be relevant to the latter problem but not necessarily to the former.

In Cameron's (1973) geographical study of industrial change in the Clydeside conurbation over the period 1958–68, data were collected on every manufacturing establishment that employed more than five employees and was in existence at some time during the period. Given the scale of the location grid used (100 m square), it was possible to investigate the process of the decentralisation of employment in considerable spatial detail.

Cameron has found that in 1958 three out of every four plants were located in the central city. By 1968 the picture had changed. The total number of plants had fallen by 8 per cent, the most marked reduction occurring in the area within 2 km of the centre of Glasgow where a quarter of the total disappeared. In the rest of Glasgow the overall picture was one of numerical stability. Elsewhere in the conurbation, outside the city of Glasgow, the subcentres and three of the four non-urban quadrants increased their share both relatively and absolutely, with especially marked gains occurring in East Kilbride and in the north-east and south-east quadrants.

The main explanation of the changed distribution was the pattern of new openings. Whereas 70 per cent of all establishments in the conurbation were sited in the central city, only just over half of the new plants were set up within this area. In the rest of the conurbation the subcentres picked up more than their 'expected' share of new plants, and comparative gains were also made in all the non-urban quadrants. The study also found that the new plants located in the centre of the conurbation tended to be smaller than those on the periphery. Thus, although the central city of Glasgow picked up more than one out of every two new plants in the conurbation, this only represented one-quarter of new plant employment. Later work on the birth of new plants using this data will be reported by Cameron in Chapter 15.

7.4 Labour market indicators

The analysis of labour market indicators can throw further light on the decentralisation of population and employment. For example, where the resident labour force in a conurbation declines more rapidly than total employment, then, *ceteris paribus*, increasing labour shortages may be expected with rising vacancies, falling unemployment, and possibly increased wage inflation relative to the regional average. Where total employment in a conurbation declines more rapidly than the resident labour force, the opposite conditions may be expected to pertain.[4]

However, within these broad trends there may be considerable variation between one part of a conurbation and another. In Greater London, for example, employment in the east end has been declining rapidly with the gradual closure of the docks. In the peripheral areas to the west of the metropolis, on the other hand, there has been a considerable growth of employment. The statistics presented below have therefore been analysed to bring out, so far as possible, any differences within conurbations.

One problem with an analysis of this kind is the direction of causation. While it is true, for example, that a more rapid decentralisation of workplaces than of workpeople may give rise to unemployment, it is equally true that a high rate of unemployment may give rise to the emigration of workpeople. Tyneside, Clydeside, and

[4]There has been a considerable debate about the labour market consequences of the decline of population and employment in conurbations for those who continue to reside in them. This debate has been somewhat confused, as the following comment by Foster and Richardson (1973) suggests:

The resident population of London has been falling for many years. More recently, it would seem that the number of people working in London has also started to decline. We have heard it suggested that a faster emigration of work people than work places would cause labour shortages and hence problems for Londoners. We have also heard it suggested that a slower emigration of work people than work places would cause labour surpluses and hence problems for Londoners. We have even heard both suggestions from the same sources, almost simultaneously. (p. 87).

their associated regions have suffered above-average unemployment rates for the entire postwar period, and the relative population decline of the Northern region and Scotland reflects this fact. Furthermore, where a region is declining in population there is likely to be a general deficiency of demand in that region, and this in itself may be expected to give rise to unemployment. In addition to comparisons between conurbations and the regions in which they are located and between different parts of the same conurbation, it is therefore also important to make comparisons between different conurbations and the national average.

For the purpose of making geographical comparisons the question arises as to whether the analysis of unemployment is more appropriately based on unemployment levels than on unemployment rates. In general, unemployment levels are more appropriate for assessing the scale of the problem in a particular area, whereas unemployment rates provide a better measure of its intensity. The traditional emphasis on unemployment rates is justified provided that the unemployment rate is a realistic indication of the risk of the typical economically-active person being unemployed; but if the unemployment register is static with the same group of people on the books all the time, more attention needs to be given to the geographical distribution of the unemployed population. In reality of course the true position is somewhere between these two extremes, and for this reason both sets of statistics are relevant.

The measurement of unemployment rate differences within conurbations is bedevilled by the problem of defining separate and distinct local labour-market areas. The Department of Employment has traditionally refrained from quoting unemployment rates for areas smaller than whole travel-to-work areas, on the grounds that the number unemployed is recorded by place of residence (since for the most part unemployed persons register at the Department of Employment local office nearest to their home), whereas the number of employees in employment is recorded by place of work. Unemployment rates, when defined as the ratio of the number unemployed by place of residence to the number of employees in employment by place of work, are liable to be distorted by commuting patterns.

Also, for areas smaller than whole travel-to-work areas unemployment rates, however calculated, cannot be reliably used as a proxy for job availability. Variations in unemployment rates between different parts of a travel-to-work area may, for example, reflect the preponderance of the unskilled among the unemployed and the disproportionate concentration of such people among the residential populations of particular localities. Lower unemployment figures in outer than in inner London, for example, do not necessarily indicate that jobs are any more readily available to the unskilled population living in outer London. Such figures may only indicate that the employees resident in outer London include higher proportions in the occupations that are most in demand in Greater London. (Many employees living in outer London do of course travel from their homes to work in inner London.) The use of residential unemployment rates (defined as the number of registered unemployed or out of employment in an area as a percentage of the economically active residents) for comparing different parts of a conurbation is open to the same objections.

7.4.1   *The distribution of the unemployed population*

Statistics of registered unemployment are compiled regularly for the English metropolitan counties and for the west-central Scotland Special Development Area in the case of central Clydeside (see Table 7.10).

These areas accounted for more than 40 per cent of all registered unemployment in Great Britain in April 1976. Greater London alone accounted for nearly 12 per cent of the total and, as noted above, there were in fact more unemployed persons in Greater London than in the whole of Scotland at that time. This concentration of unemployed persons in Greater London is not new, as Table 7.11 makes clear.

At the 1971 census the seven conurbations accounted for about 40 per cent of all those in Great Britain in the out-of-employment (other than sick) category. The proportion was a little lower in the boom year of the 1966 census. Greater London accounts for a higher proportion of census than of registered unemployment as, apparently, does central Clydeside (see Table 7.12).

7.4.2   *Unemployment rates (registered unemployment)*

In April 1976 the Great Britain total registered unemployment rate was 5.4 per cent. This figure was exceeded by three of the English

Table 7.10 Unemployment in metropolitan counties and the rest of Great Britain: males and females, April 1976

Area	Males		Females		Total	
	No.	% of GB total	No.	% of GB total	No.	% of GB total
Greater London TTWA	118,457	12.4	28,461	10.5	146,918	11.9
Greater Manchester MC	51,620	5.4	10,962	4.0	62,582	5.1
Merseyside MC	57,194	6.0	15,603	5.7	72,797	5.9
Tyne and Wear MC	33,351	3.5	9,314	3.4	42,665	3.5
West-central Scotland SDA	55,676	5.8	18,848	9.3	74,524	6.1
West Midlands MC	66,617	6.9	18,332	6.7	84,949	6.9
West Yorkshire MC	36,007	3.7	9,123	3.4	45,130	3.7
Total of above	418,922	43.7	110,643	40.7	529,565	43.0
Rest of Great Britain	540,216	56.3	161,437	59.3	701,653	57.0
Total (Great Britain)	959,138	100.0	272,080	100.0	1,231,218	100.0

Note: TTWA = travel-to-work area; MC = Metropolitan County; SDA = special development area; GB = Great Britain.
Source: Department of Employment Gazette (May 1976).

Table 7.11 Unemployment in Greater London as a percentage of the total for Great Britain, 1960–75 (October each year).

Year	1960	1961	1962	1963	1964	1965	1966	1967	1968	1969
%	11.4	13.0	12.5	11.4	11.0	11.5	11.8	13.1	11.9	10.9

Year	1970	1971	1972	1973	1974	1975	1976[a]
%	10.2	9.4	9.7	9.7	9.8	11.1	12.1

a April figure.
Source: Department of Employment Gazette.

metropolitan counties[5] (Merseyside, 10.1 per cent; Tyne and Wear, 7.9 per cent; and West Midlands, 6.0 per cent) and was in excess of the rates in the others (Greater London, 3.7 per cent; South Yorkshire, 5.3 per cent; West Yorkshire, 5.0 per cent; and Greater Manchester, 5.2 per cent). The unemployment rate in the west-central Scotland special development area at the time was 7.9 per cent.

In order to compare unemployment trends in conurbations Table 7.13 presents details of unemployment rates as a proportion of the national average, for October in each fifth year between 1960 and 1975, for the travel-to-work areas comprising the seven major conurbations[6] and for the standard regions in which these conurbations are located. Not surprisingly, unemployment rates in the conurbations have moved diverse ways. Some areas have improved against the national average; others have worsened or remained fairly steady. Some individual conurbations are unquestionably facing severe unemployment problems; but equally, others are well placed in relation to the national average. However, the most striking impression from the tables is that three conurbations, namely, Clydeside, Merseyside, and Tyneside, have experienced worse unemployment than Great Britain as a whole consistently throughout the period. Greater London, on the other hand, has

[5]The numbers unemployed in counties are aggregates of the numbers recorded at employment offices and careers offices within the counties. The unemployment percentage rates are for the nearest areas that can be expressed in terms of complete travel-to-work areas.

[6]The boundaries of the travel-to-work areas are changed from time to time to reflect changes in commuting patterns. This sometimes results in the splitting up of such areas into two or more smaller ones or in the amalgamation of two or more areas. Data for earlier years are therefore not necessarily comparable.

Table 7.12 Out of employment (other than sick) in the conurbations and rest of Great Britain: males and females, 1961, 1966, and 1971

Area	Males				Females			
	% of GB total			No. (thousands) 1971	% of GB total			No. (thousands) 1971
	1961	1966	1971		1961	1966	1971	
Greater London	15.3	15.0	14.8	84.6	18.3	15.9	17.3	52.6
Central Clydeside	8.7	6.1	7.4	42.2	5.9	3.8	4.7	14.4
Merseyside	6.4	4.5	4.9	28.1	4.3	3.4	3.8	11.6
South-east Lancashire	4.1	4.0	5.5	31.4	4.8	4.3	4.9	15.0
Tyneside	3.0	2.5	3.2	18.2	1.9	1.7	1.9	5.8
West Midlands	3.5	3.0	5.1	29.2	3.4	3.8	4.8	14.7
West Yorkshire	2.2	2.4	3.9	22.5	2.5	2.4	3.2	9.6
Total (conurbations)	43.2	37.4[a]	44.9[a]	256.2	41.1	35.3	40.8[a]	123.7
Rest of Great Britain	56.8	62.6	55.1	314.5	59.8	64.7	59.2	179.7
Total (Great Britain)	100.0	100.0	100.0	570.7	100.0	100.0	100.0	303.4

[a] Column does not add because of rounding.
Note: GB = Great Britain.
Source: Census of Population.

Table 7.13 Unemployment rate as a percentage of the Great Britain total rate: males and females, 1960–75 (October in each fifth year)

Area	1960	1965	1970	1975
Greater London	53	57	50	63
South-East	*67*	*64*	*62*	*71*
Birmingham	60	50	100	133
Dudley			69	76
Walsall	60	50	81	98
West Bromwich	33	21	73	84
Wolverhampton	53	50	127	133
West Midlands	*60*	*57*	*92*	*108*
Bradford	47	57	131	112
Dewsbury	60	64	100	84
Halifax	60	36	62	67
Huddersfield	40	36	65	69
Keighley			85	102
Leeds	53	64	96	94
Wakefield	60	50	85	76
Yorkshire and Humberside	*66*	*79*	*116*	*98*
Ashton under Lyne	66	79	88	94
Bolton	66	93	73	96
Bury	27	36	73	78
Manchester	66	71	85	100
Oldham	87	57	69	82
Rochdale	40	29	65	114
Liverpool	240	193	177	204
North-West	*113*	*107*	*108*	*127*
Tyneside	167	179	196	149
North	*173*	*171*	*177*	*141*
Glasgow	233	207	212	135
North Lanarkshire	300	221	204	159
Paisley	227	136	131	98
Scotland	*220*	*193*	*173*	*118*
Great Britain	*100*	*100*	*100*	*100*

experienced unemployment rates that are low in relation to the national average.

To a considerable extent unemployment trends in individual conurbations are reflected in (or are a reflection of) regional trends. Thus, unemployment rates in Scotland and the Northern region in common with those in Clydeside and Tyneside respectively, have been consistently higher than they are nationally. Unemployment rates in the South-East region have been consistently below the national average, while unemployment rates in Greater London have been consistently below the average for the South-East.

7.4.3 Labour market mismatch

There has been a great deal of discussion as to whether metropolitan labour markets are in some sense more unbalanced than other labour markets because of a 'mismatch' between the characteristics of job vacancies on the one hand and of the unemployed population on the other. The sensible discussion of this question is only possible provided that 'mismatch' is defined precisely. In principle, unemployment may be classified into three components: frictional, structural, and demand deficiency. Cheshire (1973) has defined these as follows:

1. *Frictional unemployment* consists of all those unempIoyed persons for whom there appear to be vacancies in the categories in which they are registered. The frictionally unemployed in any occupation are thus the number unemployed or the number of vacancies, whichever is the smaller, and the total for the labour market area is the sum of these numbers across all occupations; frictional unemployment stems partly from inadequate information flows within the labour market.

2. *Structural unemployment* consists of those for whom there are no vacancies in their own category in the labour market area, but for whom there would be if they could change their category (e.g. through training). The number of them, so defined, is the total of excesses of vacancies over unemployment in all occupations where there is such an excess, or of unemployment over vacancies (where there is such an excess), whichever of the two is the smaller.

3. *Demand-deficiency unemployment* is the number of unemployed for whom there are no vacancies in the labour market even if they change their occupations. It is the excess of total unemployment over total unfilled vacancies, if there is such an excess. If not, demand-deficiency unemployment is zero.

Total unemployment is the arithmetic sum of (1), (2), and (3). Labour market mismatch may be defined as the arithmetic sum of (1) and (2) – i.e. frictional plus structural unemployment.

Cheshire has hypothesised that the extent of labour market mismatch will be less when the typical unemployed person is near to a great many workplaces than when he is near to only a few. If this were so, then, for areas with comparable demand pressure, labour market mismatch (defined as the sum of frictional plus structural unemployment) would be higher in sparsely than in densely populated areas. Using local unemployment data for the Development Areas, Cheshire has been able to devise some empirical support for this hypothesis.

7.4.4 *Residential unemployment rates*[7]

As suggested above (p. 174), there are objections to the use of residential unemployment rates as a means of measuring labour market differences between one part of a travel-to-work area and another. In particular it cannot necessarily be assumed that because, say, residential unemployment rates are higher in inner than in outer areas that jobs are more readily available in the latter than in the former. The residents of inner and outer areas are to a large extent looking for jobs over the same labour-market area. The alternative explanation is that inner areas have among their residential populations higher proportions of people who are vulnerable to unemployment regardless of where they live. However, for employment policy purposes it is important to establish how much weight should be attached to these alternative explanations. In order to do this it is necessary to examine residential unemployment-rate differences within the conurbation.

A detailed analysis of residential unemployment rates using 1971 census small-area data has been carried out by the Department of the Environment, the findings of which have been summarised by Holtermann (1975). The basic spatial unit used in this analysis was the census enumeration district (ED). Within the conurbations it is the inner areas that contain the highest proportions of the worst unemployment EDs. Table 7.14 shows that in each case the inner area contains a higher proportion of the worst unemployment EDs than of all EDs. In Greater London, for example, the inner boroughs account for only 48 per cent of all Greater London's EDs but of 86 per cent of the worst male-unemployment EDs and 73 per cent of the worst female-unemployment EDs.

[7]Residential unemployment rates refer to the number of registered unemployed or out of employment in an area as a percentage of the economically active residents.

Table 7.14 The worst 5% of each conurbation's EDs (% in inner areas)

	Greater London	Central Clydeside	Merseyside	South-east Lancashire	Tyneside	West Midlands
Male unemployment	86	69	82	73	65	89
Female unemployment	73	55	75	56	46	81
% of all EDs in conurbations in inner area	48	58	54	29	42	64

Note: The inner areas were defined as follows: Greater London – the former County of London less Greenwich LB plus Newham LB; central Clydeside – Glasgow City of County; Merseyside – Liverpool CB and Bootle CB; south-east Lancashire – Manchester CB and Salford CB; Tyneside – Newcastle upon Tyne CB and Gateshead CB; West Midlands – Birmingham CB, Walsall CB, and West Bromwich CB (where LB = London Borough and CB = County Borough).
Source: Holtermann (1975).

The interpretation of this difference between inner and outer areas is important for employment policy purposes. Of the two alternative hypotheses the second – namely, that inner areas have among their residential populations higher proportions of people who will be vulnerable to unemployment regardless of where they live than do outer areas – is the easier to test. For example, if it could be shown that unemployment rates among groups of persons having similar personal characteristics were the same in inner and outer areas, it would be reasonable to assume that this hypothesis is the correct one. In order to do this it is necessary to obtain data on residential unemployment rates by personal attribute and by area.

A number of studies (Metcalf and Richardson, Chapter 8; Northern Region Strategy Team, 1975) have noted that skill and age are the two most important factors making an individual vulnerable to unemployment. Department of Employment unemployment statistics give a great deal of information about the composition of the unemployed population in terms of their sociodemographic attributes. For example, the regular unemployment statistics provide details about the occupations that unemployed persons are seeking, their age, and their country of origin. These statistics are supplemented from time to time by sample surveys.

These statistics are, however, difficult to interpret. For example, one notable finding of the June 1973 sample survey was that areas with high average unemployment rates on the whole have higher proportions of unemployed men with 'good or fair prospects of obtaining work' than areas of lower unemployment. This, at first sight unexpected, result is accounted for by the fact that high unemployment areas have a lower percentage of older unemployed workers; men aged 55 and over were 40 per cent of the total in low unemployment areas (unemployment rates less than 2 per cent) but only 28 per cent in high unemployment areas (unemployment rates 3.5 per cent and over). The turnover of the unemployment register is rapid even in high unemployment areas, and younger men are considered to have much better prospects of obtaining work than older men. As might be expected, however, the proportion in each age group having good or fair prospects of obtaining work is lower in high unemployment areas than in low unemployment areas.

The Northern Region Strategy Team (1975) has noted that unemployment rates tend to increase broadly in line with declining levels of skill. A comparison of the seven conurbations showed up the coincidence of high overall unemployment rates and large percentages of the labour force in the unskilled category (see Table 7.15). Of the seven conurbations, those in the traditionally assisted areas (Tyneside, Merseyside, and central Clydeside) consistently displayed this same combination of characteristics in postwar censuses. There are a number of reasons for expecting unskilled workers to have higher-than-average unemployment rates. Oi (1962) has argued that skilled workers have more firm-specific training than unskilled workers and that employers therefore tend to hoard skilled labour, or at least to lay off unskilled workers prior to skilled workers. Reder (1955) has suggested that skilled workers experience lower unemployment than unskilled, essentially because skilled workers are able to do unskilled workers' jobs but not vice versa. The dual labour-market hypothesis suggests that the unskilled, because their jobs are boring and offer little prospect of career advancement, tend to have higher quit rates, with job changes frequently involving a bout of unemployment. The unskilled are more likely to be on the unemployment register than others because the level of unemployment and other types of benefit is higher relative to their anticipated net earnings and there is therefore less incentive for them to work. Finally, because of the narrowing of pay differentials it is possible that the marginal cost of employing an unskilled worker is more likely to exceed the marginal product; consequently, employers are reluctant to employ them. Whatever the reason, the unskilled are much more prone to unemployment than other groups wherever they are living. Skill seems to be a far more important determinant of unemployment than location does.

A comparison of unemployment rates by the same socioeconomic groupings as in Table 7.15 with the socioeconomic structure of the labour force shows that a major part of the differences within conurbations in overall residential-unemployment rates can be explained by variations in the structure of the labour force between boroughs. One of the most obvious factors is that inner boroughs generally have higher proportions of the fifth socioeconomic grouping (mainly unskilled manual workers) than do outer ones. Within Greater London, for example, 22 per cent of the economically active residents of Tower Hamlets fall into this category; the equivalent figure for Sutton is only 7 per cent.

Thus, column 1 of Table 7.16 shows the actual overall unemployment rates by borough and conurbation. These are generally

Table 7.15 Out of employment (total) as a percentage of the economically active by socioeconomic grouping (males and females): English conurbations and Great Britain, 1971

Socioeconomic grouping (SEGs in brackets)	Greater London	Merseyside	South-east Lancashire	Tyneside	West Midlands	West Yorkshire	Great Britain
Managerial and professional (1, 2, 3, 4, 13)	1.9	2.0	1.9	2.9	1.6	1.6	1.9
Other self-employed and skilled manual (8, 9, 12, 14)	3.7	6.1	4.4	6.8	3.7	3.7	3.9
Other non-manual (5, 6)	2.3	2.9	2.3	2.6	2.0	1.9	2.2
Service, semiskilled manual and agricultural (7, 10, 15)	3.2	7.1	4.3	6.9	3.6	4.5	4.0
Unskilled manual, armed forces, and indefinite (11, 16, 17)	20.2	30.1	25.0	28.5	22.8	21.9	21.6
All groupings	4.6	8.4	5.3	8.2	5.1	5.1	5.2

Source: 1971 Census of Population.

Table 7.16 Unemployment by socioeconomic grouping in the English conurbations: males and females, 1971

Conurbation and boroughs	Overall unemployment rate (%)		
	Actual	Adjusted for class structure differences	Adjusted for class unemployment rate differences
	(1)	(2)	(3)
GREATER LONDON			
City of London	5	5	4
Barking LB	4	5	4
Barnet LB	3	4	4
Bexley LB	3	4	4
Brent LB	5	4	5
Bromley LB	3	4	4
Camden LB	6	5	6
Croydon LB	3	4	4
Ealing LB	4	4	4
Enfield LB	3	4	4
Greenwich LB	4	5	4
Hackney LB	6	5	5
Hammersmith LB	7	5	6
Haringey LB	5	4	5
Harrow LB	3	4	4
Havering LB	3	4	4
Hillingdon LB	3	4	3
Hounslow LB	4	4	4
Islington LB	6	5	5
Kensington and Chelsea LB	6	4	6
Kingston upon Thames LB	3	4	3
Lambeth LB	6	5	5
Lewisham LB	5	5	4
Merton LB	3	4	4
Newham LB	5	5	4
Redbridge LB	3	4	4
Richmond upon Thames LB	3	4	4
Southwark LB	6	6	5
Sutton LB	3	4	4
Tower Hamlets LB	7	6	5
Waltham Forest LB	4	4	4
Wandsworth LB	5	5	5
Westminster LB	5	5	5
Conurbation average	4.6	4.6	4.6
MERSEYSIDE			
Birkenhead CB	7	7	6
Wallasey CB	7	6	7
Bebington MB	4	5	5
Ellesmere Port MB	5	7	5
Hoylake UD	3	4	4

| Conurbation and boroughs | Overall unemployment rate (%) | | |
| | Actual | Adjusted for class structure differences | Adjusted for class unemployment-rate differences |
	(1)	(2)	(3)
Neston UD	5	5	6
Wirral UD	3	4	5
Bootle CB	8	8	6
Liverpool CB	9	7	8
Crosby MB	6	6	7
Huyton with Roby UD	9	7	8
Litherland UD	7	7	7
Conurbation average	8.4	8.4	8.4
SOUTH-EAST LANCASHIRE			
Stockport CB	5	4	5
Altrincham MB	4	4	4
Dukinfield MB	4	5	4
Hyde MB	5	5	5
Sale MB	3	3	5
Stalybridge MB	5	5	5
Alderley Edge UD	2	3	3
Bowdon UD	2	3	2
Bredbury and Romiley UD	3	4	3
Cheadle and Gatley UD	3	3	5
Hale UD	3	3	4
Hazelgrove and Bramhall UD	3	3	4
Marple UD	3	3	4
Wilmslow UD	3	4	3
Disley RD	5	4	5
Bolton CB	5	5	5
Bury CB	5	4	5
Manchester CB	8	5	6
Oldham CB	6	5	5
Rochdale CB	6	5	5
Salford CB	8	6	6
Ashton under Lyne MB	5	5	4
Eccles MB	5	5	5
Farnworth MB	6	5	6
Heywood MB	5	5	5
Middleton MB	5	5	5
Mossley MB	5	5	4
Prestwich MB	4	3	5
Radcliffe MB	4	5	4
Stretford MB	7	5	6
Swinton and Pendlebury MB	4	4	4
Audenshaw UD	4	4	4
Chadderton UD	4	4	4
Crompton UD	3	4	3
Denton UD	4	4	4

Table 7.16 - *cont.*

Conurbation and boroughs	Overall unemployment rate (%)		
	Actual	Adjusted for class structure differences	Adjusted for class unemploymen rate differences
	(1)	*(2)*	*(3)*
Droylsden UD	5	4	5
Failsworth UD	5	4	5
Horwich UD	4	4	3
Irlam UD	4	5	4
Kearsley UD	5	5	5
Lees UD	5	4	5
Littleborough UD	4	5	4
Little Lever UD	3	4	4
Milnrow UD	4	5	4
Royton UD	2	4	2
Tottington UD	2	3	3
Urmston UD	3	4	4
Wardle UD	2	3	3
Westhoughton UD	4	4	4
Whitefield UD	4	4	4
Whitworth UD	4	5	3
Worsley UD	5	4	4
Conurbation average	5.3	5.3	5.3
TYNESIDE			
Gateshead CB	8	7	7
South Shields CB	8	7	8
Jarrow MB	11	8	10
Felling UD	7	7	7
Hebburn UD	9	8	7
Wickham UD	5	6	6
Newcastle upon Tyne CB	9	8	8
Tynemouth CB	8	8	7
Wallsend MB	6	7	6
Whitley Bay MB	6	5	8
Gosforth UD	4	5	6
Longbenton UD	5	7	5
Newburn UD	5	6	5
Conurbation average	8.2	8.2	8.2
WEST MIDLANDS			
Dudley CB	3	4	3
Walsall CB	5	4	4
West Bromwich CB	4	4	4
Wolverhampton CB	5	5	5
Aldridge–Brownhills UD	4	4	4
Birmingham CB	6	5	5
Solihull CB	3	3	4
Sutton Coldfield MB	3	3	4
Warley CB	4	4	4

Conurbation and boroughs	Overall unemployment rate (%)		
	Actual	*Adjusted for class structure differences*	*Adjusted for class unemployment-rate differences*
	(1)	*(2)*	*(3)*
Halesowen MB	3	4	4
Stourbridge MB	3	4	3
Conurbation average	5.1	5.1	5.1
WEST YORKSHIRE			
Bradford CB	6	4	6
Dewsbury CB	5	4	4
Halifax CB	5	4	4
Huddersfield CB	4	4	4
Leeds CB	6	4	5
Wakefield CB	5	4	4
Batley MB	5	4	4
Brighouse MB	2	3	2
Keighly MB	6	4	5
Morley MB	3	4	3
Ossett MB	4	4	4
Pudsey MB	3	3	3
Spenborough MB	4	3	4
Aireborough UD	4	3	4
Baildon UD	4	3	4
Bingley UD	4	3	4
Colne Valley UD	3	3	3
Denby Dale UD	1	3	1
Denholme UD	4	5	3
Elland UD	4	4	3
Heckmondwike UD	3	4	3
Holmfirth UD	3	3	3
Horbury UD	3	3	3
Horsforth UD	3	3	3
Kirkburton UD	2	3	2
Meltham UD	3	3	4
Mirfield UD	3	3	3
Queensbury and Shelf UD	4	4	3
Ripponden UD	3	3	3
Rothwell UD	3	3	3
Shipley UD	4	4	4
Sowerby Bridge UD	3	4	3
Stanley UD	3	4	4
Conurbation average	5.1	5.1	5.1

Note: CB = County Borough, LB = London Borough, MB = Municipal Borough, RD = Rural District, and UD = Urban District.
Source: 1971 Census of Population, 10% sample.

higher in inner than in outer boroughs, and in Merseyside and Tyneside than in the other conurbations.

The columns 2 and 3 of the table demonstrate the influence of differences between boroughs within the same conurbation in the socioeconomic composition of the resident labour force and in the incidence of unemployment by socioeconomic grouping respectively. Column 2 was calculated by weighting the borough unemployment rates for the five socioeconomic groupings by the average proportion of the labour force in each of the five in the conurbation as a whole. A comparison of the figures in this column with the actual unemployment rates in column 1 shows that differences in the socioeconomic structure of the labour force between boroughs within the same conurbation account for a good deal of the overall unemployment-rate differences. In Greater London, for example, actual unemployment rates in 1971 ranged between 3 per cent in Enfield and a number of other outer-London boroughs and 7 per cent in Hammersmith and Tower Hamlets. However, after allowances have been made for differences in the composition of the labour force it can be seen (in column 2) that no borough would have had an overall unemployment rate lower than 4 per cent or higher than 6 per cent.

Column 3 is less interesting. It was derived for each borough by weighting the conurbation unemployment rates for the five socioeconomic groupings by the proportions of the labour force in each of the five in the borough. This column shows what the overall unemployment rate in each borough would have been on the assumption that each borough's labour force experienced unemployment rates for each socioeconomic grouping that were similar to each group's average for the conurbation as a whole. These rates are, as might be expected, more similar to the actual unemployment rates shown in column 1 of the table than are the rates shown in column 2.

In general there appears to be no obvious tendency for unemployment rates by socioeconomic groupings to be higher in inner than in outer boroughs. In London, for example, the lowest unemployment rates among those in the fifth socioeconomic grouping (mainly unskilled manual workers) are in Kingston and Westminster and the highest in the City of London, Hammersmith, and Sutton. On the other hand, column 2 of Table 7.16 shows that, while differences in the structure of the labour force account for a substantial part of the differences in overall unemployment rates between inner and outer boroughs, they cannot account for all of them. This may be because an analysis based on five socioeconomic groupings cannot capture all the relevant differences between areas in the personal characteristics of the labour force; such an analysis cannot, for example, take account of age and race differences. Alternatively, it may be because of genuine spatial differences in the availability of employment. In the absence of unemployment data more disaggregated by personal characteristics, a conclusive answer is likely to remain elusive.

The discussion of this problem will be pursued in more detail by Metcalf and Richardson (Chapter 8) and Evans (Chapter 9). They, however, deal only with London. Table 7.16 demonstrates that similar kinds of analysis could be carried out with respect to the other conurbations, and similar arguments are therefore applicable. London is not necessarily a special case.

7.5 Conclusion

The most obvious characteristic of the conurbations when compared with the remainder of the country is the decline in their population. (This is not a new phenomenon and has affected inner areas in particular for many years.) From the evidence presented above a number of working hypotheses emerge for further investigation.

First, the immediate cause of the decentralisation of population and employment appears to have been the demand for space for better housing and industrial and commercial expansion. Rising incomes and improvements in transport have given rise to demands for better housing in less-congested surroundings, while improvements in transport and communications have enabled employers to look for suitable sites for expansion over a wider area than previously.

Second, the concentration of the unskilled and the out of work in inner areas probably owes a good deal to the operation of the housing market. It is, however, a moot point how far the unskilled and out of work are tied to the cheaper housing in inner areas and how far the environment of inner areas inhibits the development of the skills and aptitudes of those who lead their early lives there.

Third, over and above the general problem of inner areas, where there may be strong similarities across all conurbations, there is also the fact that certain conurbations as a whole (notably Clydeside, Merseyside, and Tyneside) suffer from problems of unemployment associated with a general deficiency of demand in the regions of which they are part.

8 Unemployment in London

David Metcalf and Ray Richardson

8.1 Introduction[1]

This chapter reports on an analysis of the causes of male unemployment in a specific area (the thirty-two London boroughs) in 1971. Although the dependent variable is the rate of unemployment, the discussion goes behind the information on rates and emphasises that the unemployment rate is the outcome of four probabilities:

(a) the probability of being laid off, made redundant, or dismissed (involuntary separations);
(b) the probability of quitting (voluntary separations);
(c) the probability of being offered a job; and
(d) the probability of accepting an offer.

The first two elements determine the number of people entering the unemployed state and the last two the duration in that state. It is believed that such a treatment is an important innovation towards understanding the nature of unemployment.

[1]The research assistance and comments of Carol O'Cleireacain and Hen-fong Hayllar, and helpful discussion with Christopher Foster and Steve Nickell, are acknowledged with thanks. The evidence presented in the chapter is drawn from a wider study of the London labour market financed by the Social Science Research Council.

8.2 Male unemployment in London

An important feature of unemployment is the persistence of a settled geographic pattern of relative unemployment rates. This has, for example, been demonstrated for the British regions by Cheshire (1973), who has stated that 'the relative position of regions has been remarkably stable for fifty years' (p. 1). Hall (1970) has reported a similar finding concerning the structure of unemployment among the cities in the United States. London boroughs are no exception; the Spearman rank correlation between male unemployment rates across the thirty-two London boroughs in 1966 and 1971 was 0.92 ($t = 12.8$, significant at the 1 per cent level).[2]

The structure of unemployment differentials in London boroughs in 1971 was similar for males and females (the simple correlation was 0.891), all females, married females, and, more interestingly, when the sick were excluded from the economically inactive. The Spearman rank correlation between the total male unemployment rate and the male unemployment rate when the sick were excluded was 0.937 ($t = 34.1$, significant at the 1 per cent level).

8.2.1   The analysis

When explaining geographic unemployment differentials it is important to isolate the characteristics of the area (e.g. the industry mix) from the characteristics of the population. Cheshire (1973, ch. 1) has found that the pattern of regional unemployment differentials is *not* attributable to the different industrial structures; rather, all industries in high unemployment areas tend to have unemployment rates above the UK average for those industries. While this may be attributable to the inferior economic quality of the population in high unemployment regions (perhaps caused by over a century of net emigration), Cheshire has suggested that the explanation lies in the fact that unemployment rates are not industry-specific; hence, a high unemployment rate in, say, shipbuilding will tend to spread out over all the other industries in a depressed

---

[2]It is interesting that the dispersion of unemployment across the thirty-two boroughs was very similar in the two years:

	Mean unemployment	Standard deviation	Coefficient of variation
1966	2.19	0.83	0.38
1971	4.72	1.73	0.37

region. In the model that follows the importance of area characteristics and personal characteristics were examined with respect to unemployment in London.[3]

Differences in percentage unemployment arise from two sources: the probability of becoming unemployed, and the duration of unemployment. Clearly, both will be determined by both demand and supply influences. More specifically, the percentage unemployment rate is determined by the four probabilities listed in section 8.1.

The variables that can be observed as measuring these theoretical determinants of unemployment can be divided into *personal characteristics* and *area characteristics*. The first group includes:

1. *Age*   Although it is often held that young and old workers suffer higher unemployment than prime-age workers, no such hypothesis was made in the analysis, *ceteris paribus*. Young workers have higher separation rates (especially voluntary quits) and lower unemployment duration than prime-age males, while older workers have lower separation rates but much higher unemployment duration.[4] The dual labour-market hypothesis (see, for example, Gordon, 1972) asserts that young workers experience relatively high unemployment rates; for example, Hall (1970) has suggested that some teenagers in the United States exhibit 'pathological job instability' caused by their moving from one dead-end job to another and often experiencing unemployment between moves. The data used provided a test of this hypothesis. There is a problem in isolating the effect of age on unemployment, especially for old workers. If an old worker becomes unemployed (perhaps because he is made redundant) he may 'bump down' the skill ladder in an effort to secure employment (Reder, 1955). The influence of age on unemployment may then be masked by the skill variable. This possibility was tested by excluding the skill variable in some of the regression equations.

2. *Marital status*   The conventional hypothesis that the marginal utility of income relative to leisure is higher for married than for

[3]Labour is more mobile among boroughs within London than among regions of Britain, and area characteristics may therefore be expected to be less important in explaining differences in unemployment within London. It would be interesting to carry out an intermediate level of analysis using cities as the unit of observation.
[4]For evidence on the duration of unemployment by age, see Cripps and Tarling (1974).

unmarried men was adopted in the analysis. Married men are therefore less likely to become voluntarily unemployed, and the duration of any unemployment that they experience will tend to be shorter. Further, on the demand side it is possible (but unlikely?) that, *ceteris paribus*, the employer discriminates in favour of married workers (on equity grounds) when making hiring and firing decisions. It was therefore expected that marital status would be inversely related to unemployment.

3. *Number of dependants*   This variable exercises two conflicting influences on unemployment. On the one hand, identical arguments to those advanced for marital status work to reduce unemployment for individuals with a relatively high number of dependants. On the other hand, supplementary benefits are positively related to family size, which may result (from the supply side) in increased unemployment because the higher supplementary benefits lower the cost of becoming unemployed and of prolonged unemployment.

4. *Immigrants*   The influence of race on unemployment is complicated and may vary according to country of origin.[5] From the supply side it may be hypothesised that immigrants have migrated to improve their welfare; they will tend to work harder and are therefore less likely to be unemployed. Against this view, however, it has sometimes been asserted that immigrants are lazy and so more likely to be voluntarily unemployed. Also, recent migrants may have poorly-developed labour-market information networks (see Rees, 1966) and may therefore have to spend relatively large amounts of time in labour-market search activity, although the poor information may lead to inferior jobs rather than overt unemployment.

5. *Skill*   Supply side influences will tend to cause unskilled workers to have relatively high unemployment rates. They may have poor information or may be inefficient at search. The dual labour-market hypothesis suggests that the unskilled, because their jobs are relatively boring, will tend to have higher quit rates, with job changes frequently involving a bout of unemployment. The demand side arguments pull in the same direction; the well-known specific-training arguments initiated by Oi (1962), and Reder's

[5]The data used in the regressions refer to immigrants and therefore exclude non-whites born in Britain. Some tests were undertaken to see if immigrants from Ireland experienced different unemployment rates from those from Africa, Asia, or the West Indies.

(1955) hypothesis of 'bumping down' the skill hierarchy, both appear to have merit in explaining why the unskilled suffer higher unemployment rates than the skilled.

The second group of variables comprises the characteristics of the area, which include:

6. *The proportion of employment in manufacturing industry* Employment in manufacturing in London recently declined substantially (see Foster and Richardson, 1973). An important question concerning this rundown in manufacturing is whether, as suggested by Eversley (1973), it resulted in considerable hardship (including higher unemployment) or whether it was primarily in response to people leaving first and jobs following them, as suggested by Foster and Richardson. A positive significant coefficient for the variable measuring the proportion of the labour force that was resident in a borough and working in manufacturing in 1966 is consistent with Eversley's view being correct.

7. *Redundancies*[6] It is important to know whether, *ceteris paribus*, areas that suffered a relatively high number of redundancies in the years immediately before 1971 also suffered higher unemployment in 1971. If they did, action to reduce their labour supply (e.g. by providing information) or to increase their demand for labour (e.g. by relaxing zoning laws) may be necessary. Redundancies may also be positively associated with unemployment because of the existence of redundancy payments, although no such association has been found by Mackay and Reid (1972).

8.2.2 Results of the analysis

The results of the regressions are presented in Table 8.1. Equations 1 and 2 indicated the importance of personal characteristics in explaining interborough differences in unemployment. The variables for marital status, dependants, and the proportion of unskilled workers all had significant coefficients and show that boroughs with a high proportion of unskilled workers, a large number of children in relation to male workers, and a small proportion of married men tend to have higher unemployment than boroughs with the opposite

[6]Redundancies refer to the redundancies in the borough, while the dependent variable is unemployment by residence. The inclusion of redundancies therefore did not cause estimation problems.

Table 8.1　Regression results for equations explaining male unemployment in thirty-two London boroughs, 1971

Independent variable	Correlation coefficient Equation 1	Equation 2	Equation 3	Mean standard deviation
% of male labour force:				
Aged 15–24	−0.108	−0.280	0.035	15.74
	(1.03)	(1.13)	(0.31)	(1.50)
Aged 54+	0.289	0.169	0.054	23.10
	(0.64)	(1.62)	(1.25)	(1.79)
Married	−0.281	−0.572	−0.217	66.39
	(6.13)	(6.37)	(3.48)	(6.45)
All persons aged 0–14				
as % of males aged 15–64	0.071	0.209	0.057	64.85
	(3.89)	(6.50)	(2.97)	(10.37)
% of male labour force:				
New Commonwealth	−0.035	−0.079	−0.016	9.88
immigrants	(1.91)	(1.86)	(0.69)	(5.51)
Unskilled	0.249	—	0.257	8.82
	(11.10)		(10.27)	(3.94)
Employed in manufacturing,	—	—	−0.018	—
1966			(1.07)	
No. of male redundancies:				
1966–69	—	—	−0.011	—
			(2.47)	
1970	—	—	0.045	—
			(2.28)	
Constant	17.934	30.444	12.006	
	(4.40)	(3.25)	(2.50)	
R^2	0.97	0.82	0.98	

Notes:
1. The dependent variable was the unemployment rate for male residents in April 1971.
2. The regressions were estimated by ordinary least squares and expected signs were negative for percentage married and positive for percentage unskilled (see text).
3. t-ratios are shown in brackets.

Sources: Census of Population, 1971 (Office of Population Censuses and Surveys, 1973); Greater London Council (1971), and special data supplied on skill and employment in manufacturing for 1966; Department of Employment, data on redundancies; London Boroughs' Association and Salvation Army, data from survey of hostel accommodation.

characteristics. The coefficient for the unskilled proportion indicates that, *ceteris paribus*, an increase of 4 percentage points in that proportion (e.g. from 9 to 13 per cent) will raise the unemployment rate by 1 percentage point (e.g. from 4 to 5 per cent). The hardship caused by the higher unemployment rate experienced by the unskilled will be compounded by the imperfect capital market (i.e. higher borrowing rates) that they face.

The sign on the variable for numbers of dependants hints that the influence of this factor in cheapening the cost of unemployment outweighs the influence that causes men with large families to 'need' to be in work. In view of the importance of this finding, for both social and economic policy, an experiment was made with an alternative definition of dependants to check the robustness of the result. The definition chosen was the proportion of a borough's population living in households with five or more people. If individuals with a relatively large number of dependants are really likely to have a higher propensity to be unemployed, the coefficient for this variable should have a significant positive sign. In the event, its coefficient while positive was non-significant ($t = 1.27$), which suggests that the result in the equations shown must be treated with caution.

The results with respect to age are as predicted, in that they suggest that, *ceteris paribus*, neither young nor old workers are more likely to be unemployed than prime-age males.

The results also suggest that, *ceteris paribus*, immigrants do not have a higher unemployment rate than people born in the United Kingdom. This important result was sustained when the variable was split into four categories according to area of origin (West Indies, Asia, Africa, Ireland) and each category was entered in equation 1 separately; in no case did the variable have a significant coefficient. This hints that, where labour market discrimination exists, it occurs via lack of training opportunities for immigrants (to enable them to become skilled workers) rather than via hiring and firing policies within a given (e.g. unskilled) grade of labour. Further, as immigrants are disproportionately unskilled ($r = +0.37$), the unemployment experienced by immigrants is attributable to those factors which make them unskilled, such as discrimination in the education system, or a high rate of time preference, or wage discrimination causing the rate of return on training to be relatively low. Discrimination does not result in higher unemployment within a skill group.

The area characteristics were added in equation 3. They did not change the results found for the personal characteristics. Despite the rundown of manufacturing industry in London, there was no association between the proportion of a borough's labour force (by residence) working in manufacturing in 1966 and 1971 unemployment. This hints that the rundown in manufacturing employment did not cause hardship in those areas experiencing the decline.[7]

This result is supported by the fact that boroughs experiencing a large number of redundancies over the years 1966–69 had a relatively low unemployment rate in 1971. This can be attributable to a variety of factors; for example:

1. New employers may move into a high redundancy area.
2. Redundant workers may move away (which could result in hardship).
3. Individuals made redundant may thereafter have a lower propensity to quit, possibly because they have exhausted their assets while unemployed.
4. Individuals living in high redundancy boroughs may have a low propensity to quit.
5. The Department of Employment may put more resources into an area of high redundancies to speed the search process.

This last point may be consistent with the dual labour-market hypothesis in that firms operating in the so-called primary sector, with well-developed internal labour markets, will tend to give the Department of Employment and their employees advance warning of forthcoming redundancies, so that action may be taken to avert their consequences.

On the other hand, boroughs experiencing a relatively large number of redundancies in 1970 suffered relatively high unemployment in 1971.

8.2.3 Extensions to the model

Some extensions were also made to the basic model. When the semiskilled proportion of the borough's labour force was added to the unskilled proportion, the combined variable was positively and significantly associated with unemployment ($t = 4.54$) in an equation similar to equation 1. However, wealth, which influences unemployment from the supply side, had an ambiguous effect. On the one hand, the return from greater wealth reduces the cost of unemployment; but on the other hand, it may enable the individual to buy more or higher quality information, get more contacts, engage in bribery, etc., which would tend to reduce unemployment.

[7]See the debate in Foster and Richardson (1973), Eversley (1973), and O'Cleireacain (1974).

The proportion of the borough's population living in owner-occupied houses was used as a (poor) proxy for wealth. It was not significantly related to unemployment when added to equation 1; but this reflects problems of multicollinearity, as it was highly correlated with the unskilled proportion ($r = -0.80$) and with marital status ($r = +0.75$).

Area characteristics have been given more prominence in explaining labour market disadvantage by those who believe in the dual labour market or the radical paradigms than by those who accept the neoclassical explanations of disadvantage. Gordon (1972) has suggested that a rundown area reflects the fact that individuals have no control over their own destiny; and he has emphasised the problem of multiple disadvantage, incorporating such factors as poor transport, poor housing, and poor information. Given its diffuse nature, it is difficult to test this hypothesis. However, two proxies for the 'rundownness' of an area were added to equations 1 and 3 to provide a blunt test. These were (a) the number of hostel places per thousand of the borough's population, and (b) the infant death rate (for legitimate, illegitimate, and all infants).[8] These variables were never significantly related to unemployment. While this should not lead us to reject entirely the importance of area characteristics in explaining unemployment, the result does suggest that explanations of labour market disadvantage not based on conventional theory ought to be defined more rigorously to facilitate a fair test of their predictions.

8.3 Conclusions

The results suggest that male unemployment in London is primarily determined by certain individual characteristics, especially skill and marital status. Once these variables have been controlled for, race, age, and area characteristics appear to be unrelated to unemployment.

[8]These variables could also act as proxies for wealth. The hostel places variable might be endogenous; hostel places are provided, in part, in response to demand by disadvantaged individuals. The variable was entered both as a dummy (with a value of unity when the ratio was >1 and zero when <1) and as a continuous variable. Some alternative variables to represent 'rundownness' might include the proportion of a borough's residents receiving social security, family income supplement, or rent rebates, or the proportion in multioccupied houses or houses lacking specific basic amenities.

It is necessary to consider why individuals with a high propensity to be unemployed live where they do (which, in broad terms, is in the inner boroughs). The answer is found by examining the differences between boroughs in housing stocks. Individuals who are unlikely to be unemployed live disproportionately in owner-occupied houses, and therefore boroughs with a high proportion of owner-occupied houses have low unemployment rates. Conversely, the unskilled tend to live in low rent housing (between the percentage of public housing and the percentage unskilled, $r = +0.80$), and therefore boroughs with a high proportion of public housing suffer high unemployment rates. Inner city problems occur because individuals who suffer labour market disadvantage live disproportionately in the inner city, because that is where the largest stock of cheap housing (especially public housing) is found. The problems are a function of the housing stock accumulated over the last 150 years. Further, the problems become circular, because boroughs whose residents tend to suffer labour market disadvantage build a large amount of public housing in an effort to look after the welfare of their residents. This accounts for the observed temporal stability of the structure of unemployment within London.

In the United States inner city unemployment is usually attributable to employment suburbanisation, housing segregation, inadequate public-transport systems, poor labour-market information and discrimination (see Gordon, 1972, ch. 1). The results of the present analysis suggest that the problem of labour market disadvantage in London is caused, more narrowly, by the given housing stocks rather than by all the factors listed by Gordon.

This chapter has made a modest start on analysing the problem of labour market disadvantage in urban areas. Much more needs to be done, in particular:

1. The problem of multiple disadvantage needs to be analysed, to determine the extent to which unemployment, low pay, poor health, low participation rates, underemployment, poor information, poor housing, inferior local government services, etc. are inter-related.
2. There is a need for an analysis of the problem of labour market disadvantage that takes account both of the lifetime pattern of disadvantage (it is clearly more serious if the same individuals fare badly all their life than if the problems come only at particular times, such as at old age) and of family characteristics.

3. Unemployment *rates* must be broken down into numbers flowing on to the register (by analysing quit functions and layoff functions) and duration (by analysing the probability of getting a job, which in some large part will depend on vacancies). Sensible measures to reduce unemployment or alleviate its consequences are entirely different according to whether the problem is numbers or duration.

One way by which all the above aspects of unemployment could be examined is via a cohort analysis. All (or a sample of) the individuals coming on to the unemployment register on a particular day (or week) could be surveyed in regard to such factors as their personal and family characteristics, location, and previous job history. They could then be followed for, say, five years to get details of their labour market experience, including bouts of unemployment and their duration, job aspirations, actual jobs, pay, skill, etc. Although this would be costly, there is a fair chance that the social rate of return on such a survey would, via the policy measures that it would indicate to alleviate the problem of labour market disadvantage, be handsome.

9 A Portrait of the London Labour Market

Alan Evans with the assistance of Lynne Russell

9.1 Introduction

In the past few years increasing concern has been expressed at the level of unemployment in London, particularly in inner London. Inner London boroughs have made representations to the Greater London Council (GLC), and with them the GLC has made representations to central government, all the London governments arguing that inner London is no longer one of the most prosperous parts of the country and that, even if central government could not see its way to giving it more favourable treatment than other regions, at least it could be given less unfavourable treatment. This lobbying has, moreover, been to some extent successful, in that some policies now allow funds to be directed towards the creation of jobs in inner London (e.g. the small-firms employment subsidy).

The consensus of opinion seems to have been that the unemployment problems of London occur because of the decentralisation of manufacturing industry from the inner city and that these problems have been exacerbated in London's case by the operation of Industrial Development Certificate (IDC) policy, which discourages the opening of factories in London and the South-East, and by the more positive aspects of regional policy that are intended to steer industry to the development areas.

The role of manufacturing industry in London is discussed in two other chapters in this book. In Chapter 2 Dennis has discussed the nature and causes of changes in employment in manufacturing industry in London, and in Chapter 3 Gripaios has examined industrial decline in a particular sector of London. This chapter is complementary in that it examines directly the employment situation in the London labour market, using data on unemployment and vacancies, and can therefore only indirectly throw light on the causes of these changes, e.g. the movement of manufacturing industry.

9.2 Unemployment in London

The higher rate of unemployment in inner London is not a recent phenomenon. The male unemployment rates in the area of Greater London in 1951 are mapped from Census of Population data in Figure 9.1. The map clearly shows that the average unemployment rate in the inner London boroughs was higher than that ruling in outer London. Moreover, a similar pattern has persisted until the present day, or at least until the 1971 census, as Figure 9.2 demonstrates.

Why should this pattern persist? Metcalf and Richardson (Chapter 8) have shown that variation in unemployment rates between London boroughs is highly correlated with variation in the personal characteristics of the population. Most of the variation between areas can be statistically 'explained' by differences in the family characteristics and the skill levels of the residents.

First, young single people are more likely to be unemployed at any one time than older people with household and family responsibilities, although it is known that their periods of employment are likely to be shorter even though more frequent. Younger people are more willing to change jobs and are able to bear the cost of short periods of unemployment between jobs; older people with more family responsibilities are considerably less willing to take risks and less able to bear periods of unemployment. Table 9.1 gives the unemployment rates in 1971 in Greater London for different age groups and clearly shows that the probability of unemployment varies greatly with age. It follows that the unemployment rate in a borough will vary with the age structure of the borough and that the unemployment rate is for this reason likely to be lower in the outer boroughs.

Second, the less skilled are more likely to be unemployed than the more skilled. There seem to be three or four possible explanations for this, as listed below, but the evidence tends to confirm the last of these and to conflict with the first two:

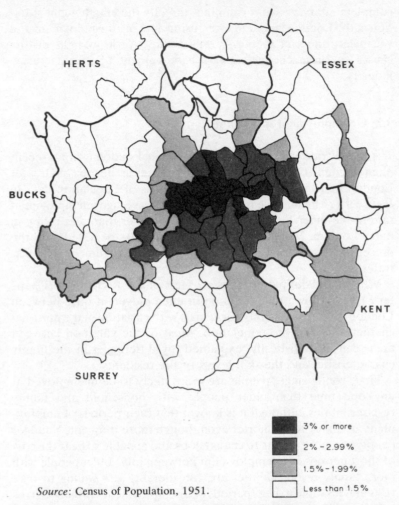

Source: Census of Population, 1951.

Fig. 9.1   Male unemployment rates in local authority areas in the Greater London conurbation, 1951.

1. Because unemployment benefits are a higher proportion of possible earnings for the unskilled than for the skilled, the disincentives to becoming unemployed – and, if already unemployed, to remaining unemployed – are greater for the skilled than the unskilled. Hence, the skilled are more likely to attempt to avoid becoming unemployed – and, if unemployed, to find a job more quickly – than the unskilled. As a result, the higher the skill level,

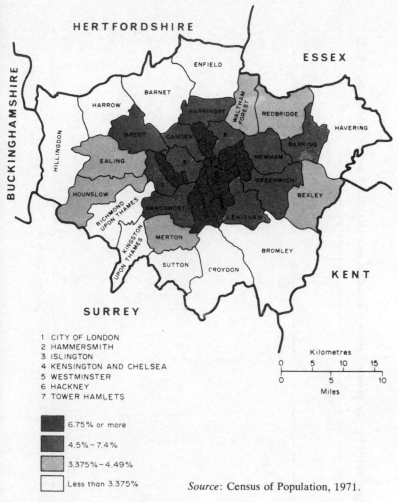

1 CITY OF LONDON
2 HAMMERSMITH
3 ISLINGTON
4 KENSINGTON AND CHELSEA
5 WESTMINSTER
6 HACKNEY
7 TOWER HAMLETS

■ 6.75% or more

■ 4.5% – 7.4%

▨ 3.375% – 4.49%

□ Less than 3.375%

Source: Census of Population, 1971.

**Fig. 9.2   Male unemployment rates in Greater London boroughs
and the City of London, 1971.**

the lower will be the level of unemployment. Against this it can
be argued that the more skilled person, once unemployed, may
remain unemployed for longer because there are fewer jobs
available requiring his specific skill (but see below).

2. Less skilled workers, if out of a job, may find it difficult either to
   move to a new job (because of the conditions of tenancy of
   housing) or to travel to it (because of the high cost of transport).

Table 9.1 Male unemployment rates by age group: Greater London and selected London boroughs, 1971

Age	Greater London	Outer London		Inner London			
		Barnet	Bromley	Camden	Kensington and Chelsea	Lambeth	Tower Hamlets
15	22	17	18	22	30	29	22
16	10	9	9	12	16	12	10
17	7	6	6	10	10	9	7
18	6	6	6	9	9	10	8
19	7	5	5	9	9	10	7
20	7	5	5	8	9	8	8
21–24	5	4	4	7	8	9	9
25–29	5	3	3	6	7	7	9
30–34	5	3	3	7	6	8	8
35–39	4	2	2	6	7	7	8
40–44	4	3	2	6	6	7	8
45–49	4	2	2	6	6	6	8
50–54	3	2	2	5	5	5	8
55–59	4	3	2	5	6	5	9
60–64	7	5	6	8	8	7	11
65–69	3	2	2	4	4	4	5
70+	4	3	3	4	5	4	4

Source: Census of Population, 1971 (Office of Population Censuses and Surveys, 1973, pt I, table 18).

Higher-paid workers are more likely to be able to move and to be able to bear the cost of travel. Thus, if a factory closes somewhere in London, the more skilled workers will find it easier to find alternative employment than the less skilled, who will be 'trapped' at that location. Hence, the average unemployment rate of the less skilled will be higher than that of the more skilled.

3. (a) Because the more skilled person can take jobs at lower skill levels he can always do this if he finds it difficult to find a job at his own skill level. The range of jobs that is open to him is therefore wider than that open to someone with fewer skills. Thus, in a situation where unemployment is widespread the probability of unemployment is likely to be lower the higher the skill level.

    (b) On the demand side, if the employer can find no one to do a particular skilled job, instead of raising the pay offered he can modify the qualifications thought to be required to do the job and hence take on a slightly less-skilled person. Obviously, this is less possible at low skill levels when the qualifications required are minimal. Thus, in a tight labour market the most-skilled job vacancies are likely to be filled first, and the higher the skill level of workers the lower the probability of unemployment.

A corollary of the second argument is that the unemployment rates of unskilled workers should vary much more widely across an urban area than the unemployment rates of skilled workers, and that the two rates should be more or less equal in some areas and widely different in others. The evidence suggests that this is not so, and this can be discounted as the main explanation for the variation in the probability of unemployment with skill level. Table 9.2 summarises data on the unemployment rates of five social classes or skill levels in parliamentary constituencies in south-east England in 1971. These social classes were constructed by amalgamating the socioeconomic groups (SEGs) used in the censuses of 1961, 1966, and 1971:

Social class

Managers and professionals	(SEGs 1, 2, 3, 4, 13)
Other non-manual	(SEGs 5, 6)
Skilled manual	(SEGs 8, 9, 12, 14)
Semiskilled manual	(SEGs 7, 10, 15)
Unskilled manual	(SEG 11)

Table 9.2   Male and female unemployment by social class: Britain and the South-East, 1971

Social class	National average unemployment rate[a](%)	Constituencies in the South-East		
		Mean unemployment rate[b](%)	Standard deviation (%)	Coefficient of variation
Managers and professionals	1.88	1.80	0.87	0.48
Other non-manual	2.21	2.01	0.86	0.43
Skilled manual	4.04	3.08	1.45	0.47
Semiskilled manual	4.13	2.81	1.27	0.45
Unskilled manual	9.24	4.89	2.90	0.59

[a] The national average unemployment rate for a social class is the number unemployed in that social class divided by the number in that social class – the normal calculation.
[b] The mean unemployment rate of the constituencies in the South-East for a social class is the average of the averages and is therefore calculated in a way that can introduce a bias.
Source: Census of Population, 1971, unpublished data.

It can be seen that the mean unemployment rate generally rises as the skill level falls. The standard deviation of the unemployment rates also rises as the unemployment rate increases, but the coefficient of variation does not, and that is the more important statistic in this context. The coefficient is approximately the same for four classes and only slightly higher for the fifth. This indicates that the variation in unemployment rates for different skill levels is no more than would be expected given the differences in the average levels of unemployment.[1]

The data for the five social classes or skill levels are mapped in Figures 9.3 to 9.7. Four important points about the London labour market can be made with the aid of these maps.

First, they show that, even when the influence of skill level has as far as possible been eliminated, it is clear that there is still a persistent difference between the unemployment rates prevailing in inner London and those prevailing in outer London. As the maps are drawn, this pattern is particularly striking in the case of the first social class (Managers and professionals) (Figure 9.3); but the prevalence of the pattern at all skill levels tends to refute at least one of the explanations of the higher unemployment rates in inner

[1] These data on unemployment by social class were obtained by Richard Webber of the Centre for Environmental Studies, and grateful thanks are extended to him for making them available.

Fig. 9.3   Unemployment of male and female professional workers, employers, and managers in Greater London parliamentary constituencies, 1971.

London that have been put forward, namely, that those at low skill levels are 'trapped' in inner London as industry decentralises, being unwilling or unable to move from rent-controlled accommodation or local authority housing and unable to afford transport to jobs in the suburbs. This may be a plausible explanation of high unemployment rates in Stepney and Poplar, but it is an implausible explanation, to say the least, of the high rates of unemployment of professionals and managers in Hampstead. Some other forces must be at work. One such has already been mentioned, i.e. the greater likelihood that those living in inner London will not be encumbered with family responsibilities. It is surely not coincidental that the area of high unemployment delimited in the maps, particularly those for the first two social classes (managers and professionals, and other non-manual), is strikingly similar to the area with high levels of immigration by young people (in Evans, 1973; or Milner Holland, 1965), which can be recognised as covering the bed-sitter areas of north and west London.

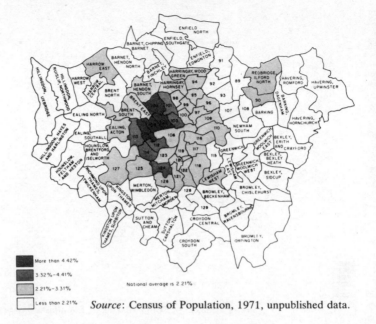

More than 4.42%

3.32%–4.41%

2.21%–3.31%

Less than 2.21%

National average is 2.21%

Source: Census of Population, 1971, unpublished data.

Fig. 9.4   Unemployment of other male and female non-manual workers in Greater London parliamentary constituencies, 1971.

Second, the maps show that, at least at the time of the 1971 census, the unemployment situation in London of the more skilled was worse *relative to the national average* than that of the less skilled. The maps are drawn in such a way as to demonstrate this clearly; the shaded areas in each map have unemployment rates that are higher than the national average for that social class. Figure 9.3 shows that the unemployment rate for professionals is greater than the national average in most of inner London and large parts of outer London. Figure 9.7, on the other hand, shows that the unemployment rate for unskilled manual workers is greater than the national average in only five parliamentary constituencies in the whole of Greater London. Taking a wider but more formal perspective, the situation in the South-East as a whole is illustrated in Table 9.2, which shows the mean unemployment rates by social class for all constituencies in the South-East compared with the national average unemployment rates by social class. It can be seen that the mean unemployment rate for professionals in the South-East is virtually the same as the average for the country as a whole, but that the unemployment

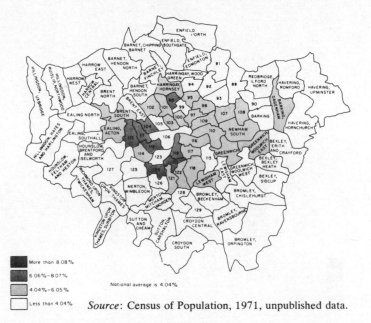

Source: Census of Population, 1971, unpublished data.

Fig. 9.5 Unemployment of male and female skilled manual workers in Greater London parliamentary constituencies, 1971.

rate at other skill levels improves relative to the national average as the skill level drops. Why should this be? The most plausible explanation is that at the lowest skill levels the spatial extent of a labour market is likely to be coincident with a travel-to-work area, but that the labour market tends to become a national market as the skill level increases. For example, the market for university academic staff is clearly a national market; posts are advertised nationally, and many staff (although not all) expect to move accordingly. A similar national market exists for managers, doctors, teachers, etc. Most studies of migration and mobility confirm that nearly all inter-regional movement is by higher-paid people. The lower the skill level, the more likely it is that the labour market for a job is limited to an individual travel-to-work area. There are two reasons for this. In the first place, a less skilled job (or worker) is likely to be more common than a more skilled job (or worker) in a particular travel-to-work area, so that the incentive for workers (or employers) to look elsewhere is lower. Moreover, at low skill levels workers with differing skills are more likely to be substitutable than

More than 8.26 %

6.20 % – 8.25 %

4.13 % – 6.19 %

Less than 4.13 %

National average is 4.13 %

Source: Census of Population, 1971, unpublished data.

Fig. 9.6   Unemployment of male and female semiskilled manual workers in Greater London parliamentary constituencies, 1971.

at higher skill levels. In the second place, at lower skill levels the costs of movement are higher relative to the benefits, so that, even if vacancies exist in other areas, unemployed workers with few skills are less likely to move. It is here that argument 1 above (p. 206) – the level of unemployment benefits – interacts with argument 2 – the cost of transport and mobility – to provide an explanation for the wider national variations in the unemployment rate of less skilled workers than more skilled workers. Obviously, if movement to a job means only a small increase in income relative to unemployment benefit, as well as giving up local authority housing and starting again at the bottom of some other housing list, it isn't worth moving. On the other hand, it will be worth moving if unemployment benefit is a small proportion of prospective earnings and if movement means realising the capital gains tied up in an owner-occupied house.

Note, however, that the variation in the absolute and relative differences in unemployment rates between regions does tend to refute argument 1 – unemployment benefits – as the sole, or even

Fig. 9.7 Unemployment of male and female unskilled workers in Greater London parliamentary constituencies, 1971.

the main, explanation of the inverse relationship between skill levels and unemployment rates. Indeed, the maintenance of this relationship between regions but the diminution of its importance from one region to another suggests that arguments 3(a) and 3(b) – the variation in the acceptability of lower skills – are the most plausible explanations for the existence of the relationship. In general, full employment is maintained at the highest skill levels, but variations in demand over both time and space are accommodated by variations in the skill level that employers require of applicants for less skilled jobs.

Third, the maps show that the areas with the worst unemployment problems, after allowance has been made for the skill levels of the residents, may not be the areas with the highest (aggregate) unemployment rates. As Figure 9.2 shows, the area with the highest aggregate unemployment rate in 1971 was Tower Hamlets in the east end of London (excluding the City of London with its peculiar characteristics). However, Figures 9.3 to 9.7 show that at that time there were only two constituencies in Greater London that had higher unemployment rates than the national average at all skill levels, and both were in north-west London, namely, Hammersmith North (113) and St Pancras North (101). Ten other constituencies are shown by the maps to have had higher unemployment rates than the national average at four out of the five skill levels: Kensington North (111), Hampstead (102), Islington North (98), Hackney North (95), Stepney and Poplar (110), Bermondsey (116), Dulwich (118), Lambeth Vauxhall (119), Lambeth Central (120), and Lambeth Streatham (121).

These twelve constituencies are marked with asterisks in Figure 9.8. Their location throws some light on the existence of an inner-city employment problem. In effect there appears to be an outer–inner city problem, for the constituencies tend to be located in inner London (the former County of London or the present area of the Inner London Education Authority) but around its outer edge; this outer–inner location is particularly evident along the northern boundary of inner London. An alternative way of demonstrating the existence of this ring is also used in Figure 9.8. 'Standardised' unemployment rates were calculated and are mapped in the figure. These are the unemployment rates that would have existed in each constituency if the residents had been allocated equally to each skill group, while the unemployment rates for each skill group remained the same. This procedure gives a greater weight to the unemployment rates of less skilled, and particularly unskilled, workers because the average unemployment rates for the lower skill groups are higher, and the variation is greater absolutely. Hence, a map, not reproduced here, of the unemployment rates of unskilled workers with somewhat more disaggregation than is shown in Figure 9.7 reveals much the same pattern as Figure 9.8, namely, an outer–inner ring of high unemployment areas, which are largely coincidental with those indicated by asterisks. The procedure seems fair, however, in that greater concern is expressed over the unemployment of less skilled workers, primarily because their unemployment rates are higher and the absolute variations are greater. Moreover, the first method used above – of tallying up the number of skill groups in each constituency with above-average unemployment rates – does not have this bias but reveals, as already remarked, a similar pattern.

Fourth, the maps reveal some of the dangers of the case study approach in that the site chosen for the London inner-area study, in Lambeth Central constituency, is in an area with an abnormally high unemployment level even for inner London.

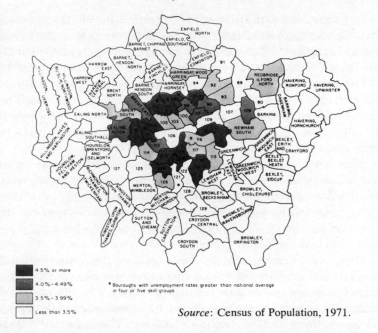

■	4.5% or more
▨	4.0% – 4.49%
▨	3.5% – 3.99%
□	Less than 3.5%

*Boroughs with unemployment rates greater than national average in four or five skill groups

Source: Census of Population, 1971.

Fig. 9.8   Male and female unemployment rates with standardised social-class structures, by Greater London parliamentary constituencies, 1971.

9.3 Changes over time

The evidence on unemployment rates in 1971, and earlier years, shows (a) that there have always been higher levels of unemployment in inner London, probably because of the personal characteristics of the people who live there, but (b) that apart from this there is probably an 'inner-city employment problem' of higher unemployment levels in an outer-inner ring. Perhaps, in this ring the decline in manufacturing has been fastest, and the fall in employment has not been compensated by the possibility of proximate employment in commerce and services. The analysis in section 9.2 is static, however, while the hypothesis above refers to changes over time. Can, then, the effects of these declines in manufacturing be identified in changes in the unemployment situations of different areas over time? Curiously, as will be shown, it is difficult to distinguish a peculiarly inner-city employment problem by these methods.

Two sources of data are used in this section: the published census data on unemployment rates, and the data on unemployment and vacancies collected by local employment exchanges and filed at the Statistics Office of the Department of Employment at Watford.[2]

First, census data were used to investigate the pattern of change between 1966 and 1971. Figure 9.9 maps the indices obtained for each London borough by dividing the male unemployment rate in 1971 by the male unemployment rate in 1966. The map reveals no clear inner-city employment problem. Instead, it shows a Y-shaped pattern in which the greatest increases in unemployment are in the south-east (Kent) sector of Greater London and along the Thames, along a line running through inner–south London into south Middlesex and up the Lea Valley in east London. In contrast, the situation has improved in north London, particularly in the inner area, and in outer–south London.

There are a number of differences between the census data and the data collected by the Department of Employment. The questions in the census have to be answered by law, while no one is compelled to register as unemployed. Moreover, the census figures on unemployment relate to the residents of an area, so that an unemployment rate can be calculated; but anyone registering as unemployed can do so at any exchange that he wishes, so that unemployment rates for small areas can be meaningless. In the calculations below the data on vacancies notified to exchanges are used, and again notification is voluntary and may be at any exchange. Despite these differences, and despite the fact that situations are compared ten years apart, not five years, Figure 9.9 reveals a pattern of change similar to that shown in Figure 9.10. For the latter map the ratio of (adult male) unemployment to (adult male) vacancies in June 1974 was found and divided by the ratio of (adult male) unemployment to (adult male) vacancies in June 1964. Areas where this index has increased may be assumed to have a worsening employment situation since unemployment has risen relative to vacancies; where the ratio has decreased, unemployment has fallen relative to vacancies. Despite the differences in the nature of the data and in the length of the period, a Y-shaped pattern of deterioration is again revealed, the base being in the south-east sector, with one arm extending up the Lea Valley in north-east London and the other running through inner–south London and fading out in south

[2] A debt of gratitude is owed to the staff at Watford for their helpfulness in making the data accessible and in explaining the systems used.

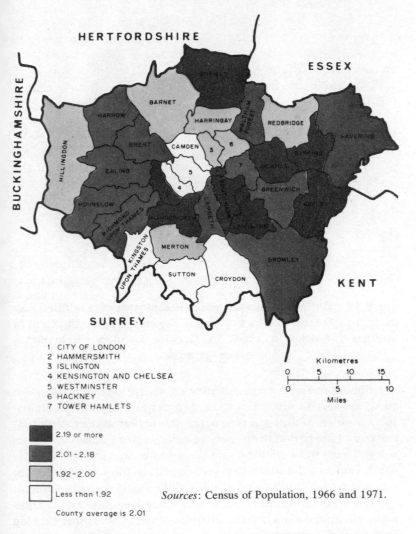

1 CITY OF LONDON
2 HAMMERSMITH
3 ISLINGTON
4 KENSINGTON AND CHELSEA
5 WESTMINSTER
6 HACKNEY
7 TOWER HAMLETS

	2.19 or more
	2.01 - 2.18
	1.92 - 2.00
	Less than 1.92

County average is 2.01

Sources: Census of Population, 1966 and 1971.

Fig. 9.9 Male unemployment rates in 1971 as a ratio of the unemployment rate in 1966 in Greater London boroughs.

Middlesex. The maps suggest that the sector of London studied by Gripaios (Chapter 3) may be exceptional, just as the earlier maps indicate that the area of Lambeth chosen for the Inner Area Study was also exceptional. The maps showing the ratios of unemployment to vacancies at the beginning and end of the 1964–74 period

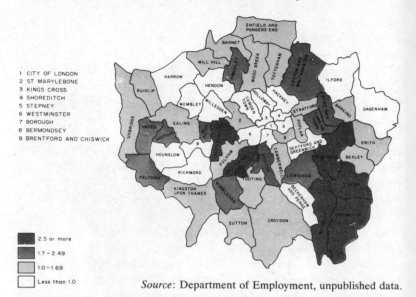

1 CITY OF LONDON
2 ST MARYLEBONE
3 KINGS CROSS
4 SHOREDITCH
5 STEPNEY
6 WESTMINSTER
7 BOROUGH
8 BERMONDSEY
9 BRENTFORD AND CHISWICK

2.5 or more
1.7 – 2.49
1.0 – 1.69
Less than 1.0

Source: Department of Employment, unpublished data.

Fig. 9.10   Ratio of registered male unemployment to notified vacancies in 1974, divided by the ratio of registered unemployment to notified vacancies in 1964, by Greater London employment-exchange areas.

are not reproduced here; but they show, curiously enough, that there appeared to be much more of a definite inner-city employment problem at the beginning of the period than at the end of it. By the end of the period the pattern of deterioration shown in Figures 9.9 and 9.10 was dominant, and the worst areas were again inner–south London, the south-east sector, and up the Lea Valley. The maps show that at the end of the period inner–north London, in contrast to inner–south London, had a relatively favourable employment situation and that the situation of this area of inner London had improved over the period.

9.4 The inner area

The contrast between inner–north London and inner–south London suggests that a more detailed study of the changing employment situation in these areas would be worthwhile to discover why it occurs. Two areas of inner London each made up of five employment exchanges – one area to the north, the other to the south – were compared. The five exchanges in north London were Camden Town, Holloway, Hackney, Shoreditch, and King's Cross, and the five exchanges in south London were Battersea, Brixton, Camberwell, Fulham, and Tooting. The Department of Employment at Watford made available the monthly analyses of registered unemployment and notified vacancies at these exchanges. The totals were analysed by industry and by occupation. The dates chosen for comparison were June 1964 and June 1974. It was hardly possible to choose a later date because legal and social changes have made comparisons with earlier dates virtually meaningless. First, since December 1975 it has in most cases been illegal to distinguish between the sexes in notifying vacancies. Second, since 1975 it is apparent that an increasing proportion of females have registered as unemployed. Thus, legal changes make separate comparisons impossible, and social changes make joint comparisons useless. In the hope that such a comparison might throw some light on the contrast in the changing situations of these areas, and on the argument that the decline of manufacturing industry in inner areas has been a direct cause of higher unemployment in these areas, the changes in the industrial composition of the registered unemployed and notified vacancies in the two areas are first discussed, followed by an analysis of the occupational composition.

9.4.1 Industrial analysis

Table 9.3 shows the analysis of registered (male) unemployment and notified (male) vacancies in the two areas by industry, disaggregated to Order level of the Standard Industrial Classification (SIC). The totals show that in inner–south London the number unemployed almost doubled between 1964 and 1974, while vacancies increased slightly. In inner–north London, on the other hand, the number of vacancies more than doubled, but unemployment increased by very little. The contrast between the employment situations of the two areas is very great. The reasons for the contrasting changes are not at all clear, however; indeed, the table is almost more notable for what it does not show than for what it shows; certainly, there is no clear evidence linking the changing employment situation with changes in manufacturing industry.

According to the table, manufacturing industry accounted for just under 20 per cent of unemployment in the south in 1964 (and

Table 9.3 Male unemployment and vacancies by industry: inner London, 1964 and 1974 (no. in June of each year)

Industry	Inner–south London				Inner–north London			
	Unemployed		Vacancies		Unemployed		Vacancies	
	1964	1974	1964	1974	1964	1974	1964	1974
Agriculture, forestry, and fishing	6	14	2	—	4	7	—	—
Mining and quarrying	1	4	—	—	7	1	—	—
Food, drink and tobacco	109	146	75	40	125	119	30	62
Coal and petroleum products	6	21	9	3	4	6	1	4
Chemicals	41	69	25	80	49	51	11	21
Metal manufacture	23	48	11	36	19	34	13	10
Mechanical engineering	86	69	153	93	128	104	111	117
Instrument engineering	9	27	22	31	40	32	38	68
Electrical engineering	83	132	84	86	82	106	44	70
Shipbuilding and marine engineering	5	3	1	—	9	4	2	—
Vehicles	25	35	31	7	25	29	15	6
Metal goods not elsewhere specified	86	148	59	161	120	148	104	197
Textiles	6	30	5	11	14	43	13	17
Leather, leather goods, and fur	9	11	4	15	38	25	39	65

Clothing and footwear	29	39	13	19	275	224	156	738
Bricks, pottery, glass, cement	20	61	29	52	50	49	13	12
Timber, furniture	51	66	42	59	250	219	163	242
Paper, printing, and publishing	60	344	24	44	127	276	53	101
Other manufacturing	54	86	37	41	100	83	51	112
Total in manufacturing	702	1,335	624	778	1,455	1,552	857	1,842
Construction	599	1,327	262	185	645	806	158	161
Gas, electricity, and water	40	106	68	16	31	34	23	17
Transport and communications	261	451	177	99	319	397	153	1,119
Distributive trades	505	742	243	302	667	502	288	514
Insurance, banking, and finance	73	259	22	104	68	208	37	156
Professional and scientific services	112	287	40	87	175	276	34	147
Miscellaneous services	626	1,093	334	302	773	773	137	311
Public administration	230	317	56	81	192	247	47	158
School leavers	414	953	—	—	524	805	—	—
Total	3,569	6,888	1,828	1,954	4,860	5,608	1,734	4,425
% in manufacturing	19.7	19.4	34.1	39.8	29.9	27.7	49.4	41.6

Source: Department of Employment, unpublished data.

the proportion was the same in 1974) and for 30 per cent of unemployment in the north in 1964 (and for the same proportion in 1974). Thus, not only did the proportions remain the same instead of increasing as might be expected, but also the proportion of the unemployed coming from manufacturing was highest in the area with the more favourable employment situation. The only interpretation of these figures that would favour the common view is as follows. Since employment in manufacturing has declined by a substantial amount, so that it now accounts for a smaller proportion of total employment than it did, then, if manufacturing unemployment has remained the same proportion of total unemployment, the employment situation of these employed in manufacturing industry must have deteriorated. Their unemployment rate has risen relative to the unemployment rate of those employed in services etc. Note, however, the conflicting behaviour of manufacturing vacancies. These have increased both absolutely and as a proportion of the total in the south; and although the proportion has fallen in the north, the total number of vacancies in manufacturing industry has more than doubled. Thus, although it is possible to interpret the unemployment figures as implying a worsening due to the decline in manufacturing industry, it is virtually impossible to interpret the vacancy figures in this way.

It is equally difficult to attribute the changes in the total employment situation to changes within particular industries, since the overall changes seem to be reflected in more or less equiproportionate changes in each industry. Some industries can be picked out as having changed by greater proportions than others. In both areas it is clear that 'Paper, printing, and publishing', with a sixfold increase in unemployment in ten years in the south and a twofold increase in the north, is the weakest manufacturing industry, and this finding fits in with casual empirical knowledge. More surprising is the increase in unemployment in 'Insurance, banking, and finance' in both areas – a fourfold increase in the south and threefold increase in the north.

Particular industrial changes can be identified in the north. Thus, there is a decrease in unemployment and a large increase in vacancies in the furniture, women's clothing, and leather goods industries. All three are concentrated in the area and have been decentralising. The absence of any increase in unemployment or any decrease in vacancies is therefore surprising. The most startling change in the area is in 'Transport and communications', with an eightfold increase in vacancies in the period. The figures for the individual exchanges disaggregated to the SIC Minimum List Heading level show that this can largely be attributed to an increase in vacancies in rail transport at Camden Town from 62 to 127, an increase in vacancies in road passenger transport at Holloway from 8 to 531, and an increase in vacancies in postal services at Camden Town from 0 to 253.

From the study of the industrial analysis of unemployment and vacancies in the two areas it is not possible to derive any clear answers to the questions posed before the analysis . In general, it appears that the analysis of the changes is unhelpful because the aggregate changes in the two areas are reflected in the changes in the industries in the two areas rather than the reverse, the changes in the particular industries located in each area explaining the difference between the aggregate changes. Why should this be so? The most probable reason is that people do not stay in one industry and take jobs only in that industry. If unemployed because of redundancies in one industry, they may, and often will, seek employment in another. The evidence on industrial mobility surveyed by Hunter and Reid (1968) suggests that only between a third and a half of the total number of job changes remain in the same industry. Thus, if a factory closes, initially there may be seen an increase in unemployment in that industry; but most of the redundant workers will find jobs in other industries so that reductions in vacancies in these industries will occur, and unemployment in these industries will occur as all unemployed workers will find it more difficult to find jobs. Thus, in a short time the effects of unemployment in a particular industry will be a higher rate of unemployment in all industries and a reduction in vacancies. A relatively larger increase in unemployment in the particular industry that started the chain will be hardly noticeable – only widespread changes of the kind observed in inner London. Only in one case is the unemployment likely to persist, and that is when the skills of the redundant workers are specific to a particular industry and when they can command high wages in that industry. Then they have a strong incentive to continue looking for employment in that industry and are unlikely to receive acceptable offers of work in other industries. The printing industry appears to be such an industry, and this may explain why unemployment in that industry is so noticeable.

9.4.2 Occupational analysis

In many respects the occupational data in Table 9.4 give a picture similar to that shown by the industrial data, if only because occupations and industries tend to coincide. In general the numbers unemployed in each occupational group, and the numbers of vacancies, change within each area more or less equiproportionately. The reasons for this are precisely the same as in the case of the industrial data. According to the studies surveyed by Hunter and Reid (1968) only about a third to a half of the total number of job changers remain in the same occupation. Hence, any large redundancies in a particular occupation will be only visible in the statistics for a short time before the process of job changing disperses the unemployment over the other occupations. Some particular changes are visible – mostly the same as those indicated by the industrial data. The weakening of the market for printing workers in both areas is noticeable, as well as the vast increase in the number of vacancies in inner–north London for transport workers and postal workers. A deterioration in the relative employment situation of 'Construction workers' is noticeable in both areas and is not evident in the case of the 'Construction' industry.

The most interesting figures are those for the two 'mopping-up' classifications of 'Labourers' and 'Professional, scientific, technical, and administrative workers'. The table shows that the number of unemployed labourers in the north fell by one-third even though total unemployment increased, and that the number in the south increased by less than a third even though total unemployment nearly doubled. It appears that in both areas the employment situation of labourers improved in relation to that of other workers. The reverse is true of professionals; the unemployment of professionals more than trebled in each area, with of course a deterioration relative to the situation in other occupations in the north.

9.5 The influence of residential changes

Summarising the position now reached, the evidence appears somewhat contradictory. It shows:

(a) that the employment situation has deteriorated recently in inner–south London but improved in inner–north London;

(b) that there is no strong evidence that the employment situation of manufacturing workers has deteriorated markedly in these two inner areas; and

(c) that the employment situation of labourers has improved in these two areas, but that of professionals has deteriorated considerably, particularly in inner–north London.

The most plausible explanation for these seemingly inconsistent changes in inner–north and inner–south London is that they are largely due to changes in the socioeconomic structure of the resident labour force, mainly resulting from the process of gentrification. Table 9.5 clearly shows that the proportion of the population in the higher social classes has risen considerably in the northern boroughs of inner London but not to the same extent in the southern boroughs. Since the higher skill groups have lower unemployment rates than the lower skill groups, the effect of gentrification – the displacement of lower skill groups by higher – will be to reduce the average unemployment rate in the area. Thus, the gentrification occurring in inner-north London will lead to a reduction in the rate of unemployment there. The change in the socioeconomic structure of the area might also lead to improvements in the employment situation of the less skilled workers remaining in the area as the total number is reduced, provided that the total number of less skilled jobs in the area does not decline at a faster rate. Thus, the immigration of professional workers is unlikely to improve their employment situation and may cause some deterioration, but that of the less skilled workers may possibly improve theirs.

9.6 Conclusions

The findings of this chapter are as follows. First, while the average level of unemployment is higher in the inner city than in the suburbs, this is not a recent phenomenon but has been so for at least the last quarter of a century.

Second, the unemployment rate tends to be higher in inner London for each social class, so that the higher average unemployment rate in the inner area is not only due to higher levels of unemployment among the unskilled. This tends to contradict the view that the higher average unemployment rates in inner areas are caused by the less skilled being 'trapped' in the inner areas while

Table 9.4 Male unemployment and vacancies by occupation: inner London, 1964 and 1974 (no. in June of each year)

Occupation	Inner-south London				Inner-north London			
	Unemployed		Vacancies		Unemployed		Vacancies	
	1964	1974	1964	1974	1964	1974	1964	1974
Farmers, foresters, and fishermen	4	24	23	16	6	26	3	1
Miners and quarrymen	3	1	0	0	4	3	0	1
Gas, coke, and chemical makers	1	6	18	4	2	5	1	0
Glass and ceramics makers	1	50	7	8	11	40	14	27
Furnace, forge, foundry and rolling mill workers	8	7	8	13	7	9	8	5
Electrical and electronic workers	84	166	37	47	50	70	48	44
Engineering and allied trades workers	168	400	371	405	179	322	274	506
Woodworkers	43	75	60	100	95	110	182	222
Leather workers (incl. shoemakers)	6	10	1	5	45	87	54	85
Textile workers	3	11	1	2	2	23	20	10
Clothing workers	29	32	20	14	124	91	118	335
Food, drink, and tobacco workers	13	42	14	20	31	24	7	17
Paper and printing workers	18	98	18	21	23	94	28	43
Makers of other products	12	58	15	16	22	27	10	42

Construction workers	48	598	28	62	65	345	24	70
Painters and decorators	83	290	86	40	120	146	19	30
Drivers of stationary engines:	11	48	5	9	16	32	8	2
(i) Air and water transport workers	14	6	9	0	13	4	4	0
(ii) Railway workers	1	16	28	1	0	1	19	119
(iii) Road transport workers	169	382	204	132	254	368	187	652
(iv) Public service, road transport workers	2	15	28	13	5	6	5	104
(v) Communications workers	76	92	63	22	159	100	32	313
Warehousemen, storekeepers, packers, and bottlers	89	196	55	112	183	225	123	338
Clerical workers	440	643	87	166	429	412	155	299
Sales workers	89	206	113	143	93	89	96	131
Service, sport, and recreation workers	270	608	141	243	328	662	72	736
Professional, scientific, technical, and administrative workers	202	734	34	70	211	695	37	54
Labourers	1,594	2,006	362	215	2,269	1,545	155	192
Total	3,481	6,820	1,836	1,899	4,746	5,561	1,703	4,378

Source: Department of Employment, unpublished data.

Table 9.5 Economically active male residents in non-manual occupations: Greater London and selected boroughs, 1961 and 1971 (%)

Area	Employers and managers		Professionals		Intermediate non-manual		Total senior non-manual		Junior non-manual		Total non-manual	
	1961	1971	1961	1971	1961	1971	1961	1971	1961	1971	1961	1971
Greater London	11.6	13.9	4.7	6.1	4.8	6.5	21.1	26.5	18.2	17.0	39.3	43.4
Inner–north London:												
Tower Hamlets	4.3	5.0	0.9	1.3	1.2	1.6	6.4	7.9	10.6	11.1	17.0	19.0
Hackney	6.3	7.7	1.7	1.9	2.1	3.0	10.1	12.6	14.1	14.1	24.2	26.7
Islington	5.1	7.9	1.5	3.5	2.3	5.4	8.9	16.8	14.5	15.3	23.4	32.2
Camden	12.5	14.6	6.3	9.6	6.4	8.8	25.2	33.0	17.8	17.3	43.0	50.3
City of Westminster	17.3	20.3	7.7	9.4	6.1	7.2	31.1	36.9	19.0	17.2	50.1	54.1
Kensington and Chelsea	16.8	20.7	10.1	13.2	8.8	9.6	35.7	43.5	20.0	18.2	55.7	61.7
Hammersmith	7.5	10.0	2.9	4.4	4.1	6.3	14.5	20.7	16.5	17.6	30.9	38.4
Inner–south London:												
Wandsworth }Lambeth }	8.9	10.4	3.2	4.5	4.4	6.6	16.5	21.5	20.0	18.9	36.5	40.4
Southwark	6.0	7.8	1.7	2.4	2.5	4.0	10.2	14.2	15.0	15.0	25.3	29.2
Lewisham	8.5	10.6	2.9	3.8	4.3	6.0	15.7	20.4	19.7	18.0	35.5	38.4

Source: General Register Office (1965), *Census 1961, England and Wales, Occupations Industry and Socio-Economic Groups – County Leaflets: Greater London* (London: H.M.S.O.); Office of Population Censuses and Surveys (1975), *Census 1971, England and Wales, Economic Activity – County Leaflets: Greater London* (London: H.M.S.O.).

jobs decentralise. The difference between the rates for inner and outer areas, for all social classes, almost certainly results from the influence of the other characteristics identified as important by Metcalf and Richardson (Chapter 8 of this book), particularly age and family status.

Third, looking at changes over time, there is no evidence of a deterioration in the employment situation in the inner city in contrast to the rest of the urban area. The situation has tended to improve in inner–north London and outer–south London and deteriorate in inner–south London and outer–south-east London.

Fourth, looking at the changes in the characteristics of the unemployed and of vacancies in inner–north and inner–south London, there is no clear evidence that the employment situation in manufacturing industry has been markedly different from that in services.

Finally, the improvement in the employment situation in inner–north London, in contrast to inner–south London, probably results from gentrification, which results in the replacement as residents of people with lower skill levels and a high probability of being unemployed by people with higher skill levels and a lower probability of being unemployed.

In general the findings of this detailed investigation of the London labour market support those of Metcalf and Richardson. Within the London conurbation most of the variation in unemployment rates between different parts of the conurbation is due to differences in the characteristics of the population that is resident in these different parts. In particular, because the young and the unskilled live in the inner city, and because the probability of being unemployed is high for these groups, the average rate of unemployment is high in the inner city. The implications of this view of the employment problem will be discussed by Evans (Chapter 20).

10 Employment in a Changing Labour Market

Richard Berthoud

10.1 Introduction

If employment statistics could be considered simply in aggregate, there ought not to be any inner-city employment problem. The great conurbations typically offer a large concentration of jobs in the centre – far more jobs than can be filled by the residents of the conurbation centre or even of the inner ring. Since there are more central jobs than people seeking jobs, large numbers of workers have to be imported from further out, causing a transport problem but apparently indicating a healthy employment situation.

Unfortunately, this happy picture based on an aggregate view of statistics disappears when they are inspected in detail, for the excess employment in the city centre is based on a large and growing tertiary sector: commerce, professional and scientific services, public administration, and so on, employing a high proportion of professional and managerial staff serviced mainly by white collar workers, often women. For the male manual worker who has depended on manufacturing industry for his livelihood, this growth of the tertiary sector offers no advantages.

On the contrary, the growth of the tertiary sector is itself one of the several pressures that can influence the decline of manufacturing industry in the inner city. The demand for office space can force up the price of land, making it less economic for industry to remain in the centre. At the same time changes in production methods requiring larger scale units, and changes in transportation systems,

232

may both tend to encourage existing industry to move out of the city and to discourage new industry from replacing it. Third, there is the national decline in manufacturing industry; between 1961 and 1977, while the number of jobs in financial, professional, and scientific services rose by 69 per cent, the number of jobs in manufacturing industries fell by 13 per cent[1] Department of Employment, 1977b. Fourth, although manufacturing industries as a whole decline slightly, certain industries decline rapidly, while others grow to replace them. Since it is old industries that tend to decline, it is probably the residents of old employment centres who tend to suffer. Employees of declining industries in the inner city would therefore have to change both their job and their home in order to profit from such changes in the industrial structure.

Many of these changes are inevitable, and many of them are desirable in the general economic interest. While it might be necessary to guide the course of industrial change, it is probably neither possible nor desirable to attempt flatly to oppose it as a long term strategy. Nevertheless, what is good for the national prosperity is not necessarily good for all the individuals affected.

The inner-city employment problem seems to consist of male manual workers on a sticky employment wicket; as the old industries decline they are forced either to remain in jobs that are below average in pay or to seek new skills, perhaps having to tear up their roots and move to a new and expanding area. The alternatives are routine clerical work at very low pay or 'scavenging' industry – small firms depending on a buyer's labour market for their existence. The problem can be summarised as the change in employment happening faster than the human population can comfortably adjust to it. The change is occurring nationally; but inevitably there are some areas where it is moving faster, causing greater frictional stress, and the old inner city areas may be among the worst affected.

The foregoing is an attempt to summarise some aspects of the inner city problem suggested by geographers and economists who have contributed to this book. In this chapter it is intended to introduce a discussion of the aspects of employment that are not peculiar to the inner city. If it is correct to assess the inner city problem in terms of manual workers' difficulties in adjusting to change in the labour market, the problem is part of a wider issue

[1]Source of data – Department of Employment Gazette.

with social as well as economic implications – the issue of matching opportunities to skills and aptitudes in the most effective possible way. In general this would be served if employers and workers sought each other in conditions approaching a perfect market. On the other hand, if there is a series of artificial or accidental obstacles hindering a meeting of employer and worker, that is likely to be inefficient and to result in inequalities between workers that are unnecessary and unfair.

The remainder of this chapter is therefore devoted to a brief review of some of the problems experienced by manual workers in their search for employment.[2] Given a number of workers in declining jobs on the one hand, and the existence of better jobs in growth industries on the other, what external influences are there that hinder the movement of the one to the other? If these could be identified, policies could be proposed that, by removing or reducing the hindrances, would help to ensure that more people gained from industrial change and fewer lost.

10.2 The advantages of job mobility

Since much of the concern about manual workers' employment is expressed in terms of preventing employees from being sacked, it first needs to be argued that changing jobs is a 'good thing' for the worker concerned. It may well be that those who have to seek a job from the insecurity of unemployment or the threat of unemployment, tend to accept a job that is no better, and perhaps worse, than the previous one. It seems reasonable on the other hand to suppose that those who choose a new job from the security of an existing job will not move unless the new job is on the whole better than the old – sufficiently better to overcome any disadvantages ensuing from the change itself. Thus, although enforced job changes are undesirable for most workers, voluntary job changes are to be encouraged. Minimising the incidental costs of changing jobs is one way of encouraging them. Quite a lot of manual workers do change their jobs – 12 per cent of them in a year (Department of Employment, 1976b). Unfortunately, it is not known how many of them do so voluntarily and how many out of necessity; nor is it known how

[2]Obstacles facing a manual worker in seeking senior non-manual jobs, with which the inner city is so well endowed, are beyond the scope of this chapter. It is assumed that the manual worker is seeking another manual job.

Table 10.1 Proportion of male manual workers with their current employer less than twelve months, by age

Age	21–24	25–29	30–39	40–49	50–59	60–64
%	20	16	12	8	5	3

Source: Department of Employment (1976b).

many gain and how many lose in the course of moving. It is known, however, that job mobility declines rapidly with increasing age (Table 10.1).

Although one would expect job stability to increase through the earlier years of a man's working life, there is no necessary reason for such a steep and steady drop in mobility right across the age range. The older the manual worker, the less likely he is to be able to profit from a change in job. Moreover, the signs are that such job changes as do occur in middle age are more and more likely to be enforced (and damaging) and less and less likely to be voluntary (and profitable), as shown in Table 10.2. Although this table would be based for preference on all workers or all job changers, rather than on the unemployed, it does in combination with Table 10.1 suggest that voluntary movement between jobs becomes rarer as middle age advances.

10.3 The decline of earnings with age

All this can be tied back to the earlier hypothesis about the potential advantages of voluntary job movement, by reproducing the well-known statistics on earnings by age (Table 10.3). Among manual workers, those aged 30–39 earn more than anyone else. From 50

Table 10.2 Unemployed workers' reasons for leaving last job, by age (%)

Reason for leaving	Up to 25	26–35	36–45	46–55	Over 55
(a) Voluntary	58	57	49	44	31
(b) Redundant	17	21	29	29	42
(c) Other	25	22	21	26	26
Ratio a:b	3.4	2.7	1.7	1.5	0.7

Source: Daniel (1974).

Table 10.3 Gross earnings by age, 1977 (£)

Type of worker	21–24	25–29	30–39	40–49	50–59	60–64
(a) Manual workers	65.4	71.9	75.8	74.5	70.1	64.1
(b) Senior and intermediate non-manual workers	63.0	83.4	101.2	111.0	112.6	101.2
Ratio a:b	1.04	0.86	0.75	0.67	0.62	0.63

Source: Department of Employment (1977).

onwards the drop is quite steep. While 24 per cent of 30–39-year-olds earned less than £60 per week in 1977, 34 per cent of 50–59-year-olds and 47 per cent of 60–64-year-olds were below that figure (Department of Employment, 1977).

These statistics are usually interpreted in terms of rising and falling incomes over the lifecycle. As children leave home and wives go out to work there is less motive for the employee to increase his earnings through overtime etc. On the other hand, this does not explain the continuing drop beyond the age of 50. Moreover, only about one-quarter of manual workers have the option to vary the amount of overtime worked (Daniel, 1975). Alternatively, earnings are said to drop through failing health, which leads to less overtime, slower piecework production, downgrading, or even a forced drop in occupational status. Without denying the value of either of these explanations it is possible to suggest a third: that the older the worker, the more likely he is to be employed in a stagnant or even declining industry, in a stagnant or declining district, and the less likely he is to be able to get out of that trap through a profitable change of job. Not only does his work potential tend to be reduced with advancing age, but also the work he is used to doing, which he is by now forced to continue doing, is no longer of such value in economic terms as it was twenty or thirty years ago. Its value may not actually fall, but it fails to increase at the same rate as the work performed by younger men in more vigorous industries.

This hypothesis may be brought into sharper focus by an analysis of the average wage increases received by men of different ages (see Table 10.4). Looked at in this way, while everyone's earnings increase even in real terms, the rate of increase lessens steeply with age up to about 40, after which the rate of increase lessens more

Table 10.4 Average increased wage received by male manual workers of different ages, 1970–77

Age in 1970	Average wage in 1970 (£)	Average wage of the same cohort in 1977 (£)	% increase	% real increase
20	19.5	71.9	269	48
25	25.1	74.5	197	19
30	27.8	75.5	172	9
35	28.6	74.8	162	5
40	28.3	73.4	159	4
45	27.9	71.2	155	3
50	26.9	68.0	153	2
55	25.8	64.1	148	0

Source: Department of Employment (1970, 1977).

slowly. Older workers' earnings do not so much go down as fail to keep up with the healthy rate of increase experienced by younger workers. It is these latter increases that cause the general average to rise, leaving the older workers relatively worse off.

10.4 Skill levels and age

Lower wages for older workers can be seen, then, as partly a consequence of secular trends in the employment structure from which the worker cannot escape, if also partly as a consequence of the individual's aging process. The problem is well illustrated by the fact that in 1971 skilled workers formed 67 per cent of the male manual workforce at age 25–34, falling to 53 per cent at age 60–64 and 36 per cent at age 65–70; meanwhile, the equivalent figures for unskilled workers rose from 11 per cent to 20 per cent and 34 per cent respectively (1971 census). On the aging process theory this would be explained in terms of failing health enforcing a drop in skill level, but this would scarcely account for the drop in the proportion of skilled workers that occurs steadily throughout the healthy years of youth and early middle age, as well as continuing through towards old age. It seems, then, that it is a comparison of current job opportunities with those of thirty or forty years ago that is critical.

Let us compare the number of men reporting manual jobs at various levels of skill in the Censuses of Population of 1961 and 1971. The general shift from manufacturing to service industries has led to a decline in the overall number of manual workers, although the trend towards higher levels of skill has meant that the decline in the number of skilled jobs has been proportionately lower than that for unskilled jobs. Nevertheless, there were fewer skilled workers in 1971 than in 1961. The question is: how was this change organised? Did industry train young skilled men in smaller numbers, so that the loss to the skilled workforce was effected through deaths and retirement? What happened to skilled workers as they became ten years older?

Table 10.5 shows the flows in and out of the three manual-worker categories between 1961 and 1971. It is not an easy table to read, so an annotated summary has been provided. The table shows that industry had to go on training young men to an extent that exceeded natural wastage. Indeed, (not shown in the table) some 10 per cent *more* young men appear to have been trained between 1961 and 1971 than in the previous ten-year period. This was because there was a tendency for men who had been skilled ten years earlier not to be members of that category by 1971. Many of them left the manual group altogether – some perhaps promoted to staff status, others to take jobs in non-manual or service occupations. However, it appears that many of the older men who ceased to be skilled may have become semiskilled or unskilled. In spite of the fact that the total number of unskilled workers decreased by 15 per cent over this period, and in spite of the fact that the number of older (aged 55–64) unskilled men also decreased by 10 per cent, the number of unskilled workers within the cohort that aged from 45–54 to 55–64 *increased* by 20 per cent.

It appears, then, that an early training does not provide a skill ticket for life. Men leave their skilled occupations throughout their careers; and although among the younger men this may be for positive reasons, for older men it is probably not from choice and may often lead to downgrading, the loss of earnings and job satisfaction, and the risk of unemployment. While this may be partly caused by physical incapacity or perhaps by lower motivation when children leave home, it may also be partly caused by the process of obsolescence, which is the theme of this chapter. The figures suggest that a workspan of forty to fifty years is too long for initial training to be valuable, so that there is a constant process of young men being

Table 10.5 Male movement in and out of manual occupational groups: ages 20–64, 1961–71 (thousands)

Age group		Skilled/foremen			Semiskilled			Unskilled		
In 1961	In 1971	Joined	Died,[a] retired	Left	Joined	Died,[a] retired	Left	Joined	Died,[a] retired	Left
10–19	20–29	1,120[1]			367			200[5]		73[8]
20–34	30–44		–2	138[4]		–1	60		–2	
35–44	45–54		83	98[4]		32	20	9[9]	15	
45–54	55–64		172	102[4]		82	32	41[9]	40	
55–64	65–74		727			432			280	
Total		1,120	980[2]	338	367	545	112	250	333[6]	73
Net Loss			198[3]			290			156[7]	

a Or migrated.

Notes:

1. Among *skilled* manual workers the number of young men who joined the group between 1961 and 1971[1] exceeded the number who left through natural wastage[2]. There was nevertheless a net loss to the group[3], because there was a net movement out of the skilled group among men who were of working age at both dates[4]. This movement out affected younger and older workers about equally.

2. Among *unskilled* manual workers the number of young men joining the group[5] was less than the amount of natural wastage[6], and this would nearly have accounted for the small reduction in the numbers of unskilled men[7]. Among workers of working age at both censuses, however, there was a net tendency to leave the unskilled group for those still in the first half of their careers[8], but there was also a tendency for *older* men to *become* unskilled[9].

Sources: Census of Population, 1961 and 1971.

Note on the preparation of the table

Census, 1961 and 1971. All figures are based on economically active and retired males aged 20–64 at either date.
Each section of the table is derived as follows:

| Age group | | Joined | Died,[a] retired | Left |
In 1961	In 1971			
10–19	20–29	A		
20–34	30–44	E	B	D
35–44	45–54	E	B	D
45–54	55–64	E	B	D
55–64	65–74		C	

[a] Or migrated.

A   The number of young men aged 20–29 in 1971, who were too young to have been members of the 20–64 age group in 1961.

B   The number in each cohort who died or migrated. It is assumed that the percentage loss (or gain) in each cohort is the same for each group of manual workers as it was for the male population as a whole, for the same age cohort.

C   The number of older men aged 55–64 in 1961, who were too old to have been members of the 20–64 age group in 1971.

D,E   The reduction (D) or increase (E) in the size of the age band, compared with the ten-years-younger age group ten years previously, after allowing for death (or migration).

trained in new skills, while those in their 40s and 50s are being 'retired' from skilled work ten or twenty years before they are due to collect their pensions. A man may lose his skilled job as a consequence of the secular industrial changes outlined above; following the decline in the demand for his skill or his product, or the removal of his employer to a greenfields site, he becomes redundant. As a result both of the general obstacles to job mobility and retraining, and of the tendency of employers to recruit and train younger men, the older man is forced to accept a job at a lower level, even though he may be in perfect health.

Thus, the lower wages of older manual workers can largely be accounted for in terms of the skill level that they were able to reach in the employment climate of their earlier years and also, by extension, in terms of the current prosperity of the particular occupation and industry in which they were trained. To illustrate by exaggeration, the 60-year-old worker is still riveting boilers on Tyneside, if he is lucky, while the 35-year-old worker is making cars in Coventry, and the 20-year-old is learning to make computers in the home counties. It is the failure of older workers to obtain these newer and more remunerative jobs that causes both a social problem and an economic problem in restricting the availability of skilled labour for new and growing industries.

So one contribution to the employment problem of inner cities, or anywhere else facing industrial decline, would be a package of policies designed to encourage workers to change jobs before they are forced into it by redundancy. To the extent that the age trap is a function of real lifecycle changes – personal inertia, lower adaptability, lower trainability, or declining health – this would mean focusing mobility on the younger and more flexible worker, leaving the older men on a firmer base and protecting them from total unemployment. On the other hand, if there are external factors that hinder the older worker's flexibility, policy can and should be directed to removing these factors, so that the older worker can obtain positive advantages from industrial change.

10.5 Training and retraining

Perhaps one of the most serious obstacles is the reluctance of employers to recruit, and if necessary to retrain, workers who are

Table 10.6   Proportion of unemployed having found a job four to six weeks after random selection, by age

Age	Up to 25	26–35	36–45	46–55	Over 55
%	38	25	23	12	9

Source: Daniel (1974).

past the first flush of youth. This is well known and is illustrated by the difficulty that older people experience when they do apply for a job, as shown in Table 10.6. No wonder there is such concern about job preservation, when the problems of finding another job are so acute. Yet employers' attitudes seem illogical. A 45-year-old still has twenty years of work left in him. Moreover, judging by the figures in Table 10.1 an employer ought to expect about 58 per cent of his 25-year-old recruits to have left him within five years, against only about 34 per cent of his 45-year-old recruits.[3] The 45-year-old is a better long-term bet, against which the upper limit of twenty years seems rather irrelevant.

In view of these problems, one of the possibilities is to encourage workers in their 40s and even 50s to retrain for more modern jobs with more up-to-date wages, either through government sponsorship or by encouraging employers to take a more realistic attitude to the middle-aged. Daniel (1974) has found that in his sample nearly a third of the unemployed had considered the possibility of retraining, and interest did not fall off until the very oldest age group. Moreover, half of those considering it had applied for a course but had often been unable to get one (Table 10.7). Thus, the demand for retraining exceeded the supply; and in view of the modest supply it is not surprising that half of those who had not considered the possibility did not even know that facilities existed (Daniel, 1974). The figures in the table represent an underestimate of the demand among the unemployed.

For that matter it should not be the unemployed in particular at which retraining policies should be aimed. It seems unnecessary to wait for the shock of unemployment before workers are retrained.

---

[3]These figures are on the crude assumption that, in any age group, those who have just joined an employer are neither more nor less likely to move again. At the end of one year, for instance, 16 per cent of 25-year-old recruits will have left, 84 per cent remaining. After five years 58 per cent will have left, 42 per cent reamining.

Table 10.7   Attitudes to retraining among the unemployed, by age (cumulative percentages)

Attitude towards retraining	Up to 25	26–35	36–45	46–55	Over 55
On a course	5	5	10	5	2
Applied for a course	22	24	21	17	4
Considered a course	37	39	36	34	11

Source: Daniel (1974).

If they are approached when redundancies are announced, or even when the possibility of redundancies is envisaged, they will be able to consider their options in a more positive frame of mind. Once unemployed a man may be deterred from retraining either by desperation or by fatalistic resignation. Moreover, at the pre-redundancy stage it is possible to select those who would benefit most from retraining, leaving the less flexible in command of the remaining jobs at the firm. Paradoxically, it may even be that retraining the young is the best way of helping the middle-aged. Nevertheless, the middle-aged could be retrained in spite of their feeling that they may be too old at 40 (Daniel, 1974).

Training and retraining schemes already exist of course. Since the early 1970s and the creation of the Training Services Agency and its Training Opportunities Scheme (TOPS), the number of courses has greatly increased, although Britain had a lot of catching up to do before it could compare with the record of some other European countries (Mukherjee, 1972, 1976). Much of the new effort has been devoted to training in clerical work, but the number of courses at Skillcentres providing skills to the manual workers considered in this chapter, has doubled during the 1970s. Skillcentres, however, cater far more for the young and never skilled worker than for the middle-aged and formerly skilled worker. A recent study suggests that the courses are not always as effective as they might be, largely because assistance to the trainees stops abruptly when they complete their courses. The Skillcentres could offer extended help both in locating job opportunities and in supporting the former trainees during the difficult early months of their new careers (Berthoud, 1978).

Table 10.8   Time taken in journeys to work in London, by occupational group (cumulative percentages)

Time taken (minutes)	Managerial and professional	Other non-manual	Skilled manual and supervisory	Semi-skilled manual	Unskilled manual
Up to 5	8	6	9	8	8
Up to 10	18	16	24	23	20
Up to 20	37	34	50	49	43
Up to 30	54	50	69	69	61
Up to 45	71	71	84	85	80
Up to 60	86	88	94	93	91
Median (minutes)	28	30	20	21	24
Mean[a] (minutes)	34	35	28	27	30

[a] Estimated from grouped data.

10.6 Personal and residential mobility

Of course, retraining workers, whether by public or by private bodies, will not make up the whole of a policy to aid workers in declining industries. Policy on supporting and/or relocating industry is the subject of other chapters in this book; this chapter is concerned with the individual worker. He, however, has to consider job mobility in the context of two other kinds of mobility, although the importance of the first is not clear. These are, first, mobility in the journey from home to work and, second, residential mobility.

10.6.1 Mobility in the journey to work

While it is obvious that the journey to work imposes a constraint on a worker's choice of job, it is not clear how serious that constraint is. If the range of jobs that is open to him within a reasonable radius is similar to the whole possible range of jobs, the constraint is slight. Similarly, if the better jobs outside that radius are sufficiently superior, they may justify a move of home (see section 10.62), and again the constraint imposed by the journey to work is slight. It is between those two margins that the constraint lies. It is not clear how great it is, although it almost certainly varies considerably by location, by occupation, and with the individual.

At first sight it appears that difficulties in interpreting variations in journeys to work are a little academic. In London there is not

Table 10.9 Method of travel for journeys to work in London by occupational group (%)

Method of travel [a]	Managerial and professional	Other non-manual	Skilled manual and supervisory	Semi-skilled manual	Unskilled manual
Car driver	57 ⎫ 61	40 ⎫ 44	52 ⎫ 58	34 ⎫ 43	24 ⎫ 32
Car passenger	4 ⎭	4 ⎭	6 ⎭	9 ⎭	8 ⎭
Underground	14 ⎫ 28	17 ⎫ 34	7 ⎫ 13	9 ⎫ 14	10 ⎫ 17
British Rail	14 ⎭	17 ⎭	6 ⎭	5 ⎭	7 ⎭
Bus	6	13	14	23	28
Walk/pedal	4	9	12	20	22
Other	1	—	3	—	1
Total	100	100	100	200	100

[a] The method of travel is that used for the longest leg of the journey.
Source: Greater London Council (1971–72).

much variation between different occupational groups, as shown in Table 10.8. Although all three manual groups show slightly lower journey times than either non-manual group, the differences, although perhaps significant in the statistical sense, do not seem very important. A maximum difference of 8 or 10 minutes is not large when the overall range of travel times is from under 5 minutes to well over 1 hour. While the average for manual workers as a group is a little less than the average for non-manual workers, there is not much than can be concluded about the journey time facing any individual.

However, the method of transport used does vary quite substantially between occupational groups, as Table 10.9 shows. Let us consider these figures in two stages: first, whether workers travel by car or not. On the face of it car driving declines rather irregularly with status, while getting a lift increases slightly; but if the extent of car driving is related to the incidence of car ownership, it appears that those of lower social status are more and more likely to use a car if they have one (see Table 10.10). While the last figure in the table obviously does not make literal sense, it seems that manual workers almost always drive to work if they have a car, while non-manual

Table 10.10 Car ownership and use of car for travel to work, by occupational group (%)

	Managerial and professional	Other non-manual	Skilled manual and supervisory	Semi-skilled manual	Unskilled manual
(a) Car driving to work[a] (London)	57	40	52	34	24
(b) Car ownership b (Great Britain)	93	61	61	38	23
Ratio a:b	0.61	0.66	0.85	0.89	1.04

[a] Data are for all work journeys made by males.
[b] The General Household Survey table gives car ownership for all households, including the retired. The figures given here are recalculated on the assumption that within each SEG group the level of car ownership among the economically inactive is half of the level among the economically active.
Source: Greater London Council (1971–72) and Office of Population Censuses and Surveys (1975).

workers quite often opt for an alternative mode. The manual workers' greater tendency to get lifts is in line with this.

One interpretation of the non-manual workers' tendency to leave the car at home is that the road network, especially congestion towards the centre, is not helpful for the journeys that non-manual workers have to make. An alternative interpretation is that the public transport network is enough in their favour for them to be in a position to make a choice. Either way the tendency for manual workers to use a car if they possibly can suggest that it is the best mode for them and that limited car ownership constitutes a constraint on accessibility to employment for the lower status groups.

The second stage of the analysis of method of travel is to look at the choices made by those who did not travel by car, ignoring 'other' methods of travel (Table 10.11). High occupational status is associated with use of either of the railway systems, low social status with buses or walking. The variation in car usage among car owners may therefore be a function of the suitability of the alternative fast mode. High status workers tend to undertake journeys where rail forms an efficient alternative; for low status workers the alternative is often a bus journey or even walking.

Since 89 per cent of managerial and professional workers use a fast mode, compared with only 49 per cent of unskilled manual

Table 10.11 Choice of alternative methods of travelling to work by non-car travellers, by occupational group (%)

Method of travel	Managerial and professional	Other non-manual	Skilled manual and supervisory	Semi-skilled manual	Unskilled manual
Railway (LondonTransport or British Rail)	74	61	33	25	25
Bus	16	23	36	40	42
Walk/pedal	11	16	31	35	33
Total	100	100	100	100	100

Source: Greater London Council (1971–72).

workers, the relative consistency between occupational groups in terms of their journey times must now be seen in rather a different light. If manual workers use slower modes, they must travel a shorter distance in a given time. Estimates suggest that the average managerial or professional worker travels about 1½ times as fast as the average semi- or unskilled manual worker.

One reaction to all these figures is that semi- and unskilled workers are remarkably lucky to live within so short a distance of their work – a fifth of them within walking distance. On the other hand, travel by bus or on foot is so slow that this distance advantage scarcely translates itself into a time advantage. The advantage of the shorter journey will mainly be felt in terms of financial costs – an item that could be balanced by higher wages.

The alternative interpretation may be that, because of the relative arrangement of their homes and their jobs, manual workers are unable to benefit from the radial railway network. If they have no car, they are compelled to seek a job within bussing or walking distance of their home – a distance limited by the amount of time that can reasonably be devoted to travel at the beginning and end of the day. If the radius of movement of a managerial or professional worker is half as large again as that of a semi- or unskilled manual worker, the latter can seek a job within a circle whose area is 2¼ times as great as that of the former. This may indicate a constraint on the range of jobs available to the manual worker, which would in turn restrict his occupational mobility.

Neither this analysis, nor the inferences based upon it, are watertight. However, if it is true that the transport network imposes constraints on the job choice of manual workers, there are obvious implications for transport policy. The extent of the constraint is far from clear, but the possibility of its existence is supported by two other pieces of information. First, unemployment rates vary between inner London boroughs to an extent that can probably be explained only in terms of the unemployed in one borough being out of range of the jobs in some other (Census of Population, 1971). Second, Daniel (1972) found that when men were made redundant in south-east London their new jobs involved an increase of 23 per cent in the journey-to-work distance, at the same time as a 15 per cent decrease in real earnings. For those aged 46–55 the journey-to-work distance increased 48 per cent. Evidently, the range of jobs within their habitual radius of movement failed to satisfy their requirements, even though they were prepared to lower these requirements following redundancy.

10.6.2 *Residential mobility*

If better jobs are so far away from home as to impose an intolerable journey time, a worker has the option to stay where he is or to obtain a better job by moving home – theoretically at least. Housing mobility for job reasons is remarkably rare; contrary to popular stereotype the senior occupational groups are not constantly moving from town to town to further their careers. Only 2 per cent of managerial/professional households move for job reasons in a year (Office of Population Censuses and Surveys, 1975), suggesting less than one move-for-job per household per lifetime. Even that figure is rather substantial compared with other non-manual households (0.6 per cent), skilled manual households (0.4 per cent), and semiskilled/unskilled households (0.4 per cent again). This suggests that less than one manual worker in five ever moves for a job throughout his life. (These figures exclude moves made by young men first setting up a household and also transient workers who, living in lodgings or a hostel, do not set up a household at all. While both of these are important to the general flows of labour about the country, they are not relevant to the middle-aged manual worker trapped in the inner city.)

In view of these statistics it seems that encouraging workers to move in search of better jobs is going to be rather an uphill struggle.

On the other hand, this massive inertia not only is a sufficient explanation of the severe frictional stress imposed by industrial change but also suggests that anyone prepared to make a move will find a substantial reward for doing so. Yet, only 1 per cent of all households were even considering a move for job purposes. Even among the unemployed (out of work on average for twelve months) 71 per cent had not even considered the possibility (Daniel, 1974). The reasons given suggest personal inertia rather than external hindrances. 'This is my home, why should I move?' just about sums it up.

Thus, reluctance to move home to another area constitutes perhaps the greatest obstacle to occupational mobility, and this will have to be respected in the development of policy. On the other hand, the difficulties of obtaining accommodation may be one of the reasons for the inertia. Certainly, if it were easier to move home, at least those who did consider the possibility would be enabled to do so. For instance, of the small number of unemployed workers who had located a job outside their local area but had not taken it up, nearly a quarter had rejected it because of inability to find a home (Daniel, 1974). If there are ways in which geographical mobility is hindered at present – or conversely, if there are ways in which it could be encouraged – policies aimed at removing hindrances and encouraging mobility would be good not only for the workers concerned but also for those preferring to remain behind.

There may be constraints on geographical mobility for home owners in the wide variation in house prices between areas and also in the artificially high incidental costs of buying and selling. However, on the assumption that most of the manual workers with whom this chapter is concerned are out of reach of owner occupation, it is rented housing that is more relevant.

Privately rented accommodation is of course the tenure that presents greatest ease of access to the geographically mobile; it accounts for 14 per cent of all households' accommodation but plays host to 23 per cent of all moves (Office of Population Censuses and Surveys, 1975 and Central Statistical Office, 1974). On the other hand, the disadvantages of private rental, particularly in areas of excess demand, are well known. Perhaps less often clearly appreciated is the rent differential between tenants who have been living a short or a long time in one house or flat, shown in Table 10.12. There is clearly a considerable difference between the level of rents of those with long-standing tenure and the rents available on the open market. This represents a premium on moving

Table 10.12 Average rent of tenants of different length of residence in the City of Westminster, 1972 (£ per week)

Type of rental	Over 10 years	5–10 years	Less than 5 years
Council tenants	4.4	4.5	5.5
Private unfurnished	5.7	8.4	11.2
Private furnished	4.3	5.9	12.8

Source: Hedges *et al.* (1974).

that presumably acts as a constraint on mobility. Nevertheless, private rental remains the tenure with the greatest ease of access, and its decline may play a part in hindering people from moving, at least unless or until public housing can play a more positive role.

At present, although moves into and between council houses are almost as common as moves into and between owner-occupied homes, the regulations governing entry to council homes favour moves within the same local authority area rather than true geographical mobility. For instance, council housing accounts for 26 per cent of all tenures in London and receives 35 per cent of all the movers within London, but it receives only 11 per cent of migrants into London and is the source of only 13 per cent of migrations out of London (Office of Population Censuses and Surveys, 1975 and Central Statistical Office, 1974). On the other hand, council lettings, which are controlled by local government and subject to influences by central government, could be made more freely available to migrant workers if public policy were directed to that end. This could be either through a general relaxation of the rules or through an energetic effort to attract workers to particular towns. New towns are of course an existing example of the latter policy; and if the comparative reluctance of manual workers to move home in order to get a better job indicates a relative home orientation, perhaps they could be encouraged to change jobs in order to get a better home.

This is not intended to suggest that there should be a mindless rush to move relatively 'strong' workers out of declining areas, leaving only the weak behind. Moving jobs into such areas may be a more important aim of policy than moving people out. Nevertheless, there will be many cases where a move for the worker may be best for all parties, and in these cases there could be a policy to make a move easier.

Table 10.13 Variations by age and occupation in the fortunes of the redundant (%)

| | By age at time of interview | | | | | By occupational status | |
	Up to 25	25-35	36-45	46-55	56-65	Non-manual	Manual
Had not found a new job before dismissal took effect	43	52	56	56	74	41	65
Increase (+) or decrease (−) in real earnings	+15	−1	−9	−13	−29	−4	−14

Source: Daniel (1972).

10.7 Conclusions

The theme of this chapter has been that geographical imbalances in the employment of manual workers are a function of industrial change occurring faster than the individual workers can comfortably adjust to it. Although a worker may originally have chosen the right occupation in the right place, by the time he reaches middle age change has overtaken him. If he were free to choose again, he would take a different occupation in a different place, but by this time the choice is no longer open to him. About the only advantage remaining to him is his long-term job security, but in extreme cases redundancy deprives him even of that. These points are well illustrated by the Political and Economic Planning (PEP) study of the effects on workers of the series of major redundancies that occurred in south-east inner London in the late 1960s (Daniel, 1972).

Perhaps the most telling finding concerned the age of these redundant workers; 60 per cent were 45 or older on dismissal compared with 39 per cent of all male workers. At the same time 82 per cent had been in manual occupations compared with 69 per cent of all male workers. Clearly, the middle-aged manual worker is most likely to be affected. He is also likely to be the most seriously affected. Table 10.13 shows how the middle-aged worker was most likely to have a period out of work following redundancy and most likely to suffer a relative drop in earnings; manual workers also tended to suffer on both of these counts.

In conclusion, the evidence suggests that, although nothing can persuade the middle-aged manual worker to learn to love industrial change, a more active labour-market policy could at least mitigate its worst social consequences.

11 Labour Migration, Housing, and the Labour Market

John Salt

11.1 Introduction[1]

One of the key processes in the adjustment of supply and demand in the labour market is labour mobility. Often, this refers to a simple change of job between occupations or local employers without any change of residence, but it also includes migration in a geographical sense, i.e. movement that involves a simultaneous change of both job and home. Labour migration of this kind results in the relatively long-distance relocation of skills and thus has an important bearing on regional contrasts in economic change. It involves a move from one community to another, making an important impact on the social life of the families and communities involved. Finally, it is likely that the pressures encouraging labour migration will become increasingly strong in the future as current social and technological changes foster greater mobility in the workforce.

A large amount of interurban migration goes on in Britain (Harris and Clausen, 1967; Johnson, Salt, and Wood, 1974). This is characteristic of a modern industrial economy where technological and ensuing industrial change necessitate the redistribution of labour, both occupationally and geographically, in accordance with changes in demand. During the last half-century, for example, the older industrial areas on the coalfields of the north and west have declined economically while expansion has occurred in the towns of

[1]This chapter is based on joint research carried out by J.H. Johnson, J. Salt, and P.A. Wood.

253

the Midlands and south England. Hence, there has been a regional shift in the demand for labour not matched by a parallel shift in supply (Eversley, 1971). This regional economic imbalance by no means provides a full explanation for labour migration. Over the last twenty years fundamental changes have taken place in urban trends in population and employment. Decentralisation, first of population and then of employment, has taken place. Most often this has been a suburban movement; but frequently, as in movement from urban core to outer ring, the distances moved have been great enough to necessitate labour migration (Department of the Environment, 1976). Increasingly also, the organisation of modern labour markets leads to increased mobility between them. For some occupational groups migration between similar types of urban centre has become normal and expected behaviour and is not a response to spatial economic imbalance (Wood, 1976).

Labour migration may thus be viewed in several ways. A worker may be attracted to another labour market by a vacancy there, offering perhaps the prospect of promotion; such moves may be to another branch of the same firm. Alternatively, the move may be for other reasons, such as an improved social life, with employment considerations secondary. Labour migration may also be looked upon as a means of escape from actual or threatened unemployment. It is in this last sense that government policy towards labour migration has developed.

In discussions of labour migration housing is frequently assumed to act as one of the most important barriers to movement; but the actual relationship between housing and labour migration is far from clear, and the evidence is conflicting (Cullingworth, 1969). At first sight 'housing shortage' seems to be the key variable, but there is no satisfactory way of measuring shortage, partly because there is no commonly held view of what constitutes an acceptable standard of housing provision. This difficulty is also the result of various physical and social policies that distort the housing market, making it impossible to assess the real demand. Attempts to measure surpluses and shortages of housing by comparing the number of households and number of dwellings recorded in the Census of Population oversimplify the very complex situation that exists in reality, with the national housing market being divided up into a series of spatial submarkets. These local housing markets include different types of accommodation, and problems often arise from the distribution of households within the available dwelling stock. For example, it has been shown that within the London housing market in 1971 there were enough dwellings to allow a reasonable density of occupancy, but mismatches occurred between household incomes and dwelling costs (Greater London Council, 1974). Such imbalances may help to explain how an analysis of migration rates and dwelling stock change for London boroughs between 1961 and 1971 showed a lower level of correlation (goodness of fit 0.71) than might have been expected (Gilje, 1975).

Any change of home poses problems for the household, and as the distance of move increases the problems are compounded. The basic difficulties may be summarised in terms of finance, information, and time. Access to finance is crucial in purchasing property. Heavy expense can be involved in searching and negotiating for new accommodation, paying legal fees, and moving to a larger property, which may be in a more expensive housing market. The extent to which such costs are recoverable, either through assistance in paying moving expenses or through higher income after the move, will strongly influence the migration decision. If the financial costs are not recoverable, other perceived benefits will need to be correspondingly high. The importance of information availability is hard to measure, especially as there are two variables to consider: the amount of information a migrant has, and the way in which he assesses it. Most people know a fair amount about their local area and, with exceptions, less about areas further away. Ignorance of housing conditions in other labour markets not only restricts the area of search but also influences the potential migrant's perception of possible destinations. The information sources used are also important, e.g. whether or not reliance is placed on formal or informal channels. The time that a potential labour migrant has available largely determines the information that he is able to receive and use. Does the move have to be made in a hurry? How much time can be allowed off work to search for housing? Clearly, migrants wishing to move greater distances may often find more timing problems than those whose moves are local.

When long distance moves between the broader regions of the country are distinguished from local intraurban moves, the discussion of the relationship between housing and labour migration frequently centres on tenure. There is some evidence that home ownership facilitates inter-regional migration, while the inhabitants of local authority houses experience a low level of inter-regional movement, and that those in privately rented accommodation are more commonly involved in short distance moves (Cullingworth, 1965; Pennance and Gray, 1968). Nevertheless, it is clear that the actual situation is much more complicated than can be explained by a simple correlation of mobility with any one factor. Housing is a complex phenomenon when regional differences in the housing market, the preferences of various social classes, and their differential accessibility to housing finance are all considered. Movements of population are equally complex when they are disaggregated to reveal the different socioeconomic and demographic attributes of the people involved, the distances moved, and the varying characteristics of origin and destination areas.

Unlike most contributions to this book, this chapter does not focus specifically on employment in the inner city. It seeks instead to examine a relationship – between labour migration and housing – that bears directly on the employment problems of all labour markets, including that of the inner city. Although there have been a number of empirical studies of migrants in Britain (e.g. Donnison, 1964; Cullingworth, 1965; Woolf, 1967; Harris and Clausen, 1967), attention has not been focused specifically on the problems faced by those moving long distances (labour migrants) until recently (Johnson, Salt, and Wood, 1974). This chapter draws upon the empirical evidence for labour migration and housing collected by the Housing and Labour Mobility Study.[2] Surveys were conducted in 1972 of 551 labour migrants into four labour markets in England (High Wycombe, Chatham, Northampton, and Huddersfield), chosen for their contrasting employment, migration, and housing conditions. The aim here is to use these data to examine the relationship between labour migration and the housing market for different types of labour migrants and to suggest some of the main implications of the findings for the development of housing and migration policies.

11.2 Employment of labour migrants

A substantial minority of labour migrants in the sample (28 per cent) were moved by their firm and were cushioned from the

[2]A joint research study carried out at the Department of Geography, University College London, in 1970–74 and largely financed by the Joseph Rowntree Memorial Trust.

problems of moving by financial help, advice, and information by the employer. However, 66 per cent moved to a new employer. Hence, not only did the move of home and job require a search for new accommodation by all migrants, but for nearly seven out of ten it also implied a search for new employment. For those changing employer the area of search was surprisingly limited. Just over 50 per cent of them only searched for a job in the area to which they moved; 17 per cent looked in both the old and the new area; and a further 18 per cent restricted their search to the new area and to two others. In general the higher income and socioeconomic groups (SEGs) had a wider area of search than others. This restricted search area must be put alongside the reasons for choosing a particular area. Only 18 per cent indicated that their ability to find a house controlled their choice of area, although the proportion ranged from 25 per cent in Chatham, through 19 per cent in Northampton and 16 per cent in High Wycombe, to 12 per cent in Huddersfield. In contrast, 50 per cent of those labour migrants who changed employer claimed that reasons connected with employment guided their choice of area in which to buy or rent the new home. This factor was most marked among migrants who went to High Wycombe and Huddersfield (56 per cent).

Labour migrants who stayed with the same employer also had, of course, some choice in the move. About one-third asked to be transferred; for four in ten of the rest the move implied promotion or better prospects. In 23 per cent of cases the employer had a vacancy that it required the mover to fill, while 14 per cent moved when the whole office was transferred. It should be noted, however, that in the total picture of labour migration promotion with the same organisation was relatively unimportant, applying to only 8 per cent of the total number of labour migrants.

Among the labour migrants the unemployed were conspicuously absent. Only 3 per cent had been out of work before moving, although a further 8 per cent had not previously been employed (mostly students). Virtually all labour migrants were in full time employment following the move; less than 2 per cent were unemployed. Although other moves may have been made in response to redundancy threat, these results suggest that unemployment is not directly a major determinant of labour migration despite the frequent use of unemployment rates in forecasting inter-regional migration.

11.3 Socio-economic group, income, and motivation

Most studies of long distance migration show marked differences
between socioeconomic groups in the propensity to migrate (e.g. for
the United States, Tarver, 1964, and Ladinsky, 1967; for Britain,
Friedlander and Roshier, 1967) – a pattern confirmed by the Housing and Labour Mobility Study. More labour migrants were in the
higher socioeconomic groups, though there were marked disparities
between the different labour market areas (Johnson, Salt, and
Wood, 1974, p. 158). For example, the proportion of managerial
and professional workers was 54 per cent at High Wycombe but
only 27 per cent at Chatham. Conversely, the proportion of labour
migrants who were manual workers was 12 per cent in High
Wycombe, while Chatham had 27 per cent.

It seems reasonable to suppose that those with high incomes
would be better able to surmount barriers to migration. British
evidence tends to support this supposition (Willis, 1968; Woolf,
1967; Cullingworth, 1965) in contrast to some American studies
(Lansing and Morgan, 1967; Bogue, 1959) that found an inverse
relation between income and labour migration. The results of the
Housing and Labour Mobility Study confirmed earlier British findings, although there was considerable variation in the average
income of labour migrants between the four areas. In general also,
labour migrants tended to improve their income upon moving; 22
per cent of the migrants specifically mentioned improved income as
the main benefit from moving, and a further 18 per cent mentioned
other job-associated benefits. However, it is interesting to note that
labour migration did not lead to higher income for all migrants,
especially where career betterment was not the main reason for
undertaking the move. In other words, a substantial minority of
labour migrants were moving for reasons not primarily of employment and were not experiencing gains in income either.

Reasons connected with employment were the single most
important set, although their significance varied between the four
areas (Johnson, Salt, and Wood, 1974, p. 206). About half of the
sample moved specifically for job reasons (including setting up
businesses). The next most important category may be referred to as
'home town' reasons (13 per cent) including migrants who moved
back to an area lived in previously or who were attracted to an area
by the presence there of friends or relatives. Housing reasons were
given by 11 per cent of the sample, and 10 per cent mentioned

convenience for travelling – usually the journey to work. Others (7 per cent) claimed that they liked the area, and 6 per cent moved for personal reasons. These proportions are of interest in themselves because of the paucity of such information on labour migrants, as distinct from all migrants, to whom housing reasons associated with the lifecyle are more important (Cullingworth, 1965; Donnison, 1964; Harris and Clausen, 1967). However, the combined analysis of reasons for migration and of the characteristics of migrants provides more perceptive insights into the labour migration process.

It is of particular interest to compare those who were primarily motivated by employment with those who moved for other reasons. There is no evidence that job-motivated migrants implied any special need to move away from poor economic circumstances; in fact, rather the contrary seems to be true since most job-motivated migrants enjoyed higher incomes than average before moving. Conversely the migrants who were not primarily job motivated included a larger proportion than average of low-income labour migrants. An exception was the group, mostly moving to High Wycombe and Chatham, who moved for journey-to-work improvements; they tended to have higher incomes. Many of those whose chief motivation was a return to a former area of residence – Huddersfield was a frequent destination for this type of move – were among the less well off, while housing reasons were the main motivation for medium income households. Perhaps of greater significance for the study of labour migration are the contrasting results of the moves on incomes. Job-motivated movers improved their incomes more markedly than others, whereas there was little overall improvement in the incomes of those moving for non-job-motivated reasons.

The evidence for a significant improvement in income and status for job-motivated movers was further strengthened when the socioeconomic structure of the sample before migration was examined in relation to reasons for moving. A dichotomy emerged between SEGs 1–5 (employers, managers, professional workers, and intermediate non-manual workers) and the others. The higher-status occupational groups were more likely than average to move for reasons of job improvement (they made up 55 per cent of job-motivated movers compared with 47 per cent of the whole sample). On the other hand, manual workers and other workers together included a much lower proportion of job-motivated movers than expected from their share of the sample (14 per cent compared with 23 per cent). After movement the predominance of SEGs 1–5 had increased among the job-motivated movers (72 per cent compared with the sample proportion of 59 per cent), and a much smaller proportion remained in SEGs 6–9 (junior non-manual and skilled manual). In contrast, the proportions of SEGs 6–11 (junior non-manual and all manual) grew markedly as a result of labour migration among those moving primarily for non-employment reasons. Although the proportion of the sample in SEGs 6–11 was only 36 per cent after the moves it was 66 per cent of the home-town-motivated movers and no less than 77 per cent of the housing-motivated movers.

Thus, in terms of both income and SEGs, labour migration for job reasons was a very positive agent of upward mobility for managerial, professional, and intermediate non-manual groups. These people tended to be job motivated, to have a high income and social status before moving, and to improve their position with the move. In comparison, those who moved for other reasons (mostly junior non-manual and manual workers) appeared to achieve little improvement in income or socioeconomic status. Labour migration thus seems to have had the effect of polarising the socioeconomic structures of the differently motivated groups still further. A large number of migrants in the sample underwent the upheaval of changing the location of their homes and jobs – their whole physical and social environment – for reasons unconnected with financial or occupational reward. Some of these, especially in south-east England, were prosperous professional and managerial families moving to reduce the daily journey to work, but many more were lower-paid manual workers who gave a variety of personal, social, and housing reasons in explanation of their moves. This form of working-class labour mobility, allowing households to adjust their location to meet social and housing rather than economic needs, represents a significant aspect of labour migration to be contrasted with the movement of professional and managerial workers, who dominate the national pattern. It may help to explain the migration of manual and lower-paid white-collar workers from areas of housing and employment stress, such as parts of the inner city.

11.4 Housing tenure

The sample results confirmed the different propensities of people in different tenure categories to become labour migrants. Owner-occupiers purchasing their dwellings and private rented furnished tenants were more mobile than average, while private rented unfurnished and local authority tenants were very much less mobile. The rent-free sector was also associated with a higher degree of mobility. However, again there were marked differences between the four areas for all tenure categories; council housing was obviously easier to obtain at Huddersfield than elsewhere and particularly difficult at High Wycombe. Private renting was more important at Northampton and rent-free accommodation more common at Chatham (Table 11.1).

In contrast to some other studies (e.g. Woolf, 1967), which indicate that most migrants remain within the same tenure group, over half of the labour migrants (54 per cent) changed tenure, the figures ranging from 60 per cent in Northampton to 49 per cent at High Wycombe (Table 11.2). Most of those who did not change were owner-occupiers, it being less common for those who had been renting to transfer to accommodation within the same tenure. Only one-third of those who had been local authority tenants were still local authority tenants after the move. Of those who had been renting private unfurnished accommodation, over half became owner-occupiers and only one in seven did not change his tenure. Tenants of private rented furnished accommodation were also likely to become owner-occupiers although a quarter of this group did remain in the same tenure. Of households living in tied accommodation over a half changed tenure, especially to owner-occupation. These results, indicating differences in tenure distribution between labour migrants and the rest of the population, including short distance migrants, complement those of the National Movers Survey reported in Gilje (1975). This showed that among migrants leaving London (and therefore probably labour migrants) the largest group was of owner-occupiers, with few migrants in or out being local authority tenants.

11.5 Motivation and housing

A major aspect of the housing changes resulting from labour migration was the increased cost of housing. In general, before migration there was no significant difference in expenditure on housing between job-motivated movers and the rest of the sample. After moving, expenditure on housing by all migrants increased sharply, especially for the job-motivated; thus, to offset their higher earnings after migration the job-motivated spent more on housing. The

Table 11.1 Tenure of labour migrant households after moving

Tenure	Chatham		High Wycombe		Huddersfield		Northampton		Total	
	(no.)	(%)	(no.)	(%)	(no.)	(%)	(no.)	(%)	(no.)	(%)
Owner-occupier with mortgage	61	48.4	102	57.3	47	61.8	93	54.4	303	55.0
Owner-occupier without mortgage	6	4.8	9	5.1	3	3.9	7	4.1	25	4.5
Local authority tenant	9	7.1	2	1.1	9	11.8	5	2.9	25	4.5
Rents privately furnished	18	14.3	20	11.2	4	5.3	28	16.4	70	12.7
Rents privately unfurnished	6	4.8	8	4.5	6	7.9	18	10.5	38	6.9
Rent-free, with parents, in-laws, housekeeper	16	12.7	14	7.9	4	5.3	7	4.1	41	7.4
Tied cottage, goes with the job, etc.	6	4.8	18	10.1	1	1.3	9	5.3	34	6.2
Lodger	4	3.2	5	2.8	2	2.6	4	2.3	15	2.7
Total	126	100.0[a]	178	100.0	76	100.0[a]	171	100.0	551	100.0[a]

[a] Rounded.
Source: Own Survey.

Table 11.2 Tenure change upon moving (%)

Effect of move on tenure	Chatham	High Wycombe	Northampton	Huddersfield	All areas
Kept same tenure	42.4	50.5	40.3	49.6	45.7
Became owner-occupier	30.1	19.6	26.9	26.4	24.8
Became local authority tenant	0.8	0.6	1.2	7.7	2.2
Became private rented furnished tenant	11.8	8.4	11.7	1.2	8.9
Became private rented unfurnished tenant	4.6	4.5	8.2	6.4	5.6
Became rent-free tenant	7.1	6.2	4.1	5.0	5.8
Took tied accommodation	0.8	5.0	2.3	1.2	2.3
Became lodger	2.4	1.1	1.7	2.5	1.8
No information	—	4.1	3.6	—	2.9
Total	100.0	100.0	100.0	100.0	100.0

Source: Own survey.

housing costs of the groups moving for reasons other than employment displayed marked contrasts. Before moving both home-town movers and those who moved for housing reasons had low housing costs; after moving the former group retained their share of low cost accommodation (probably because many were staying with relatives), but the latter group increased their outlay on housing. Those moving for improvements in journey to work tended to pay more for their housing. When new housing cost was examined as a proportion of income, it was seen that job- and journey-to-work-motivated migrants had only marginal increases in the proportion spent on housing, while those who moved for housing reasons, and who tended to be in lower socioeconomic and income groups, found the heaviest burden of actual housing costs as a result of labour migration.

In general three groups of labour migrants may be identified from their housing experiences. The first group consists of those, especially in higher social status and income groups, who moved for employment reasons. Their search for accommodation followed an earlier decision to change job and took place in the context of rising income, so that many could afford a more expensive house. In the second group were those for whom the search for better housing was a prime reason for moving. Many of these people were employed in fairly generally available occupations, especially in manual and lower-paid non-manual jobs. They tended to be worse off financially after moving, paying a higher proportion of their incomes for accommodation. Thus, for them migration imposed economic costs that either had to be recovered in other ways, perhaps by the wife going out to work, or could be offset by other benefits, such as an improvement in social life. A third group gave priority to improvements in general living environment, but the primary motivation varied. They included both low-paid workers, many returning to a home town, and those who were better off and sought improved travelling conditions. The common element in this group is that the acquisition of job and accommodation were by-products of other decisions to move. Consequently, attitudes to the search for accommodation are heavily influenced by income and status before moving, the move itself bringing comparatively little change in material circumstances.

11.6 Consequences of moving

In the sense that all labour migrants found somewhere to live the search for accommodation could be regarded as successful. However, degrees of satisfaction with the new housing varied. About six in ten of migrants felt that the housing that they occupied after migration was similar to what they had had in mind when they decided to move, and hopes were more often fulfilled by the acquisition of self-contained property and by owner-occupation than other tenures. The failure of rented accommodation to provide what was envisaged was especially marked in private rented furnished property, indicating the significance of this sector as fallback accommodation for some migrants. Both small and large households found their requirements difficult to fulfil, and low to middle income groups were less satisfied. The latter were also more constrained in their choice, more often having to accept what was available. Housing gains were seen as the most important gains from moving by those moving into owner-occupation. Those moving to private rented accommodation most frequently failed to see any general improvement in their lifestyles as a result of moving. Those moving to local authority, rent-free, and tied accommodation regarded income improvement as a more important benefit than housing. The benefits of migration may be related to socioeconomic group. Employment improvements (including those of income) were most noticed by professional and senior non-manual groups. Manual and junior non-manual groups appeared to gain most in housing and in their social life.

11.7 Housing problems during the move

About one-third of the sample experienced no difficulties in moving. Of those with difficulties, housing was the most important reason, with 45 per cent of the sample mentioning various types of housing problem. Among housing difficulties the main group of problems arose from the need to acquire temporary accommodation during the course of the move to the new area. It was sought by 65 per cent of the migrant sample, most commonly for a period of one to three months, but with 20 per cent of the labour migrants staying in such accommodation for over three months. Longest periods were spent in temporary accommodation by the highest and lowest income groups; the former mainly used hotels, boarding houses, flats, or houses, while the latter tended to rely on friends and relatives, hostels, or caravans.

Overcoming the problems of moving was linked to assistance provided for migrants, usually by the new employer (85 per cent were so aided). The higher socioeconomic groups with higher incomes received most assistance in covering the cost of moving.

Frequently this included help in finding and paying for temporary accommodation, e.g. in a hotel, while owner-occupied property was being sought. In contrast, lower-paid workers received assistance less frequently (only a quarter of skilled manual and a third of unskilled and semiskilled workers received help), were more reliant on their own savings, and were forced into cheaper and less conventional types of temporary accommodation. Overall, the biggest subsidies to labour migration, both financial and otherwise, went to the higher income and social groups, while those who were most in need of assistance were more often forced back entirely on their own resources.

11.8 Policy implications and further study

This review of some of the salient aspects of labour migration and its relationship to housing raises several issues. First is the need to develop housing and migration policies that are more compatible than exist at present. Particular attention should be paid to the need to facilitate moves between council houses in different parts of the country and to the importance of private rented accommodation in aiding migration, provided that it is available on a short term basis.

Over the years government involvement in the housing market has steadily increased. A significant result of this has been to restrict entry by labour migrants into the rented sector. This has worked in two principal ways. First, many local authorities already have long waiting lists for housing, and the priority given to those displaced by slum clearance and redevelopment means that waiting lists fall only slowly, if at all. For example, in Greater London in 1972 the waiting list was 190,000 but only 48 per cent of council house allocations that year went to waiting list cases; in inner London the figure was only 40 per cent (Greater London Council, 1974). Because of this pressure local authorities have adopted residence qualifications for the allocation of council houses, which include the need for households to have lived in the local authority area for a set period – in some cases five years or more. Migrants from other areas are thus, by definition, frequently barred from council housing in their chosen destination area. Second, rent controls on private rented unfurnished housing have probably encouraged many tenants to sit tight, thus lowering turnover and hence the access of migrants to this rented accommodation. The Housing Act 1974 gave security for the first time to tenants in the private rented furnished sector – an important source of accommodation for labour migrants. The result has been to reduce the availability of such accommodation, repeating the pattern for the private rented unfurnished sector and erecting a further housing barrier to labour migration. Thus, it is in those sectors of the housing market where government has taken most control, and which provide cheap accommodation, that there is most restriction on entry for migrants. Yet, at the same time these are the sectors that are most likely to provide for those workers (the lower paid and unemployed) at whom the government's migration policies, operating through the Employment Transfer and Job Search Schemes, are aimed.

This contradiction, as well as the lack of government commitment to a migration policy (the cost of the policy is only about £12 million per annum), means that the pattern of labour migration that exists is very much the result of *laissez-faire* policy and has to find its own adjustments to the constraints imposed by housing. If the government is seriously to consider providing more assistance to migrants as part of an attempt to 'manage' the balance of supply and demand in high unemployment areas, which include some parts of the inner city, there needs to be a change of emphasis in its housing policies, so that the special cases of low income migrants are allowed for. This would involve the frequently-called-for abolition of length-of-residence qualifications for council housing (Ministry of Housing and Local Government, 1969; Burn, 1972). A better means of information exchange in the council sector is required. A central clearing house for information on council house exchange would cost comparatively little but fill a yawning information gap. Ideally, local authorities ought also to provide a stock of accommodation specifically for allocation to migrants, part of which could be short term to satisfy the need for temporary accommodation.

Policies also need to be considered in the light of local conditions. A preliminary study of the four labour markets (Hadjifotiou and Robinson, 1972), and the survey results, showed a wide range of local experience, and some labour markets are clearly easier to move to than others. Hence, in the formulation of policy it is important to bear in mind the degree of spatial variation in housing and labour market conditions and to develop sets of policies sensitively related to them. For example, migrants going to some places will be in need of more assistance than if they went elsewhere. Where there are job vacancies but housing is expensive, provision could be made for easier mortages for lower-paid migrants. These mortgages could be from local authorities or from building societies with security provided by national or local government or through some insurance scheme. In areas where private rented stock is small and under severe pressure, greater flexibility in the allocation of council housing to migrants would facilitate movement.

Finally, two groups may be isolated for further study. First, more sociological information is required on the willingness to move among a wide variety of potential movers as a prerequisite for the development of suitable policies. A weakness of most migration studies is that they have focused on those who successfully moved, and usually there are few data on those who failed to surmount barriers such as housing. For example, how many people really are trapped in inner city areas and wish to leave? Second, a substantial minority of labour migrants had low-middle incomes and moved either to cheap owner-occupied housing or to rented property. For many of them migration brought no financial or occupational reward. In no sense were they 'spiralists' like many of the professional and managerial groups whose migration is much better understood; nor were they immobile like many low-paid and low-skilled workers. There is a need to examine more closely their patterns of behaviour, their experiences in moving, and the manner in which subsidies and information flows affect their propensities to migrate.

IV The Inner Area Studies

12 Employment Problems in Lambeth

Glen Bramley

12.1 The Lambeth Inner Area Study

This chapter is an attempt to summarise the findings of the Lambeth Inner Area Study (IAS) on a range of employment issues with the benefit of hindsight and in the light of other work. In the available space full justice cannot be done to all the relevant work lying behind the conclusions reached; so, the interested reader may wish to refer also to the Lambeth IAS final report (Shankland, Willmott, and Jordan, 1977) and indeed to the more detailed working papers (Lambeth Inner Area Study, 1975a, and 1977a). Detailed references to these documents are omitted.

The Lambeth IAS was a multidisciplinary project intended to address the whole range of inner city problems through both research and action focused on a particular area. It was one of three such studies commissioned by the Department of Environment but undertaken by consultants in co-operation with the local authorities. The author was a member of the study team set up by the Shankland Cox Partnership with the Institute of Community Studies between 1973 and 1976 and was responsible for most of the work on employment and related issues referred to below. The Lambeth IAS was based on a study area of 50,000 population in the central part of the London Borough of Lambeth, comprising Stockwell and parts of Brixton, Clapham, and Vauxhall, but of necessity the work on employment encompassed much wider areas. A variety of types of evidence were generated, and of particular

271

relevance were the 1973 household survey in the study area, 1971 and earlier census data, Department of Employment records, and an interview survey of forty larger private-sector employers in inner-south London in 1975.

12.2 Some major issues

The economic or employment problems of inner London have been and remain a controversial topic, although with more information and analysis the debate has shifted somewhat from an earlier concern with the factual delineation of problems to a greater concern with causality, with policy implications, and with implementation. Six main issues that have been or are subject to debate may be briefly sketched out:

1. *Is there a problem?*   Are inner London residents relatively disadvantaged in terms of unemployment rates and in terms of earnings or incomes? Because of difficulties with the data for sub-areas of London, the answer to this question was less clearcut in the early 1970s than it is now; but as section 12.3 shows, some fairly clear conclusions can be drawn in Lambeth.

2. *Are employment problems central?*   The 'inner city problem' is widely believed to be primarily a result of economic decline, and the government's policy response appears to accept this (Department of the Environment, 1977b). This issue begs questions beyond the scope of this chapter. One example is the role of unemployment, underemployment, job instability, and low pay in accounting for poverty and multiple deprivation. While section 12.8 touches on this, other Lambeth IAS reports (Shankland, Willmott, and Jordan, 1977; Lambeth Inner Area Study, 1975b, 1977b) analyse the extent, incidence, causes, and correlates of multiple deprivation more fully. Other questions that are worthy of mention but not resolved here include the impact of employment problems on housing conditions, on private sector services, on the rate base and public services, and on migration and population structure.

3. *Why is unemployment high in the inner area?*   Explanations of unemployment are complex, and there is a distinction between explanations at the individual and at the area level. The essential debate in London is about unemployment propensities being a function of 'where you are' as well as, or rather than, 'who you are'.

One school of thought stresses personal characteristics such as age, skill, colour, family situation, and other less measurable individual attributes (see section 12.5) and argues that spatial concentrations of unemployment reflect concentrations of people with certain characteristics, which in turn reflect the impact of the housing system on residential location patterns (Metcalf and Richardson, Chapter 8; Evans with Russell, Chapter 9). This view implies that London is spatially a single labour market, although it may be linked to non-spatial concepts of segmentation, particularly the dual labour market thesis (Bosanquet and Doeringer, 1973). The other school argues that labour markets in London are localised (see section 12.4), that employment decline has led to deficient demand in some local areas (Shankland, Willmott, and Jordan, 1977; Lomas, 1974; Eversley, 1973), causing higher unemployment (section 12.6), and that higher demand for labour can overcome individual disadvantages (Hill *et al.*, 1973). Changes in labour demand patterns may also be invoked by explanations that stress the occupational segmentation of the labour market, whether or not localised, and that perhaps point more towards manpower policies. There is also debate about whether the decline of manufacturing jobs plays a crucial role (Metcalf and Richardson, Chapter 8 of this book; Eversley, 1973) or whether it is service industry decline or perhaps shifts between occupations within industrial sectors.

4. *Why are earnings low in the inner area?* As will be shown in section 12.8, there is a crucial distinction between earnings classified by workplace as opposed to residence. This emphasises the relationship between the housing market, residential location, and incomes in the inner city (section 12.7). Also of interest is what bearing the structure of employment, particularly in terms of industry, and changes in this over time have on earnings. Finally, the implicit assumption that low income is another side of the same problem as unemployment needs to be questioned, through considering whether earnings are sensitive to demand and supply conditions in the local labour market (Mackay *et al.*, 1971).

5. *Why is employment declining in inner London?* Despite the greater volume of evidence that is now available there remains uncertainty and dispute about the reasons for the large job losses from inner London in manufacturing and other sectors. Yet, understanding here seems to be crucial to the prospects for a policy of regeneration. Three general types of reason suggest themselves. First, the structure of London's industry either at the sectoral or at

the micro (plant) level may be such, given national economic trends and pressures, as to make decline inevitable. Second, inner London may well be a very poor location for industry, old or new. Third, regional and local planning policies may have had a cumulatively serious effect on industry in London. In section 12.10 the evidence on this issue, particularly from inner-south London, will be examined.

   6. *What are the prospects for a policy of economic regeneration?* Clearly, this issue follows closely on the previous one, but it also returns to all the issues raised previously. It may well be argued that industrial regeneration in inner London should not be the only or even the main plank of policies designed to correct problems of unemployment, low income, bad housing and environmental conditions, and all the other ills of areas like Lambeth. There is still scope for challenging the view that London should retain such a large population and workforce rather than seek to achieve a better balance within a smaller total (Shankland, Willmott, and Jordan, 1977). Furthermore, there are serious questions to be asked about the feasibility of industrial regeneration and appropriate policy instruments to bring it about (Lambeth Inner Area Study, 1977a; Foreman-Peck and Gripaios, 1977). It will be argued in section 12.11 that housing, manpower, and education policies are as important as industrial and land policies.

12.3 Unemployment and incomes in Lambeth

With more information becoming available at the small area level there is less scope for debate about the existence of concentrations of unemployment and low incomes in areas like Lambeth. This section will therefore confine itself to a brief summary of the evidence, bearing in mind the sensitivity of particular figures to the area definitions used (e.g. employment exchange areas as against boroughs) and the sources and definitions of indicators.

   The study found that male unemployment rates were somewhat higher in Lambeth than in the country as a whole and markedly higher than in London and the South-East (Greater London Council, 1975). While the Brixton area stood out to some extent, this was part of a general pattern of unemployment, which was higher in inner than in outer London (5 per cent compared with 2.7 per cent in 1971). Also, male unemployment appeared to have worsened between 1966 and 1975 in relative as well as absolute terms, although national cyclical fluctuations were replicated locally, with the result that the 1973 household survey picked up a rather low rate. Female unemployment rates appeared to be lower in relative as well as absolute terms. Other evidence reinforced the view that the main problem was with jobs for men, and in particular there was found to be a very high participation rate among married women. Within age bands, the activity rates for this group for Stockwell were 3–12 percentage points higher than those for Greater London and 7–20 points above those for Great Britain. Among males unemployment was particularly high in the younger age groups, due both to higher registration rates and to longer durations on the register, but it was less of a problem in the older age group (Greater London Council, 1975). In part this reflected the concentration in Lambeth of young West Indians with abnormally high unemployment rates (Community Relations Commission, 1974), although the household survey evidence on unemployment by colour was less clearcut.

The main conclusion from the 1973 survey data on incomes was that the earnings of study-area resident males were low, the median being 17 per cent below the national level, while double the national proportion were low-paid (i.e. less than £24 per week). Women in Lambeth were better off relative to national averages, but despite this and the high activity rates household incomes were about 12 per cent below the national average. The evidence for males was consistent with a Department of Health and Social Security sample survey of earnings for sectors of London, which showed markedly lower earnings in most of the inner sectors (Simon, 1977).

12.4 Geographical definition of the labour market

Part of the reason for the 'who you are' versus 'where you are' debate, referred to earlier, lies in the difficulty of defining the labour market spatially within the larger conurbations. The job market that is relevant to Lambeth residents is that part of London to which they can reasonably travel, which of course varies greatly for individuals depending on their income, car ownership, time constraints (e.g. shift workers travelling at unsocial hours, or women with children needing local part-time work), and other factors. However, the typical Lambeth worker, lacking a car and with lower-than-average potential earnings, is confined to a zone that is much smaller than London as a whole – probably the inner-south sector plus the central area. This conclusion emerged from a mapping of public transport accessibility from Stockwell in terms of time and cost contours and was confirmed by the pattern of actual work journeys (Lambeth Inner Area Study, 1975a). In 1966, 44 per cent of Stockwell workers had jobs in inner-south London; the proportion was raised to 87 per cent including central London. Work journeys appeared to be lengthening by 1973 with more dependence on the central area, especially among women, while journeys beyond this zone were mainly by higher-paid men. In an interesting analysis of London travel to work, Berthoud (Chapter 10) has elaborated on the disadvantages of lower-paid and manual workers, particularly those without a car, in reaching jobs, especially in non-radial directions.

So, it can be strongly argued that London is not a single labour-market area, although clearly local markets overlap. In particular the central area draws workers from the entire region and not just one radial segment. It was also interesting to discover from employers in south London that many of their workers – notably managerial, professional, and technical staff but also many skilled men – travelled in from the suburbs. However, in so far as there is particular concern over the less skilled and mobile inner-area residents' job chances, it seems fair to stress the localised nature of their market. Journey-to-work considerations are probably reinforced by time and cost constraints on job search and by the key role of 'informal' sources of information on job openings,[1] which are by their very nature localised.

12.5 Characteristics of the workforce

To understand the nature and the causes of employment problems in a particular area it is important to know the composition of the workforce in terms of a variety of characteristics (e.g. age, skill, and colour) and to examine the association between these characteristics and people's experience of employment difficulties. This sec-

[1] See the General Household Survey, 1974 (Office of Population Censuses and Surveys, tables 3.20–3.22); Daniel's study of the unemployed (1974); Dunnell and Head's study of employers' recruitment preferences and practices (1975); and such American studies as Rees and Shultz (1970) and Rees (1966).

tion focuses particularly on factors associated with unemployment, low pay being discussed in section 12.8.

Age has already been touched on, where it was pointed out that unemployment in Lambeth was particularly concentrated in the younger male group. This reflected a growing national problem since 1967, documented elsewhere (Mukerjee, 1974; Manpower Services Commission, 1977), but was more acute in this area and not apparently a function of the age structure of the workforce. Three reasons may be suggested for this phenomenon: labour demand, racial disadvantage, and education/vocational preparation. To an extent that is probably increasing, due to union pressure and national legislation, existing jobs are protected, so that the declining labour demand in this area (see section 12.6) took the form of wastage and non-recruitment (confirmed by most employers interviewed). This was at the expense of new entrants to the labour force and of those who changed jobs frequently – groups largely comprised of young people. Many young workers in Lambeth are black and suffer from multiple disadvantages, chronicled elsewhere (Community Relations Commission, 1974), including not only discrimination but also language and literacy problems, the lack of qualifications and skills, and perhaps inappropriate attitudes and aspirations. Finally, the levels of educational attainment in the area appeared to be very low, while employers complained not only of this but also of young applicants' lack of preparation for the realities of job seeking and work.

The skills of the workforce are usually regarded as central to employment prospects. The population of the Lambeth study area was more working class and less skilled than the national population, although less dramatically so than might be expected (Shankland, Willmott, and Jordan, 1977), and this can be explained by the operation of the housing market. While other studies (Metcalf and Richardson, Chapter 8) argue that the low skills of the inner area population account for its high unemployment, this explanation can be criticised (Holtermann, 1978; Bramley, 1979), and in Lambeth as in other inner areas it was found that *within* most skill groups unemployment was higher than regionally. That is not to say that the less skilled workers were not more vulnerable to unemployment nor that many of the unemployed were not relatively lacking in skill (Lambeth Inner Area Study, 1975a), although it should be stressed that registered unemployment statistics considerably exaggerate the number of wholly unskilled workers. It is argued here that the skills of the workforce should be set against the pattern of demand for different skills (section 12.6) and that attention should also be paid to the processes by which skills are, or are not, created. Lack of demand is likely to reduce training and lead to a wastage of existing skills (Berthoud, Chapter 10 of this book; Daniel, 1972), while the institutional problems of vocational training (e.g. the lack of Skill-centres in the Lambeth area and the lack of incentives for firms to take on trainees) and the inadequacies of education are also relevant.

The large coloured immigrant communities in inner areas like Brixton are also commonly seen as an explanation for high unemployment, and this is most clearly so in the case of the young West Indians. In fact the evidence of the household survey did not imply employment difficulties for all coloured men over and above the level of disadvantage suffered by white men living in the study area. Whether in terms of having experienced unemployment in the previous year or having low earnings, it was only in the (broad) skilled manual category that coloured men showed a significant disadvantage, which implies perhaps that discrimination is more acute in the skilled trades, as this was also the impression gleaned from interviewing employers. Fairly clear evidence of discrimination by London employers has been revealed by the Political and Economic Planning (PEP) studies (Smith, 1974).

A number of other individual attributes have also been invoked as being relevant to unemployment. Married men tend to be less prone to unemployment (Metcalf and Richardson, Chapter 8). Men with lower earnings potential and large families may have little financial incentive to work (Metcalf and Richardson, Chapter 8 of this book), especially if heavy travelling costs are necessary, and some evidence of this emerged from the Lambeth household survey and follow-ups (Lambeth Inner Area Study, 1975a, 1975b). The study area had relatively high proportions of single people of working age and of large families (Shankland, Willmott, and Jordan, 1977). Sickness and disability are often associated with unemployment; but as Hill, Harrison, Sargeant and Talbot (1973) have argued, these should not be divorced from the state of demand in a locality. The proportion of respondents reporting disabilities in Lambeth was about average. Another factor is that frequent job changing by a minority of workers does account for a noticeable part of the total level of unemployment in any area at any one time. Although it was not easy to compare job changing in Lambeth with wider areas, it was seen to be concentrated in certain occupations and industries, particularly construction and personal services, which were in turn well represented in the local workforce (Lambeth Inner Area Study, 1975a). Finally, there are a range of personal attributes or behaviour patterns that are less measurable but may also be more concentrated in the inner areas, e.g. criminal records, alcoholism, mental disorder, and illiteracy.

12.6 The demand for labour

There were a number of reasons for trying to establish the level and pattern of demand for labour in Lambeth and the neighbouring areas relative to the wider regional position. Central to this concern was the debate as to whether people's liability to unemployment was affected by where they lived as well as by their individual characteristics. Only then was it possible to begin to resolve whether job losses from the inner areas were causing hardship, to whom, and in what ways. The argument in section 12.4 that job opportunities should be seen in a local context within London provided a spatial framework for this analysis. It was also seen as important to disaggregate employment totals in terms of skill levels and types of occupation, so that a problem of general demand deficiency could be distinguished from a more likely problem of imbalance or mismatch. Even if a simple supply and demand model were to be questioned, demand would still be a relevant concept; for example, the dual labour market thesis implies that there is no shortage of less skilled and low-paid jobs, but rather a shortage of 'good' jobs, to which access is restricted (Watchter, 1974). Also, as has already been suggested, the impact of personal disadvantages on actual unemployment experience may be heavily conditioned by the local state of demand, as indeed may the existence of apparent disadvantages (e.g. a lack of skill or work experience).

The appropriate measurement of labour demand raises both conceptual and practical difficulties, which may be why this issue has not often been addressed. In the light of the earlier discussion, unemployment itself cannot be regarded as an unbiased indicator of demand. In principle unfilled vacancies provide perhaps the best measure, but the Department of Employment's vacancy statistics are not generally seen as very reliable, understating true vacancies in most but not all circumstances but to a varying and unknown degree (Department of Employment, 1974a). Also, it is difficult to match area boundaries and occupational groupings when combining the Department's with census data. Major notified redundancies are another indicator from Department of Employment sources; but because of the predominance of wastage as a means of reducing workforces, perhaps this is too partial an indicator to be reliable. Annual Census of Employment data are now available to give recent trends in employment; but these are only classified by industry, whereas it is the occupational disaggregation that is most useful. Hence, it is necessary to rely on the Census of Population, now rather out of date, to measure trends in different kinds of jobs in particular local areas and to relate these to trends in the workforce. This was done in the Lambeth IAS for the period 1966–71. More qualitative indications of labour demand conditions were also obtained through the interviews with local employers.

Table 12.1 presents an analysis in terms of four indices of demand – vacancies plus three census indicators – for six broad groupings, based on census socioeconomic groups (SEGs) 1–11, that distinguish non-manual from manual work and broad levels of skill. The analysis referred to males only, compared inner-south London (Lambeth, Southwark, and Wandsworth) with Greater London or Great Britain, and also included two alternative estimates of unemployment rates for men in these groups. In terms of *areas*, the table shows that inner-south London had a less favourable position for most groups on all indicators when compared with Greater London or Great Britain. The 1971 job–worker ratio is perhaps misleading in that most of central London was excluded, and the vacancy rate for SEGs 1–5 was also biased for this reason. However, in terms of *skills* the relative disadvantage of inner-south London was most noticeable in the unskilled category and to a lesser extent in semiskilled and junior non-manual occupations, while the demand for skilled, professional and managerial workers was more favourable. Other more detailed analyses filled out the picture by distinguishing particular skills and by showing how some groups (transport, clerical, and service) could benefit by travelling into a wider area (Lambeth Inner Area Study, 1977a).

The local position was broadly confirmed by employers interviewed in 1975, who had then or (more likely) in the past experienced recruitment or wastage difficulties, but mainly with skilled, non-manual, or female staff. So the evidence confirmed that there was a local shortage of job opportunities, but the picture was not one of deficient demand across the board, nor indeed of a

Table 12.1 Selected indicators of the demand for labour and unemployment (male), by socioeconomic grouping: inner-south London (ISL), Greater London (GL), and Great Britain (GB), 1971 and 1973

Indicator		Professional managerial, and technical (SEGs 1–5)	Junior non-manual (SEG 6)	Personal service (SEG 7)	Skilled manual (SEGs 8, 9)	Semiskilled (SEG 10)	Unskilled (SEG 11)
Demand for labour							
1973 vacancies as % of 1971 jobs	ISL	0.10	1.07	1.43	1.47	1.11	1.04
	GB	0.61	1.52	4.31	1.71	1.34	2.11
1971 job/worker ratio × 100	ISL	125	86	53	96	88	63
	GL	119	130	116	113	120	102
1971 jobs (workplace)/1966 jobs ratio × 100	ISL	109	84	101	85	78	70
	GL	114	83	102	88	84	84
1971 job/worker ratio ÷ 1966 job/worker ratio, × 100	ISL	99	89	100	102	97	88
	GL	106	101	105	101	101	99
Male unemployment							
1973 registered unemployed	ISL	1.04	1.95	2.46	1.88	2.40	11.2
Index (all SEGs = 100)	ISL	38	70	89	68	87	404
1971 census unemployed[a]	ISL	3.14	2.82	3.84	4.76	5.26	7.08
Index (all SEGs[b] = 100)	ISL	66	60	81	100	111	150

[a] Estimated for males only.
[b] Excluding SEG 17.
Source: Shankland, Willmott, and Jordan (1977), table 20.

surplus of 'bad' jobs and a shortage of 'good' jobs as in the dual market model. There was rather an imbalance of demand and supply with the less skilled male manual worker increasingly in excess supply, and a shortage of jobs in the immediate area for the less mobile groups. These factors were argued to be part of the explanation for Lambeth's relatively high unemployment rate, along with some of the social, ethnic, demographic and other factors considered earlier. Regression analyses of unemployment rates across all thirty-two London boroughs, reported elsewhere (Bramley, 1979), indicated that measures of demand at the sectoral and borough level played a part in explaining differences in male unemployment. Thus, the Lambeth conclusions may not be untypical of much of inner London.

Reasons for the apparent imbalance or 'mismatch' could be seen on both the demand and supply sides of the market. About half of the loss of semi- and unskilled male manual jobs from inner-south London between 1966 and 1971 can be attributed to industrial decline, one-third of which was in manufacturing and two-thirds in selected services (e.g. transport and distribution). The other half must have been due to shifts *within* industries in the types of labour employed, with more non-manual and technical staff as against less unskilled manual labour. One major local employer – the Borough of Lambeth – was a significant example of this shift; between 1967 and 1974 salaried employment rose by 95 per cent while manual jobs grew by only 30 per cent. It is thus a misleading simplification to identify industrial, or more specifically manufacturing, decline as the prime cause of labour market problems in inner London. The role of the public sector in exacerbating imbalances in the labour market may also have been significant (Department of the Environment, 1975). On the supply side, the problem was characterised by an inadequate supply of labour skills (and according to some employers, of quality). In part this was attributed to the inadequacies of education and training, but part of the problem was associated with the housing system, which the following section will consider.

12.7 Housing and labour supply

Traditional urban residential location models (Evans, 1973) have predicted that lower income and lower status groups would tend to live in the inner rings of the city, and the Lambeth IAS evidence showed that this was broadly the case in London (Lambeth Inner Area Study, 1975c). However, these models assume a free housing market and a concentration of employment activity in the central area, both of which assumptions are far from the realities of London in the 1970s, with massive public intervention in housing and increasing decentralisation of jobs. The need to explain the continued concentration of low income and low skill groups in inner London is sharpened by labour market considerations, for the evidence on labour demand and unemployment, discussed above, implied that it would be beneficial if more of these groups could move out of the inner area. This would improve their job prospects, reduce competition for the diminishing number of appropriate jobs in areas like Lambeth, and create a little space in the housing stock for groups of workers in greater demand. Housing and environmental considerations, e.g. the need to reduce child densities, pointed in the same direction. The evidence up to 1971 was that the emigration that was proceeding rapidly was very unbalanced in terms of skills; for example, inner-south London residents migrating to outer-south London or the outer metropolitan area in 1965–66 included 6.15 per cent professional and managerial men, 2.95 per cent of skilled manual men, but only 1.15 per cent of the unskilled manual group (Dugmore, 1975).

Public intervention in housing in Britain has progressively increased during this century; yet, it has paid little heed to employment considerations by tending to inhibit mobility in general and in some situations by systematically housing particular groups in the wrong place. Arguably, inner London is an example of the second phenomenon as well as the first. Barriers to movement into and between housing tenure groups are central to the problem. Access to owner-occupation depends on a household having sufficient income to obtain a mortgage for most of the price of a suitable house, which meant £3,000–3,500 per annum in the London area in 1973. Of households in the Lambeth study area, 90 per cent were tenants; and of these 11 per cent were above the £3,500 income level, while 80 per cent were below the £3,000 level. Thus, quite apart from other problems of buying, e.g. deposit requirements and mortgage eligibility, very few residents could expect to buy their way out of inner London.

Privately rented housing is concentrated in the inner area of London, and this sector's decline has meant that there have been few new lettings, many of which have been allocated through personal contact networks or rationed by premia. Meanwhile, the public sector has operated mainly on the principle of rehousing within boroughs, with very little interborough transfer activity. While in principle the Greater London Council (GLC) could perform the strategic role of providing opportunities for publicly rented housing in outer London, in practice its stock has been increasingly concentrated in inner London, and its willingness and ability to build or acquire in outer London have dimished. Similar remarks apply to the growing housing-association movement. New and expanding towns have provided opportunities for those willing to move longer distances; but again the programme is being run down, and the allocation of tenancies in these areas has tended to exclude less skilled workers.

So there were very real barriers to emigration by the less skilled and lower-paid groups in Lambeth. There may also have been disincentives that in the short term discouraged individuals from trying to move. Examples of these include the tendency of rents on new lettings or mortgages to be high relative to existing housing payments (Berthoud, Chapter 10), uncertainty about job and housing opportunities elsewhere, possibly longer work journeys and the need to use a car, a possible lack of female jobs, and so on. However, the widely held view that working-class inner-city residents do not want to move was clearly refuted by the Lambeth IAS survey evidence. Between a quarter and a third of residents wanted to move out, for reasons primarily to do with housing, environment, and community breakdown, but many of these clearly perceived housing cost or availability as the critical barrier. These aspirations to move were fully shared by the lower socioeconomic and income groups, although there were differences in terms of household types, colour, and tenure.

12.8 Employment, income, and poverty

Much of the discussion so far has taken unemployment to be the problem at issue, but there was another dimension to the employment-related problems of Lambeth residents. About a quarter of families in the study area were in poverty, defined by reference to current supplementary benefit scales net of rent, and this above-average liability to income poverty was associated with other deprivations (Shankland, Willmott, and Jordan, 1977; Lambeth

Inner Area Study, 1975b, 1977b). While many of these were elderly or single-parent families, a higher proportion than nationally were couples with children, probably headed by a man in low-paid employment. Low pay could be seen as a more pervasive problem than unemployment. Certainly, this was so in 1973 when 15 per cent of full time men earned less than £24 per week, whereas only about 3 per cent were unemployed at the time of the survey and 9.2 per cent had experienced some unemployment in the previous year.

Much the same basic question ('who' versus 'where') can be asked about the reasons for Lambeth residents' low earnings as was asked about their higher unemployment. Were male earnings low because of the characteristics of the men who lived in Lambeth or because of the fact that they lived there rather than somewhere else? If it were the former, one would expect to be able to explain low earnings in terms of residents' lack of skills and qualifications, their age structure, and the industries they worked in, and then to explain their presence in Lambeth mainly in terms of the housing opportunities that were open to lower-paid workers. If the latter were significant, one would expect job opportunities that were accessible to men in the local labour market to be low-paid, either because of their occupational and industrial composition, or because of the particular characteristics of local firms, or because of the state of demand for labour in that local market. The evidence was not sufficiently good to provide a complete answer, but certain tentative points could be made.

Rather surprisingly, it was not possible to explain the low earnings of study area men in terms of their occupations, at least not from a broad socioeconomic-group breakdown, and in fact substantial shortfalls were evident within each SEG. Industrial composition could explain part of the shortfall because of the high proportion of manual men working in five low-paid service industries (distribution, financial, professional services, miscellaneous services, and public administration). Whatever the reasons for low pay at the individual level, the arguments in section 12.7 provide a convincing explanation in terms of the housing system for finding a resident population drawn from the lower end of the earnings distribution. Certainly, the evidence of the earnings of people *working* in Lambeth and its neighbouring areas from the New Earnings Survey and the employers' survey carried out for the present study was that local job opportunities were not on average low-paid (Simon,

1977). Discussions with local employers suggested a strong tendency for their more highly-paid workers to commute in from the suburbs and beyond.

So, in the case of low earnings the explanation appeared to be mainly one of 'who' (and housing) rather than 'where', but one or two qualifications should be added. First, the industrial composition of manual jobs in the labour market area was somewhat biased towards low-paying industries, parallel to the findings relating to residents' earnings. However, this bias did *not* appear to have increased as a result of employment changes between 1966 and 1971, because both high- and low-paying industries declined over this period. Second, it could be argued that jobs in inner-south London were less highly paid than would have been expected on the basis of London's 14 per cent cost-of-living differential and in the light of theoretical models that predict a wage gradient declining from the centre of the city to the periphery. Third, the higher differentials for male residents compared with national averages in the less-skilled manual and manufacturing categories may have been attributable to declining or low demand. Finally, if there is any truth in the argument that low demand reduces the opportunities for people in Lambeth to gain or retain skills, the 'individual characteristics' explanation cannot be completely separated from the 'area' explanation.

12.9 Jobs in the inner area

Before moving on to consider the reasons why employment in the area around Lambeth has been declining it is important to know some of the characteristics of existing employment. The inner-south sector lacked really large-scale industrial concentrations, unlike other parts of London; nor was it dominated by major individual employers. Although it lacked manufacturing in general (22.7 per cent of jobs in 1971), inner-south London had substantial employment in the food and printing groups. Employment in most manufacturing groups declined much more than in the country as a whole from 1966 to 1971 (by 16 per cent), and rapid decline has since continued. Inner-south London was more dominated than London as a whole by construction and by most services, but particularly by wholesale distribution, education, health, and local government. It had relatively low shares in 'other' transport (road haulage, docks, etc.), financial and business services, private professional services, and some of the 'miscellaneous' services (entertainment, betting, hairdressing, dry cleaning, charities, etc.). In many services employment again declined faster than nationally, in part no doubt as a response to falling population, but the area performed better than Britain in road passenger transport, posts and telecommunications, private professional services, and national government services. Its performance in the cases of laundries, railways, and construction, although declining, was not much worse than the national trend in each case.

The interviews with thirty-nine larger private-sector employers in inner-south London suggested certain other characteristic features of local employment. The manufacturing sample, although small (twenty-six firms), was fairly representative, but the thirteen service firms were mainly drawn from the distributive and miscellaneous services groups. Of the manufacturing firms, 70 per cent were owned by a parent company; but as many as 77 per cent of the plants visited were firms' headquarters. This partly explains the very striking finding that nearly 40 per cent of the 'manufacturing' jobs were non-manual, i.e. office jobs, and this may be a general characteristic of inner London. Half of the manufacturing firms had other plants – an average of four each – around the country. None of the manufacturers had started as a new firm at the premises in question, but most had been there for more than ten years. Of those moving premises recently, the normal pattern was one either of very local moves or of moves outwards from central London, both associated with the need for bigger or better premises or the pressure of redevelopment. Linkages with other firms in London were weak on the supplier side but strong on the customer side, even in the case of manufacturing. As already noted, in many cases much of the workforce, including many skilled men, was not locally resident, which may to some extent have been associated with the high proportions (17 per cent in manufacturing, 40 per cent in services) of employees who did not work on the premises (e.g. salesmen, service engineers, installation fitters, drivers, homeworkers, cleaners). This again is probably characteristic of inner London firms. Finally, firms were asked about pay levels, and what was striking about their replies was the very wide range *within* skill groups between different firms; for example, semiskilled males varied from £36 to £85 per week. As in other studies (Makay *et al.*,

1971), the evidence did not show local market pressures equalising wages, although low-paying firms had more labour supply difficulties. Overtime and strong union influence were factors related to high-paying plants.

12.10 The decline of employment

As already shown, much of the debate about inner city policy has hinged on the diagnosis of the 'problem' of industrial decline. The focus has tended to be on manufacturing, and the Lambeth IAS was no exception in that respect. There are good reasons for concentrating on manufacturing, including its rapid decline in London (*not* explained by industrial structure; Greater London Council, 1975), its 'basic' character, its potential for providing well-paid skilled and semiskilled manual jobs, and indeed its key role in the government's industrial strategy. Some of the reasons for employment changes in services are better understood, but it is not denied that these had important labour market consequences in Lambeth at the time of the study.

As a first stage in explaining the loss of jobs it is helpful to do an accounting exercise to show the impact over a period of openings, closures, relocations, and *in situ* changes on the employment of firms. Dennis (see Chapter 2) has reported on a Department of Industry analysis of manufacturing employment changes in London for the period 1966–74, to the effect that closures were the dominant item, with relocations and *in situ* declines accounting for a lesser part of the change. While not directly comparable, the Lambeth IAS's tracing of the thirty manufacturing firms approached for interview in inner-south London suggested a different picture of the substantial (about 27 per cent) drop in employment between 1970 and 1975; only 23 per cent was attributed to closures, compared with 58 per cent to relocations and 19 per cent to *in situ* decline. If there is a significant difference of view here, it is that relocation – broadly defined to include shifts of production lines between existing plants and firms changing their name or product slightly – may be more significant for inner London than is implied by the Department of Industry's figures.

However, the accounting exercise was of itself none too helpful in explaining why things happened, and it was here that the detailed case study material provided by the interviews was very useful. Only four cases of closure were picked up, and these were mainly a result of technological change, declining demand, or international competition. However, even in these cases of economic failure such factors as labour shortage and obsolete premises played a part. Twelve cases of relocation (actual or potential, and often partial moves) were analysed, and here again varied and complex reasons were given. However, two general types of reason came up very frequently, and these were: first, a shortage of space (or unsuitable premises); and second, difficulties of labour supply. The space constraint particularly affected growing firms, and the costs or difficulty of rectifying it on site or locally were seen to be great. The labour constraint was sometimes more qualitative then quantitative and could be linked to other considerations like pay, travel to work, and local amenities. Many other locational disadvantages were mentioned by respondents, particularly factors relating to transport and congestion (e.g. parking, access for lorries, public transport). Policies were not directly responsible for many actual or potential moves, and these were mainly local authority action – i.e. redevelopment or planning refusal – rather than central controls – i.e. Industrial Development Certificate (IDC) or Office Development Permit (ODP). Once firms had decided to move or set up a branch, the attractions of new towns and development areas clearly played a part.

When the reasons why employment was tending to decline within firms that remained were considered, there was a tendency to come back to the same factors as affected relocation. In other words, economic or structural explanations of decline were not strongly supported either by the shift-share analysis of employment changes (Greater London Council, 1975) or by the examination of the case studies. Table 12.2. summarises the pattern in relation to changes in output, productivity, and employment between 1970 and 1975. Category 1 represented structural reasons for decline and accounted for less than a third of firms, even that being exaggerated by the severe 1974–75 recession. Productivity was increasing in many firms, so that in terms of output these firms were performing better than their employment might have indicated. The most significant finding was the large number of firms that said that they were constrained not by demand but by other factors, which were mainly again space and, to a lesser extent, labour supply.

An assessment was made of the future prospects of firms as employers of labour on their present scale in inner-south London against a long list of criteria. This suggested that between a quarter

Table 12.2 Changes in employment in 39 larger private sector firms in inner-south London, 1970–75

Category	Manufacturing firms	Service firms	All firms
1. Demand declining or productivity increasing more than demand – falling employment	8	3	11
2. Demand and productivity static or off-setting – static employment	3	3	6
3. Demand increasing more than productivity – rising employment	5	3	8
4. As 2 or 3 but subject to constraints	10	4	14
Total	26	13	39

Source: Author's own survey.

and a half of manufacturing firms or jobs were vulnerable, but a rather lower proportion of service firms. It was difficult to identify any particular characteristics of the vulnerable group, apart from an interesting tendency for it to employ more white collar and fewer unskilled workers (parallel with the comparison between growing and declining firms). This could be interpreted as a tendency for private sector firms to be responsive to labour market conditions and to 'follow the workers' to some extent.

12.11 Policy implications

The preceding analysis of employment and related problems in Lambeth led the IAS team to conclude that a three-pronged attack was needed, corresponding to the complex and in some ways paradoxical nature of the problem. The three elements were:

(a) industrial and employment generation or retention;
(b) raising the skill level of the workforce; and
(c) a more balanced dispersal of population.

   1. *Employment generation* Nine policy measures were identified to stem or reverse the decline of inner area industry and

to improve local job opportunities for less skilled men in particular.
These were:

(a) positive statements by both levels of government in favour of
   industry in inner London;
(b) the elimination of IDC controls in inner London;
(c) the relaxation of planning controls over industry and commerce
   in inner London;
(d) the permitting of selective office development in areas with a
   surplus of clerical workers;
(e) the allocation of more land in inner London for industry and
   commerce, and local authority provision of industrial estates
   and advanced workshops;
(f) local authority provision of advice and other services to small
   businesses;
(g) the protection of areas containing small firms against wholesale
   clearance;
(h) the protection, or even creation, of mixed use zones; and
(i) the revival of the construction industry through increased housing rehabilitation in inner London.

Two general points need to be made about this list, which are
perhaps more apparent now as the authorities get to grips with
trying to implement some of the proposals. It was not the view of the
Lambeth IAS team that a dramatic reversal of trends was feasible,
and clearly these policies would take time to have a significant
impact. Also, it was very clear that serious conflicts would arise
between these and existing policies of other kinds. In particular, the
need for better access and parking might conflict with traffic
restraint policies and an unwillingness to build roads into the inner
area. Allocating the substantial amount of extra land needed for
industry was infeasible in some boroughs and usually would conflict
directly with housing and open space policies. There is a more
general conflict between favouring industry and trying to improve
the environment. Partly for these reasons and partly because of
what the analysis of labour market problems implied, the study
team sought to emphasise the other two elements of policy more
strongly.
   2. *Training and education*   It is perhaps in the training field that
there have been the greatest developments since 1973, with a
number of major initiatives by the Manpower Services Commission

and its agencies. Of particular note are the Youth Opportunities Programme (Manpower Services Commission, 1977), the expansion of the Training Opportunities Scheme (TOPS) (Manpower Services Commission, 1976), and the proposals for Training in Vital Skills (Manpower Services Commission, 1978). Undoubtedly, the problem of low educational attainment offers no easy solution, reflecting as it does a combination of adverse factors in the school, the home, and the environment, which were not subject to systematic examination in the Lambeth IAS. However, with the shift away from unskilled manual jobs towards white collar jobs being so pronounced in inner London, and indeed with the basic standards of literacy and numeracy being regarded as essential for any skill, this problem should receive high priority study and action research.

3. *Balanced dispersal* The third element of policy was more contentious but strongly argued, because the case for it rested on a number of distinct arguments. The aim was to overcome the 'housing trap' that prevents less-skilled lower-income people from moving out of inner London to the suburbs and beyond. This could be achieved through a 'common allocations policy' for public housing throughout London, supplemented by a 'national housing mobility pool', as long as additional public housing was acquired or built on a substantial scale in outer London and in the wider region.

It is inevitable that with the benefit of hindsight one seeks to put a different emphasis on conclusions reached previously. Two important changes of context have taken place since 1973. First, the strategy that these recommendations represented depended for its success upon the national economy operating at a high level of demand, as in the mid-1960s and in 1973–74. In fact Britain has not recovered from the recession of 1974–75, the effects of which on the demand for labour have been catastrophic (Moore, *et al.*, 1978). The Lambeth IAS did not shrink from making recommendations about national policy, so that, in the light of what has happened and is forecast to happen to unemployment nationally, a change of macroeconomic strategy should be treated as the primary and over-riding measure needed to begin to deal with the inner-city employment problem. Second, the whole drift of planning and housing policies is against balanced dispersal, and for political reasons the GLC is disengaging itself almost completely from its strategic role. Are any substitute vehicles available to carry this policy forward? The Housing Corporation could become more active in the outer areas, but this is unlikely, as is large-scale inner-borough building in the suburbs. Special assistance with house purchase might help some groups, but only those already close to the margin of owner-occupation.

So, on present evidence the Lambeth IAS policy package is not to be implemented in full, and the results are likely to be less than satisfactory. Nevertheless, the debate will continue; and not only will policy priorities change, but perhaps also will perceptions and definitions of 'the problem'.

13 The Impact on Workers from the Inner City of Liverpool's Economic Decline

Rupert Nabarro

13.1 Introduction

This chapter results from work carried out in the Inner Area Study (IAS) in Liverpool. The studies, intended to contribute to a 'comprehensive approach' to the problems of British cities, were commissioned by the Department of the Environment. Similar projects were undertaken in Small Heath (Birmingham) and Lambeth (see Chapters 14 and 12 respectively). In each case standard research techniques were combined with a series of 'action research' projects conducted within defined areas.

The Liverpool IAS area was located in parts of Liverpool 7 and 8, in an area of some 60,000 people roughly centred on Edge Hill. Included were a number of different communities, among them being one of the longest-established black settlements in Britain; an area of stable working-class housing whose residents largely seek work on the neighbouring Edge Lane industrial estate; a poor 'rooming' area offering accommodation of a kind to new arrivals to the city, including many coloured immigrants, Irish, and single-parent families; and an area of very low-quality 1930s council housing, which is among the most unacceptable public housing in the city (Liverpool Inner Area Study, 1977a). Despite the existence of a wide range of individual circumstances within the local population, the area is characterised by a very poor environment, high unemployment, and generally low living standards (Liverpool Inner Area Study, 1977b).

Unlike many studies of employment in the inner city that have concentrated exclusively on factors concerning the availability of jobs, an important part of the Liverpool IAS was to show how changes in the structure of the economy affected the work prospects of those living in the inner city. Thus, this chapter seeks to explain: how changes in the level and composition of economic demand in Merseyside affect the residents of one small area; the special features of the working of a declining labour market, and the way in which changes in demand affect different groups of workers in the inner city; the ways in which employers in areas of high unemployment adjust their recruitment and training programmes; and the effectiveness of government training and placement services, which in principle provide the link between unemployed persons and the labour market. This chapter shows how, in areas of deficient demand, the incidence of unemployment and low quality employment becomes concentrated upon certain groups and in certain areas, and how a labour market trap may form. Both regional policy and the operations of the government placement and training services tend to contribute to this process.

The first part of this chapter discusses changes in the structure of employment in Merseyside during the 1970s. The discussion is in summary form, as the reasons for changes in the economy have been treated in other parts of Liverpool IAS work (Liverpool Inner Area Study, 1977c). This is placed against the background of the area within which workers from the inner city customarily travel to work or would be able to see work. Changes in the composition of the demand for labour are then contrasted with the occupational characteristics of workers in Liverpool. The second part of the chapter attempts to develop indicators of labour market demand at different occupational levels. The last part of the chapter presents a detailed discussion of the reasons for which people are unemployed and of the attitudes of employers and government employment agencies; this is held to explain why unemployment becomes concentrated on certain groups, although not the overall deficiency of demand.

13.2 Structural change in the Merseyside economy

The economy of Merseyside has undergone major changes since the war, in part at least due to the influence of regional policy. In 1950,

14 per cent of all employment in Merseyside was in port-related activities (water transport, sea transport, shipbuilding) and a further 21 per cent in associated industries. By 1973 these proportions had fallen to 5 and 13 per cent respectively (Merseyside County Council, 1975a).

In the period 1945–71, 175 firms were introduced to Merseyside, which between them established 94,000 new manufacturing jobs. The years of most rapid development were between 1959 and 1965 when an average of nearly 6,000 jobs a year were brought to the area, accounting for approximately 17 per cent of all mobile (footloose) industry relocated in the United Kingdom in those years. Since then the scale of new investment has been rather lower, due to the smaller average size of new firms and to the lower national level of new investment. Relatively few firms have moved out of Merseyside, and these total no more than 3,000 jobs since 1945 (Merseyside County Council, 1975a).

13.3 Changing location of employment

The change in the structure of employment in Merseyside has been matched by a shift in the location of jobs. The new settlements on the periphery of the special development area have been the locus of employment growth (see Table 13.1).

The boundaries of the Liverpool Employment-Office area cover a rather larger area than the city and include some of the growth zones to the north, east, and south-east of the city. Even so there was a net loss of manufacturing employment in the area of 6,300 jobs over the 1961–71 period, compared with the growth of 26,000 jobs in the outer areas of the Merseyside Special Development Area. The position with regard to services is even more pronounced, with a heavy loss of employment in the docks, railways, construction, public utilities, and distribution. In total the Liverpool area lost more than 50,000 jobs in the decade, while the outer areas gained nearly 19,000. In 1961 employment in the Liverpool area accounted for 65 per cent of that in the Special Development Area; by 1971 this proportion had fallen to 58 per cent. The loss of jobs within the city itself continued at a very much faster rate than in the Employment Office area.

Three main trends account for the relative decline of employment in the inner parts of Merseyside. First, new jobs brought to the

Table 13.1 Employment changes by industrial sector: Merseyside Special Development Area, 1961–71

Area	% change				Change in no. of jobs	
	Manufacturing[a]	Construction[b]	Service[c]	All sectors	Manufacturing[a]	Service[d]
East group						
Skelmersdale	+193	+ 2	+434	+167	+ 5,100	+ 1,350
St Helens	+ 0.5	− 22	+ 7	− 4	+ 160	+ 1,580
Prescot	+ 10	+ 8	+ 23	+ 12	+ 1,210	+ 90
Widnes	− 7	+107	+ 76	+ 20	− 1,050	+ 900
Runcorn	+ 34	+124	+ 41	+ 41	+ 3,360	+ 2,270
Total					+ 8,780	+ 6,190
Across the water						
Wallasey	+ 29	+ 1	+ 17	+ 18	+ 1,740	+ 2,000
Hoylake	+ 27	− 41	+ 1	− 7	+ 50	+ 40
Bebington	+ 5	+ 27	+ 20	+ 12	+ 590	+ 1,640
Neston	− 6	− 28	+ 88	+ 28	− 60	+ 710
Ellesmere Park	+ 85	+ 26	+101	+ 80	+14,630	+ 5,130
Total					+16,950	+ 9,520
Liverpool group						
Liverpool Exchanges[e]	− 8	− 17	− 20	− 15	− 6,250	−50,450
Birkenhead	− 10	− 35	− 13	− 13	− 2,100	− 4,490
Total					− 8,350	−54,940

a Orders 3–19 of the Standard Industrial Classification (SIC)
b Order 20.
c Orders 1, 2, and 21–27.
d Orders 1, 2, and 20–27.
e Leece Street, Old Swan, Regent Road, Walton, Bootle, Crosby, Garston, and Kirkby.
Source: Department of Employment, unpublished data.

region as a result of regional policy located in the outer settlements where good environmental conditions were combined with modern housing, new industrial estates, and access to the national motorway network. Second, some firms already established in Merseyside moved to new premises on the periphery. Third, the declining industries of the area, especially the docks and shipbuilding but also many manufacturing firms, were concentrated in the old areas of the conurbation, i.e. Liverpool and Birkenhead. These declined in employment terms or were lost to the national economy altogether.

To some extent the effects of these losses were balanced by the growth of city centre services. Finance, professional and scientific services, and public administration provided an additional 4,000 jobs for men, although not on the whole employment of a suitable type for those laid off from manual service employment. Liverpool's growth here has not, however, been as vibrant as that of similar commercial centres elsewhere in the country or in the competing Manchester area.

The concentration of declining manual service sectors within Liverpool has been matched by a similar picture as regards manufacturing. Over the period 1961–71 male employment in manufacturing in the Liverpool Employment Office area showed a small decrease, while declining by one-third in Liverpool. Much of the loss occurred in the latter part of the decade, a major cause lying in factory closures in the electrical engineering, chemicals, and textiles sectors and a rapid rundown of shipbuilding. Male manufacturing jobs in Liverpool were lost in every sector, apart from vehicles and clothing where few people were employed and where increases were small.

13.4 The definition of labour market areas

The extent to which people are prepared or are able to travel to work is critical in defining the boundaries of urban labour markets and in determining how a given market will respond to changes in demand and employment structure. In the short term a person's mobility is determined by his ability to travel from his home to a place of work; in the longer term he may be prepared to move house. Both kinds of mobility vary between occupational, income, and demographic groups and are affected by personal preference.

There is no clear cut-off point beyond which people will not travel; the constraints are progressive (Lambeth Inner Area Study, 1975a).

In the case of Liverpool considerable difficulties exist in travelling to work from the inner area. Car ownership in the IAS area was low (18 per cent of men travelled to work by car in 1971 compared with 24 per cent in the city as a whole), and the majority (52 per cent) of work trips were made by bus. A very high proportion of the working population of the area (83 per cent) worked within the city of Liverpool, and those travelling outside largely had access to a car. Similarly, the IAS's Survey of Unemployed showed over 90 per cent of men to have held their last job in Liverpool and over 60 per cent to have held theirs in south-inner Liverpool.

The difficulty in getting from the inner areas to the new jobs created as a result of regional policy on or beyond the periphery of Liverpool is very real. The Falkner estate is a modern council estate approximately at the centre of the IAS area. Many of its residents have come from nearby slum clearance areas. For those seeking work in the new employment growth centres and using the fastest available public transport, the travel time to Ellesmere Port is 55 minutes each way at a cost of £5 per (five-day) week, to Runcorn 40 minutes and £4.40, and to Halewood 1 hour and £2.80.[1] Each of these journeys for shiftwork outside the peak hours presents special problems; and even so the Falkner estate is relatively well placed due to its proximity to Edge Lane and the bus routes to the city boundary. Other areas do less well, especially the council estates near the docks.

13.5 The occupational mix of employment change

It is possible to show how the decline of employment within Liverpool city boundaries in the period 1966–71 has been concentrated on certain occupations. In Table 13.2 Census Workplace tables have been reclassified to provide compatibility with standard Census socioeconomic groups (SEGs). This provides an indication of the skill level of the jobs that are available in the city. Between 1966 and 1971 the total number of jobs for men fell by 18 per cent. However, the number of unskilled manual jobs dropped by 25 per cent, of semiskilled by 24 per cent, of personal service jobs by 41 per

[1]Fares existing at September 1975.

Table 13.2   Percentage change in occupational status of economically active males and of jobs available: Liverpool District, 1966–71

SEG	Socioeconomic status	Jobs available (1)	Economically active males (2)
1–4	Professional and managerial	− 1	− 1
5	Supervisors (non-manual)	+12	− 1
6	Junior non-manual	−21	−18
7	Personal service	−41	−15
8–9	Skilled manual (incl. supervisors)	−20	−17
10	Semiskilled manual	−24	−20
11	Unskilled manual	−25	−17

Source: Census of Population, 1966 and 1971, population and workplace tables.

cent, and of junior non-manual (clerical and sales) jobs by 21 per cent (column 1).

In order to compare changes in the national and local occupational composition of employment, a shift-share analysis was applied to the change in structure of male employment in Liverpool between 1966 and 1971. This shows that at the start of the period the city contained a slightly higher share of the types of job that declined nationally over the period (Liverpool Inner Area Study, 1977c). However, this would account for only some 5 per cent of the loss of jobs that actually took place in Liverpool over the period. The remainder of the loss was due to a more rapid decline in jobs in each occupation than would have been expected on the basis of figures for Great Britain. The loss was due to Liverpool's industrial structure, which contained a disproportionately large share of industries employing low-skilled labour that were in rapid decline.

13.6   The impact of the loss of low-skilled jobs

An indication of how the decline of these industries has affected workers who are resident in the inner city is provided by the Social Area Analysis (Liverpool Inner Area Study, 1977a). Table 13.3 shows the distribution by industrial sector of residents from each social area, and Table 13.4 the occupational structure of each industry. Workers from the inner council estates are concentrated

Table 13.3 Distribution of residents by industrial sector and social area: Liverpool district, 1971 (%)

Industrial sector	City mean	High status area	Rooming house area	Inner council area	Outer council area	Older terraced area
		1	2	3	4	5
Mining and manufacturing	36	26	30	33	41	39
Government and services	45	57	51	42	37	38
Construction	7	5	7	8	8	8
Transport and utilities	13	11	11	17	14	15
Total	100^a	100^a	100^a	100	100	100

^{a} Rounded.

Note: The city was divided into social areas 1–5 by means of a Cluster Analysis conducted using data from the 1971 census (see p. 305). It is to these areas that the descriptions 'high status' and 'inner council' refer.

Source: Census of Population, 1971.

Table 13.4 Distribution of residents by socioeconomic status and industrial sector: Liverpool district, 1971 (%)

Socioeconomic status	Mining and manufacturing	Government and services	Transport, utilities, and construction	All industrial sectors
Professional and managerial	5	13	6	8
Non-manual	14	49	17	30
Skilled manual	37	11	41	27
Semiskilled	34	17	17	23
Unskilled	10	11	19	12
Total	100	100ᵃ	100	100

ᵃ Rounded.
Source: Census of Population, 1971.

in the transport and construction sectors, which employ more unskilled workers than other activities in the city (Table 13.3). More detailed analysis also shows that a higher proportion of the transport and construction workers living in the inner council estates is unskilled than elsewhere. Conversely, in the outer estates the employment structure is geared towards manufacturing, and a higher proportion of workers in this sector is unskilled (33 per cent compared with 22 per cent in the inner council area). The residents of inner Liverpool, then, are concentrated both in the industries, and in the occupations within those industries, that are in rapid decline.

13.7 Measures of the demand for labour

Residents of inner Liverpool are effectively limited in their search for work to the boundaries of the city. To travel further means having the use of a car or being prepared (or able) to move home. The extent of the decline of employment and the way in which this is concentrated on certain occupations have been shown above. A number of different indicators of the level of labour market demand can be developed.

First, an analysis of Department of Employment records suggested that job vacancies in Liverpool are quickly filled. There are at all times more registered unemployed than notified vacancies, and the ratio of the two is higher than that prevailing nationally (see Table 13.5). Fewer job opportunities are available to a man becoming unemployed than would be the case elsewhere.

Table 13.5 Ratio of registered unemployed to notified vacancies, 1971–75

Date	Liverpool Employment Office	UK
April 1971	10	4
April 1972	19	6
April 1973	8	2
April 1974	6	3
April 1975	11	4

Sources: Area Management Unit, Liverpool District Council; Department of Employment.

Second, the impact of employment decline has been falling on the least skilled workers. The effect of the massive loss of unskilled work in Liverpool might have been acceptable either if the number of men seeking this kind of work had fallen also or if skills could have been acquired that would have allowed better jobs to be taken on by the unskilled. Table 13.2 has shown the changes that took place in the occupational composition of employment and in the skills of the workforce between 1966 and 1971. Jobs declined faster than the number of workers at all levels below those of a supervisory, professional, or managerial nature (SEGs 1–5).

The number of jobs available in Liverpool for every worker of the city competing for these jobs is shown in Table 13.6. Just as people from Liverpool travel out to work, so those living in surrounding areas travel in. The better jobs show the most favourable balance for local residents; there are almost twice as many jobs as residents for professional and managerial work. However, this type of work, and jobs in government, are filled largely by people travelling into the city from the more affluent suburbs and peripheral settlements. There are many fewer jobs than workers for semiskilled and unskilled jobs.

Column 3 in the table shows the change in the ratio of residents to workers that took place between 1966 and 1971. Overall, the number of jobs declined slightly faster than the number of resident workers. Unskilled workers faced a very poor position within a

Table 13.6 Ratio of jobs to workers: Liverpool district, 1966–71

SEG	Socioeconomic status	Ratio of jobs to workers		Ratio of change in jobs to change in workers,
		1966 (1)	1971 (2)	1966–71 (3)
1–4	Professional and managerial	1.90	1.85	0.97
5	Supervisors (non-manual)	1.12	1.27	1.13
6	Junior non-manual	1.69	1.62	0.95
7	Personal service	1.55	1.08	0.69
8–9	Skilled manual (incl. supervisors)	1.06	1.03	0.97
10	Semiskilled manual	1.05	0.99	0.94
11	Unskilled manual	0.77	0.71	0.92

Source: Census of Population, 1966 and 1971, population and workplace tables.

labour market providing, within the city, only 71 jobs for each 100 workers – a position that declined relatively by 8 per cent between 1966 and 1971. The position facing semiskilled workers is less good than that facing skilled, although for them too the situation deteriorated. There are more jobs available to junior non-manual workers (SEG 6) than workers in this occupation in the city, although again the ratio declined over the period. Supervisory, managerial, and professional groups are well placed in view of both the availability of jobs and their continuance over the period.

13.8 The geographical distribution of unemployment in Liverpool

Although the types of demand indicator shown above can be assumed to be common to workers living in fairly widely-spread areas, significant differences were found in local rates of unemployment. It is not of course possible to show small-area unemployment levels with Department of Employment data. Thus, local differentials may be best illustrated by reference to the Cluster Analysis of the 1971 census, which divided the city into twenty-five relatively homogeneous areas (with populations ranging from 5,000 to 67,000) that could themselves be regrouped into a fivefold system of social areas (as used in Table 13.3 above). However, it was also possible to group the original twenty-five clusters by a single set of census variables – for the study purposes those related to economic activity and economic status. The variables used are those shown in Table 13.7: the socioeconomic status of households, based on occupation; the industry in which people work; self-employment; change of occupation in the previous year; unemployment and sickness; and educational attainment. All these vary considerably in their incidence. The analysis was also based on the proportions of women at work, although these do not vary greatly across the city, and there is no perceivable tendency for high unemployment areas to have large numbers of women working.

The five economic areas form a symmetrical hierarchy of economic characteristics. Nearly two-thirds of the city's population fall in the fourth area (see Figure 13.1). The pattern is of a broadly-skilled manual and semiskilled population working chiefly in manufacturing industry. The rest of the population splits either side of this: a small hierarchy of three high status areas of professional/ managerial and non-manual workers, chiefly in services and gov-

Table 13.7 Economic areas: Liverpool district, 1971

Variable	City mean (%)	Indices of economic areas (city = 100)				
		1	2	3	4	5
Heads of household:						
Professional and managerial	10.9 ⎫	602	273	152	52	40
Non-manual	19.6 ⎪	116	190	164	78	59
Skilled manual	34.2 ⎬ 100.0a	27	63	97	115	72
Semiskilled	20.8 ⎪	9	42	68	116	124
Unskilled	14.4 ⎭	2	19	29	109	234
Males, economically active:						
Unemployed	9.1	21	48	48	105	203
Sick	1.9	24	50	51	99	227
Females, economically active	46.0	85	97	96	101	106
Married females, economically active	44.3	87	103	102	100	100
Economically active:						
Mining and manufacturing	35.8 ⎫	49	67	84	113	91
Government and services	43.6 ⎬ 100.0	173	140	118	87	99
Construction	7.2 ⎪	29	72	81	109	116
Transport and utilities	13.4 ⎭	34	73	95	105	118
Education:						
HNC or degree	5.6	634	385	146	34	36
ONC OR A-level	6.6	500	306	133	53	48
Self-employed	4.2	354	170	137	78	60
Changing occupation in previous year	6.1	70	115	102	102	80
City population (%)	100.0a	2.2	10.4	13.9	62.2	11.2

a Rounded.

Note: Economic areas 1–5 are groups of clusters in the social-area cluster analysis of the 1971 Census, as follows:

1. very high status area (cluster 2)
2. high status area (cluster 1, 5–7)
3. medium status area (clusters 3, 4, 15)
4. city average area (clusters 9, 14, 16–25)
5. high unemployment area (clusters 8, 10–13).

Sources: Census of Population, 1971.

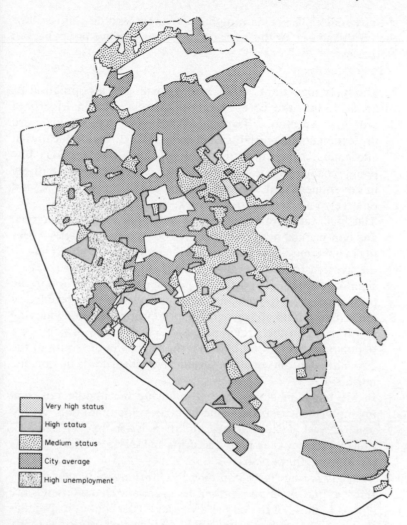

Fig. 13.1 Economic character of Census enumeration-district clusters, 1971.

Legend:
- Very high status
- High status
- Medium status
- City average
- High unemployment

ernment; and a lower status area, overwhelmingly unskilled and having very high unemployment.

The five economic areas show a strong geographical pattern. The first two (those with the highest status) are located south-east of the city centre between the river Mersey and the Woolton ridge. The fifth area (the most deprived) forms a tight ring immediately around the city centre. The remaining built-up areas include almost all of the north and east of the city and the Woolton ridge at Speke and Netherley.

In greater detail:

1. The 'very high status' area is very small with a population of about 13,000 the core of the high status area in Liverpool around Woolton. Two-thirds of its households are professional/managerial with correspondingly high educational attainment, a high proportion of self-employed, and very few people changing their jobs. The source of work is almost entirely in government and services. Unemployment is very low, and relatively few women are at work.

2. The 'high status area' is predominantly professional/managerial and non-manual households with good education, chiefly working in government and services. Unemployment is about half of the average for Liverpool (i.e. equal to the national rate). A significantly high proportion of people changed their job in the previous year, although this largely relates to the presence of areas that contain above-average proportions of people moving to Liverpool in the previous five years. The area, which has a population of about 60,000, is found chiefly in the south of the city, although one enclave around Newsham Park lies on the north side.

3. In the 'medium status' area, occupying the middle position, unemployment is at the same level as in the first area; but the general level of skill is lower, and there is a more even distribution of work between manufacturing and services. It has approximately 80,000 persons.

4. The 'city average' area contains 380,000 persons or nearly two-thirds of the city's population. Its economic characteristics are closest to those of the city as a whole; 80 per cent of its population is skilled manual, semiskilled, or unskilled, working chiefly in manufacturing, construction, transport, and utilities. This is the working class core of Liverpool, which largely determines its economic character. Educational achievement is low; unemployment is about average for the city but twice the national rate, implying that two-thirds of the city is experiencing a low level of economic activity compared with the region and country. The area covers most of the built-up area on the north side of Liverpool, the outer council estates (including the most recently constructed), and the older terraced-housing area.

5. The 'high unemployment' area has a population of 70,000, living in the inner council estates and the worst of the rooming house area. Its dominant characteristic is a male unemployment rate that is twice the city average and an even greater ratio of male sickness. It has the highest proportion working in construction, transport, and utilities, and 60 per cent of its households are semiskilled and unskilled. Educational attainment is low, as is the proportion of people changing their jobs. The area forms a continuous ring around the central area from Vauxhall to Brunswick Dock.

Above-average rates of male unemployment occur in most of the inner area and also in the newer council estates, from Gillmoss and Cantril Farm to Netherley and Speke. Much of this pattern can be explained by the level of skill of the working population. Comparisons at the cluster level show that, the higher the proportion of unskilled workers, the greater is the total male unemployment ($r = +0.83$). This finding, based on data from areas that are more homogeneous than London boroughs, is broadly consistent with the results of Metcalf and Richardson (Chapter 8).

The fifth area in the system based on economic characteristics brings together high unemployment and absence from work through sickness and low skill. It is the only one in the system to show unemployment rates and proportions of semiskilled and unskilled that are significantly above the average for the city. It exhibits poor educational qualifications, little job changing, a low level of car ownership, and heavy reliance on public transport, together with many people walking to work. The working population of this area also relies to a greater extent than other parts of the city on jobs in transport (the docks and railways) and construction, and relatively few work in manufacturing industry.

In 1971, at a time when the average rate of male unemployment for Great Britain was 4.2 per cent and that for the city of Liverpool was 9.1 per cent, the rates shown in Table 13.8 were found in different parts of this area (from the cluster analysis). The socioeconomic status of clusters 8 and 10 are close to the average for the city. The actual size of cluster 8 (the Princes Avenue area) is too small for status-specific rates to be statistically reliable, but the indications are that unemployment rates among skilled manual workers were about 31 per cent, among semiskilled workers 24 per cent, and among unskilled workers 51 per cent. This is an area that serves a residual housing function for the transient population of the

Table 13.8 Male unemployment in selected parts of the 'high unemployment' area of the Liverpool district, 1971

Cluster	Description of cluster	Unemployment (%)
11	Small groups of council blocks of flats in Everton, Abercromby, etc.	21.9
8	Multilet houses of Princes Avenue etc.	19.9
10	Parts of Granby and Princes Park	18.7
12	Main dockside council estates	18.0

Source: Census of Population, 1971.

city. There are high indicators of family instability (e.g. illegitimacy, infectious diseases, children in care) and also much serious over-crowding. There are also high proportions of new Commonwealth-born residents (ten times the city average) and of Liverpool-born blacks. The special problems that face both groups and their position in a declining labour market are returned to in section 13.9.

Contrasted with these areas is that of the dockside council estates. Here unemployment rates are exceptionally high, chiefly because of the dependence of these clusters on unskilled work. Unskilled workers in this social area are more likely to be unemployed than similar workers in, say, the outer council estates because the former rely more on jobs in services, transport, and construction industries (in particular the docks, up to a third of which are within walking distance), whereas the latter rely more on manufacturing industry.

Thus, the core of the inner area may be defined on the one hand by very large proportions of unskilled men in declining industries, and on the other by areas of social instability. However, the inner area thus defined provides only a part of Liverpool's unemployment problem. It is complemented by the wide extent of the city making up the older terrace-housing areas and the modern peripheral council estates, where employment conditions are substantially better and not tied so closely to the declining service and transport sectors, but where unemployment is still over twice the national average.

13.9 The severity of unemployment

Numbers unemployed in Liverpool have nearly doubled since 1971 – a fact that would greatly increase the percentage rates shown in the Census. A major concern of the Liverpool IAS was to under-

Table 13.9 Male unemployed by age group (%)

Area	18–24	25–34	34–44	45–54	Over 55
Study area	29	27	19	15	9
Merseyside	23	23	19	17	18
North-West	21	21	17	17	24
Great Britain	18	17	15	16	32

Source: Department of Employment (1974c), tabulations for Merseyside, North-West, and Great Britain.

stand the effects and consequences of this scale of unemployment on the opportunities of individuals. This section draws on two surveys: first, a detailed study of all the unemployed workers (Survey of Unemployed) from the study area registered at the various employment offices in Liverpool; and second, a survey among a cohort of 18-year-olds who had attended schools in the IAS area (the Edge Hill survey).[2]

Unemployment tends to affect workers of younger age groups in low demand areas more than elsewhere. The IAS area has a high proportion both of the very young and of those in the middle years of their working life among the unemployed. A rather low proportion of the unemployed fall in the older age groups. These findings are consistent with those of the Department of Employment (Training Services Agency, 1974), which has shown that in areas of low demand the impact is felt more severely by younger persons (Table 13.9).

The severity of unemployment is indicated by the total length of time for which individuals have been out of work over the last few years (see Table 13.10). In 1975, 52 per cent of those currently unemployed had been out of work for at least two years in the last five; and three times as many men as were then unemployed had known a spell out of work in the last three years (Liverpool Inner Area Study, 1977c). Unemployment can be seen to be endemic in inner Liverpool. A high proportion of the workforce know what it is like to be unemployed – many for long spells.

13.10 The sharing out of unemployment

Clearly the main explanation of the high levels of unemployment in inner Liverpool is the lack of jobs. Those workers who have stayed

[2]For details of these surveys, see Liverpool Inner Area Study, 1977d.

Table 13.10   Total time spent unemployed in the last five years in the IAS area, by age group, 1975 (% of unemployed men)

Time unemployed	20–29	30–39	40–49	Over 50	All age groups
Less than 1 year	31	28	27	26	29
1–2 years	22	18	17	10	19
More than 2 years	47	54	56	64	52
Total	100	100	100	100	100

Source: Liverpool Inner Area Study (1977d).

in Liverpool are competing for a pool of rather poor jobs, and one that is rapidly shrinking. The new work introduced into Merseyside has been located away from the older areas, with the jobs going largely to those who have moved away from inner Liverpool to the zones of postwar population expansion.

However, the analysis of the surveys and Census shows that within the inner area unemployment has become heavily concentrated on certain groups, including young people, the unskilled, and immigrants. Other groups such as young people with a poor work record, ex-prisoners, and the long term unemployed, who fare badly in the labour market everywhere, do particularly badly in inner Liverpool.

The evidence suggests that the concentration of the most obvious effect of economic decline on certain groups is caused by particular features of the way in which a declining labour market works. In an area where unemployment is high, workers react by holding on to jobs they have. Interestingly, Census information shows the areas of highest unemployment to be those with least job changing. Anecdotal evidence is provided by the long waiting lists that exist in Liverpool for jobs that are customarily difficult to fill elsewhere and by the low turnover within them, e.g. Liverpool Corporation dustmen, and milkmen. Clearly, a lower throughput of workers among existing jobs reduces the number of vacancies becoming available.

A similar attenuation of the flow of vacancies results from the way in which employment has declined. An analysis of the components of change of local employment showed 80 per cent of the loss of jobs in inner Liverpool to be due to the decline of firms *in situ* (Liverpool Inner Area Study, 1977c); only a minor part of the loss was due to closures and moves. Much of the *in situ* loss of jobs has occurred by natural wastage, i.e. by firms not replacing workers who leave. Some forty firms from Liverpool 7 and 8 were interviewed; this survey (Liverpool Inner Area Study, 1977c) indicates that the average age structure of workers in the docks, railways, and manufacturing firms in inner Liverpool is rather high. Older men are loath to leave stable jobs, and the impact of declining local opportunities falls on younger age groups. Men 50–60 years old were found to have a lower rate of unemployment than those 30–40 years old – a reversal of the picture in both the North-West and the country.

The thing *not* to do in Liverpool, then, is to fall out of work. One of the reasons for the very high levels of unemployment among the low-skilled is the fact that many unskilled jobs are short-lived or temporary. The biscuit factories and holiday camps of north Wales provide seasonal work. Short spells of building work are available, but these are intermingled with long periods of unemployment. Low-skilled workers take longer to find work and hold each job for a shorter period than more skilled workers (see Table 13.11).

Employers in Liverpool have a degree of choice in recruiting that is far greater than in more buoyant parts of the country. People are loath to leave jobs; when a vacancy does become available the

Table 13.11 Length of time since registration of unemployed and period for which last job was held, by skill groups: IAS area, 1975 (%)

Period	Junior non-manual	Skilled manual	Semiskilled	Unskilled	All skill groups
Months since registration					
Less than 6 months	50	52	45	41	48
6–12 months	28	20	27	22	22
More than 12 months	22	28	28	37	30
Total	100	100	100	100	100
Months for which last job was held					
Less than 3 months	40	31	31	37	33
3–6 months	23	16	18	20	18
6–12 months	12	18	15	19	17
More than 12 months	25	35	36	24	32
Total	100	100	100	100	100

Source: Liverpool Inner Area Study (1977d).

Table 13.12 Comparison of skill of last job with that of previous jobs held by unemployed men: IAS area, 1975

	Last job	2 jobs back	3 jobs back	4 jobs back
Last job was skilled				
Sample size (no.)	305	196	130	93
% whose last/previous jobs were skilled:				
Junior-manual	—	2	3	4
Skilled manual	100	66	65	62
Semiskilled	—	11	13	12
Unskilled	—	14	14	16
Others	—	6	5	6
Total	100	100	100	100
Last job was unskilled				
Sample size (no.)	372	251	143	92
% whose last/previous jobs were unskilled:				
Junior non-manual	—	5	6	12
Skilled manual	—	14	12	10
Semiskilled	—	26	19	22
Unskilled	100	53	55	49
Others	—	2	8	7
Total	100	100	100	100

Note: Sample size gets smaller as we go back over time because complete information is not available on the records of the Employment Services Agency.
Source: Liverpool Inner Area Study (1977d).

number seeking work leads to a flood of applicants. It is not difficult to understand how a Catch-22 situation develops for low-skilled workers. Many of the jobs that they can take are short-lived, and yet an employer looks very critically at a varied and inconsistent work record.

However, the difficulty for unskilled men is worse than this for they are competing for jobs with men with a wide range of skill levels. A significant proportion (47 per cent) of those whose last job was unskilled held a 'better' job the time before, and similarly in previous jobs 34 per cent of those whose last job was skilled had, in their previous job, done a stint of less skilled work (see Table 13.12). Many of the unskilled were not unskilled at all; they had had a training in the past and a record of some years work in a skilled job. This suggests that skilled men join less skilled in the search for unskilled jobs, that they 'fill in' with an unskilled job if they fall out of work in their own trade. An examination of the records of those who have never held anything but an unskilled job shows them to have a disastrous employment record. More than 60 per cent had been unemployed for more than half of their time in the last five years.

This competition between workers of a wide range of skills for whatever jobs are going is exaggerated by the Employment Services Agency (ESA), which misrecords the occupation of men registering for unemployment. Table 13.12 compares the occupation classification of unemployed men, as recorded by Employment Officers, with the actual occupation of the last job held.[3] The ESA classified 63 per cent of men as unskilled on the basis of their last job and listed them as such in its statistical returns. In fact only 30 per cent of those recorded as unskilled had actually been in unskilled work (SEG 11) in their last job; for 13 per cent the last job had been skilled, and for 36 per cent either semiskilled (SEG 10) or junior non-manual (SEG 6).

The impact of the limited availability of jobs also falls very severely on other groups that either are just entering the labour market or that bring some other factor to it that an employer might class as an impediment. First, young people. The impact of the decline of local industry falls most severely on the very young. The scale of the problem may be appreciated from the fact that Liverpool has customarily more young persons unemployed than Birmingham and Greater London combined.

A survey among 18-year-olds in the IAS area found 25 per cent of boys to be unemployed (July 1975). The proportion of boys who had entered a job with apprentice grade training on leaving school (23 per cent) was lower than in both Liverpool as a whole (30 per cent) and the North-West (48 per cent). These statistics partly reflect qualifications and aptitudes; the level of educational achievement of the young people from the area is certainly very low (Liverpool Inner Area Study, 1977d). However, they also reflect the low level of economic activity. The demand for apprenticeships far exceeds the supply. One firm on Edge Lane received 200 applications for the four places it was able to offer in 1975. Plesseys receive around 400 applicants a year for what used to be forty

---

[3]The description of the last job recorded on each unemployed person's record was converted to the corresponding SEG by means of the OPCS Classification of Occupations.

apprentice places but which was cut to three or four in 1975. In the inner areas a high proportion of young people, who would be getting a proper training in more prosperous areas, start life in unskilled and semiskilled jobs. They are feeding the most oversupplied sector of the labour market and are denied the basic ticket to the skilled labour force – a training at the time of leaving school. An associated problem is the connection between apprentice training and further education. Less than 40 per cent of the sample had any contact with further education after leaving school, largely because most further education for the 16–19 age group is tied to training schemes.

Unemployment, as might be expected, falls most heavily on those with the fewest personal aptitudes. The young unemployed in inner Liverpool differ in a number of respects from those in work. They leave school at a younger age (75 per cent at the statutory age compared with 57 per cent of those in work), pass fewer examinations (10 per cent compared to 43 per cent), and are less likely to have attended a further education course (17 per cent compared to 38 per cent). They also take longer to get a job in the first place (36 per cent of those currently employed having taken at least six months to find a job when leaving school). Furthermore, two personal characteristics appear relevant: (a) of six coloured boys interviewed, all were unemployed; and (b) 40 per cent of the fathers of the young unemployed in the area were out of work themselves, living away from home, or dead.

Discriminating recruitment patterns undoubtedly account for the position of coloured workers. Few immigrants among the unemployed are recent arrivals in this country. However, despite a similar level of training and educational qualification to the UK born they do worse for jobs in a number of respects. First, they are over-represented in three low-paid occupations: shops, clerical, and personal services. They also experience greater difficulty in finding jobs. Few immigrants find a job within six months, rather more find employment in the 6–12-month period, but relatively few remain unemployed for more than a year. This record of unemployment can be compared with the record in jobs. Immigrants hold jobs very much longer on average; 48 per cent held their last job for more than a year, compared with 28 per cent of the UK born.

A survey among employers in Liverpool 7 and 8 showed that only thirteen of the thirty-four firms employed coloured workers, largely in unskilled jobs. Even in medium and large manufacturing firms, which are the most likely to employ coloured workers, only one employed more than 2 per cent coloured workers, and only three employed more than fifteen coloured men. Two employers admitted to not being prepared to employ blacks, others said that coloured men very rarely presented themselves, and others claimed that few possessed the right qualifications or work record. No firm interviewed currently had a coloured apprentice, despite the fact that around 200 boys in sample firms were undergoing this form of training. The firms interviewed were operating in an area with a 13 per cent immigrant population in addition to substantial numbers of Liverpool-born blacks.

The same factors that allow employers to discriminate against coloured workers also adversely affect the prospects of others. The prospects of the long-term unemployed are grim. Around 20 per cent of the adult unemployed had a recorded prison sentence. The operations of the housing market tend to concentrate certain groups (immigrants, the low-skilled, and offenders) into the inner areas. Their position where the demand for labour is weak becomes impossible.

13.11 The employment service

In these circumstances the role of an active employment policy takes on greater importance. The placement service is the point of contact between an unemployed person and the labour market. It has an important role in disseminating information about the jobs that are available locally and in encouraging movement elsewhere. The training service may improve the attractiveness of the area to outside investors, and the opportunities that are open to individuals in competing for jobs, by maintaining and improving the levels of skill.

The need for a well-developed employment service is greatest in areas such as Liverpool, where the numbers unemployed are highest and where structural unemployment exists. The service needs to concentrate its efforts in such areas and to exercise considerable autonomy in order to be able to respond flexibly to local opportunities, to be able to appreciate the special characteristics of the labour market in which it is operating, and to develop special services for those who suffer most severely from the results of economic decline. It was concluded in the Liverpool IAS that existing government employment services at most make little impact on those affected by the decline of the Liverpool economy, and at worst contribute to it (Liverpool Inner Area Study, 1977c).

The evidence of the Survey of Unemployed shows that more submissions have been made for skilled men, and for those who have completed an apprenticeship or attended a government training centre, than for less skilled – in fact that more help is given to those better placed in the labour market. Unskilled workers and those with no training have had very few submissions made for them. The size of the unskilled register is so large in Liverpool that it is not possible for ESA Employment Officers to give individual attention to any one but the most persistent. In fact the unskilled section of the live register is very rarely consulted for placement purposes. That a situation has arisen in which employment officers give more help to those who will find it easiest to get work in any case is due to a number of factors: management procedures encourage those among the unemployed with the best prospects to be put forward for jobs; the employment officer has to meet a certain placement target each week; he also has to generate a certain number of vacancies; and no system of priorities exists, either in terms of finding jobs for specified groups or in offering special advice or support.

Leece Street, the inner Liverpool Employment Office, has many more clients than it can cater for on an individual basis. Jobs fill themselves before employment officers have made submissions for them. It is not difficult to become demoralised in looking for a job that requires few skills in Liverpool, and the ESA in effect is providing a service only to those prepared to come to the exchange each morning at 9.30 a.m. to have first bite at the vacancies going. In many ways the system is similar to the old casual-labour schemes operated at the docks.

There has been a considerable increase in the number of training places available through the ESA on Merseyside, totalling 5,500 annually in 1976–77. However, it is clear the the low proportion of the unemployed[4] to have benefited from government training is primarily related to the shortage of available places. It is difficult to evolve clear indicators of the position, but at any time a comparison between the numbers unemployed on Merseyside and the current provision for training shows that only 7 per cent of the unemployed

---

[4]Less than 5 per cent of the unemployed in the survey had attended a government training centre or Skillcentre course.

can be accommodated on a course in any year. In fact the proportion is lower than this, for courses are attended not only by the unemployed but also by those in work, and more people flow on to and off the unemployment register during a year than are out of work at any time. Within inner Liverpool (as represented by the Leece Street employment office) more than 12,000 unemployed men are competing with men from other areas for the 650 places available at Aintree (the only Skillcentre within reasonable access of the inner city) if they wish to attend a Skillcentre course.

Long waiting lists exist for most courses. It is not possible to be considered for a course within some months of application, and for more popular skills (e.g. welding) the waiting period can stretch over two years. It is thus difficult for a man who becomes unemployed to get on to a course, and many will be back in work before their opportunity for training comes up. An added difficulty in view of the poor educational qualifications and experience of many of the unskilled lies in the standard of entry qualifications. In a number of cases these are very demanding, with around 50 per cent of applicants failing to gain admission to courses for lack of suitable qualifications or experience. Even where admission standards are not prohibitive there is a tendency to prefer the best qualified in order to maintain placement rates among those completing courses. This again may lessen the prospects of low-skilled workers with indifferent work records.

The Training Services Agency and Manpower Services Commission have recently taken a clear lead in putting forward the outlines of a possible strategy for the development of services to young people (Training Services Agency, 1974). Their discussion paper indicates many of the existing deficiencies and provides a clear programme for developing preparation in schools, induction, long-term training, provision for young people not receiving training, and training for the unemployed. This would involve greater resources being devoted to the training of young people and a more equitable distribution between those entering different types of work. It would also mean a closer involvement of the Training Services Agency in most parts of the process.

13.12 Conclusions

This chapter has attempted to show how the employment opportunities of workers in inner Liverpool have been affected by the scale of decline that has taken place in recent years in the economy of the city. This decline has affected virtually all industrial sectors except city centre services but has been heavily concentrated on low-skilled employment. There has been a particularly severe loss of jobs in the old basic industries (the docks, railways, and certain manufacturing firms), which employed large numbers of semiskilled and unskilled workers.

By contrast, the growth sectors of Merseyside, heavily supported by regional policy, have located in areas to which it is very difficult for those laid off in the older industries to travel in a normal daily journey to work. The demand for labour within the city labour market for all types of job except those of a managerial, professional, and clerical nature is weak. There are very many fewer jobs than workers for those obliged to work within Liverpool; the ratio deteriorated between 1966 and 1971, and this deterioration has almost certainly accelerated in more recent years. There has been little upward mobility among workers; rather, higher-skilled workers have come to compete for lower-skilled jobs.

The effects of this adverse pattern of demand can be traced in a number of ways, although not unfortunately on wage levels. In the first place the flow of vacancies that are available to those seeking work has been much reduced. Individuals have reacted to the difficulty of finding work by being reluctant to leave the jobs that they have, and many firms have reduced their establishment by natural wastage, not replacing workers who leave. Also, in terms of the replacement of skills in the labour force, it seems clear that firms have reduced their intake of apprentices in view of the relative ease of hiring skilled labour from among the ranks of the unemployed – a situation rarely found elsewhere in the country.

From the 1971 Census it is possible to see a clear spatial pattern within Liverpool in the distribution of unemployment. A rather limited number of areas in the city are prosperous – largely middle class settlements with rates of unemployment that are no higher than the national average. Contrasted with this is an area containing around two-thirds of the city's population, where the workforce mirrors that of the city and unemployment is about twice the national rate; it is this population that is affected by the general weakness of demand in the city's economy. Contrasted again with this area is another, concentrated specifically in a ring around the city centre, where the worst effects of economic decline are to be felt. Two types of sub-area can be isolated: (a) the area around the docks where those laid off from the old basic industry of the area have failed to find work elsewhere; and (b) the area of low quality and often multiple-occupied housing in which many of the more recent arrivals to the city have located, but which also contains a large portion of the long-established black community of Liverpool and provides accommodation for certain groups that tend to be concentrated in the inner city, such as single-parent families and ex-prisoners.

It is this last area that can be said to make up the 'inner city component' of Liverpool's resident working population. Many in the area have low educational achievement, few skills, and a poor work record. They suffer from considerable discrimination, and government training and placement services are very insensitive to their needs. It may be said that in many cases a labour market trap has developed; given the severe competition for jobs, those with the least skills and those who bring an impediment to the labour market (e.g. colour or a poor work record) are pushed to the bottom. Employment for many has become an irregular occurrence, and the pattern may become firmly established early in a working life. Many workers from this environment will be the last to be drawn back into work with any reflation of demand that might result from the success of inner city policy.

The effects of concentrated unemployment are particularly apparent in the inner city. Clearly, however, the inner city has no well-defined boundaries, and the processes that affect workers there are common to workers from other areas. This is already clear in the postwar peripheral settlements such as Kirkby and Netherley. Two results of low demand deserve urgent attention. First, young people who would have received a training elsewhere in the country miss out; this is inequitable, and it fuels the already oversupplied stock of low-skilled workers in the local labour market. Second, workers with well-established skills and stable work records become downwardly mobile; this makes life even more difficult for those with less developed skills and 'wastes' their own skills.

It may be argued that many of these problems would sort themselves out if new jobs could be introduced to the city, and the restoration of growth conditions to the local economy is obviously a prime goal of policy. This may, however, be difficult to achieve and long in coming. In the meantime those currently affected by the scale of decline in Liverpool might be helped by several means: by a better matching of the skills required in work to the skills possessed by individuals; by extensive programmes to maintain the level of skill in the population, especially among young people entering the labour market for the first time; and by guarding against discriminatory recruitment practices, the scope for which increases enormously in an area of weak labour demand.

14 Employment in Inner City Areas: a Case Study of the Position in Small Heath, Birmingham, 1974

Barbara M. D. Smith

14.1 Introduction

The work that forms the basis of this chapter was commissioned in 1974 by the Inner Area Study (IAS) consultants: Llewelyn-Davies, Weeks, Forestier-Walker, and Bor. The working papers that came out of the various small projects have been published in full elsewherc.[1] This chapter summarises the findings of these projects and draws together conclusions from them on the employment situation in Small Heath, Birmingham.

The chapter first sets out the aim of the original research as agreed with the sponsors to complement their own work. A framework for this work is then presented. This involves workplaces, employers, premises, and land as keys to local employment generation and provision. The first three of these were the subjects of investigation in Small Heath, the results of which are summarised here. Much of this involved data collection, obvious in nature but nevertheless new in relation to the local area. The weaknesses, both in the data sources relied on and in the limited inductive explanation directing the research, are recognised, but a start was made in this

[1]See lists published by the Department of the Environment in the series IAS/B. For a full bibliography, see Lambert (1977a, 1977b, 1978) and Smith (1974).

case study on which other research and policy making could build. More narrowly, an employment and industry dimension was provided for the IAS itself.

14.2 The aim of the original research

The aim of the work was to investigate the volume and composition of the jobs available in the IAS part of Small Heath and its job catchment area in south-east Birmingham (or as much of this as could be included in the brief time available). It omitted any investigation of the characteristics and jobs of employed residents in the study as this was the responsibility of the consultants.

By volume and composition of jobs was meant the number of jobs, their location, hours of work, and character in terms of the kind of employees required to fill them (in terms of age, sex, skill, and other criteria). The aim, which this part of the work only went half way to meeting, was to compare the jobs in the area with the employed residents there, to judge the current match, and to see whether either the jobs or the employed residents had been changing to the disadvantage of the residents or the employers. An important factor was therefore the extent to which local residents held the local jobs, both in and out, commuting being of relevance. There was little time for refinement of theory or method, and too much should not be claimed for the precision of the findings, although there is little doubt of their general accuracy.

It was essentially a local study. Comparative research in other inner areas and especially in outer areas was lacking in 1975 and is still lacking in 1977. There was, and is, evidence too of many of the same problems in other cities and labour markets generally. This indicates that many of the economic and employment problems are national ones. These issues are relevant to any assessment of the degree of peculiarity of either the economic structure or the decline of (a) inner areas in general or (b) this particular one.

14.3 A framework

Recollecting in tranquility, it becomes apparent that in 1974 it was only possible to put the work into a framework instinctively.[2] (One of the aspects to note in the 1974 framework is the absence of refer-

[2]This framework has been more fully developed in Smith (1977a).

ence to investment.) This involves two sets of influences on the balance and provision of employment in an area. These influences operate within the primary requirement that there is a demand for the products and services created by that employment. The lack of this demand may be all or a large part of the employment problem; thus, employment-generating policies may have to start with demand acceleration at national level. Subsequently, the influences discussed here, however, may become an absolute constraint preventing demand from benefiting employment locally.

One set of influences in the framework involves jobs, the other jobtakers. The set of influences and potential constraints on the *job* side are the actual and potential supply of four factors: jobs or workplaces, employers, premises in which to provide the jobs, and land for employment-generating purposes. Those on the *jobtakers* side (the labour supply side) are the actual and potential supply of four other factors: economically active persons, households in which these persons can live, houses to accommodate these households, and land on which to provide the houses. The two sets of influences join up into a circle both where the workplaces meet the economically active and where land is allocated between employment-supply-generating purposes and employment-demand-generating purposes.

In the work undertaken the concern was with the job side of this framework. Two assessments needed to be made. The first was of the current situation in order to compare it with that of the past, and the second was of the precise nature of the influence of each of these constraints on employment. Thus, conceptually, the framework included:

1. *Workplaces* – the stock of jobs at employing concerns of all kinds in the premises on the land in the area. This refers to the total of workplaces in the area in terms of both numbers and composition (age, sex, skill, hours, pay or other employee requirements of employers). Once these workplaces have been counted and classified, the crucial issues for employment balance are: whether decline or productivity improvement is reducing the number of jobs; whether change in the employers and their employee requirements is affecting the composition of available jobs; whether any of the jobs are vacant; and, if so, whether they can be filled from the economically active population on the jobtakers' side of the equation. Clearly, the supply and composition of workplaces may

be deficient because of factors affecting employers rather than jobs directly.

2. *Employers* – the stock of employers in the premises on the land in the area. These include all employment providers including the self-employed. Here, the stage is reached at which the workplace provision is shaped into employment of a particular size and composition that are liable to change. The character of each employer and his employee requirements are crucial to the composition and change in employment; for instance, the industry of the employer will affect the likelihood of growth or decline, and the processes used, organisation, status of unit, hours, sex, pay, skill requirements, etc. will affect the kind of jobs available. However, an employer also has some recruitment discretion as to the kind of jobs offered and to whom they are made available.

Both employers and employee requirements in an area can change. Employer changes reflect: (a) births and deaths of firms; and (b) moves in, out, and within the area. Employee requirements reflect: (a) changes in employers; and (b) changes in the requirements of existing employers through their growth or decline in size, or through variations in their products, operations, costs, or labour supply situation, or through variations in recruitment policies independently of these. These changes occur within the existing stock of premises or within changes in that stock through building, demolition, or change of use. Only limited change is possible without alteration in the stock of premises.

3. *Premises* – the stock of premises on the land at the present time in use for employment-generating purposes. The crucial issues for employment provision are: what premises there are in number, size, type, and quality; whether any of these premises are vacant (idle) or not in use for employment-generating purposes; and, if idle, whether they can be brought into use. Constraints on the latter include the availability of planning permission of supply, ownership, physical nature, and suitability for the employment-generating purposes needing premises. Another issue is the density of employment-generating floorspace per acre of land. The contrast between multistorey offices and a storage yard brings home this point. The use of scarce industrial land for warehouses is often the policy issue. Has density been changing in existing premises, with consequences for employment? Density is altered by either building or demolition as well as by use and so is related to the stock of premises at different times on the same land and to its usage.

Finally, changes in the quality of the premises may affect their ability to provide jobs, and this could be influenced by the planners through Industrial Development Certificate (IDC) or planning permission supply or through rehabilitation schemes.

4. *Land* – the stock of land in the area in use, or allocated and available for employment-generating purposes. Conceptually, land for employment generation is defined more widely than specifically industrial land and includes land for shops, farms, offices, schools, etc., all of which generate employment as well as goods or services. The land is of course in units of various kinds and not homogeneous. The crucial issues for employment provision are: what land is in employment-generating use; whether any is idle; and, if so, whether it can be brought into use. Constraints on this include IDC and planning permission supply, ownership, the physical nature of the land, and its accessibility to users, sewerage, road facilities, etc. Its suitability in broad terms may perhaps be assumed from its allocation to employment-generating uses.

Logically, although it was outside the research project, the next influence on employment provision is the competition for land from housing and associated uses. Moving up the framework on the jobtakers' side, housing land provision affects house provision, which in turn affects the number and type of households and hence the number and type of economically active persons who are available to work. These, plus or minus net in-commuters, comprise the labour force that is available to fill the workplaces in the first stage of the framework. Again, the composition of this labour force needs to be considered, in terms of age, sex, skill, education, etc., and changes in this due to housing, education or industrial-training policies, and the provision of day nurseries or public transport not only in the area itself but also in areas that are relevant through commuting.

It could be argued that these influences did not constrain employment provision in Small Heath in the early 1960s when unemployment levels were low. Change may have occurred through any of these points in the framework, although it is certain, for instance, that the resident population has not increased to push up unemployment. Planners need to know the crucial constraints if they are to act on them. The identification of these will not be easy, but it will be no use providing premises if it is not premises but employers (entrepreneurs, investors) that are lacking. On the other hand, it will not be surprising if the numbers of employers and jobs have fallen if redevelopment has been causing the demolition of shops, work-shops, etc. and blighting others.

This framework identifies the subjects for investigation. It establishes that these should be in turn jobs, employers, premises, and land to arrive at the influences on jobs and that the investigation should primarily take the form of a count of these at different times to get at the present situation and recent changes. As a secondary aspect, much more information should be obtained about the composition of the stock of units and about densities, vacancies, etc. The work done in Small Heath made a start on these lines; however, it did not reach land supply or densities. Nor did it attempt to assess the economic and social factors behind any of the changes found.

14.4 Practical difficulties

There were a number of substantial difficulties to be met in translating these ideas into practice. The lack of research time, of lists of employers or premises, and of details of workplaces or jobtakers, together with instability in the employment situation in the summer of 1974, all presented problems. Evaluation also presented a major problem since only one very restricted area was being considered and little comparative information was available.

Another major issue was the appropriate employment area to cover. This affected research design and research findings. No finite travel-to-work area could be isolated in Small Heath, and in any case the Small Heath IAS area is largely residential with employment for residents provided in adjacent areas. A study of the Birmingham area indicated that jobs outside their own area were not likely to compensate Small Heath residents for adverse changes to jobs in their own area. The likelihood in 1974 was that any unemployed Small Heath residents catching buses to find work in the wider labour market would merely have passed passengers from elsewhere travelling into Small Heath to look for work because of declines in their own areas. It was considered that this made the selection of a self-contained labour-market area less crucial.

There was also the question as to whether economically active residents in the Small Heath area had been declining in numbers parallel to jobs. This could be cause or effect. There are three points here. First, the number of employed residents may not be the crucial statistic if emigrants from the area continued to work in Birmingham after moving out to live. Second, notwithstanding, a decline in the numbers of residents and their spending power would have affected the demand for services and hence the jobs in these sectors. Third, there is every indication that the emigration of population has involved people with particular employment characteristics and it looks as if the lost employment opportunities have not matched these characteristics.

Evidence from the Census of Population for Birmingham and Small Heath ward shows a considerable increase in in-commuting, larger declines in the proportion of economically active persons than in total population (population in 1971 in Small Heath was 90 per cent of that of 1966 compared with 81 per cent for the economically active, the population being maintained by the growth in the number of children under 15 years), and higher unemployment rates in Small Heath in 1971 compared with Birmingham in 1971 and compared with Small Heath in 1966 and in 1961 (in 1971, the Small Heath rate was 6.9 per cent compared with 4.7 per cent in Birmingham). Given the composition of the resident population of Small Heath ward in 1971, it is not surprising that unemployment incidence is higher there than in Birmingham as a whole, for, first, the rate of unemployment among the unemployment-prone groups was higher in Small Heath and, second, such groups formed a higher proportion of the local population. Thus, the opportunity to become unemployed was greater as well as the outcome. Unemployment caused by sickness was also more common in the inner area.

In consequence of these practical difficulties, this report is based on a number of desk studies aimed at estimating different parameters of the employment situation: the number of premises available as employing units, the employment potential of plant and shop, the movement and opening/closure of employing units, and changes in total employment and unemployment. It also includes a survey of current employment in larger enterprises in the study area and its immediate vicinity. The aim has been to examine and quantify trends by any means available, even where this has involved reliance on rather imperfect sources, although every effort has been made to check and supplement these sources. Much of the work has concentrated on the Small Heath IAS area. Where possible, information on the wider picture is presented both to help evaluation and to make some attempt to deal with the travel-to-work issue.

14.5 The research carried out

The research programme as carried out involved eight projects. Each project represented an independent exercise, drawing on either new or past work, the latter not being designed with this study in mind. All represent desk studies using secondary sources, except for the final and most important one (section 14.58). This was based on interviews carried out with employers in the study area and its vicinity about the jobs that they provided.

Accounts of these eight projects are summarised here and the implications of their findings highlighted. For definitions, methods, and sources beyond what is given here, the papers in the original report should be consulted.

In 1975 similar inquiries were carried out to extend the work to the wider Small Heath local planning district. Methods were similar. In particular this further work permitted the effect of redevelopment in St Andrews to be isolated more fully.[3] Findings basically confirmed the earlier work.

14.5.1 Large employing units

The first project was directed at larger employing units (employers rather then premises) as one of the influences on employment in the study area. It analysed the employing units with over ten employees in the study area in 1967 by industry and employment size. The inquiry was based on a list of employers by size and industry that was available for that date. It provided an elementary starting point in assessing the economy of the area narrowly defined.

The IAS part of Small Heath was found to contain 162 employing units on this basis in 1967: 55 in manufacturing, 19 in construction, and 88 in services. While all these had over ten employees, only 10 per cent had over 100 and none over 1,000. Butlers (part of the Joseph Lucas Group) making vehicle lamps, Chrysler in car part distribution, and Wimbush in bread and cake making were the three concerns with over 500 employees.

Comparison with Birmingham indicated the relative absence of large concerns, the relative presence of units with between twenty-five and ninety-nine employees in the study area, and a mix of manufacturing rather than the more usual predominantly metal-

[3]Copies of these papers – nos. 9–11 in the Small Heath working paper series – are available from the author.

processing firms of Birmingham. It was estimated that employment was biased towards construction and services, notwithstanding the omission of many small service-based units from the project.

14.5.2 Employing units over time

This project pursued the issue of employing units (here meaning premises as much as employers) with a comparison over time from 1960 to 1973–74. It examined changes in the numbers and industry of employing units of all sizes and kinds in the study area using *Kelly's Directories of Birmingham* street lists as a source. While these lists are not absolutely accurate, they enabled the small and service units not covered in other projects to be included, and accuracy was improved as one year was checked against another.

It was found that there were 1,300 employing units in the study area streets in 1960. The number declined by 20 per cent after 1960, although increases occurred in the number of garages, banks and insurance offices, cafes, betting shops, and travel agents. This 20 per cent decline occurred overall and in each broad sector: manufacturing, services, and construction. Manufacturing units fell from 142 to 113, construction from 53 to 40, and service from 1,105 to 894 between 1960 and 1973–74. The overall decline was from 1,300 units to 1,047. Retail shops declined in number from 675 to 429 but, outside distribution, service units increased in number.

Comparative evidence of the same kind is not available. However, rating evidence for Birmingham as a whole (from the *Birmingham Abstract of Statistics*) indicates a decline in shop premises of 21 per cent between 1960 and 1972 and an increase in garages of 51 per cent.

The distribution of employing units was also examined spatially, and the main decline was located as occurring in the Bolton Road vicinity where redevelopment had been proceeding. Employing units fell by 41 per cent there but hardly at all in the Green Lane and Bordesley Green area and less than overall on the main Coventry Road. This contrast suggests that planning and redevelopment policies were important influences within the more general inner-area picture.

Decline occurred principally in the early 1960s outside distribution and in the early 1970s in all sectors; the latter decline particularly affected retail shops.

Comparative evidence is needed to evaluate the redevelopment, structural, and other influences in this decline and to separate general and local influences, and all these prove very difficult to separate.

14.5.3 *Premises in manufacturing use over time*

Employment is provided in premises: no premises, no employment. Changes in the supply and use of premises could be an absolute constraint on employment in an area and an explanation for its decline.

This project took the individual premises that at some time between the late 1950s and 1974 provided accommodation for manufacturing and related jobs in the study area. (Other premises were excluded simply for lack of time and information.) By following each set of premises through the twenty years it was possible to trace the changes that occurred, first, in the premises themselves (i.e. the incidence of vacancy, demolition, subdivision, etc.) and, second, in the occupiers of the premises. Thus, a fairly precise analysis of the ingredients of job decline in a small area was obtained.

The project identified 191 premises as relevant at the end of the 1950s and 215 in 1973–4, although fewer of the latter were in industrial use at that time. Subdivision, new building, or change of use explained the net additions. The number of premises that were not in use for anything rose from 24 in 1960 to 57 in 1974, and the number in use as shops, garages, repair shops, etc. (non-manufacturing) rose from 10 to 34. This count was based on a number of sources: the list used in the first project, past factory-inspectorate data, and *Kelly's Directories of Birmingham*.

Using what employment information was available, it seems that about 2,200 jobs disappeared by 1974 out of the 5,100 estimated to have been provided in these premises at the end of the 1950s. Trading changes seem to have been more significant in causing this fall than industrial relocation. The loss of 1,600 jobs at BSA Cycles, the closure of three laundries, and the reduction of manpower at Wimbush through mechanisation in breadmaking were major factors in the decline. (The more recent closure of BSA Motor Cycles occurred 50 yards outside the study area.)

This decline in jobs was at a rate of 39 per cent over fifteen years or 2.6 per cent per annum – double the 1.3 per cent per annum decline in Birmingham employment.

Closures cost 2,430 jobs, reductions in jobs at existing works 250, and moves elsewhere 115, plus 300 office jobs recently moved to Solihull. However, openings brought in 480 jobs (net of jobs lost in the firms replaced in the same works), expansions at existing premises 90, and moves-in 300.

While the area lost BSA Cycles, it gained a Chrysler parts depot (in the old Singer Motor factory) and Smiths Industries (in the old David Harcourt works), although the latter two only added 300 jobs net to the employment in the area.

In 1974, 380 jobs had been lost from premises vacant or demolished – a relatively small part of the total (and included above).

Thus, these findings draw attention (a) to the important point that a continued supply of premises must be maintained if employment is to be provided in the area, and (b) to the specific ingredients of decline in this precise area. The limited importance of outward movement questions the role often given to regional and overspill policy in inner city decline.

14.5.4 The wider employment scene: employment change in Birmingham

The IAS part of Small Heath lies in Birmingham, and employment conditions and changes in Birmingham obviously have a profound effect on the area. An examination was made of the employment pattern in Birmingham in 1971 and of changes evidenced between 1951 and 1971 using Department of Employment ERII statistics. Comparison was made with Great Britain.

The statistics need not be repeated here. However, they made it clear that the employment prosperity that was evident in Birmingham in the early 1960s had disappeared by 1971. The decline, which started in 1967, has continued since. Thus, any decline in the inner area was paralleled in Birmingham as a whole. The economic problem is clearly wider than the inner areas and in some respects is a national one. The essential point is that Small Heath residents faced with decline in their local job opportunities could not have found compensation in the wider labour market area. In both, job loss exceeded the loss of economically active resident population.

14.5.5 Public-sector employing units

Public-sector employing units were traced in the study area. There was in practice no time to consider the employment provided by them (although it has been drawn into later work), but it is worth considering whether the public sector cannot help the employment situation directly through its own local employment and recruitment criteria.

14.5.6 Changes in employers: the flow of employers into and out of the area

Employers rather than premises were considered here using data collected in an earlier study from comparisons of names and addresses in *Rylands' Directory* of the metal trades and the employers' register, telephone directories, etc.

It has been suggested that employment problems in inner city areas are a consequence of the decentralisation of industry proceeding faster than that of population. Also relevant is the net balance between the births and deaths of concerns. This project looked at the movement of employers into, within, and out of: first, Birmingham; second, the sector of Birmingham in and around the study area; third, the Small Heath employment-exchange area (including Solihull); and fourth, the study area. The coverage in time and industry differed from one area to another, although comparisons were attempted, but it is evident that there has been a net outward movement of industry from each area and from Birmingham with a consequent effect upon employment and its location. It is also evident that there has been a good deal of movement within the city. The rates of movement and destinations vary between industries and by size of plant, with manufacturing and construction firms more likely, for instance, to move out of the Small Heath exchange area when they move.

Changes resulting from movement and closure have been considerable in recent years. For instaι.ce, 35 per cent of the employing units in Small Heath exchange area left the area between 1967 and 1973–4, either moving out or closing down (this ignores moves in, but these were very few); this may represent a loss of 18–25 per cent of the jobs in the area in 1967. As indicated earlier, closures seem to be more important than moves-out, suggesting that changes in trading conditions rather than redevelopment or regional policy are responsible, and closures neither reappear nor benefit other areas.

It is clear also that the study area (and Small Heath and Birmingham) continues to hold and attract firms; many remain in their existing premises or move very short distances when they move, and others start up in the area. It is moves-in from areas outside Birmingham that are lacking. In most instances, therefore, employers are not voting with their feet to leave either Birmingham or Small Heath.

Nevertheless, although this hopeful point is made the trend in the number of employing units was down from closures and moves-out, while other work does not suggest that any expansion of existing employers was providing either enough replacement jobs or the driving force necessary to cause the others to leave through competition for land and labour. Job decline is definite and sustained.

14.5.7 *The outcome: comparative unemployment*

This project looked at registered unemployment (the wholly unemployed) in the Small Heath employment exchange area and in Birmingham between 1961 and 1974. The Small Heath share of Birmingham's unemployment has been volatile but has increased in recent years for men and women, although the share of the latter has been lower than that for men. Meanwhile, Birmingham's unemployment rate has risen relative to that for Great Britain. From 1970 to 1973 the Birmingham rate was above the national one – a marked reversal of the previous relationship. Birmingham rates are higher now too in comparison with those of Greater London. Thus, the inner area problem in Birmingham occurs within a less favourable regional employment situation than does the locally more severe one in London.

14.5.8 *Workplaces: the composition of employment at selected local concerns, and changes in that employment*

This project was the major new contribution to the research; it was based on interviews with the larger employers in the study area or within 2–3 km of its boundaries. All the known larger employers (with over 100 employees) other than the local authority in the study area were included, together with a number of larger concerns just outside. Time prevented the inclusion of more from outside; selection was therefore mainly on the basis of size and location. This was partly because Pinder's (unpublished) study for the consultants had looked specifically at small manufacturing concerns. (The 1975 work took in Pinder's small firms, local authority and public sector employment, and other concerns mainly within the same spatial area to cover 33,000 jobs.)

In 1974, 37 employers with 49 plants and 26,606 employees were included overall. Of these, 23 employers employing 4,416 people in 27 premises were located in the study area, and the other 14 with 22 premises and 22,200 employees were located just outside. The employment provided had particular characteristics of importance to study-area employment well-being. These jobs were of course complemented in practice by the employment that was available at concerns not included in the survey, particularly by employment elsewhere in Birmingham and in service establishments in the local area in sectors not represented in the survey (mainly because of their small size). Nevertheless, this account deals with jobs of substantial importance to employed residents of the study area. It has in mind the notion that the characteristics of these jobs should broadly match those of the employed population if there is to be adequate employment provision in the area.

A number of points with important implications for local employment came out of this comparison:

1. There was some contrast between the jobs provided in the often smaller study-area concerns and those just outside. The latter were larger concerns, employing proportionately more men and more works personnel (as opposed to office workers) than the others.
2. Office jobs formed one-third of those in the study area concerns interviewed. This was a higher proportion than nationally and than in the concerns interviewed outside the study area (25 per cent). However, it was suggested that many of these office jobs were held by in-commuters rather than by local residents. Evidence from the 1971 Census of Population and the 1974 Inner Area Social Survey (Morton-Williams and Stowell, 1974) suggest that only 21 per cent of Small Heath residents were in standard socioeconomic groups (SEGs) 1–6 and 13 (employers, managers, and professional and non-manual groups) compared with 35 per cent in Birmingham as a whole and 36 per cent in Great Britain. This left 79 per cent in manual work in the local area, compared with 65 per cent in Birmingham and 64 per cent in Great Britain.
   Using census data analysed by both socioeconomic group

and industry, it was found that some 5,540 (50 per cent) of the 10,930 employed of both sexes in Small Heath ward in 1971 were in manual work in manufacturing (SEGs 7–11 and 15). The proportion in Birmingham was 40 per cent.

Thus, the office—staff job proportion in the concerns interviewed was much higher than in the economically active resident population in the area. This could explain the in-commuting reported (in 1971 nearly 50 per cent of all jobs in Birmingham County Borough in SEGs 1–6 and 13 were held by in-commuters into the borough). So could the lower educational attainment reached overall and in most socioeconomic groups in Small Heath compared with Birmingham.

The converse applied too. While 67 per cent of the jobs at these concerns were for works or manual personnel, the census showed the economically active population of Small Heath ward to include 79 per cent in these kinds of jobs, although only 50 per cent were specifically manual workers in manufacturing. It therefore seems likely that some manual worker residents have to travel out to work because of the mix of local jobs.

3. Female jobs formed 35 per cent of those in study area concerns – a similar proportion to that in Birmingham overall, but higher than in the concerns interviewed outside the study area (28 per cent) despite the inclusion of a hospital among the latter. There seemed to be a generous share of female manufacturing jobs in the study area itself, resulting from four concerns employing mainly women.

4. This means conversely that male manufacturing jobs in the study area concerns were less frequent and that this was compensated for in the concerns just outside, where *both* office staff and works jobs were dominated by men.

5. There were few part-time jobs for women in these firms, although seven in the summer of 1974 ran popular evening shifts for women – but not any longer it is thought. The Census of Population, however, shows that women in Small Heath ward in 1971 had part time jobs in the same proportion as women in Birmingham as a whole, although it also shows female activity rates to have been somewhat lower in Small Heath than in Birmingham. However, more women with children under 5 years were working and were working full time. The employment position for women in the study area vicinity looks less favourable when the census data is analysed in such detail.

6. There was a good deal of shiftwork for men. About 39 per cent of male manual workers at the concerns interviewed worked nights permanently or in rotation. This seems to be well above the national average of 20 per cent (Department of Employment, 1974b).

   Shiftworking raises earnings but often restricts overtime working and the employment of women and school leavers. It may also complicate domestic and social arrangements (as may female evening shiftworking). Some men, however, sought permanent nightwork. Shiftworking provides one means of adding to employment densities on the same floorspace and industrial land. It is therefore important to land shortage areas like the study area, or to areas like Saltley where redundant industrial land is being held idle or turned over to warehouses for capital and current profits; 81 acres in Saltley owned by nationalised industries were reported to be in this position (Community Development Project, 1975c).

   Shiftworking firms may find their manual labour costs relatively important, and this may make location in areas like the study area more attractive if this point is appreciated. The Canning Town Community Development Project has suggested that such points were overlooked by Standard Telephones (Community Development Project, 1975a).

7. Some of the characteristics described above derived from the bias in the sample of the survey employers towards manufacturing and large concerns, although the majority of Birmingham employees work in large manufacturing concerns. Included in the survey, however, were a large hospital and Post Office supplies stores.

8. There was a low proportion of skilled manual jobs in these concerns – 22 per cent of the works complement, compared with a national 43 per cent (excluding the hospital and defining skilled as apprenticeship trained). Relatively more jobs than nationally were in the unskilled category at these concerns. This may provide jobs that can be filled specifically by local residents, encouraging employers and residents to remain in the area. On the other hand, it restricts training opportunities and earning prospects and may encourage labour turnover and the incidence of unemployment.

9. Immigrants were estimated to hold roughly 11 per cent of the total jobs at these concerns – some 3,000 jobs in all out of

26,600. This was 14 per cent of the male and 8 per cent of the female jobs. Immigrants formed the majority of the male works labour force only in perhaps five concerns in the study area and two outside. Immigrants tended to hold the unskilled and semi-skilled jobs. Distribution seems to have been uneven for this and other reasons.

However, the 1971 census indicates that economically active men with parents born in the New Commonwealth formed 24 per cent of the economically active in Small Heath ward and that other immigrants, including the Irish, formed another 14 per cent. Thus, to a disproportionate extent immigrants seem likely to have to travel out of the vicinity to find work.

10. At least five of the larger firms seemed unlikely to recruit manual workers over the age of 50 or 55, although there was no suggestion that they would dismiss their own employees at this age. This implies some restriction on the ability of an employee dismissed from an existing job, at this age, to find another.

11. There were few jobs in these concerns for school leavers and young people of either sex, with or without training. In concerns employing between them 26,600 people only just under 300 openings for young people were found. Most of these involved training as some employers shut their doors completely to the employment of untrained young people, perhaps for paternalistic reasons, but ignoring the fact that 78 per cent of their works personnel were semi- and unskilled manual workers. Factors influencing this were the lack of the use of apprenticeships as a means of supplying future skilled labour (as firms expected to 'poach' skilled workers when these were needed), the lack of applicants for apprenticeships (vacancies existed), a low percentage of skilled jobs in total employment, the availability of women and immigrant men to do unskilled work, and the supposed reluctance of school leavers to do unskilled factory work for the wages available. Some trade unions oppose the employment of young people as their high turnover imposes a burden on their adult members.

More information is needed (and is being collected) on what school leavers do for a living *before* they become unskilled factory workers at 18 or 21 (Smith, 1975). Consideration also needs to be given to why enough suitable applicants for apprenticeships cannot be found.

On the assumption of a closed labour market, all young persons aged 16 and 17 resident in the study area and seeking employment would need to find it at these concerns. A total labour force of 26,600 could be expected to contain about 1,000 employees of 16 and 17 divided equally between the sexes across all industries; but the interviewed concerns produced only 300 jobs in all, indicating a marked deficiency. Moreover, the age structure of the population, especially of the immigrant population, in Small Heath shows an increasing number of school leavers relative to those retiring from the labour force. Thus, job demand is going to rise sharply from the existing population in the near future. This makes the job deficiency for young people in the interviewed concerns look even more serious.

12. About 120 job vacancies were found at the interviewed concerns with normal labour turnover, however, producing (in 1974) a regular flow of vacancies at many firms. While these would not give all the local unemployed a job, many individuals could obtain one. However, in 1974 the position was tightening; a no-replacement policy was spreading, and there were also redundancies and more short-time working, starting with the dismissal of part time women.

Natural wastage as a means of reducing a labour force hits particularly those seeking to enter the labour force and those made redundant at another firm.

13. Six employers out of the thirty-seven said that they were prepared to take on non-English-speaking employees; another fifteen were not (unless shortages became desperate). Many had additional and often quite demanding requirements of recruits even for semi- and unskilled work. Some employers insisted on checking references and on medical tests, while the food factories made fairly rigid cleanliness demands. Many concerns used an application form to screen applicants, especially callers. This was a useful expedient for jobs where written credentials were lacking, but at a seminar with career teachers in Small Heath this was felt to be an insurmountable barrier to many school leavers and thus discriminatory. So, a low level of literacy should be added to lack of knowledge of spoken English as a problem. The incidence of these conditions in the local population is unknown.

14. About fifteen employers had overt systems under which less skilled employees could be upgraded to fill vacancies as these

arose. At least three other concerns upgraded employees less formally. Elsewhere, this may be called promotion from within. Such a system meant that most jobs offered outside these firms were either unskilled (and often menial, e.g. a janitor or sweeper) or 'scarcity' occupations (e.g. craftsmen, accountants) where skill could not be picked up on the job and where there were often professional or craft associations or unions restricting the entry of dilutees. This system provided some means of career and earnings advancement for the unskilled, but it could keep out from jobs in such firms those already possessing experience unless they were prepared to enter at the lowest level and await promotion.

15. Methods of recruitment varied but had a significant influence on the kinds of jobs available to those applying in particular but different ways. Recruits were obtained either from internal upgrading, the employment exchange, press advertisements, callers, or friends of existing employees according to the skill requirements of the jobs, the practice of the firm, and its labour supply situation. The latter varied in 1974 from acute shortage in one or two firms (when school leavers and immigrants were recruited) to superfluity (when a waiting list existed and few jobs reached the exchange or press advertisement).

The discretion of the 'gatekeepers' was important in determining whether particular applicants obtained jobs and where the applicants were drawn from – leaving aside how the firm decided what jobs were vacant and to be filled and what recruitment requirements had to be met by applicants. The 'gatekeepers' included personnel reception, personnel managers, departmental foremen, and for some the employment exchange staff. Attitudes and practices seemed to vary randomly from firm to firm.

16. Earnings for a 40-hour week on days ranged widely at the concerns interviewed, jobs in the bakery trade being among the lowest paid. (The working paper on this project listed earnings, including overtime, shift, and threshold payments in dozens of local jobs for men and women.) Earnings could be substantially added to by overtime working (not available, though, at a number of concerns at any time), and by shiftwork and nightwork (also not available to many). For some, 10 hours overtime could add 37 per cent to weekly earnings at time-and-a-half rate, and shiftwork 10–25 per cent. Earnings of £40 a week in 1974 could be boosted to £62 (before tax) if both overtime

and shifts were worked in the same week. Women were less well paid in terms both of lower rates and of less overtime and shiftworking, although their income was needed by many families.

17. It seems likely that skilled and office employees in local firms tended to be in-commuters, not residents, and that some ex-residents held on to local jobs after moving house elsewhere. Thus, all jobs at these concerns were not available to current local residents.

18. The main attraction of the area to employers seems to be the supplies of unskilled and semiskilled employees, including men prepared to work nights. A policy of locating offices or skilled-worker-employing firms in the area may yield little local benefit unless recruitment and training discriminates in favour of local residents. Two concerns have moved their offices out of the vicinity to Solihull in recent years, ostensibly to move nearer employees.

19. Taking the periods 1969–74 and 1974–79, five of the concerns interviewed were new to the area, and seven (possibly nine, including the Chrysler parts depot with 1,100 jobs) expected to depart in the future.

20. Employment had changed recently at many of these concerns, but the expansions in jobs mentioned in 1974 had not balanced the declines. Employment at the concerns interviewed had fallen by 2,800 jobs or 10 per cent in five years. In the recent past twelve concerns had expanded employment to the present level, while that at seven had declined. One firm, Wilmot Breedon, had cut employment by a third in five years, and after the survey it shut down a complete factory making more people redundant. The first was due to rationalisation and the second to trade recession, but the factory space has gone on the market. BSA was another major source of job loss in the area. Newcomers were Dolland and Aitchison, makers of spectacles for their own optician shops, and Smith Industries; both took over existing works and so were replacements, not additions, to employing units.

Future growth even in 1974 suggested a bare 160 jobs, excluding the hospital (where wards were built but unstaffed).

So, expected losses exceeded expected gains. Replacement expansion possibilities were limited by the fact that seven large concerns in 1974 had reached the end of their space and two expected any growth to be located in their development area plants. Others had land but depended on the planning authority's attitude for its development.

21. Although employment at only a limited local group of concerns was examined and the coverage could usefully be widened, a useful picture of the job supply situation facing residents in the study area emerged.

14.6 Sources of employment gain and loss

There are two forces here: the expansion or contraction of concerns *in situ*, and the movement of concerns, both having an effect on employment. It is time to consider the reasons behind each of these at the general level, these reasons being relevant to the design of remedial measures.

Expansion or contraction in situ

The causes of expansion and contraction *in situ* can be listed as:

1. Changes in the demand for the product of the factory or concern   These changes may be due to competition won or lost or to structural change in demand affecting the whole industry. It is difficult to absolve management from some responsibility for failure to deal even with structural change. Demand changes have been important in the study area, e.g. increasing car demand and decreasing cycle and motorcycle demand.

2. Changes in output per employee (usually upwards)   Unless demand can be increased, increases in productivity will reduce jobs. Capital investment is encouraged by labour costs and shortages and has been fostered by government through investment incentives. The fact that there may still be room for improvement does not preclude a substantial past effect. This may qualify enthusiasm for investment that turns out to be just labour saving. Another aspect of this is the relationship between employees and space. Investment in space-consuming machinery and facilities must reduce employment unless additional space is available on the same site or on idle industrial land in the vicinity. Both these aspects will be welcome to the firms concerned and to the national economy, but the effect may be serious on employment at existing, often prosperous, concerns. Alternative jobs, and hence additional land on which to locate these jobs, are needed. Both are also an impetus to movement if the existing site is deficient. The arithmetic is frightening to an employment planner. One counterbalancing factor is an increase in shiftworking.

3. *Changes in organisation within firms that affect the output and employment mix at particular plants*   Closely related to productivity changes, the term 'rationalisation' embraces changes not necessarily linked with improvements in productivity although presumably aimed at reducing costs and labour somewhere. Here again there is a link with movement, for included would be the hiving-off of departments to or from other locations and plants.

Movement

The causes of movement may be similarly summarised. Movement is usually caused by some deficiency developing in the existing premises or location rather than, pure and simple, the attraction of another site. Firms do not move without good reason. Deficiencies in the existing premises that may cause a move may be divided into five kinds:

(a) lack of space to accommodate expansion, either immediate or future;
(b) poor quality of the existing premises in various respects, pushing up costs and prompting a move when these cannot be remedied economically on the site;
(c) deficiencies relating to the locality of the premises in terms, perhaps, of labour supply, transport links, or suppliers;
(d) deficiencies in relation to company or group organisation that suggest, often irrespective of the position in the premises affected, that the plant should be closed; and
(e) redevelopment or demolition caused by road schemes and the like, which may be direct or anticipated – or even mistakenly anticipated.

Where movement out of premises is involved these deficiencies will operate at the study area premises; with moves-in, at a plant elsewhere. In either case these are relative deficiencies and are conditional on the identification of a better alternative.

While probably more movement results from a lack of space than from other causes, total movement, and the balance between causes, will change according to the economic climate and the circumstances of the particular area and firm. The present economic climate may have reduced the incidence of growth but made firms more aware of quality and cost factors and generated rationalisations. In the past few firms have moved from the study area because of defects in their location. It was their premises that were defective, and such firms could be satisfied with alternative premises nearby. Industrial land zoning and allocations and the ability to obtain an IDC and planning permission can constrain this, while financial and other incentives to movement to development areas and even to overspill areas may encourage longer moves or the opening of branch plants further off (Smith, Ruddy, and Black, 1974; West Midlands Regional Study, 1972).

The present situation in the study area with redevelopment, road plans, old premises, and limited alternative premises must generate a continuing movement flow outwards; and within Birmingham, for the same reasons, a similar trend is evident. Moreover, the trend in the study area at least must continue as none of the processes is likely to be reversed; and as alternative premises at low rents or prices become scarcer in Birmingham movement out is likely to be over extending distances, carrying jobs further from their present locations and causing redundancies in Birmingham.

While in the past there was criticism of Birmingham Corporation for not matching its public relations claims that it was making every effort to retain its firms, much more sympathetic policies are now evident in a positive attempt to help employment. Unit factory provision, the postponement of road schemes, rehabilitation replacing redevelopment, emergent industrial-renewal policies, and efforts to foster existing employers will all help, and Birmingham's schemes are being supplemented by the West Midlands County Council as the structure plan proposals indicate. However, finance is a constraint on what can be done; and if it were not, the supply of industrial land might soon prove to be one.

Regional policy – controls on the building of new production floorspace above a certain amount in the conurbation combined with incentives to build elsewhere – may not be a crucial factor in the local employment situation directly, although indirectly it will have deterred factory modernisation and encouraged the building of warehouses on the limited land. This seems likely to be the case because of the greater influence of trading conditions and the lack of growth and because of IDC limitation to new floorspace when there are premises on the market. Nevertheless, regional policy is a decline-reinforcing factor and hinders remedial measures. Exemption from refusals or subsidies for training might be given to inner areas. The Industry Act 1972 might be used to foster local concerns to avoid closure or to expand them, but the ramifications of this are wide.

Another approach entirely might be directed to improving the take-up of training opportunities by local residents so that they could fill a wider range of local jobs. Many of these suggestions have in fact been taken up in governmental and local initiative since this chapter was completed.

14.7 Conclusion

This chapter records a deteriorating employment situation in the study area within a deteriorating Birmingham one – and the situation has worsened since 1974. It is difficult and perhaps misleading to separate the two situations. The study area decline may be merely part of the Birmingham one, or it may have special features superimposed. This is partly a matter of definition, for it is difficult to distinguish in the individual firm the real reasons for decline or to decide, in Birmingham's case, the responsibility of trading changes (structural changes perhaps exacerbated by management failings and regional policy) and of inner area problems (redevelopment and decentralisation perhaps also exacerbated by regional policy). The events at BSA, for instance, have been crucial to the study-area employment situation; 1,600 jobs were lost when cycle production went and 2,000 (plus probably another 1,500 if comparison is made with the 1950s rather than merely mid-1971) when motorcycle production collapsed, neither having so far been replaced. This was due to trading changes together with competition from Japanese producers and the increase in car ownership, and expansion at the time at car plants in Birmingham (some in or near the study area) ought perhaps to be seen as compensation. These job losses were not due to redevelopment or industrial relocation. Nor were they due to regional policy, although that has diverted car plant and other expansion to development areas, including expansion at groups with study area plants.

The extent to which redevelopment and roadbuilding plans and practice have been responsible for employment loss in either Birmingham or the study area is not clear. The analysis of moves referred to above has not involved asking firms why they closed or moved, and the evidence quoted in this report relates to a smaller number of concerns questioned after they had moved. Information about closures is always limited as there are no managers to question, and it is these closures that have produced the gross loss of jobs. However, although causes may be complex and difficult to determine, there is no doubt that the trend is towards further employment loss from firms moving out, closing when their premises are redeveloped or for internal reasons, and reducing their labour forces following productivity improvements.

The study area has three assets: its relatively central location, its supplies of unskilled and semiskilled shiftworking labour, and its inexpensive premises. The demand for each of these, however, is declining in the long term, and the supply of premises is being reduced by redevelopment and old age. There is some danger too that employees may show increasing reluctance to work shifts and to have factories amidst their houses, ignoring the impact on their own employment. A supply of industrial premises and land is a prerequisite for retaining employment, let alone increasing it. The training of labour may also improve the supply of other kinds of local labour to fill existing vacancies.

It would be wrong to emphasise simply the employment declines. It is clear that, due in part to population decline, unemployment has not rocketed in either Small Heath or Birmingham, although it has risen. The economically active population was finding work in 1974 despite the trend towards greater output *per capita* and fewer employees per acre that has reduced employment at otherwise flourishing concerns. A few firms have moved in; others are remaining in their existing premises or moving locally. The number 'voting with their feet' has been few.

The study area situation is in many ways a microcosm of the Birmingham one; and while minor but significant adjustments can be made at the local level, the key influences on employment well-being are the general economic climate and the future of particular industries and firms. Moreover, the decentralisation process – affecting jobs, employers, and people both directly and indirectly – reflects long term trends in industrial location factors and costs that will be difficult to halt or reverse.

V New Firms and the Inner City

15 The Inner City: New Plant Incubator?

Gordon C. Cameron with the assistance of
Mary Latham

15.1 Introduction[1]

The New York Regional Plan Study (Hoover and Vernon, 1960) –
that classic portrayal of what makes an urban economy function –
has come to the firm conclusion that the inner areas of New York
have acted as incubators for new small firms. Thus, Hoover and
Vernon (the two principal authors of the study) have argued that
'The process, as we see it, is one in which persons aspiring to go into
production on a small-scale have found themselves less obviously
barred by a high cost structure at the centre of the urban area than at
the periphery' (p. 47).

   This work and the subsequent writings by Hoover (1975) and
Lichtenberg (1960) suggest that there are two distinct but related
factors in this incubation process. The first is that the inner city
attracts new manufacturing companies and new plants in *external
economy* industries. These industries are prepared to pay the high
costs demanded for space at the centre in order to minimise the
costs of access to suppliers and to customers. In such industries
customers gain from the firms being in a spatial cluster, because
they can compare products easily and also demand immediate
product modification to suit their changing needs. Typically, the
customer, who may be an intermediary between producer and final
consumer, orders small batches and requires product differentiation and speedy product delivery. The consequential shortness of

[1]The author wishes to acknowledge the extensive help of J. R. Firn in preparing this
chapter and also the improvements made to an earlier draft by the editors.

and variation in the production run favour a high labour–output ratio and also generate variable input demands. In turn this favours the creation of specialist suppliers (i.e. backward linkages) who can deliver specialist products speedily and flexibly in response to the changing input requirements of the producer. Thus, the customers reap benefits from the spatial production cluster through flexibility to compare products, and the producers reap benefits from the spatial production cluster through their ability to draw upon a range of physically close suppliers who can deliver their specialist products not only quickly but also at a price that is lower than the producer could possibly supply them internally. Thus, the system is symbiotic, each producer gaining from the presence of the other.

Generally, in addition to these specific industry factors, the authors of the New York study have suggested that the core areas provide *urbanisation economies* for many new small firms that are not in external economy industries. They have argued that such areas possess a supply of factory space suited to small firms, much of it in small flexible units, and some of it in areas due for redevelopment where rentals reflect the fact that the properties are old and the environment is ugly. Similarly, the diversity of the external economy industries creates a demand for diverse labour skills, so that the core becomes an area where skilled labour can be obtained without the expense of training. Finally, the core areas, because of the very density of production and of producers, become areas in which information on changes in technology, commerce, and production is freely available, thereby creating a favourable environment for the new small-scale entrepreneur who is keen to minimise the risks of his enterprise.

Several conclusions may follow from this simple diagnosis. First, as long as there are external economy industries in which there are company/plant births, and as long as the central areas retain some net input/output access advantages for such industries, the locational birthrate for such industries may be expected to be highest in the inner areas. This will not be true *in general* for non-external economy industries. However, it may be expected that at least an average proportion of non-external economy industry births will occur within the inner city because of the suitability of premises, low hiring costs, and a general production environment that is conducive to small scale enterprise. Taking together the combination of a very high birthrate for external economy industries and at least an average birthrate for non-external economy industries, the inner areas may be expected to have an *above-average* birthrate compared with other parts of metropolitan space. This is here termed the *birth hypothesis*.

Second, it may be expected that new plants as they grow will not only require more production space but also increasingly substitute internal economies of scale for external economies of scale and for urbanisation economies. The substitution will be most pronounced in non-external economy industries, so that early growth within an inner area will have a high probability of being followed by a locational shift away from the inner area. In contrast, firms or plants in external economy industries that wish to expand may have to seek more production space beyond their original central location but will be more inclined to locate as close to this locale as possible so as to continue obtaining the advantage of ready access to linked producers and perhaps to customers and buyers. This is here called the *mobility hypothesis*.

Empirical research into this hypothesis of inner area 'incubation' and mobility has cast some doubt upon its validity. Struyk and James (1975) and Leone and Struyk (1976) have shown that, while there was some support for the hypothesis in New York and Cleveland, the same was not true for Boston, Minneapolis, St Paul, or Phoenix. The basic problem with these findings, as the authors themselves have conceded, was that the data used typically covered a very short run of years and were therefore liable to be affected by both general investment cycles and specific-industry investment cycles. This throws some doubt on the reliability of their findings. Furthermore, the nature of their data did not permit them to explain *causality* in location decisions. The present analysis seeks to remedy both these deficiencies by using data drawn from eleven consecutive years and by focusing upon explanations of, rather than inferences from, the observed location pattern. More specifically, this chapter will examine:

(a) whether the inner areas only attract new firms/plants in the industries already clustered there;
(b) whether the inner areas perform the more general function of facilitating the location and early growth of some non-external economy plants;
(c) whether there is a marked difference in the mobility characteristics of external economy and non-external economy industries after their initial location in the inner areas; and
(d) whether the location decisions made by new plants can be modelled.

15.2 The data and the area

This study relates to the central Clydeside conurbation plus the new town of Cumbernauld during the years 1958–68 inclusive.[2] Data were collected relating to all manufacturing plants that employed five or more employees. Included were all plants in existence at 1 January 1958, all those which were born or moved into the area between then and the end of 1968, all deaths and all movements between areas of the conurbation and to areas outside the conurbation. Data on employment changes in all categories of plants were also recorded. Thus, a complete record was compiled of manufacturing births, deaths, movements, and *in situ* employment change by 100 m grid reference points, all of which can be aggregated into any spatial unit thought appropriate.

In practice there is no agreed definition of an inner area. For this study it is taken to mean the zone that interlaces with and surrounds the central business district – in more precise terms the area of the central city (Glasgow) that is within a 4 km radius of the centre point. The remaining 4 km of the central city are termed the outer central city. In addition two kinds of smaller decentralised nodes have been separated out: the old urban centres that have their own central core peaks; and two new nodes, namely, the new towns of East Kilbride and Cumbernauld. The spatial disaggregation is completed by four non-urban quadrants that represent an urban/rural interface and contain limited urban concentrations of labour.[3]

Using this spatial breakdown for all the 2,492 establishments at the beginning of 1958 it can be shown: that almost three-quarters (1,844) were in the central city (Glasgow); that the highest concentration of establishments (1,424 or 57 per cent) was in the inner area (rings 1–4); that the old subcentres contained approximately one-seventh of all plants and exhibited the same fall-off in density as the

[2]The Clydeside conurbation is in west-central Scotland. It had a population of 1.7 million in 1971 and a manufacturing labour force of over 300,000. The Census of Population defines it as Glasgow County of City; Dunbarton County (part) – Clydebank LB, Bearsden SB, Kirkintilloch SB, Milngavie SB; Lanark County (part) – Airdrie LB, Coatbridge LB, Hamilton LB, Motherwell and Wishaw LB, Rutherglen LB, Bishopbriggs SB, East Kilbride SB, No. 6 DC, No. 8 DC, No. 9 DC; Renfew County (part) – Paisley LB, Barrhead SB, Johnstone SB, Renfrew SB, First DC, Second DC. This study includes the new town of Cumbernauld in the area of the conurbation. The approximate dimensions of the area covered by the study are 50 km from west to east and 30 km from north to south.
[3]A diagrammatic map is printed in Cameron (1973).

Table 15.1 New developments 1958–68

Type of development	No.
Branch developments:	
Conurbation companies	44
Other UK companies	110
Total branch developments	154
New companies	353
Headquarters establishments	19
Total	526

Source: Own survey.

central city; that the new towns, not surprisingly, contained hardly any plants; and that the non-urban quadrants were sparsely populated except for the south-east quadrant. Thus, the conurbation was a standard type of old metropolitan area with a high density of plants at the centre, a sharp fall-off in plant density away from the centre, smaller subcentres of activity, and a low density of plants at the peripheral sites (see Table 15.2, first two columns).

During the period 1958–68, 526 new establishments came into existence. The ownership of these establishments is shown in Table 15.1. The bulk of these were in totally new companies, with a smaller proportion being formed as branches of existing conurbation or non-conurbation companies and the remainder being formed as headquarter establishments by existing companies.

In this chapter external economy industries are defined in a rational but slightly arbitrary fashion. As already noted, 57 per cent of all plants were in the inner area of the conurbation in 1958; so where an industry had more than 57 per cent of its establishments within the inner area in 1958 it is here defined as an external economy industry. On this basis seven industries at Standard Industrial Classification (SIC) Order Heading level – 'Clothing and footwear' (Order 15), 'Leather goods and fur' (14), 'Instrument engineering' (8), 'Paper, printing, and publishing' (18), 'Timber and furniture' (17), 'Food, drink, and tobacco' (3), and 'Chemicals' (5) – are classified as being external economy industries in 1958. In some parts of the chapter this approach will be refined by disaggregating the data to a Minimum List Heading level and by ranking industries in terms of the *average linear distance* from the centre point of the conurbation of all plants in these industries.

Table 15.2 Location of existing establishments, 1958, and initial location of new establishments, 1958–68

Area	Existing establishments, 1958		New establishments, 1958–68		
	No.	% of conurbation total	No.	% of conurbation total	Birthrate[a] (%)
Inner area:					
Ring 1	576	23.1	82	15.6	16.3
Ring 2	429	17.2	52	9.9	14.0
Ring 3	239	9.6	40	7.6	16.5
Ring 4	180	7.2	22	4.2	13.3
Total (all inner area)	1,424	57.1	196	37.3	14.8
Outer central city:					
Ring 1	127	5.1	21	4.0	21.3
Ring 2	88	3.5	19	3.6	21.2
Ring 3	117	4.7	34	6.5	26.1
Ring 4	98	3.9	19	3.6	20.4
Total (all outer central area)	430	17.2	93	17.7	21.3
Old subcentres	374	15.0	80	15.2	21.9
New subcentres	12	0.5	42	8.0	113.5
Non-urban quadrants:					
North-east	19	0.8	25	4.8	80.6
North-west	65	2.6	17	3.2	25.0
South-west	27	1.1	8	1.5	32.0
South-east	141	5.7	65	12.4	41.1
Total (all non-urban quadrants)	252	10.2	115	21.9	41.1
Total (all conurbation)	2,492	100.0	526	100.1	21.9

[a]The birthrate is measured as the number of new-establishment (initial) locations as a percentage of the 1958–68 average stock of

15.3 New plant location

The starting point is the absolute number of new establishments that located within the defined area between 1958 and 1968. Their location pattern is shown in Table 15.2.

At first sight the table appears to lend support to the notion that the inner area is an incubator zone of new establishments. No less than 196 (37.3 per cent) of the total of 526 new establishments located within the area. Indeed, no other single ring or area could match the innermost ring in 'playing host' to eighty-two establishment openings.

Most of these openings were in the form of very small establishments; and as predicted, the inner area tended to pick up many of the smallest-sized plants and very few of the largest establishments (see Table 15.3). Of course, one possible reason for this concentration of smaller plants in the inner area is that external economy industries, which contain many small plants, bias the overall location of small plants. However, although the smallest plants in non-external economy industries did not congregate in the inner area to the same extent as small plants in the external economy industries, there was nevertheless a similar and very clear tendency for the smallest of them to locate there, whereas this was not the case with medium and large plants.

The second finding, as Table 15.4 shows, is that the inner area

Table 15.3 New establishments within the inner area by size group, 1958–68

Size group (no. of employees)	Conurbation		Inner area	
	No.	%	No.	% of conurbation no.
5–9	123	23.4	57	46.3
10–24	196	37.3	86	43.8
25–49	94	17.9	34	36.2
50–99	53	10.1	13	24.5
100–249	36	6.8	3	8.3
250–499	14	2.7	2	14.3
500–999	4	0.8	1	25.0
1,000–4,999	6	1.1	0	0.0
Total	526	100.1	196	37.3

Source: Own survey.

Table 15.4 Inner area: percentage of total new establishments by type of industry, 1958–68

External economy industries			Other industries		
SIC trades by order	No. attracted	% of all conurbation	SIC trades by Order	No. attracted	% of all conurbation
18 Paper, printing, and publishing	21	83.3	4 Petroleum products	1	100.0
14 Leather goods and fur	5	72.5	7 Mechanical engineering	25	45.8
15 Clothing and footwear	50	61.7	9 Electrical engineering	12	29.4
8 Instrument engineering	4	50.0	19 Other manufacturing	7	29.3
17 Timber and furniture	26	44.8	16 Bricks, pottery, glass, etc.	6	26.9
3 Food, drink, and tobacco	10	26.4	12 Metal goods	13	26.1
5 Chemicals	2	15.4	6 Metal manufacture	2	22.0
			11 Vehicles	1	8.7
			13 Textiles	11	6.7
			10 Shipbuilding	0	0.0
Total	118	52.2	Total	78	26.0

Source: Own data.

attracted companies from a wide range of industries and not solely from external economy industries.

However, on more careful scrutiny of the data three factors stand out clearly. First, although the number of new plants established in the inner area was very high, the *birthrate* of new plants in the inner area was low by comparison with the conurbation average. As Table 15.2 shows, it was in fact only two-thirds of the overall average rate. In contrast, the birthrate was almost exactly equal to the overall rate in the outer central city and exactly equal to the average in the old centres. The birthrate was exceptionally high in the new towns and in the non-urban quadrants, although of course this can be partially explained in that, in the case of the new towns at least, the number of plants in existence in 1958 was very small. As a general rule, however, the birthrate increased from the centre of the conurbation. When this low inner-area birthrate is disaggregated by Order Heading level, it is found that in nearly every individual industry the same finding holds valid. Thus, as Table 15.5 clearly shows, the inner area only attracted an above-average rate of births in two of the seventeen industrial sectors. In contrast, the non-urban quadrants achieved above-average performance in no less than fourteen of the seventeen Orders; and even if the definition of the inner area is widened to include the rest of the central city, the birthrate performance is still below average.

Another possibility is that the birthrate would be higher in the inner area for entirely new companies starting up without existing input–output linkages. These, it could be argued, would be more likely than the branches or divisions of existing companies to need the urbanisation economies of the inner area. There is no reason why the branch factory of, say, a British car manufacturer should require the same locational advantages as a firm set up by a Scottish printer. However, Table 15.6 indicates that, while entirely new companies did tend to locate more heavily in the inner area than branches, thus to some extent confirming this argument, their birthrate was still below the conurbation average.

This low birthrate in the inner area together with a high concentration of small new establishments there resulted in the inner area attracting relatively few 'new' jobs. Thus, Table 15.7 shows that 15.5 per cent of all jobs in new plants were located in the inner area, while 35.3 per cent of all conurbation jobs were there in 1958. This compares with the fact that 37.3 per cent of all new plants were located in the inner area, while 57 per cent of all plants were there in 1958. Moreover, 45.8 per cent of all new companies located there.

Table 15.5 Birthrates by area and main Order Heading, 1958–68

Industry Order	No. of births	Birthrates by subdivisions of conurbation (%)					
		Conurbation	Inner	Outer	Old Centres	New Centres	Quadrants
3 Food, drink, and tobacco	38	12.8	5.8	8.3	9.6	50.0	45.2
4 Coal and petroleum products	1	5.1	11.1	0.0	0.0	0.0	0.0
5 Chemicals	13	13.9	4.1	22.7	6.9	200.0	42.9
6 Metal manufacture	23	18.3	4.6	22.6	19.7	0.0	43.2
7 Mechanical engineering	85	25.4	21.0	10.4	27.6	122.2	45.4
8 Instrument engineering	8	20.5	14.3	40.0	0.0	200.0	25.0
9 Electrical engineering	41	42.7	28.9	38.1	30.8	150.0	47.6
10 Shipbuilding	3	5.6	0.0	0.0	40.0	0.0	11.6
11 Vehicles	15	21.4	6.1	29.6	10.8	0.0	40.0
12 Metal goods	59	29.9	14.8	37.0	23.1	100.0	78.9
13 Textiles	24	17.4	14.8	15.8	19.4	0.0	14.8
14 Leather goods and fur	6	11.8	11.8	0.0	0.0	0.0	28.6
15 Clothing and footwear	69	27.8	24.4	23.5	51.9	80.0	57.1
16 Bricks, pottery, glass, etc.	23	19.1	14.8	7.7	30.8	400.0	20.3
17 Timber and furniture	58	24.1	16.7	37.3	25.4	66.7	54.5
18 Paper, printing, and publishing	34	16.3	14.6	26.4	0.0	111.1	11.8
19 Other manufacturing	26	39.1	21.5	37.5	80.0	66.7	63.2
Total (All manufacturing)	526	21.9	14.8	21.3	21.9	113.5	41.1

Source: Own data.

Table 15.6 Births by area and type of establishment, 1958–68

| | New companies | | | Branches | | |
| | | | Birthrate[a] | | | Birthrate[a] |
Area	No.	%	(%)	No.	%	(%)
Inner area	137	45.8	10.7	64	29.0	5.0
Outer central city	40	13.4	9.1	46	20.8	10.5
Old subcentres	51	17.1	13.9	30	13.6	8.2
New subcentres	19	6.4	51.4	22	10.0	59.5
Non-urban quadrants	52	17.4	18.6	59	26.7	21.1
Total (all conurbation)	299[b]	100.1	12.5	221[b]	100.1	9.2

[a]The birthrate is defined as the number of *each* kind of establishment as a percentage of the 1958–68 average *total* stock of plants.
[b]These two types of companies total 520 since six companies could not be adequately classified.
Source: Own survey.

Table 15.7 Employment in new plants by area, 1968

Area	No. of employees	%
Inner:		
Ring 1	1,815	5.4
Ring 2	1,403	4.2
Ring 3	1,538	4.6
Ring 4	444	1.3
Total	5,200	15.5
Outer:		
Ring 1	643	1.9
Ring 2	313	0.9
Ring 3	1,358	4.1
Ring 4	707	2.1
Total	3,021	9.0
Old subcentres } New subcentres	8,523	25.5
Non-urban quadrants	16,708	49.9
Total	33,452	99.9

Source: Own survey.

To summarise: First, it was found that the inner area attracted an *absolutely* large number of small new establishments and especially entirely new companies. Although these were drawn from nearly every industrial sector, a high proportion of these location decisions arose from a very limited set of industries. Thus, there was a marked tendency for the industries already strongly represented in the inner area to attract new units from their own industry to the area. In contrast, industries that were not initially strongly located within the inner area tended not to locate new units there. Seen in terms of *birthrates* the inner area did not, as hypothesised, have above-average birthrates. The really strong contenders for incubator status on this measure were the new towns and non-urban quadrants. When birthrates were measured in terms of new employment created, the inner area came out particularly badly since a low birthrate of plants coupled with a small average establishment size resulted in a very limited proportion of all new jobs being located there.

15.4 The mobility characteristics of new plants

The second hypothesis outlined above – relating to the mobility characteristics of new plants – is that plants in external economy industries will tend to seek their new location, if expansion leads to a move, on sites as close to the inner area as possible. In contrast, new plants in other industries will shift away from the high-rent inner area when expansion and the consequent increase in size mean that internal economies of scale and experience can substitute for the advantages of access and other urbanisation economies of the inner area.

To test this the mobility characteristics, particularly the length and direction of moves, of all new establishments that initially located within the inner area were examined. The mobility rate of these new plants was high (34.7 per cent), suggesting that one out of every three initial locations was followed within the time period (up to eleven years) by a move. This compared with a mobility rate for all other plants of 37.1 per cent. However, the most interesting finding is that nearly all the new plants stayed within the inner area. No less than seven out of every ten moves that originated within the inner area ended up within the inner area. Indeed, almost 30 per cent of these intra-inner area moves were in a more central direction.

Table 15.8 Movement destinations of new and all inner-area plants, 1958–68

Moved from inner area to	All moves (no.)	All moves (%)	All moves minus new (no.)	All moves minus new (%)	New (no.)	New (%)
Inner area	300	63.7	253	62.8	47	69.1
Outer central city	107	22.7	99	24.6	8	11.8
Subcentres	43	9.1	38	9.4	5	7.4
Non-urban quadrants	21	4.5	13	3.2	8	11.8
Total	471	100.0	403	100.0	68	100.1

Source: Own survey.

This overall tendency for a high degree of short distance moves was almost exactly paralleled by the movement patterns of all other inner area plants, as Table 15.8 makes clear. However, for study purposes the crucial finding was that very few moves that originated within the inner area ended up outside the inner area. Therefore, there is little point in distinguishing between external-economy industry moves and other industry moves. Thus, at least over the time period involved in this analysis, no support for the mobility hypothesis was found.

15.5 Explaining the location pattern

The final objective of the study was to explain the location pattern of new plants. Cameron (1973) has shown that new plants tend to mirror the locational pattern of their parent industry with regard to linear access to the central point. This was shown in the present study by ranking all plants, classified by industry to SIC Minimum List Heading level, with regard to their average distance to the centre. These ranks were calculated for existing plants in 1958 and for all new plants. A high rank correlation between these two sets indicated that centrally located industries tended to attract new plants in these industries to similar locations, whereas decentralised industry-location patterns were mirrored by the locations of new plants in these same industries.

Given this finding it was concluded that the inner area appears to possess locational advantages for certain types of activity and, conversely, that decentralised sites have net advantages for other types of activity. It follows that a location theory should be adopted that reflects net differences in input/output access at given sites, *and* differences industry by industry in the demands for these sites, depending primarily upon the production characteristics of the industry and the growth characteristics of the company making the decision.

To test this a very simple model was formulated, based upon three propositions:

1. An industry will tend to decentralise if it is growing very rapidly since growth necessitates new space, which is most widely available away from the centre.
2. An industry will tend to be centralised if it is dependent upon variable product demand and colocation economies,
3. An industry will tend to require the access advantages of the centre if labour costs form a high proportion of total costs or if it has a need for special types of labour.

Accordingly, the following four proxies were selected for the variables in a regression equation

$$C = f(G, I, L)$$

1. *Demand for centrality (C)*   the dependent variable was the employment-weighted average logarithmic distance from the centre point of every Minimum List Heading industry that had more than 60 per cent of all employment in 1958 within 8 km of the centre point of Glasgow. Only plants within Glasgow were included in the calculation.
2. *Growth (G)*   As a measure of growth the rate of growth of net output *per capita* over 1958–63 (G_1) was used, the assumption being that rapid productivity growth is associated with a need for additional space. An alternative way of specifying this was also used, namely, the level of net output per head in 1963 (G_2).
3. *Interdependency (I)*   There is no adequate measure of colocation economies and of the need for flexible communications. Therefore, three proxies were chosen: the proportion of net output being sold as intermediate goods (I_1), the proportion of communication costs in net output (I_2), and the proportion of transport costs in net output (I_3).
4. *Labour (L)*   The assumption here was that the centre point is the area of maximum labour access; and accordingly, in industries in which labour demand varies frequently and/or there is a

need for a special category of labour, the central areas will be attractive because of ease of hiring. The proxies used were the percentage of labour costs in net output (L_1) and the percentages of females (L_2), of skilled workers (L_3), and of administrative, clerical, and technical workers in the labour force (L_4).

All the variables (G, I, and L) were drawn from Census of Production data for the United Kingdom. The regression equation was therefore of the form

$$C = f(G_1, G_2, I_1, I_2, I_3, L_1, L_2, L_3, L_4)$$

This equation explained 67 per cent of the variance, and all the signs were as expected except for I_1, which was positive, suggesting that the higher the proportion of intermediate sales the more decentralised the industry. This perhaps suggests that the proxy used for colocation economies is defective. The most significant were G_1 (productivity growth), accounting for 28.83 per cent of the variance, and the percentage of females in employment, L_2 (15.62 per cent). The total results are shown in Table 15.9.

Table 15.9 Significance of variables in the regression equation

Variable		% of variance explained
Rate of productivity growth	(G_1)	28.83
% female labour	(L_2)	15.62
% intermediate sales	(I_1)	9.89
% labour costs	(L_1)	4.52
% communications costs	(I_2)	4.28
High productivity	(G_2)	1.62
% administrative, clerical, technical labour	(L_4)	1.56
% skilled labour	(L_3)	0.11
% transport costs	(I_3)	0.03

Interpreting this equation is risky, but it probably indicates that:

(a) the faster the rate of growth in an industry, the more likely it is that the plants in the industry will be found in decentralised sites;

(b) the more firms in an industry require female labour, the more likely they are to be centralised; and

(c) the more firms in an industry require extensive communication networks, the more likely they are to be centralised.

15.6 Conclusions

Two simple hypotheses have been tested, and an attempt has been made to model industrial location choice within the city. It has been shown that the inner area is neither an incubator zone in the sense that it has an above-average birthrate nor an area of major growth of new location employment. However, it has been shown that the inner area continues to be attractive to certain kinds of external economy industries; more generally, it attracts small plants and especially entirely new companies, probably because of urbanisation economies. For many of these small plants relocation occurs after an initial phase of growth, but for the vast majority this is achieved through a short distance move. This also suggests the continued importance to small companies of external economies and urbanisation economies.

The policy implications of this diagnosis are simple. The inner area should continue to be planned so as to contain zones for industrial activity, but the pervasive tendency to decentralised workplaces should be recognised by zoning a growing proportion of industrial land in areas outside the inner area.

16 Finding a Place for Small Enterprise in the Inner City

Nicholas Falk

16.1 Introduction

The problem of unemployment and the inner city are interwoven and therefore hard to disentangle. As a consequence, despite the mountains of research carried out within academic and government circles there is still fundamental disagreement over whether action is required to halt the decline, what should be done, and who should do it. However, there is really no need to resolve the 'chicken and egg' dilemma of whether it is the fault of the individual or of the system and whether it is the environment that causes the economy to decline or vice versa. The fact is that both industry and the cities are going through changes that may seem in retrospect like a second industrial revolution, with the difference that this time both industry and the cities are contracting.

16.2 Decline of the inner city

One of the major indications of the economic changes has been the decline in employment, now declining faster than population in the inner areas of all the great metropolitan conurbations like London, Manchester, and Birmingham (Table 16.1). It is the loss particularly of manufacturing employment that has given rise to the greatest concern, for this is where the greatest job losses have been (Lomas, 1974; Community Development Project, 1976). Further-

Table 16.1 Population and employment change by urban zone, 1951–61 and 1961–71

Area	1951–61				1961–71			
	Population change (no. in thousands)	(%)	Employment change (no. in thousands)	(%)	Population change (no. in thousands)	(%)	Employment change (no. in thousands)	(%)
Urban cores	486	1.9	902	6.7	–729	–2.8	–439	–3.1
Metropolitan rings	1,721	13.3	293	6.6	2,512	17.2	707	15.0
Standard metropolitan labour areas	2,207	5.7	1,196	6.7	1,784	4.4	271	1.4
Outer metropolitan labour areas	245	3.1	–14	–0.4	786	9.8	130	3.9
Metropolitan labour areas	2,451	5.3	1,182	5.6	2,569	5.2	401	1.8
Unclassified areas	–22	–0.9	–57	–5.5	–32	–1.4	–7	–0.7
Britain	2,430	5.0	1,125	5.1	2,537	5.0	394	1.7

Source: Goddard and Spence (1976).

Table 16.2 Employment in Greater London by broad industrial and occupational groups, 1961 and 1971

Industrial/occupational group	1961 (no. in thousands)	(%)	1971 (no. in thousands)	(%)
Manufacturing				
Operatives	877	61.4	623	57.0
Office workers	385	26.9	354	32.4
Others	167	11.7	116	10.6
Total	1,429	100.0	1,093	100.0
'Growth' services[a]				
Operatives	119	10.0	123	8.6
Office workers	630	52.9	781	54.6
Others	441	37.1	527	36.8
Total	1,190	100.0	1,431	100.0
Other industries and services				
Operatives	511	28.9	418	26.8
Office workers	389	22.0	392	25.1
Others	867	49.1	750	48.1
Total	1,767	100.0	1,560	100.0

[a] 'Growth' services comprise insurance, banking, finance, business services, professional and scientific services, public administration, air transport, postal services and telecommunications, miscellaneous transport services, and storage.
Sources: Census of Population, 1961, GLC special tabulations, corrected for bias; Census of Population, 1971.

more, manufacturing employs a higher proportion of operatives and pays higher wages than service employment (Tables 16.1 and 16.2). It is also an accepted part of government policy to expand the manufacturing sector to help the balance of payments.

16.2.1 Loss of large establishments

A great deal of the job loss has been due to the rationalisation of large multiplant firms that have closed their older inner-city factories and offices. In Wandsworth, for example, seven-eighths of the job loss in recent years was due to ten large firms closing their plants (London Borough of Wandsworth, 1976). Large firms have come to dominate most of the manufacturing sectors, mainly as a result of mergers and takeovers. Thus, the top 100 firms have doubled their share of output in the last forty years; their average number of plants rose from twenty-seven to seventy-two between 1958 and 1972 (Prais, 1976), whereas the minimum scale of efficient plants has not risen nearly so rapidly.

Two factors have encouraged the closure of branch plants. First, operating costs in the inner areas are higher. Inner city areas have typically smaller and older plants than elsewhere (Vernon, 1960; Martin, 1969). Their sites are cramped as the surrounding area has usually been built up. It is often difficult for employees to get to work, particularly those living in the suburbs. Goods movement is also difficult in many places. Second, the property boom, at least up to 1973, and the willingness of local authorities to buy land for housing provided an additional incentive to move or close, since a high price could be secured for the old factory site. For example, developers expected inner areas like north Southwark and the western part of Tower Hamlets to take the overspill from the city (Ambrose and Colenutt, 1975) and were prepared to pay for more than the value of a site in industrial use.

Even where plants have not been closed, multiplant firms tend to concentrate expansion outside inner areas where resources are easier to come by.

A further factor is that improved communications have made traditional central locations irrelevant. The food and drink industries, for example, no longer need to be on the river; motorways have made rail connections unnecessary; telephones and data transmission services mean that factories can be distant from their head offices.

At the same time the decline in manufacturing is no longer being offset by the rise in service and office employment. There are a number of reasons why the office sector is not likely to grow in inner areas. With the decentralisation of population and rising transport costs there is no longer much need to retain many of these activities in the centre. The banks and insurance companies, which accounted for much of the growth, are now moving the bulk of their administration to out-of-town locations where costs are lower and it is easier to attract the labour that they require. Those which require regular and easy contacts with other firms stay, but the departments that move tend to be the very ones that employ the most unskilled in routine clerical functions. Surveys showed that the rate of inquiries for office space in 1976 was only one-third of the 1975 level, and supply was far in excess of demand, with peak rents down to one-third of their level of three years earlier after adjusting for inflation.[1]

A further cause of decline is that clerical jobs are often just as vulnerable to change as manual jobs, in terms of both mechanisation and decentralisation. Indeed, they may well be more dispensable than many manufacturing jobs that rely on the co-ordination of hand and eye (Simon, 1960). The computerisation of many repetitive functions can only be held back so long as labour is cheap and readily available.

The past growth in the tertiary sector may have been at the expense of manufacturing industry, when set against the overall decay of industry in the United Kingdom. Between 1960 and 1973 the proportion of workers in manufacturing industry fell from 48.8 to 42.3 per cent (Organisation for Economic Co-operation and Development, 1974). There is reason to suppose that office and service employment has risen faster than the nation can afford, bearing in mind the growing imports of manufactured goods (Bacon and Eltis, 1975).

16.2.2 Loss of small firms

Returning now to the fate of manufacturing in the inner city, as well as the closure of large factories and their movement out of the city there has been an equally significant loss of small firms. (The Bolton Committee on Small Firms's definition of a small manufacturing firm is one with under 200 employees.) Of course a few large firms closing down or rationalising operations take the headlines and command government interest, but each large firm that collapses tends to bring down many small firms that provided it with materials or services of some kind. Much of the decline has been in industries associated with relatively small-scale production, sometimes in markets that are expanding. For example, Redding (1971) has shown that between 1954 and 1968 – a period of only fourteen years – the number of factories in inner London (excluding the smallest units) fell by 39.4 per cent in the clothing industry and 52.6 per cent in electrical engineering.

It is hard to say for certain how many people are employed by small firms as the statistics are unreliable. However, it seems that small firms play a significant part in the manufacturing sector of the city economy (Hall, 1964; Boswell, 1971; Merrett and Lehr, 1971).

Analyses of the manufacturing firms in three London boroughs

(Hackney, Islington, Southwark) showed that 50 per cent of the firms employed less than 10 people and 90 per cent less than 50 people. Some of the major industries meeting basic human needs (clothing, furniture, printing) are largely made up of tiny firms. The 1968 Census of Production revealed that 40 per cent of people in manufacturing in London worked in small units, and this is bound to understate the figures as it excludes units employing less than eleven people. Many of the functions associated with smaller firms tend to be ones traditionally associated with inner areas (Table 16.3).

The loss of small manufacturing industry is even more disturbing than the loss of large firms because the inner city should be an appropriate location for many kinds of small enterprise – appropriate in terms of both the needs of small firms and the needs and resources of the inner city. The next two sections consider in turn the benefits that small firms offer both locally and nationally and why they are disappearing.

16.3 The need for small firms

In an age entranced by size, small firms may seem an archaic hangover from Victorian times and out of place in modern cities. It is very hard to make up one's mind about a form of activity that ranges from sweet shops to sweat shops, from the shape of things to come to the reminder of days gone by.

However, it seems that, despite increasing scale and concentration in the twentieth century in all areas of activity, small businesses are still of some significance in the economy as a whole and are still a dominant form of activity in parts of the older cities. The Bolton Committee of Inquiry on Small Firms (1971) has recognised that 'small firms account numerically for the vast majority of all business enterprises. Their diversity is even more striking than their number'. Thus, according to the 1963 Census of Production, 94 per cent of the employers and 20 per cent of the employment in manufacturing were accounted for by small firms, and the proportion of employment was even more significant in retailing (96 and 49 per cent respectively) and construction (89 and 33 per cent). Taken in

Table 16.3 Male earnings in London by broad industrial and skill groups, 1974 (£ per week)

Industrial group	Manual	Non-manual	All skill groups
Manufacturing	48.2	62.8	53.8
Growth services	40.0	66.8	61.4
Other industries and services	44.0	56.2	49.5
Transport and communications	47.3	63.2	53.6
All non-manufacturing	44.4	63.3	55.3
All industrial groups	45.9	63.2	54.9

Source: Department of Employment (1974b).

aggregate therefore, small firms are big business. However, certain economic myths have grown up that have caused small firms to be neglected.

16.3.1 Myths of scale

An argument that was current in the 1960s was that the solution of Britain's economic problems depended on the growth of larger firms, often with international connections, and the modernisation of production processes in large single-storey factories located far away from the cramped inner areas. This has lain behind the thinking of many of the public authorities who have helped to shape the fate of inner areas. For example, the Docklands Development Team (1975) has reflected the conventional wisdom when stating that:

> A large part of the decline of industry in East London has been the result of concentration of adverse factors in one area. Not only are sites and premises small and inappropriate for modern methods but many firms are small and find difficulties acquiring the capital needed for modernisation. Also, modern technology, if it is to be fully exploited, requires operations to be on a larger scale than in the past.

There is a common argument that larger firms are needed in order to exploit the economics of scale that modern technology has made possible. Certainly, there are some kinds of goods and services that can only be supplied efficiently through very large organisations, e.g. the production of energy supply. However, the return on assets in manufacturing is higher in small firms than in large firms and has been for some time (Bolton Committee, 1971; Samuels and Smyth, 1968). This points to the fact that, although there are technological economies associated with large organisations, there are also certain diseconomies of scale relating to efficiency and flexibility, which call into question the desirability of an economy based solely on large organisations.

As far as efficiency is concerned, in many industries technological economies of scale are reached fairly rapidly, and there is some evidence that the minimum efficient scale of plant is falling (Bain, 1966). At the same time there are considerable organisational problems in developing a sense of common purpose in large organisations and in avoiding their becoming top-heavy with administration. Large companies may have flexibility between plants, but they are often more inflexible within them (Leibenstein, 1966; Beynon, 1973). Implementing a consistent and yet sensitive set of corporate policies throughout seventy-two plants (the average number for the top 100 companies) can outstrip the managerial resources that are available, particularly where there are differences in the background and wants of the workforce in different parts of the country.

In terms of flexibility it can be argued that large firms are taking over because of their greater capacity to adapt to changing consumer tastes and also to plan and organise production and to weather economic storms. This latter proposition has been put forward by, for example, Galbraith in *American Capitalism* (1957) and later works (Galbraith, 1967), where he has stated that:

> The size of General Motors is in the service not of monopoly or the economies of scale but of planning. And for this planning – control of supply, control of demand, provision of capital, minimisation of risk – there is no clear upper limit to the desirable size. It could be the bigger the better. (p.76)

However, this may no longer be so, due to changes in the economic factors that shape industrial development: rising raw material and energy prices, the economic recession, and increasing conflict within industry, which favours a profusion of smaller units.

In future, subdued rates of economic growth, along with increasing competition from countries with low wage rates, will inevitably force firms to change what they produce. The continued expansion of choice will make consumers more discriminating (assuming that import curbs are not introduced). The only viable response is for firms to seek out niches where they have a competitive edge, and this is proving difficult. In the industries where there is comparatively little product differentiation (e.g. steel, chemicals) British firms can only compete if they can match foreign competition in quality, reliability, and price; on all these scores (except perhaps price) most British firms seem weak. While the large firms, particularly ones that rely on highly specialised assembly processes, are geared to meeting steady mass demands at low costs, they get into difficulties when circumstances change radically, as witnessed by British Leyland and Chrysler. There is evidence that the prevailing management style of large companies is inappropriate to the management of complex unpredictable situations and to the resolution of conflicting demands. As Caves (1969) has put it in *The Brookings Report on the British Economy*: 'Business is a second choice (for the best people) . . . they tend to retain the Civil Service as their model and settle into a trustee role of gentlemanly responsibility that is hardly conducive to rapid innovation.'

The trend towards concentration in industry has in part been due to economic rationalisation, but it has also been greatly accelerated in recent years by the spate of mergers and takeovers. It is now being discovered that it was wishful thinking that Britain's economic problems could be solved by the white heat of technology and by merging competitors under the control of a seemingly successful firm, as Alfred Herbert and Leyland have shown. Despite the arguments used to justify mergers, few have in fact shown production economies. As Kitching (1967) has shown in his classic study of 'Why do mergers miscarry?', the tangible benefits have been in the greater financial resources that have been available to the group, the reduction of competition, and perhaps some economies in distribution.

Successive governments have encouraged the concentration of industry into ever larger units. Although large scale industry normally pays considerable taxes, it also receives considerable help from the government in the form of investment grants and incentives, as well as the spinoffs from the new towns programme and building of motorways between cities. The total government assistance has been estimated by some Cambridge economists as £2,500 million (Roy, 1974), which is biased disproportionately towards large firms. The large firms with their specialised staff are better able to know and exploit the various grants and tax allowances. Yet, despite public support big industry has not delivered the goods.

16.3.2   Economic benefits

Let us consider in contrast where the small firm has an advantage. The smaller firm offers four main benefits to the consumer, which will continue to be important and perhaps assume increased significance.

First, they can be more flexible and responsive to particular needs than larger firms (Schumacher, 1974; Simmons, 1976). These needs tend to fall into five main categories: the luxury market (e.g. racing cars); unusual demands (e.g. cars for disabled persons); the exploitation of new technology (e.g. electronic petrol-injection equipment); products that require very close liaison between the customer and the design and production staff, which range from high technology components (e.g. transistors) to handmade items incorporating considerable artistic or craft skills (e.g. jewellery, harpsichords); and finally, the whole field of service and repair, which is likely to assume ever greater importance given the rising stocks of goods and increasing replacement costs, which justify the reconditioning of many kinds of product.

Second, small firms are often more resilient and less vulnerable to disruptions (e.g. by industrial action). There are several reasons for this. Many small firms, particularly in engineering, can turn their hand to a wide variety of products, whereas a car production line, for example, cannot easily be altered. The small firm is less dependent on a large number of inputs being available as and when they are required. Thus, even during the three-day week in 1974 small firms survived, with, for example, some furniture firms in High Wycombe turning to steam power! Also, there is less chance of the management losing touch with the shopfloor for they are literally working together.

Third, small enterprises are an important source of innovation, developing new products or services that large companies would often suppress. Large production processes involving what Jacobs (1972) in *The Economy of Cities* has described as a 'sterile division of labour' are unlikely to encourage innovation and produce new work and techniques because of the dominance of each part of the process by the requirements of the whole. In addition the unsatisfying nature of the work itself and the lack of opportunity for creative self-expression may mean that inventiveness and the interest in exploiting new ideas may be greater in small organisations than in large hierarchical ones. The Bolton Committee found no overwhelming evidence one way or the other, but studies in the United

States have shown that small firms introduce more successful inno-
vations than very large firms, which may well sit on an idea to
prevent a competitor from stealing an advance (Scherer, 1965;
Mansfield, 1963; Cooper, 1964; Nelson, 1969; Burns and Stalker,
1961; Jewkes, Sawers and Stillerman, 1969; Adams and Dirlam,
1966). This is certainly the case with alternative forms of motor
vehicle, and it should not be forgotten that, although transistors
were developed in the large Bell Laboratories, it took what at the
time was a small Japanese entrepreneur (Sony) to realise their
potential use in pocket radios. A good deal of research effort in
large firms is wasted, whether it be drug companies indulging in
'molecule manipulation' to evade patents, people writing their PhD
thesis in the company's time, as Robert Townsend of Avis observed
in 'Up the Organisation' (Townsend, 1970), or people working on
irrelevant projects.

Finally, there are the benefits that come from there being a wider
range of jobs close at hand. One of the effects of the growth of large
firms has been to make employees more dependent on the results of
decisions taken far from the place where they work. A firm like
Ford Motor Company, for example, considers not only the short-
term economic benefits that may result from transferring production from one manufacturing plant to another, but increasingly also
the advantages from undertaking the work in a country with lower
labour costs and more trouble-free operating conditions. The growing dominance of firms with many locations encourages rationalisation and results in fewer choices for the employee in terms of both
the numbers of employers and the types of work and working
conditions that are available.

16.3.3 Social benefits

Turning now to the potential of the small firm in the inner city,
despite, and in many ways because of, the economic recession there
are opportunities for substantially expanding the small firms sector
in a way that is unlikely in the case of larger manufacturing firms
(Boswell, 1971; Falk and Martinos, 1975; IBM/Urbed; 1977).
There are two great appeals of such a policy. First, small enterprise
is uniquely well suited to the conditions of many inner-city areas
where the problems are concentrated. Its operations are intensive in
terms of both the relationship between labour and capital and the
space that it occupies. Thus, small firms can operate in multistorey

and often old premises where large firms would demand new single-storey factories with space alongside for potential expansion (Keeble, 1976). Second, unlike large firms, many small firms actually need to be near the centre of large cities in order to be close to both customers and a range of specialised suppliers, as well as to a pool of trained labour (Birch *et al.*, 1974). Many of the resources that small firms require and complain are difficult to obtain, such as premises and personnel, are now potentially available and standing idle. Also, the economic situation in certain ways increases the chances of small firms setting up. Young people find it more difficult to get jobs with large organisations or are unwilling to work in what they perceive as soulless bureaucracies making things of little apparent worth. A new spirit of enterprise can be found among certain immigrant groups and those concerned with forming an 'alternative society', which is reminiscent of the kind of drive that created the industrial revolution (Rolt, 1970). Older people, including managers and those with technical skills, are made redundant and are well aware of the enormous scope for filling gaps in the marketplace or producing existing products or services in a better way. For these reasons depressions are usually associated with the formation of an increased number of small businesses in the most surprising fields.[1]

At the same time the concentrated and diverse character of cities creates the essential conditions for entrepreneurship and innovation to flourish. This point is well illustrated in Jacobs's *The Economy of Cities* (1972), where she has argued that innovation is a byproduct of work: 'New goods and services, whether criminal or benign, do not come out of thin air. New work arises upon existing work, it requires "parent work" ' (p. 55); and 'they depend upon large numbers and great diversity of economic organisation, some of which of course grew large in their heydays' (p. 79).

Small firms also help to pay for the services provided in urban areas. At a time when local government is faced with rising demands for services and falling sources of revenue it should not be forgotten that small businesses can be an important source of rates. Unlike many residents, small businesses are likely to contribute more than they cost; they pay a higher rate in most urban areas and make few calls on local authority services that they do not pay for directly.

[1]See, for example, *In the Making*, published from Acorn, 84 Church Street, Wolverton, Buckinghamshire, or *Undercurrents* magazine.

During the last few years many local authorities have been compelled to encourage the comprehensive redevelopment of former industrial areas (e.g. north Southwark) because of their falling rate yields (Ambrose and Colenutt, 1975). This is in part due to industries leaving the area. Thus, the overall decline in the industrial proportion of rate income between 1966–67 and 1973–74 was from 15.8 to 10.6 per cent in Southwark and from 25.7 to 19.7 per cent in Tower Hamlets, compared with a more modest decline of from 14.3 to 12.1 per cent for England and Wales as a whole (Docklands Development Team, 1975). While the contribution of small businesses cannot readily be singled out, they are undoubtedly important to the financial viability of the cities.

Finally, there is the contribution that smaller firms make to keeping things in balance. In any industrial system some concerns will grow and flourish while others stagnate or decline, just as in nature. By having a diversity of concerns operating in different markets the community insulates itself from overdependence on the success of one unit, just as wise farmers avoid overdependence on any one crop. Again as in nature, the various parts support each other, giving vitality and resilience to the whole. Significantly, the small firm is more tied to its location (movements as opposed to deaths accounted for 36 per cent of the closures of manufacturing firms in south-east London employing more than fifty persons, compared with 22 per cent those employing less). When the smaller firms move they also tend to move only half as far on average as the larger firms (Gripaios, 1977a). It is a tragedy that in some inner-city areas the death of small firms and the low replacement birthrate have left large firms with an excessive influence. For example, in Canning Town 75 per cent of the jobs of the 60,000 people who worked there in 1974 were controlled by fifteen firms (Community Development Project, 1975a).

It is not surprising that, in such a situation, half the workers experienced redundancy between 1966 and 1972. The more concentrated the area, the more rapid is the rate of extinction. Thus, Martin discovered, when he returned in 1975 to the large factories that he had studied in 1954, that 42 per cent of the factories in Ealing were still in use by the same firm compared with only 22 per cent in Southwark (Martin and Seaman, 1975). Most of the sites lay derelict, contributing to the general air of desolation in inner urban areas that were once industrial centres.

While a full cost–benefit analysis has not been attempted, there is enough evidence to suggest that a further fall in the number of small firms operating in inner areas would be undesirable for the urban community as well as for the nation at large.

16.4 Why small firms have disappeared

The loss of small firms is the result of the interplay of national and local forces. Nationally, small firms have lost ground as a source of employment; small firms accounted for approximately 19 per cent of national employment in manufacturing and small plants for 30 per cent. The UK share seems to have declined further and faster than that of other countries (Figure 16.1); for example, West Ger-

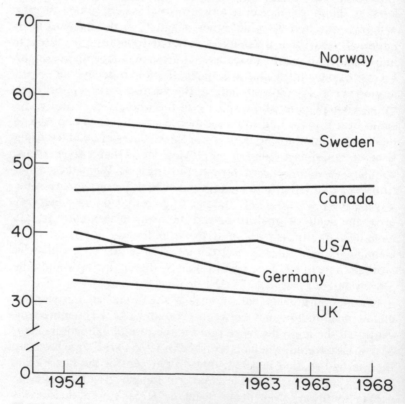

Fig. 16.1   International comparisons of the proportion of manufacturing employment in small firms.

Source: Bannock (1976).

nany has 40 per cent more small firms *per capita*. To make another comparison, the United States has two to three times the birthrate and only one-quarter of the deathrate of firms, compared to the United Kingdom. The comparison is even more disturbing at the level of tiny firms (under ten employees) in relation to the population; there are one-third more in the United States and twelve times the number in West Germany, compared with the United Kingdom (Bannock, 1976). The reasons usually given are the various disincentives to entrepreneurship, such as the high cost of finance and tax rates, which bear heaviest on the small firm. The lower birthrate and higher deathrate of small firms in the United Kingdom compared with, say, the United States are certainly bound up with the business environment, as a recent study by the firm of A.D. Little (1977) clearly points out. Comparing the poor showing of 'new technology–based' firms in the United Kingdom and West Germany with that of such firms in the United States, he has pointed to the US advantages of: a very large domestic market that is conducive to rapid growth and development; the availability of private wealth as a source of seed capital for new ventures; a fiscal framework that encourages the flow of private risk capital into new ventures; the existence of an active (over-the-counter) market for the trading of shares in new ventures; social and behavioural attitudes that encourage entrepreneurship and the mobility of individuals between academic institutions and industry, as well as the willingness of scientists to set up their own businesses in order to exploit their technical knowledge; and 'a large and active government expenditure programme in high technology areas which provides significant opportunities for new technology based firms' endeavour, particularly through government procurement programmes'. There may also be a greater personal aversion to taking risks and getting one's hands dirty in the United Kingdom, although this is by no means universal. These factors, and others examined below, have led to the loss of small firms even in growth sectors where they are economically and technically viable; but equally, if not more important, there are also local disincentives, particularly in finding premises, personnel, and finance (Falk, 1978a).

16.4.1 Premises

It has become increasingly hard to find a place to work at a price that small firms can afford. This is largely the result of redevelopment and rising accommodation costs – both rents and rates. In the past the inner areas acted as natural seedbeds for innovation and as nurseries for new enterprise (United States Temporary National Economic Committee, 1941; Lichtenberg, 1960; Hoover and Vernon, 1959; Vernon, 1960; Martin, 1966). Entrepreneurs found it easiest to start in secondhand premises on a small scale, taking advantage of close proximity to customers and suppliers (Hall, 1964; Riley, 1973). Now, starting in business is harder. Many of the customers have moved out. Redevelopment schemes have sought to remove non-conforming uses and to provide more room for housing and open space. In the process they have cut the supply of cheap workshop premises. They have also caused many established firms to go out of business and in the process severed vital networks and linkages and reduced the viability of other firms. Various surveys suggest that between one-third and one-half of firms affected by redevelopment go out of business (Zimmer, 1964; Berry, Parsons and Platt, 1968; Darley and Saunders, 1976). Neither the private nor public sector has replaced the premises lost.

16.4.2 Personnel

Paradoxically, personnel can also be a problem for small businesses. The Docklands Development Team's consultative paper on *Work and Industry in East London* (1975) refers to the apparent contradictions between the views of employers expressed in discussions, namely, that their chief problem was a lack of skilled workers, and the views of the local population, who saw the chief problem of the economy as a lack of jobs. 'Both views are true and result from looking at different aspects of the very rapid changes taking place' (para. 37). Small firms find it particularly difficult to keep skilled workers when there are more secure and better-paid jobs in the public sector or in large firms; the side effect of Ford's new plant at Halewood, for example, was to attract away skilled craftsmen from small firms, thus weakening Merseyside's indigenous economy (Department of the Environment, 1976; Beynon, 1973). Small firms also find it hard to attract and keep young people who are prepared to work hard at learning a trade; in consequence many of them are firms run by old men whose businesses will disappear when they retire.

There are a number of other reasons for the shortage, although it is not yet possible to assess their relative importance. First, wages, opportunities for overtime, and fringe benefits are almost certainly lower than in large firms operating in more oligopolistic market conditions, which can pass the cost on to the consumer. Second, working conditions are often unattractive, with many workshops appearing Dickensian – cramped, dirty, and cold. Third, young people have come to want clean office jobs or jobs in large factories where they can work with their 'mates'; while small business may appeal more to middle class radicals and conservatives alike, it is not so in line with the self-image of most working-class teenagers of English background anyway. Fourth, small firms operating in inner areas suffer from the general shortage of skilled workers. This in part reflects the generally low levels of training and the reduction of apprenticeships in the United Kingdom. It is also due to the movement out to the suburbs of the more skilled, which is compounded by the deteriorating public transport services and the obstacles placed in the way of people driving to work. It is difficult for small firms to make contact with people who might be interested in learning the business or taking over the management when the owner retires. Fifth, finding staff is in many ways similar in its problems to finding a spouse. Personal contact is the main method, and this suffers when communities break up. Labour exchanges do not communicate the subtleties of the very specialised work that most small firms do and are little used by the small firm (Dunnell and Head, 1975). Advertising is beyond the means or interest of the small firm, which can hardly compete with firms like Fords or Marks and Spencer. Small firms make little use of public employment services (Urbed, 1978a).

16.4.3 Finance

A further problem is that of securing finance for starting up and expansion, although opinions differ greatly on this. With higher rates of taxation and higher levels of investment it is certainly harder now than in Victorian times to save enough to start a small business or to borrow it from friends. Of probably even greater significance is the brake provided on firms' expansion by the high cost of capital in the United Kingdom and the shortage of equity or risk capital (Brown *et al.*, 1976). The clearing banks are essentially interested only in giving secured loans, usually for short periods. Merchant banks and venture capital organisations generally have a dismal record in backing new ventures, as opposed to taking over substantial ongoing firms. Furthermore, in the United Kingdom finance is generally available on terms that require borrowers to take personal risks that are greater than in, say, the United States and certainly greater than the average Briton is prepared to take. The value placed on the results of success simply do not compensate for the costs of failure. The great managers of personal savings – i.e. the insurance companies and pension funds – have preferred to invest in commercial property, and increasingly abroad, because of the low returns on investment in the United Kingdom combined with continual exchange-rate devaluation. Even specialised finance organisations such as Industrial and Commercial Finance Corporation provide little help to the mass of small firms, as they tend to be interested in larger loans than many small firms require (because of the risks and the cost of administration). There is, however backing available for high technology (through Technological Development Capital and the NRDC), but here the problem is said to be a lack of men who have entrepreneurial flair as well as good ideas. Generally, it is far easier for a large organisation to generate internal finance, and it can also borrow money on better terms than a small struggling one. This is because the institutions that manage finance are reluctant to take risks and see their responsibilities as protecting their investors rather than encouraging industrial growth. This is in marked contrast to countries like the United States, Japan, France, and West Germany, where small business benefits from finance on favourable terms and preferential public procurement policies and where banks are more closely involved with industry at both the national and local level. One final point, which applies to all the resources that a small firm requires, is that the small firm is less likely than the larger one to *know* what help is available and has less capacity to find out. Information, then, is a further key resource in the birth and growth of small enterprise (Boswell, 1971; Falk and Martinos, 1975; IBM/Urbed, 1977).

16.5 Fostering small firms

If it is considered that the benefits of retaining small firms in inner areas outweigh the costs, a number of changes must be made in government policies and practice. Securing the right balance between a mass of competing demands for scarce resources in conditions of great uncertainty will always be difficult; but there are different ways of planning and organising urban change that can lead to substantially better results than at present, and in many cases successful precedents already exist.

16.5.1 New policies

A priority should be to widen the choice of employment opportunities through attracting new industry and making it easier for small firms to set up and grow (in both services and manufacturing). With few resources at their disposal they need a supportive environment. Access to resources, including premises, personnel, finance, and information, must be made easier. To take personnel, for example, the government training services can fill an important gap by providing more relevant training to the groups that find it hardest to get jobs (basically the under 25s, over 45s, and West Indians) and by encouraging large firms to train 'for stock'. Transport authorities can improve accessibility by focusing on the problems of getting to work and of moving goods within cities. Above all, however, more small units of accommodation are needed at rents that small firms can afford, as demand far outstrips supply (Urbed, 1977). This is a field in which local authorities have both the power and the resources, and so it is worth exploring in more detail.

Paradoxically, despite the shortage of small workspaces in inner areas there is an abundance of empty buildings and vacant sites that would be better used for industry than other purposes. Thus, there are over 35 million sq. ft. of empty industrial floorspace in the South-East, mainly in Greater London and usually in factories that are far too large for any likely occupant. Once they were rehabilitated and converted, many of these could provide cheaper and better premises for new and growing firms than building afresh, providing a vital first rung on the ladder (Eley *et al.*, 1978). Action is required in four main areas:

1. *Control over industrial development* should be modified. For example, Industrial Development Certificates (IDCs) would be better handled at the regional level, e.g. by the Greater London Council, so that their issue could be linked with local planning, and IDCs should be dropped altogether for rehabilitation schemes involving subdivision.
2. *New sources of finance* are required to back such development. The scale is too large for the individual small firm, but the

returns are inadequate to attract most developers, especially at present interest rates. Immediate action would involve local authorities guaranteeing rents. Central government could also help by reducing the rates on finance for investment that provided relevant employment in areas that needed it and possibly also by providing a source of finance, analogous to housing improvement grants, to offset the cost of meeting statutory requirements, which account for about 30 per cent of the cost of conversion (Eley *et al.*, 1978).

3. *Certain planning and building controls* also need to be relaxed. Local authorities should be encouraged to allow non-conforming uses and the mixed use of buildings where there is no local objection. A review of the various building regulations (e.g. health, fire) would establish those which are no longer cost effective. An analysis of the division of powers both within and between authorities would determine how far present organisational arrangements are responsible for excessive uncertainty and delay with regard to both rehabilitation and new development; for example, Slough Industrial Estates has shown that it takes twice as long and costs on average 25 per cent more to build the same-sized factory in this country as in other industrial nations (Mobbs, 1976). Most important of all, redevelopment schemes involving the disturbance of small firms should be dropped, except where absolutely necessary on environmental grounds, for it is far harder to create than to destroy.

4. *Excessive rental expectations*, which lead to the overvaluation of empty buildings and sites, are a major cause of urban dereliction. Ways must be found of bringing these sites into use as rapidly as possible by purchasing empty space at existing use values and by fostering more realistic expectations about both land use and rental growth.

16.5.2 New agencies

Policies are not going to be adequate by themselves, unless they are backed up with new approaches to organisation that match the task in hand. Whereas in the past local government planning has tended to be reactive and restrictive, it will have to become more positive and catalytic in areas that have lost their locational advantage for private enterprise. Here are four kinds of organisations that are needed:

1. *Industrial housing associations*   At present, although it is often viable to convert old buildings to new uses there is no established form of development agency. What is needed is a financing capability and perhaps an institution that could take on the role of the housing associations in the industrial field. The most logical sources of this finance are the pension funds and insurance companies that invest so much in new buildings, but they will need a great deal of underwriting before finance is available on anything like the scale needed to stop the empty buildings from deteriorating beyond the point of no return. The aim should be to create 'working communities' in which a complementary range of small firms share the same building and, where appropriate, common services. There are certainly enough successful experiments in different parts of London – e.g. Covent Garden, Clerkenwell, Chiswick, and Rotherhithe – to show that this approach can work (Franklin and Stafford, 1977). However, it needs fostering if it is to be more than a set of isolated examples.

2. *Industrial parks*   At the same time new industrial estates and flatted factories will also be required in some areas to accommodate growing firms. The land is certainly available, ranging from the vast former docklands, railway marshalling yards, and gasworks to former larger factories, often on main roads. The problem here is acquiring it at its existing use value, and a number of local authorities complain that the 'statutory undertaker' has been particularly self-centred in the past. The finance and expertise for development are available from the private sector, but it is the local authorities that will need to bear part of the risk and act as catalyst through partnership arrangements with private developers or institutions, as some are clearly beginning to do (Falk, 1974). The key to success is finding local resources and tapping them. These can include, for example, technological universities, polytechnics, and industrial research establishments, which abound in and around London; there is nothing yet akin to the Stanford Industrial Park in Palo Alto or the string of high technology firms around Boston, which draw many of their products and some of their personnel from the creative work of the university laboratories. There are, however, a few fledgling projects – e.g. industrial estates in Cambridge, Edinburgh, and Warrington – that offer some promise (Warrington Development Corporation, 1975; Urbed, 1978b).

3. *Small enterprise centres*   Providing premises will be insufficient if small firms, particularly the fledgling ones, are still weak.

One way in which small enterprises can become stronger is through collaboration. Many small enterprises face similar problems to those encountered by large firms but have no one to turn to for help. By joining together, just as small shopkeepers and farmers have done, they can begin to get equal treatment with the larger firms. Collaboration can involve sharing basic services such as secretarial facilities and reception within the same buildings, or the same approach can be applied to a whole area. It can also involve combining on certain business functions, such as purchasing or distribution. In some areas chambers of commerce may take the lead; in others new 'third force' organisations are needed, such as the evolving small-enterprise centre in Covent Garden, applying the principles of community development to the business sphere (Lessem, 1977; Falk, 1978b).

4. *Local economic planning and development*   Just as local authorities already accept the responsibility for housing lower income groups and encouraging related services through community workers, so a similar effort is needed in the industrial and commercial field. Many local authorities have already accepted the need to do something about employment, formulated industrial policies, and appointed industrial development officers and in some cases employment officers. Nevertheless, good intentions will have little influence if they are not backed up with action. The designation of industrial improvement areas, followed by a coherent set of measures to overcome local business grievances, can be a vital first step (Falk and Martinos, 1975; Rochdale Metropolitan Borough, 1974[2]). This will typically involve improvements to public transport, flexibility with regard to parking restrictions, appropriate housing for key workers, and environmental improvements to make a rundown area 'come alive'.

Mounting an effective strategy will depend on concentrating on either a particular geographical area or a business sector and uniting all the departments involved. To succeed, such an effort must have top level backing, its own small team and budget, and close links with local business and union leaders. There are now signs that many local authorities recognise the problem. There is still time to ensure that small enterprise has a permanent place in the life of the cities, but it will require a massive switch in attitudes and practices before business is once again a vital part of a balanced and self-sustaining community.

[2]See also various articles in 'Opportunity docks', feature in *Architectural Design* (February 1975).

17 Asian Shopkeepers as a Middleman Minority: A Study of Small Businesses in Wandsworth

Howard Aldrich

17.1 Introduction

A comprehensive explanation of the conditions under which ethnic or racial minorities enter small shopkeeping in large numbers requires the consideration of four factors:

(a) demographic changes in the size and distribution of the minority and majority group populations;
(b) changes in a society's industrial and occupational structure;
(c) the employment opportunity structure for the minority population; and
(d) the organising capacity of the minority population.

The second factor is subsumed in theories of industrialisation and societal growth and is not examined in this chapter. Taken together, the other three factors comprise two strands of theorising and research that have traditionally been treated separately: models of *ecological succession*, accounting for the process by which minority groups replace majority group residents of a residential area; and models of '*middleman minorities*', accounting for the tendency of certain ethnic minorities to enter small shopkeeping in societies to which they have emigrated. The literature on residential ecological succession in the United States has previously been reviewed

389

(Aldrich, 1975), and space does not permit a summary here. This chapter focuses on the middleman minority model, after a brief review of the results from a test of two hypotheses from the ecological succession model. Hypotheses were tested on two samples of small businesses and shopkeepers in Wandsworth – one of the boroughs of Greater London. Comparisons are made between findings from research in the United States and England.

The area chosen for a study of New Commonwealth-origin shopkeepers was the Borough of Wandsworth, with a population of 302,247 residents in 1971. Wandsworth lies just south of the river Thames, below Westminster and Chelsea, and is bounded to the east by Brixton – another area with a relatively high concentration of New Commonwealth-origin population. Wandsworth was chosen for two reasons. First, in 1971 its twenty wards varied from 2 to 17 per cent in Commonwealth-born population and 2 to 21 per cent in New Commonwealth-origin population (i.e. both parents born in the New Commonwealth).[1] Second, an investigation by the Wandsworth Community Relations Officer in 1974 found a large number of Asian-owned shops in the borough, and also it was known that a large number of Asians had settled in Wandsworth after their expulsion from Uganda.[2]

In December 1975 a complete enumeration of *all* businesses in Wandsworth was made, based on a direct observation of the commercial activity on each street. There were 2,590 commercial establishments in Wandsworth, with 2,351 owned by whites (both native and foreign born), 195 by Asians, 28 by Chinese, 2 by Japanese, and 14 by West Indians. All the Chinese and Japanese shops were either restaurants or food sales establishments. They were excluded from further consideration.

17.2 The succession model and ethnic enterprise

Research on American cities indicates that the ecological succession model of residential population change fits fairly well the changes observed in the small business population in racially changing areas (Aldrich and Reiss, 1976; Aldrich, 1975). Ecological

[1] Information on the population composition of the twenty wards was obtained from the 1971 Census of Population, Small Area Statistics (Ward Library), which is based on a 100 per cent count of the population.
[2] 'Asian' in this chapter refers to people of Indian or Pakistani descent, excluding Chinese, Japanese, and the like.

succession in the residential and business populations of the inner city is an aspect of the more general processes of urban differentiation and change. The two processes are quite similar, both being orderly sequences of change through which communities pass as a consequence of population growth and movements. For study purposes the ecological succession model was extended to cover the process by which New Commonwealth-origin businessmen – Asians and West Indians – are replacing native whites as shopkeepers in British inner cities.

Major differences exist between the American and English cases, the central difference being that Asians have traditionally played a middleman minority role (Bonacich, 1973) in the societies to which they have emigrated, whereas blacks in the United States have been employed as unskilled and semiskilled workers. West Indians in England are quite similar to American blacks in this respect, and they also differ from Asians in being much less prominent as small shopkeepers. Consideration of the middleman minority argument will be delayed until results from the succession model have been summarised.

Two hypotheses concerning the application of the ecological succession model to understanding the penetration of minority businesses into the business population of an area have been tested in a previous paper (Aldrich, 1976a). First, in the *ethnic composition hypothesis* it was hypothesised that there is a strong positive correlation between the ethnic or racial composition of an area and the proportion of minority-owned shops. To the extent that shops were *not* found predominantly in ethnic areas the middleman minority model's stress on organising capacity was favoured. Using the twenty wards in Wandsworth as units of analysis, the correlation between the percentage of New Commonwealth-origin population and the percentage of shops owned by Asians and West Indians was 0.38; and if only children under 14 were included, the correlation increased to 0.48. This is a moderately large correlation, but at the same time it leaves a great deal of the variation in the proportion of minority shopkeepers unexplained.

The association between racial composition and minority ownership results *not* from white owners leaving racially changing areas at an increased rate but rather from the failure of whites to buy into the area. As the white residential population of an area declines, the shops left vacant through the normal process of business turnover are not occupied by new white owners. Potential white owners define the racially changing area as undesirable, and consequently the market for vacant shops is made up almost entirely of minorities. A follow-up study in June 1977 of the 1975 Wandsworth sample confirmed this interpretation. Of the twenty-nine previously white-owned shops sold to new owners in the 'high minority' wards (15 per cent or more New Commonwealth-origin population),48 per cent were sold to Indians or Pakistanis. In the 'low minority' wards (less than 15 per cent New Commonwealth-origin population) only one of the nine shops that were available was sold to an Asian.

Second, in the *deteriorating area hypothesis* it was hypothesised that minority-owned shops tend to locate in economically deteriorating areas. This hypothesis, as well as the first, has been strongly confirmed for urban areas in the United States (Aldrich and Reiss, 1976). It was also supported for Wandsworth, using the percentage of all white-owned shops that were chain owned as an indication of an area's economic potential and attractiveness. The correlation between the percentage of white-owned retail shops that were chain owned and the percentage of all shops owned by Asians or West Indians was -0.37. (Note that a part-whole correlational confounding was avoided by using the percentage of *white*-owned shops that were chain owned rather than the percentage of all shops.) Taken together, the relative size of the youthful New Commonwealth-origin population and the percentage of chain ownership accounted for about one-fourth of the variation in the percentage of New Commonwealth-owned shops (corrected $R^2 = 0.24$).

These results lend strong support to the hypothesis that similar patterns of residential succession in the United States and England are producing similar patterns of business ownership among black and brown minority populations in the two societies. (For other discussions of similarities and differences in racial residential succession between the United States and England, see Dalton and Seaman, 1973; Lee, 1977; and Goering, 1978.) As stated, the two ecological succession hypotheses require very few assumptions to be made about the social and cultural characteristics of the racial or ethnic group moving into business opportunities in changing areas. The middleman minority model complements the succession argument by directing attention to the fact that some minority groups are in a better position to benefit from residential succession than others.

17.3 The middleman minority model and ethnic enterprise

Research on migrant communities in foreign countries indicates that some ethnic groups are more likely than others to establish themselves in small business enterprises. Bonacich (1973) has commented that:

> . . . there is a general consensus that a number of ethnic groups around the world have occupied a similar position in the social structure (i.e., middleman minorities or middleman trading peoples). Among these are the Jews in Europe . . . the Chinese in Southeast Asia, Asians in East Africa, Armenians in Turkey, Syrians in West Africa, Parsis in Africa, Japanese and Greeks in the United States, and so on. (p. 583)

In contrast, Frazier (1957) has commented on the lack of a 'tradition of enterprise' in discussing black business in the United States:

> Although no systematic study has been undertaken of the social causes of the failure of the Negro to achieve success as businessmen, it appears from what we know of the social and cultural history that it is the result largely of the lack of traditions in the field of business enterprise. (p. 410)

However, attributing lack of success to 'lack of traditions' is of course simply to beg the question of what accounts for the alleged 'lack of traditions'.

The middleman minority model focuses on two of the four factors listed earlier as part of a comprehensive explanation of the conditions under which an ethnic minority enters small shopkeeping in large numbers: the employment opportunity structure for the minority population, and the organising capacity of the minority population. 'Organising capacity' refers to values and orientations, family organisation, and other group attributes that affect a minority group's ability to concentrate resources to form small businesses.

In the remainder of this chapter four hypotheses based on the middleman minority model will be tested, with a brief rationale presented for each. A complete discussion is given in Aldrich (1976b).

17.3.1 The Wandsworth interview sample

A sampling list of Asian businessmen in Wandsworth was obtained from a complete enumeration of all Indian and Pakistani shopkeepers prepared by the Wandsworth Community Relations Council in

1974. This list was supplemented with additional shops on the basis of a business census of Wandsworth in December 1975, which generated a list of all businesses and the ethnicity of their owners. The final sampling list was reduced because of extensive demolition in the areas and shops failing since the Community Relations Council list was compiled. The target sampling list included 132 addresses, and interviews conducted by Asian interviewers were obtained at seventy-four sites for a completion rate of 56 per cent. Not all these interviews were with Asians as a few shops had been sold to whites and a few others to Cypriots since the original list was compiled.

A white-owned sample was drawn from the business census list in a way that maximised its comparability with the Asian sample. First, all chain-owned or multiple shops of more than five sites were excluded. Second, as Asians were concentrated in a few lines of trade rather than spread over the same industries as whites, the white sample was limited to the following industries: grocery and food sales, newsagents, confectioners and tobacconists, restaurants, clothing shops, chemists, and consumer household durables. The final sample was drawn by taking every seventh business on the census list, excluding industries not specified above. After omitting those chain-owned shops inadvertently selected and sites out of business, the sampling list totalled 105 businesses. Interviews conducted by white interviewers were obtained at forty-seven sites for a completion rate of 45 per cent. As with the Asian sampling list, a few shops had changed hands or been misclassified, and thus some of these interviews were with non-whites.

17.3.2   Do Asians serve a protected market?

The first middleman minority hypothesis deals with the ethnic composition of the market served by minority businesses. It was hypothesised that black shopkeepers in the United States are much more dependent upon a protected minority market than Asian shopkeepers in England. Moreover, while special consumer tastes may account for a partial protected market for Asians in England, such tastes are less important than the absence of white competition in accounting for the market for black shopkeepers in the United States. This *protected market hypothesis* suggests a strong continuity in the kind of market served by Asians in most of the host societies where they have settled – namely, service to the majority group –

whereas black shopkeepers in the United States are hampered by not having a very large distinctive market to serve that will compensate for the other disadvantages that they face.

This question was investigated by asking shopkeepers to estimate what proportion of their customers were white, Asian, West Indian, and of other ethnic origins. If Asian shops benefited from serving a protected market, the percentage of white customers that they served should have been significantly lower than that of white-owned shops. Note that the hypothesis is that the proportion of white customers served will not differ significantly between the two groups.

The average proportion of customers who were white, as estimated by white shopkeepers, was 65 per cent. Asian shopkeepers estimated that they served a 60 per cent white market, which was not significantly different from the estimate of white shopkeepers ($F = 0.83, p > 0.10$). In the food sales sector, where proponents of the 'special consumer tastes' argument would predict the most likely existence of protected markets, white grocery and food shop owners estimated that 68 per cent of their customers were white, while Asian grocery and food shop owners estimated that 58 per cent of their customers were white. In the restaurant sector – the other likely 'protected market' – there was a larger difference, but a small number of cases and missing data hampered the analysis. Among the four white restaurant owners answering the question the average estimate was 87 per cent, while among the seven Asian restaurant owners the average estimate was 61 per cent.

A more sophisticated version of the protected market hypothesis asserts that Asian shopkeepers benefit from serving a customer group that white shopkeepers can't or won't serve namely, West Indians. However, this hypothesis also was not supported; white shopkeepers reported that an average of 18 per cent of their customers were West Indian, while Asian shopkeepers reported an average of 21 per cent ($F = 0.44, p > 0.10$).

There were no significant differences by type of business; for example, among white-owned grocery stores the average reported was 18 per cent and among Asian grocery and food shops it was 26 per cent, and this 8 percentage point difference was the *largest* difference across the five industry categories.

An alternative explanation for the proportion of Asian or West Indian customers making up the market of a small business is that it depends on the ethnic composition of the neighbourhood or area.

This hypothesis was supported, as the correlation between the percentage New Commonwealth-origin population in a ward and the proportion of a shop's customers that was white was −0.34 ($p<0.001$). Especially significant is the fact that the correlation was essentially the same *within* the two groups of shops, being −0.29 among white-owned shops and −0.39 among Asian-owned shops.

There was thus little indication that Asian shopkeepers depended on or benefited from a protected market, as the ethnic composition of the market that they served was essentially the same as that served by whites. The only hint of the possibility of a protected market, due to special consumer tastes, was in the restaurant sector, but even there the difference was not large and the number of cases was small.

Other evidence against the protected market hypothesis was obtained when shopkeepers were asked how they accounted for the ethnic mix of the customers that they served. If a shopkeeper estimated that his proportion of white customers was less than 50 per cent, he was asked: 'Why is your proportion of white customers so low?' As only a minority of shopkeepers in either group reported that less than 50 per cent of their customers were white, the number of cases was small. Among the eight white shopkeepers with a minority of white customers, six accounted for this in terms of the high percentage of Asians and West Indians living or working in the area, and the other two said that they carried a product that catered to the tastes of Asians or West Indians and didn't appeal to or wasn't used by whites. Among the seventeen Asian shopkeepers with a minority white clientele, seven (or 41 per cent) thought that they carried a product that appealed to Asians or West Indians rather than whites. Note that these seven cases of a 'protected market' made up only 11 per cent of the Asian sample.

Shopkeepers estimating that 50 per cent or more of their trade was with whites were asked: 'Why is your proportion of white customers so high?' Their answers are reported in Table 17.1. A higher percentage of white than Asian shopkeepers attributed their predominantly white clientele to the high proportion of whites living in the area, but the most interesting difference lies in the high proportion of Asian shopkeepers citing 'good service' or 'late hours' and the lack of such responses by white shopkeepers. About one-quarter of *each* group believed that they had a largely white trade because the product carried catered to the tastes of whites and didn't appeal to Asians or West Indians or was not used by them.

Table 17.1 Responses to: 'Why is your proportion of white customers so high (i.e. 50% or more)?' by owner's ethnicity (% responding).

Response	White	Asian
Mostly whites living/working here	56	39
Product caters to white tastes	24	29
Good service/late hours	3	26
Product too expensive for Asians	9	2
Other	9	4
Total	101	100

Notes: N of cases = 34 (white) and 49 (Asian); χ^2 = 10.76; $p < 0.05$.
Source: Own interview survey.

The fourteen cases of Asians making this argument represented 21 per cent of all Asian-owned shops, which was nearly double the proportion (11 per cent) arguing that they enjoyed a protected market among non-whites.

About the same proportion of shopkeepers in each group reported that they had competitors in their area. The major difference between Asian and white shops is that Asians face competition not only from whites but also from other Asians, whereas whites are much less likely to have Asian competition. It might be expected that the more intense level of competition facing Asian shops would lead to the adoption of more vigorous competitive practices, and this possibility has been explored in Aldrich (1976b). Briefly, it was found that Asians in competition with other Asians were open longer, worked more hours per week, were open more often on Sundays, made deliveries and extended credit to a greater extent, and were more likely to employ their children than Asians not in competition with other Asians. Only two of these six results were statistically significant, but the pattern is nevertheless instructive. Competition with other Asians is a spur to more intensive competitive behaviour.

The information presented in this section supports the view that Asian shopkeepers in Wandsworth do *not* depend on a protected market for their survival. They serve about the same proportion of white customers as their white competitors, and indeed a higher proportion of Asian shops are oriented towards an exclusively white market than towards an exclusively non-white one. This situation contrasts sharply with that of black shopkeepers in US cities, who rely almost exclusively on black customers for their trade.

17.3.3 Ethnicity and competitive practices

The second middleman-minority hypothesis posits that, in so far as there are special culturally-transmitted skills that facilitate the successful operation of a small business, these may be observed more often among Asians than among West Indians in England or blacks in the United States. The study was limited to observing the *effects* of this skill rather than the skill itself, e.g. being open more days of the week and longer hours, refusing to extend credit and thus avoiding carrying a burden of unpaid bills, or in general paying more attention to competitive practices. A thorough-going test of this *intensive competitive-practices hypothesis* must await two conditions:- (a) obtaining a larger sample of West Indian shopkeepers than in the present study; and (b) assembling the relevant information on US black small businessmen. Information for the latter test is available from previous US studies (e.g. Aldrich, 1973) but has not yet been brought together with the present study because of resource limitations.

The present study did permit an indirect test of this hypothesis, however, as a comparison could be made between the business practices of Asian and white shopkeepers. To the extent that Asians possess 'special' skills, this should be apparent in a comparison with whites operating small shops in a deteriorating inner-city area such as Wandsworth. Indeed, associations of white shopkeepers often claim they are being driven out of business by Asians using 'unfair' business practices, implying that Asians possess some business resources that are not available to local whites. To the extent that Asian business practices did not differ significantly from those of whites, this criticism was blunted. This finding also calls into question any argument about Asian success being dependent on 'special skills'.

Information in the first two rows of Table 17.2 confirms the casual visitor's impression of the services offered by Asian shops; they are open a half-day more per week and an hour per day more than white-owned shops. In spite of being open about 12 hours per week less than Asian shopkeepers, white owners and managers asserted that they worked almost 64 hours per week – the same number as Asian owners and managers. Either white respondents were overestimating or Asians were underestimating the hours that they worked, with the latter the more likely the case, given the hours per week that Asian shops were open. The pattern of longer hours

Table 17.2 Ethnicity of owner and business practices.

Business practice	White	Asian	P[a]
Days open per week	5.8	6.3	0.001
Hours open per day	9.2	10.4	0.001
Hours worked per week	63.7	63.9	n.s.
Open on Sundays (%)	26	48	0.03
Making deliveries (%)	51	26	0.01
Selling on credit (%)	26	18	n.s.
No. of part time employees	0.74	0.72	n.s.
Total no. of employees	2.07	2.38	n.s.
Total no. of family members employed	0.86	1.18	0.05
No. of employees working without pay	0.36	0.27	n.s.
Spouse working in business (%)	58	58	n.s.
Children working in business (%)	14	22	n.s.
Business premises in below-average condition (%)	36	8	0.01
Located on mainly commercial street (%)	55	59	n.s.

[a] Significance test based on either difference-of-means test or chi-square; n.s. = not significant.
Source: Own interview survey.

of operation held across all types of business (industry-specific data are not presented in Table 17.2).

Almost half the Asian shops were open on Sunday – a recent innovation in English retailing – compared to about one-quarter of the white-owned shops. The next two items also tap an essential difference between the traditional mode of running a small business and more modern methods. First, 51 per cent of white-owned shops still made deliveries to customers, while only 26 per cent of Asian-owned shops did. Delivery service is a convenience for customers, but it is doubtful if it is economically justified in view of the added costs involved for the small shop. Second, 26 per cent of the white-owned shops sold some goods on credit, compared to 18 per cent of the Asian-owned shops. This difference was not statistically significant, and both figures are probably lower than for shops a decade ago. High interest charges and the cost of collecting bad debts place locally owned shops at a severe disadvantage in offering credit to customers, compared with the resources of chain-owned stores, which accept credit cards and sometimes have their own credit operation.

Asian and white-owned businesses may have differed in the services that they offer, but they employed approximately the same number of people, differing only in the extent to which they used family labour. The average number of part time employees was the same in both groups, indicating that each had the same flexibility built into its mode of operation. Asian shopkeepers employed a significantly higher number of family members; and as other information in Table 17.2 shows that Asian and white shopkeepers were equally likely to have their spouses working in the business (58 per cent), the difference in relatives employed must have been due to the number of children and other kin employed from the extended family.

The final two items in Table 17.2 concern the physical situation of a business – the business premises and the street on which it was located. Based on interviewer judgements, a higher proportion of white than Asian-owned shops were located in premises that were 'bad' ('dark and dingy, jumbled stock, etc.') or 'poor' ('fairly clean, but jumbled stock, etc.') (This may have been partially a function of management skills.) Roughly the same proportion of Asian and white-owned shops were located on mainly commercial streets, i.e. 'high streets', and other major traffic arteries.

The analyses reported in this section lend support to the hypothesis that Asian shopkeepers are engaged in more intensive competitive practices than whites, e.g. longer hours, and have adapted more readily to 'modern' business practices, e.g. being open on Sundays and not making deliveries to customers. By inference, this behaviour is a result either of greater skills or of the interaction of skills with high achievement motivation.

17.3.4 *Ethnicity and socioeconomic background*

The third middleman-minority hypothesis concerns expected differences between the socioeconomic characteristics of Asian and white shopkeepers. Because of barriers to economic opportunities in the white-dominated occupational structure, minority shopkeepers are predicted to be of (relatively) higher socioeconomic background than local white shopkeepers. White shopkeepers are expected to be much like local white small businessmen in the United States: aged, of relatively low education, and recruited from previous blue-collar employment. The *higher socioeconomic-background hypothesis* expects that some, but not all, Asian businessmen will conform fairly closely to the traditional view of the economic entrepreneur.

Table 17.3 Ethnicity and socioeconomic background of owner

Variable	White	Asian	P^a
Mean age (years)	44.4	38.6	0.05
Standard deviation of age (years)	13.9	10.9	
Educational qualifications (%):			
No qualifications	59	36	
'O' levels	13	12	
CSE^b or finished secondary schooling	18	12	
'A' levels	0	10	
Craft or technical training	8	8	
College graduate	3	22	
Total^c	101	100	
Self-employed in last job (%)	11	25	n.s.
Employed in blue collar work on last job (%)	52	37	n.s.
Father self-employed (%)	34	44	n.s.
Father employed in blue collar work (%)	53	30	0.05
Married, widowed, or divorced (%)	88	83	n.s.
With children (excludes singles) (%)	74	74	n.s.
Mean no. of children	2.15	3.26	0.05
Children with 'A' levels or beyond (%)	23	48	0.05
Job expectations for children: (%) saying 'Don't know' or 'It's up to the children to decide'	67	42	0.10
Owning other businesses or rental property (%)	17	19	n.s.

^{a} Significance test based on either difference-of-means test or chi-square; n.s. = not significant.
^{b} CSE = Certificate of Secondary Education.
^{c} $\chi^2 = 15.4$; $p<0.02$; N of cases = 39 (White) and 59 (Asian).

Source: Own interview survey.

The average Asian shopkeeper was about six years younger than the average white shopkeeper, and the Asians were a slightly more homogeneous group (see Table 17.3). Most relevant to the third middleman-minority hypothesis is the finding that 22 per cent of the Asian shopkeepers had college degrees, compared to only 3 per cent of the white shopkeepers. Here is direct evidence for the *'blocked upward-mobility thesis'* that other investigators have commented on: barriers to entry into managerial jobs in white-owned businesses push some Asians into going into business for themselves.

A higher proportion of Asians were self-employed in their last job and had fathers who were self-employed, but these differences were not large enough to be statistically significant. The proportion of self-employed fathers for both groups was much higher than would be expected on the basis of the English occupational distribution of thirty years ago, when these shopkeepers were growing up. These figures are strong evidence for the importance of occupational inheritance in the small business sector. The proportions of white shopkeepers whose fathers were either self-employed or in blue collar work was quite similar to those in Brian Elliott's and Frank Bechhofer's study of shopkeepers in Edinburgh, lending confidence to these findings.[3]

Similar proportions of shopkeepers in each group were married and had children, but family size was significantly larger among Asians (2.15 versus 3.26 children per family). Child rearing is an area of social behaviour where observable differences in the norms and values of the two groups of businessmen might be expected, and the penultimate two rows in Table 17.3 show that this was indeed the case. Nearly half the Asian children had the higher qualifications, while less than one-quarter of the white children did. None of the white children earned a college degree, whereas one-fifth of the Asian children had college degrees. Moreover, 44 per cent of the Asians wanted their children to enter a white collar job, compared to 25 per cent of the white parents, implying higher aspirations on the part of Asian than white shopkeepers for their children. These findings do *not* accord with Bechhofer and Elliott's, as they found that white shopkeepers in Edinburgh were ambitious for their children and that their male offspring had done remarkably well in occupational mobility. The reason for this divergence of findings is not clear but may have to do with the social marginality of the shopkeepers in Wandsworth.

Asian shopkeepers were slightly younger, were significantly better educated, had larger families, and had higher educational and occupational aspirations for their children than white shopkeepers. In one significant area, however, there was little difference; about the same proportion of shopkeepers in each group owned another business or other rental property (17 per cent of the whites and 19 per cent of the Asians). About the same proportion in each group had self-employed fathers, were married, widowed, or divorced,

---

[3] Brian Elliott, personal communication.

and had children. Thus, the differences in socioeconomic background between the two groups should not be overstated. This section can be summarised by noting that the differences in skills and aspirations documented in Table 17.3 are consistent with other findings concerning differences in competitive business practices.

17.3.5 Organising capacity of the Asian population

The fourth middleman-minority hypothesis – the *greater organising-capacity hypothesis* – is that differences in the organising capacity of the Asian as opposed to the West Indian or black population account in part for the greater success of Asian shopkeepers. Differences in organising capacity will be indicated by differences in the role of family labour and in the degree of support from kinsmen and friends in raising funds to capitalise a business. Again, because of the small number of West Indians in the sample, a comparison between the two minority populations could not be made. However, the organising capacity of the Asian population could be evaluated against that of the white small-business population, the implicit model being that white shopkeepers' success depends on individual as opposed to collective achievement, and vice versa for Asians.

Asian shopkeepers made use of direct ties through friends more often than whites in learning about the availability of business sites. Whites, on the other hand, were slightly more likely to have acquired a shop through personal contact with the previous owner or to have bought the shop from a family member (see Table 17.4). Not quite half of each group made use of the more formal procedure of going through an estate agent or scanning the newspaper advertisements. The existence of a substantial within-group market in business sites was reflected in the 48 per cent of Asian shopkeepers who bought their business from another minority group member and the 94 per cent of whites who bought from other whites.

The importance of family and friendship ties within the Asian community was also shown in that 42 per cent of the Asian shopkeepers raised some of the capital to go into business from among their family and friends, compared to 22 per cent of the white shopkeepers. Note, however, that among those shopkeepers in both groups using family and friends the actual proportion of the required funds raised from each source was about the same (white shopkeepers and Asian shopkeepers raised 34 and 31 per cent of

Table 17.4 Ethnicity of owner and organising capacity

Variable	White	Asian	P^a
Previous owner was white (%)	94	52	0.01
% who raised capital through:			
Family and friends	22	42	0.01
Bank or lending association	47	57	n.s.
Personal savings	81	83	n.s.
% of capital raised through:[b]			
Family members	34	31	n.s.
Friends	33	26	n.s.
Bank or lending association	62	37	0.01
Personal savings	71	59	n.s.
% with family members owning shops	31	32	n.s.
% of shops employing non-whites [c]	64	98	0.01
% of shops employing whites [c]	58	14	0.01

[a]Significance test based on either difference-of-means test or chi-square; n.s. = not significant.

[b]Base for these percentages is only those shopkeepers using a specific source for capital.

[c]Base for these percentages is only those shops having one or more employees.

Source: Own interview survey.

capital respectively from family members and 33 and 26 per cent respectively from friends). About the same proportion of shop-keepers in each group reported using personal savings to capitalise their businesses, with the percentage raised from this source being insignificantly higher in the white group.

Most significant, from the viewpoint of an ethnic group's organising capacity, is the finding that there was no significant difference between the two groups in their use of banks or lending associations as a source of capital. Asians, indeed, were slightly (but statistically insignificantly) more likely to borrow from a bank or lending association than whites. (By way of contrast, in a US sample of black small businessmen (Aldrich, 1973; Aldrich and Reiss, 1976) only 6 per cent reported beginning their business with the help of a loan from a bank, credit association, or finance company, and a high proportion had been turned down.) Among those whites and Asians using a bank or lending association's funds, however, whites fulfilled a significantly larger share of their capital needs than did Asians. As in the United States, the most important source of capital for *all* small shopkeepers in founding a business was personal savings, with this money supplemented by family, friends, and credit institutions. Asians didn't appear to be disadvantaged in the struggle for funds, and these findings, coupled with some field data collected, demonstrate the importance of friendship networks to them.

Approximately the same proportion of each group had family members who owned shops (31 per cent for whites and 32 per cent for Asians). Many investigators in England do not seem to be aware of the high proportion of white shopkeepers who have shopkeeper relatives, as much is always made of the pattern of business ownership within Asian families as though this were somehow unique to Asians as a group.

There is one final indicator of the extent to which an ethnic group draws upon its own resources in creating and operating small businesses, namely, the degree to which members of one's own group are hired as employees. Asians differed substantially from whites in this respect, as 64 per cent of the white-owned shops with one or more employees had at least one non-white on their staff, whereas only 14 per cent of the Asian-owned shops employed any whites. This situation is quite comparable to that observed in the United States. In a previous study of small businesses in Chicago, Boston, and Washington, DC (Aldrich, 1973; Aldrich and Reiss, 1976) only one black businessman who employed *any* whites was found, whereas white-owned businesses in black residential areas had many blacks on their staffs (although not in as high a proportion as the racial composition of the area implied). Furthermore, in Wandsworth, as only 58 per cent of the white-owned shops with employees employed any whites, this means that 42 per cent employed *only* non-whites. In contrast, only one Asian-owned shop employed only whites. One of the consequences of this high degree of ethnic exclusiveness on the part of Asian employers, coupled with high Asian penetration of the staffs of white-owned shops, is that young Asian workers receive training from *both* Asian and white shopkeepers.

Information presented in this section does not reveal any major differences in the organising capacities of the Asian and white population of shopkeepers, but clearly the sample of each group was biased. (Less than 10 per cent of the white working population is employed in shopkeeping; and although estimates for the Asian population are hazardous, the proportion employed as shopkeepers can't be much higher.) A finding that bears further investigation is the relatively higher proportion of Asians learning about business opportunities by word of mouth passed on through friends and raising capital through family and friendship ties. A proper test of the fourth hypothesis requires further field work among West Indians and Asians and investigations of the non-shopkeeping population.

17.4 Conclusions

Four hypotheses derived from the middleman minority model of ethnicity and success in small businesses have been examined in this chapter. This section will review the findings concerning each. (Hypotheses regarding the ecological succession model have been summarised in section 17.2).

1. Asian shopkeepers in England were much less dependent upon a protected market than blacks in the United States, and special consumer tastes accounted for only a small part of Asian penetration into small shopkeeping. Asians served about the same proportion of white customers as their white competitors and, if anything, were more oriented towards the largely white market than the minority 'protected' market.

2. Asian shopkeepers were engaged in more intensive competitive practices than whites, e.g. being open for more days a week, especially Sundays. In a number of instances whites and Asians were very similar in business practices, e.g. in the percentage with the spouse or children working in the business, and so the overall pattern was a mixed one. The extent to which Asians differ from West Indians in business skills and practices cannot be tested until additional information is collected.

3. It was hypothesised that because of barriers to economic opportunities in the white-dominated occupational structure, Asian shopkeepers would be of (relatively) higher socioeconomic background than local white shopkeepers. This hypothesis was only partially supported. Asian shopkeepers were slightly younger, were significantly better educated, had larger families, and had higher educational and occupational aspirations for their children than white shopkeepers. However, about the same proportion of each group owned other business or rental property, had self-employed fathers (although whites had a signific-

antly higher proportion of blue collar fathers), were married, and had children. The observed differences are consistent with differences found in competitive business practices, but whether it can be concluded that it is *these* factors that provide Asians with a competitive edge it is too soon to say.

4. Differences in the organising capacity of the Asian as opposed to the West Indian (or US black) population were hypothesised to account in part for the greater success of Asian shopkeepers. Once again, this hypothesis had to be indirectly assessed by comparing Asian to white shopkeepers. In general the analysis did *not* reveal any major differences in the organising capacities of the two populations of shopkeepers under study. However, as the sample included only the whites and Asians who were successful in establishing themselves in business, it was thus biased away from finding failures in organising capacity. Further fieldwork needs to be carried out to test this hypothesis conclusively.

VI Policies for the Labour Market

18 Manpower Policy and Inner Cities

G. L. Reid

18.1 Introduction[1]

The novice who comes relatively fresh to the detailed employment problems of inner cities, and reads all the papers in the Centre for Environmental Studies (CES) Seminar series and various other analyses, is left with two over-riding impressions. These will seem absurdly simple to those in the field, but they have determined the form of this chapter. First, 'the problem' of inner city employment is incredibly complex and multifaceted. Its analysis seems to require an understanding of many disciplines and techniques, and yet an analysis that is too broadly ranging risks descending into generalities and prescriptions for thoroughly and comprehensively changing the whole social and economic structure of cities (and possibly of the nation). These may be useful as a long term guide to where policy should go; but unless they take account of resource scarcities and real world practicalities and priorities, they may not command much support from policy makers. Second, in attempting to frame solutions to inner-city employment problems many analytical studies assign a central role to policies affecting employment, and more specifically to manpower policy measures. A return will be made to both these points a little later; but this introduction will first briefly indicate, without much detail, the general role of manpower policy as it appears to be.

[1] Any opinions in this chapter are the author's and should not be taken to represent the policy of the MSC. Some alterations have been made to reflect institutional changes within the MSC in mid 1978, but the structure and argument of the chapter remain unchanged.

The Manpower Services Commission (MSC) has been charged with the responsibility for 'developing and executing a comprehensive manpower policy', and this has both an economic aspect – in enabling the development and most effective use of the nation's manpower resources – and a social aspect – in giving individuals the opportunities and services that they require to lead satisfying working lives. This is of course a general statement of intent, which has to be defined and articulated as is now happening within the MSC, but it does indicate the central role that manpower policy and the consideration of manpower issues should have at the company level, the national level, and all levels of decision taking in between. This has certainly not been the case in the past. Indeed, it is extraordinary how manpower considerations have been treated as a residual, thought about (if at all) only after all other factors, presumably in the fond hope that things would work themselves out. A few brief examples: the past use of the construction industry as an economic regulator has occurred with apparently no consideration of the serious short-term labour constraints and the inflationary consequences of overexpanding demand; the apparent unwillingness of many companies to do any manpower planning, even of the most rudimentary kind, means that they have relied on short term responses to immediate problems and thereby stored up trouble for themselves; and the past housing and transport policies of some local authorities seem to have paid scant attention to travel-to-work patterns or the distribution of employment.

Manpower policy has close links with various other social and economic policies; it affects them and is affected by them. This does not mean that all manpower considerations must somehow be structured or brought under a 'co-ordinating' framework of public policy. There are many labour market situations or movements where the participants are apparently satisfied without any policy intervention, but there must be some framework within which the instruments of manpower policy can be brought into action, and this implies an understanding of the manpower system and the flows in it. Again, the central role of manpower policy does not imply that it must always be dominant. For example, the creation of secure permanent employment depends on a wide range of economic and industrial policies of government (or, more correctly, on the corporate and individual reactions to such policies), but these in turn depend on a proper consideration of manpower aspects and on manpower policy measures being taken where necessary.

As far as the MSC is concerned, this approach to manpower policy has several important implications for the development and administration of manpower policy. First, the MSC must take a forward view of the development of the labour market and parts of it, be they geographical, industrial, or occupational, to identify so far as possible the major areas where employment problems may arise. Second, there must be a selection of strategic priorities in the basic programmes providing information, placement, training, and other conventional manpower services, although of course the modernisation and new management of these activities will mean a different level of service from that of the 1950s and 1960s. Third, while it is hoped that the days of manpower policy as a 'fire brigade' activity, called in only when something has gone wrong, are now past, the rapid response to particular short- or medium-term problems is very much the MSC's concern, and this often involves special measures in particular areas. Fourth, the central role of manpower policy demands a constant review of how successful policy actually is in meeting its objectives, and this means the evaluation of policies and ongoing consideration of the organisation of services and the overall use of resources.

The relevance of this to inner-city employment problems will, it is hoped, become clear, but of particular importance is the interaction of manpower policy with other policies. This chapter will deal with a partial approach to certain aspects of the inner city problem, and it should be recognised that manpower policy alone cannot solve these employment problems without the contribution of other interacting policies. The remaining sections of this chapter will deal with the identification of inner-city employment problems from the point of view of manpower policy, outline the present approach of policy measures, and set out some questions for discussion on the general role of manpower policy.

18.2 Identification of the problem

The employment problems of inner cities, and of wider areas within conurbations, have been exhaustively analysed in the CES Seminar series and in other publications. To summarise them very briefly, inner city areas are characterised by most or all of the following symptoms: high registered unemployment, low activity rates, declining manufacturing employment, and low pay (not dealt with in this chapter). Particular groups within the population, particularly ethnic minorities and unskilled workers, tend to be disproportionately represented.

These are the symptoms with which manpower and other policies have to deal; but what is much less clear, even given the depth of existing analysis, is why these symptoms exist and what the proximate causes are. From the literature it can be seen that *employment changes* can be divided into a number of categories of change, of which the following list is illustrative:

(a) the decentralisation of employment from the inner to the outer areas of conurbations;
(b) the declining importance of small firms and/or industrial concentration;
(c) secular changes in industrial structure (e.g. the London docks); and
(d) the decline or slow growth of certain service industries.

The explanations of these changes advanced by the analytical papers are tremendously varied. They include failures of land use planning for industry, new towns policy, past trends in regional policy and Industrial Development Certificate (IDC) controls, housing and transport policies, general or specific technological changes, industrial policy, fiscal or budgetary policy, and financial relations between local and central government.

It is difficult to judge or assess how valid these different explanations may be, but one interesting and probably unanswerable question is: what difference would the 'correct' policy have made? For example, one reason for the decline in employment or the failure of employment growth in inner city areas may be planning controls of various kinds that prevent firms with a suitable cost structure from remaining on their inner city sites. Another possibility is that there are no planning constraints but that the sites, or firms on them, cannot in any case show a comparative advantage compared with sites or firms elsewhere. This could be because of simple relative inefficiency, i.e. because, correcting for other factors, inner city firms are less efficient than others. However, leaving this aside, what kind of policy change would have been necessary to avoid these employment declines by restoring inner city firms to a competitive position, and would these policy changes have been feasible in the light of other priorities (e.g. would they have meant a dismantling of regional policy)? To look at this in another way, is there any evidence on how far inner city firms would have needed to be compensated or subsidised to retain or increase employment in the inner city, or is the policy maker faced with a fact of economic life that inner city policy can of itself do little to reverse or even alleviate?

One of the interesting CES Seminar papers[2] by Smith concluded:

> The study area situation is in many ways a microcosm of the Birmingham one, and while minor but significant adjustments can be made at the local level, the key influences on employment well-being are the general economic climate and the future of particular industries and firms.

This conclusion is a rather less pessimistic version of the question at the end of the last paragraph. While the policy issues that it raises seem well outside the scope of conventional manpower policy, the creation and preservation of employment is a relevant concern of manpower policy, and the identification of the reasons for employment decline is thus important.

Unemployment is perhaps of more direct concern to traditional manpower policy, but here again there is no real consensus about why inner city areas apparently have higher levels of unemployment. Is it because there is in these areas:

(a) a higher concentration of individuals who are vulnerable to unemployment, in the sense that their characteristics place them at a labour market disadvantage; or
(b) some form of labour market imbalance, with higher frictional unemployment; or
(c) simply a shortage of jobs for those who are able and willing to work?

Or is it because of a mixture of all three conditions? It is obviously important to distinguish between the different types of unemployment, so that the correct policy conclusions can be drawn and resources can be devoted to the real problems.

Many of the CES Seminar papers highlighted data deficiencies as hindering the more accurate identification of inner-city unemployment problems, notably the paper by Metcalf and Richardson (Chapter 8). The MSC has as one of its objectives the improvement of labour market information, but it has to be recognised that the detailed data at inner city level can be very difficult to secure. The following list outlines a few types of data that would improve the

[2]See Chapter 14 for revised version.

present understanding of inner-city employment problems and the direction of policy measures and comments on what improvements might be expected:

1. *Better unemployment data*　Registered unemployment is an imperfect indicator of the 'true' level of unemployment, and there is some indication that inner city areas are differentially affected by this variation. The only corrections that can presently be applied are from Census of Population data, and these seem likely to vary cyclically and possibly over time. There are, however, few alternatives open. Household sample surveys including all those looking for work could of course build on the data of registered unemployment, but they would be costly and would have to be limited in scope and coverage.

2. *Regular occupational data*　Planners and others operating in or analysing subregional and local areas argue that they are gravely handicapped by having occupational statistics only from census data every ten years. More regular data would allow a greater knowledge of structural change and labour market mismatch and would facilitate industrial, manpower, and planning policy. There would be great advantages in having such data, but the problems faced by their producers would be great. It would be difficult or impossible to obtain refined classification of occupational structure from employers without an enormously more complex inquiry, and employee surveys of sufficient depth to be useful at small area level would in effect mean a mini-census. Some local authorities have in fact been carrying out such surveys.

3. *Additional data*　If an ideal menu of desirable data or information improvements were being drawn up, commendable additions (with Metcalf and Richardson, see Chapter 8) would be: more intensive study of the 'lifecycle' and timepath of unemployment; employer forecasts of manpower requirements in the short run; a better knowledge of employee travel-to-work patterns; and much more attention to the demand side of the employment relationship, including employer recruitment patterns, hiring practices, and so on. None of these would be at all easy to investigate, but it is possible that some of them would add more to the knowledge of particular area problems than progressively more detailed analysis of Census of Population data.

Of course information has costs, and the utility and feasibility of data collection have to be weighed against their value in identifying problems and guiding policy. Again, the real world is a complicated place; and policy makers have to operate, and are used to operating, on the basis of information that is imperfect, often seriously so. An approach that overemphasises the complexity of the inner-city employment situation and the difficulties of defining the key problems runs the risk of nothing at all being done. There are, however, some common factors in the existing analysis, and the next section considers what manpower policy can do in the existing state of knowledge and how its role might develop.

18.3 The instruments of manpower policy

How can the existing instruments of manpower policy help with inner-city employment problems? Rather than present an exhaustive list of all the various programmes, this section will consider three problem areas where manpower measures may be able to help, building on the observation of section 18.2 that higher unemployment in inner areas could be due to characteristics of individuals or to labour market imbalance of some kind. In practice some of the broad areas of policy action are similar whatever the reason for unemployment, so that manpower measures may be considered in three broad groups: those which provide information and try to make the search process more effective, those which attempt to overcome occupational or geographical rigidity, and those which provide employment directly.

18.3.1 Information and placement activities

The more imperfect knowledge in the labour market is and the more difficult the suppliers of labour services and their potential employers find it to contact one another, the higher will frictional unemployment be. A more effective information and placement service will reduce the duration of vacancies, thus increasing output, and the duration of unemployment, so improving individual incomes. The machinery for doing this has existed for many years in the shape of the public employment service, but the network of employment offices is now being completely modernised under the control of the Employment Service Division (ESD) of the MSC.

In the past the employment exchange was a multipurpose

administrative office, one of whose main functions was to pay out unemployment benefit. They were generally in the main areas of population, which in conurbations in the period up to 1939 were usually in city centres; and for reasons of cheapness and discretion (unemployment was a very visible phenomenon when benefit was being paid out) they were not in the main streets. These offices had a placement function, but it was not a primary one, and it was difficult to exercise because of the nature of the employment exchanges at that time. Employers were reluctant to notify vacancies because they believed that the clientele of the exchanges were primarily poor-quality unemployed workers who would be unsuitable for their purposes and that the exchange might use the vacancy only to test the willingness to look for work (and thus the benefit worthiness) of the unemployed.

The benefit payment and placement functions have now been separated, and the ESD is in the process of restructuring the old employment exchanges (now called employment offices) and developing a network of new Jobcentres, with a multitier service designed to deal with a variety of employment problems. The first tier is self-service, where notified vacancies are displayed and anyone – employed or unemployed – can look around without registration and can be submitted to one of these displayed vacancies with a minimum of formality and with no ESD 'guarantee' of suitability. This self-service tier is in a sense capitalising on the known preferences of workers for informal job search and is not unlike a search through newspaper advertisements or round factory gates, with the added convenience that checking on the vacancy and introducing the jobseeker will be done by an employment adviser. The second tier in the Jobcentre involves placement activity of a more structured kind, where the employment adviser interviews and discusses with the jobseeker his requirements and work needs with a view to matching the individual with a notified vacancy. Above the second tier further services are available, including occupational guidance, placement into a training course, and specialised resettlement for those who suffer from mental or physical handicap.

The modernisation of the employment service rests on the view that the development of a good and effective placement service meeting the needs of jobseekers depends on the provision of a first-class service to employers. Without a regular supply of good vacancies the ESD cannot do as good a job as it would like for jobseekers, and a supply of good vacancies will only be forthcoming if employers are convinced that the ESD can meet their needs. When the ESD receives an order, or vacancy notification, it must satisfy the employer that it is doing its best to meet his requirements; otherwise the credibility of the organisation and its ability to achieve placements will be hazarded, and the chances of raising the low-level vicious circle of the old employment exchanges will be small.

The importance attached to meeting employer needs and increasing the placement rate has affected the structure of operations, and three points may be noted. First, Jobcentres are intended to attract jobseekers into the self-service section and have therefore been located in busy sites such as shopping areas and main thoroughfares. Their locations are related to the travel-to-work patterns and population distribution in the town or city, but they are not normally situated in rundown or decrepit city areas. This may argue that the Jobcentre could be less convenient for inner city dwellers than the old employment exchange, but against this has to be set the increased vacancy notification (about 40 per cent higher in some cases than the equivalent employment office) and the greatly improved range and quality of services on offer.

Second, the ESD is concerned to improve the quality of its information about the labour market and its information to labour market participants. In the former case this means the gradual development of local labour-market information both as an aid to the ESD's resource planning and understanding of the area in which it is operating and as a service to employers in the area. In the latter case technological developments have given a better information exchange between ESD local offices or data handling within offices. An example is the computerised system of exchanging vacancies between local offices that is being introduced in all conurbations; it effectively extends an employee's area of search at virtually no cost. A much more sophisticated approach being piloted in north-east London is the CAPITAL system. This holds details of registrants on a computer file and enables the employment officer to see and judge very quickly the records of registrants in relation to a notified vacancy in a particular area.

Third, the ESD has a management structure that decentralises responsibility for planning and resource decisions as far down the line as possible and a management information system that allows line managers to identify the costs of their operations. This is very different from the old pre-ESD management style, which involved a set of fairly standardised responses to situations, with policy determined at the centre and administered in the local areas. The new system obviously has the capability to respond much more quickly to local area problems where they occur.

What does this mean for inner city residents? One important point is that the ESD's programmes provide a range of services to meet individual needs and to improve employability, but these are not generally allocated or targeted towards particular groups in the labour market. Clearly, in ESD planning, resources will tend to be concentrated on areas with disproportionate numbers of individuals needing counselling, guidance, etc. – but not necessarily because the area as such is thought worthy of priority. A good example of this is seen in the experimental service for those with special employment needs. This gives emphasis to inner city areas because these areas contain large numbers of individuals with employability problems.

The Special Employment Needs Service represents an attempt by the ESD to test new ways of providing services for the hard-to-place. All public employment services face this problem of what their main task should be. On the one hand, it may be argued that an employment service can only operate successfully for all its clients if it retains the confidence of employers and has a steady flow of good vacancies and that this requires a realistic approach to submissions. On the other hand, others may believe that the public employment service should concentrate on the hard-to-place, try to get them into employment through a specialised approach to employers, and so form a kind of 'safety net' in the labour market as an adjunct to the social security system. The ESD has broadly accepted the first view, with an active marketing of its services to employers. This should not of course mean that only the good placement prospects get jobs. Some vacancies are suitable for those who are not particularly easy to place, and in the normal course of business the ESD places a large number of people who would not be regarded as first-class placement prospects, sometimes by speculative submission to employers who have not notified vacancies and by using their knowledge of employers' requirements and the individuals on the register.

The arguments on the balance of placement services seem quite convincing, provided of course that it does not lead to an overconcentration on high placement rates without sufficient consideration for the hard-to-place. The Special Employment Needs Service is an acknowledgement of the need for balance between the requirements of employers and those of the individuals on the register, and the ESD and the MSC are fully aware of the need to monitor the placement effort and its effect on the labour market.

18.3.2 Occupational and geographical mobility

Structural unemployment, or more general labour-market mismatch, may occur because of deficient occupational or geographical mobility, because individuals do not have the necessary skill to be employed in jobs within their own labour-market area, or because they are unable or unwilling to move outside it to jobs beyond daily travel-to-work distance. Manpower policy measures exist to try to remedy these types of immobility.

Adult retraining is frequently regarded as most desirable. Several of the CES Seminar papers suggested retraining the unemployed to give them a better chance of new employment, and international comparisons are often drawn to suggest that the UK retraining effort is much less adequate than it might be. Adult retraining is administered by the Training Services Division's Training Opportunities Scheme (TOPS) and is done either in Skillcentres (previously called government training centres) or colleges of further education, with some training also done in employers' establishments. TOPS output in 1975 was 60,700, with almost 90,000 trained in 1976 and a target of 100,000 by 1980. There are sixty-three Skillcentres throughout the country, each catering for a wide geographical area. Given the size and complexity of Skillcentres it can be difficult to site them in inner city areas, and they are normally located close to industrial establishments, e.g. on or near industrial estates. In any case it is obviously much more cost-effective to have the employees travel to the Skillcentre; and trainees get maintenance allowances during their courses, including lodging allowances if the Skillcentre is beyond daily travelling distance from their homes. Trainees who live at least 2 miles from the training establishment may be reimbursed their travelling expenses.

TOPS training has a twin objective: helping to meet national manpower requirements, and helping individuals to meet their employment aspirations. Thus, the programme too has to strike a balance between providing courses that will meet employer demands and courses that meet individ al needs. The emphasis of the TOPS programme is again on the inaividual, and no discrimination is made in favour of or against particular areas. In practice of course the distribution of TOPS trainees is not random. For one thing, those in employment or self-employment can only take TOPS courses if they leave employment to do so, and most of the people who apply are unemployed (about 65 per cent in 1978), so that the scheme is disproportionately weighted towards the unemployed. Second, there are variations between areas in the occupancy rates of Skillcentres and colleges; and waiting lists vary, so that some individuals will have more success than others with their applications. Third, like the ESD, the Training Services Division has devolved a good deal of managerial responsibility to its regional and Skillcentre managers, who are able to accord priority to cases in special circumstances. Support under TOPS is available only to people aged 19 or over, but other training arrangements exist for unemployed young people between 16 and 18 to attend courses below craft level.

What is the relevance of the TOPS scheme to inner-city employment problems? To the extent that there is a higher proportion of unemployed in inner cities, this will tend to favour them. The location of Skillcentres may tell marginally against inner cities in some regions, but they will be within daily travelling distance within most cities. In addition, since TOPS applications are processed through ESD local offices, knowledge of the scheme and ability to apply should be unaffected by Skillcentre location. Perhaps the most important factor is that the capacity of the TOPS programme is small compared with current levels of unemployment, so that even a disproportionate number of successful applications from inner cities would not be significant in absolute terms. Should a greater effort be made to train the unemployed, not necessarily by giving them priority within the existing capacity but possibly by substantially increasing the numbers in training? These questions, and others, have recently, been examined in a review of the TOPS programme.

The ideal training programme is one that meets equally the needs of individuals and labour market requirements – which identifies the skilled labour requirements of industry and mounts a large training programme to retrain those who are unemployed for jobs that now exist or will appear in the near future. To some extent this can be done, but it is not really possible to fine-tune the training system in such a precise way. Manpower forecasts are notoriously unreliable, and there may be additional geographical mismatches that prevent occupational supply and demand from being equalised. If it is accepted that it is going to be very difficult to match up precise training requirements and training provisions, the question then is whether it is worthwhile and justifiable to train the unemployed even if there are apparently no jobs in prospect for them.

On the one hand, it can be argued that giving an individual a new skill will increase his employability even if he does not immediately use that skill and that retraining will make him more adaptable to move on to other work if he does not get a job in his training trade; this would especially be so if the retraining were a basic and general course rather than a specific one. Those who argued against using training in this way would stress the practical problems of maintaining and justifying the system. It might be possible to 'sell' training on the grounds that it was preferable to immediate unemployment and could lead to employment, but this would involve a fairly radical change of approach. There would have to be a greater tolerance of high wastage rates; there would be a lowering of morale among staff in the training system if they felt that it was being used simply as a substitute for unemployment; there would be damage to the image of retraining among those who would really benefit from it; and perhaps most important, there would inevitably be low placement rates and questions about how public resources were being spent.

Finally, it is by no means clear that the full Skillcentre-type course is most appropriate to the unemployed in the inner city. While it could perhaps be combined with mobility assistance so as to improve employability and reduce structural unemployment in these areas, it can be argued that a lower level training could better meet the needs of many unemployed people in a more cost-effective way. Many such courses exist, but of course in the allocation of resources the question still remains of how far deliberate priority should be given to particular inner-city residents over unemployed people from other areas or other groups who might seem equally deserving.

A range of services for geographical mobility is offered through the ESD, of which the best known is the Employment Transfer Scheme (ETS). This applies mainly to unemployed or potentially redundant workers in the assisted areas, although non-assisted area workers can participate if they have no prospects of finding a regular job near home and there are no suitable unemployed to fill the vacancy in which they are interested. The ETS provides a set of grants and allowances for travel, settling in and separation, housing removal, rehousing and house purchase/sale expenses, and visits home during a period of separation. Another ESD scheme called the Job Search Scheme is designed to assist workers who are looking for work in another area. The client group is the same, and the assistance takes the form of fares and a contribution to expenses in connection with a job interview.

These programmes are not really very effective in stimulating or affecting geographical mobility. The ETS assisted some 16,000 moves in 1975–76, which was a tiny proportion of all job changes and a minority of inter-regional moves. It could be argued that a scheme of assisted labour mobility is less relevant in a period of generally high unemployment than when there are serious labour shortages in some areas and surpluses in others; and while the ETS could make a contribution in the upturn, recent research suggests that the majority of recipients would have moved in any case and that the ETS made no difference to the direction or timing of their moves. There are many other examples outside the manpower field where people are paid money to do what they would have done in any case, but the ETS is unselective in the types of worker to which it applies and mainly assists long distance moves.

In view of these considerations it is difficult to see the ETS as important in alleviating inner city problems, although it may have some marginal influence. In theory it would be most desirable if policy could make more of a contribution to mobility or extend the employee's travel-to-work area through some kind of ETS or travel subsidy, since it has often been suggested that restricted travel opportunity, or its cost, is important in limiting employees' job search. However, the practical difficulties do seem rather daunting. It is known from mobility research that the movement of households for job reasons is uncommon and that the psychological cost of movement is high. There seems to be no way to identify the 'marginal movers' who would move only if some subsidy were paid, although it may be more possible to identify the 'stayers' who settle happily in their new location. An increase in subsidy is costly if it applies to everyone. If it does not apply to everyone, some rules must be drawn up, and what should these rules be? This same consideration applies to travel-to-work subsidies. It may be desirable to extend the travel-to-work area of inner city residents; but is this best done by subsidies, which can be difficult to regulate and control, or by transport policy? Or is the lack of job information at the root of apparent travel problems, and will the Employment Service Division's improved service remedy this? There is a good deal of thinking still to be done about the most appropriate policies towards mobility and travel to work.

18.3.3 The creation of employment

In 1975 the MSC proposed to the government a Job Creation Programme (JCP) to provide temporary jobs of value to the communities in which they were located. The intention was to take the sharp edge off unemployment in particular areas rather than to substitute for macroeconomic employment creation, and the scheme was approved and came into operation in late 1975. The guidelines for the programme catered particularly for young people and took special account of inner city areas. A rough count of the JCP projects in mid-1976 suggested that the programme had been reasonably successful in this. About half the Merseyside projects were in central Liverpool, and about one-third of the west Scotland and North-West projects in Glasgow and Manchester respectively.

The administration of the programme did, however, make it difficult to guarantee that jobs would be created or particular groups or areas favoured. The programme responded to projects emerging from local sponsors approved by area action committees serviced by MSC staff in the region. It was therefore up to local initiative to bring forward proposals for funding; and the great majority of projects came from local authorities, although some voluntary associations were involved, and some areas and some authorities were quicker off the mark than others. The programme's contribution to alleviating the problems of an inner city area thus depended not on MSC action but on the capability of organisations within the area to take advantage of the MSC's sponsorship.

The quantitative importance of the programme should not be overstated. The peak number of jobs in existence in 1978 was 55,000 in projects averaging ten to twelve employees and lasting nine to twelve months. Although the programme had an insignificant impact on overall unemployment, it may have been considerably more important for certain groups and certain areas. The programme was a short-term and fairly small-scale reaction to the most serious unemployment position since the war. The Special

Temporary Employment Programme (STEP), set up in September 1978 is similarly quite small in scale, although more directly related to inner cities. Whether such programmes as STEP should be of this kind is a question raised in the next section.

To sum up, the instruments of manpower policy operated by the MSC have tended not to discriminate in favour of particular areas or groups. The MSC's main programmes are based on meeting the needs of individuals and improving individuals' employability by directing them to the specialist service that is most relevant to their needs. On this criterion priority towards inner city problems would thus come from a concentration of services and resources on people living in these areas who are utilising manpower services and whose needs have been properly identified. There is, however, an increasing emphasis on the new special programmes for young people and adults and on experimental and pilot approaches to particular problems. It is often easier to give such schemes a geographical focus, and the inner cities have benefited from this.

18.4 The developing role of manpower policy

One of the most common criticisms of manpower policy is that it does not meet the needs of the communities that it is trying to serve, but what exactly does this criticism mean? Does it mean that there should be full employment as traditionally defined – no bottlenecks or labour shortages even of a temporary kind, no structural employment, no individual who is dissatisfied with his position in the manpower system, and no employer who is unhappy about the quality or quantity of his labour force? Perhaps the major problem in manpower policy is identifying what the real needs of a community are, whether individual or corporate, and how far they can and should be met by policy measures. The job of the policy maker is to decide how resources should be deployed, and this means having a clear view of objectives and priorities as well as an understanding of how the services can best get to the individuals or organisations that they are designed to help. The main issues discussed in this section broaden the discussion of section 18.3 and consider in more detail possible extensions and developments of the role of manpower policy as a positive contribution to meeting inner city problems.

One point that is perhaps worth a little more discussion is the general approach to identifying and dealing with employment problems. Section 18.3 has pointed out that, while some services are relevant to groups, in particular those for the disabled, the mainstream services have been designed to improve individuals' employability. The argument here is really twofold. First, while it is possible to identify particular groups of people within the labour market who will *on average* experience some labour-market disadvantage, a structure of services based on the group approach may fail to recognise that many members of a particular group have relatively little disadvantage while certain individuals are seriously affected. The real problem is not so much with groups but with 'groups within groups', and this tends to point towards a structure that looks at individual needs rather than group needs.

Second, there are practical problems in adopting a group approach. Among the questions that arise are how to select and define groups, how to decide on priorities between groups, how to justify selection to groups who are further down the priority list and who may have within their numbers individuals who have serious employment problems, and so on. The approach of giving priority to certain groups could also lead to the confusion of objectives within programmes and to consequent difficulties of management and control. Perhaps even more important, the structure of programmes could become politicised, with different groups claiming a share of available resources not necessarily on the basis of need but on the basis of some assumed comparison with other groups. The allocation of manpower policy resources would then become a bargaining process where employment needs tended to be downgraded. The arguments in favour of an employability approach and against a group approach are strengthened in the light of what has happened in some other countries that have adopted the group approach and found the manpower policy structure virtually disintegrating under the pressure of competing 'political' demands from groups. It is of course important that the employability criterion should work and that individuals who have special labour-market disadvantages should find the services accessible to them.

This approach to the mainstream services has the considerable merit of concentrating resources where they are most needed and, it is to be hoped, of striking a balance between the competing claims on resources to give what seems to be the most satisfactory package of provision at any point in time. With its commitment to develop manpower policy, however, the MSC must also consider new approaches to manpower problems and changes in organisation so as to make the MSC's contribution more effective. A few important issues will be highlighted here, taking particular account of the recent recognition that manpower policy can play a part on the demand side of the labour market as well as on the supply side, and all are relevant to the inner city problem.

First, the MSC's Job Creation Programme was always seen as temporary and countercyclical; but the Special Temporary Employment Programme, with its particular inner-cities bias, is rather longer term. The experience of these programmes and the stubborn nature of the inner city problem raises the question of whether such schemes could be put on a permanent basis and developed to deal with particular local problems, e.g. to provide temporary jobs in association with major redundancies or in areas with continuing high general or specific unemployment. Some have suggested that there would be net benefits to the government financial account in providing a large semipermanent supported work sector and in financing this from money presently going in unemployment benefits rather than simply paying people to remain unemployed; but the relationship of such a supported sector with the normal labour market would raise some difficult but important issues. How would the work relate to normal jobs to avoid competition for workers or work; how would the wage structure relate, so that people had an incentive to move from supported work to normal work; what control mechanisms would be necessary to ensure that employers did not misuse the scheme for 'cheap labour'; how permanent would particular projects under the scheme be; how should it be targeted to individuals or areas most in need; and should the administration be decentralised and local? From the point of view of employment creation the key question is how far there is a displacement effect, i.e. how far the jobs created are genuinely additional; the answer to this question considerably affects the value for money of any scheme.

Second, the MSC has a well-established procedure for dealing with the registration, placement, and possible training of individuals involved in redundancies. Should manpower policy go further to look at the scope for employment or market expansion in particular firms in the area where the redundancy or potential redundancy takes place? This kind of exercise has been done in the context of some of the British Steel Corporation redundancies, and it is most obviously useful in that kind of major redundancy situation. Might it, however, be possible to do something of the same kind in inner cities, by identifying much more precisely and carefully possible job opportunities that to some extent match the characteristics of those on the labour market or those likely to emerge from some employment rundown? This kind of initiative would obviously require a good deal of co-operation between various interests, not least those with responsibility for industrial development, but the identification of opportunities and action to bring them into being would take place at a much more micro level than the level at which industrial policy presently operates.

Third, if in spite of all policy measures high unemployment continues, how far should attempts be made to alter the distribution of unemployment by subsidising the employment of some workers at the expense of others, as was done by the recruitment subsidy for school leavers in the winter of 1975–6, and has been done since October 1976 by the youth employment subsidy? Some have argued that the same kind of priority might be given to the long term unemployed. It would, however, be difficult to subsidise the employment of inner city residents in such a direct way, because of the complexity of travel-to-work patterns and the difficulty of knowing how the subsidy should be attached to individuals. In addition the difficulty of justifying priority to one group in the labour market at the expense of others would come up in an acute form for employment subsidies of this type, as would also the cost in efficiency terms and whether they were consistent with other social and economic objectives.

A final general area that is relevant to the problem of inner cities is the delivery of manpower services. The activities of the MSC will only be useful if services can be provided to the people who need them at the right time and the right place. This is partly a matter of marketing and ensuring that people know about the services that are available to them (and like many public services the MSC is not as well known as it should be), but it also bears on the organisation of services on the ground. There is a good deal of local criticism from all parts of the country about the fragmented state of manpower services and the various bodies that provide them.

The point is often made that 'no one has responsibility for manpower at the local level'. This is not a criticism of the staff involved nor necessarily of the services offered. It is more an indication of the very wide role for some manpower authority that people in local areas see and of the extent to which they would like a much more co-ordinated approach and much closer links between all the bodies and organisations concerned with manpower services in their areas. The MSC now has manpower services directors in the regions, whose job it is to co-ordinate the delivery of manpower services at that level. The April 1978 unification of the MSC and its agencies should bring services together. This is particularly relevant in inner cities where the regional manpower services directors represent the MSC and the Secretary of State for Employment on the official partnership committees.

There are four main ways in which the instruments of manpower policy, very broadly defined, may be brought to bear more precisely on the kind of problems that exist in inner city areas and other localities as well. These are now put forward for consideration:

1. The identification of manpower problems requires better and closer information at the local level. Census information and employment data are a good base on which to build, but the detailed knowledge of the problems of local areas presently depends on the development of the ESD's local labour-market intelligence experiments and on activities by local authorities. Is there a case for some additional manpower intelligence resource at local level?

2. The MSC already has devolution of managerial authority to regions, areas, and districts. This is obviously most desirable, since to have decisions taken at a level that is remote from the understanding of the real problems simply involves the risk that the policy measures will not provide a solution. It may be interesting to debate how far devolution of authority can realistically go. Some other countries have attempted community or regional employment strategies giving some financial autonomy to line management; and while it obviously makes sense to allow those who take the decisions to spend the money (or at least some of it), there are formidable problems of establishing employment objectives, of budgeting, and of control adherent in this kind of approach. Is this the direction in which the MSC should go?

3. In some problem areas, whether geographical or topic oriented, it appears that the relevant approach for the MSC is a task force approach. This involves the assembly of a group charged with putting together a package of measures from different parts of the organisation (and possibly from outside as well), to be kept in being for a limited time and to be disbanded if the problem

disappears. It is a truism that no administrative structure can cope with all eventualities, and a task force approach that allows a cross-section of measures to be put together for a particular purpose is a useful and flexible way of overcoming possible rigidities in the administrative structure.

4. The MSC is most concerned to recognise and identify the effectiveness of its manpower measures. This means that whatever is done in inner city areas through mainstream programmes or special approaches requires monitoring and evaluation, so that the MSC can justify to itself and to others the commitment of public resources.

There has been no attempt in this chapter to be comprehensive in describing manpower policy as it might affect inner cities. For example, the very broad and important area of training within industry, either apprenticeships or in-firm retraining has not been dealt with, nor has the activities of the industrial training boards, whose influence on companies is most significant. Again, no mention has been made of the various pilot and operating schemes of vocational preparation nor of the MSC's Youth Opportunities Programme that has been under way since April 1978. This simply emphasises the wide-ranging nature of manpower policy, even within the ambit of the MSC itself, and the variety of programmes from which relevant packages could be assembled to deal with particular manpower problems. It has been stressed, however, that many of the inner-city manpower problems need action not only by the MSC but also by others at national local and company level, in fullest co-operation and consultation with the manpower authorities.

19 A Careers Service View of Inner London

Robert Gourlay

with additional material by
Catherine Avent

19.1 Introduction

This chapter is in two parts. Robert Gourlay, in section 19.2, gives an outline of the employment situation in inner London as seen from the standpoint of the Careers Service. He does not attempt to describe the work undertaken by the Careers Service in the vocational guidance of individual boys and girls and college students, nor the advice given to employers on induction, training, and recruitment problems, nor the contribution that careers officers make to the preparation of young people for the transition from school to work before they leave their various educational establishments. It is the task of section 19.3, by Catherine Avent, to outline what she considers to be the main functions of the schools in preparing young people by adequate programmes of careers education, and in the same way this contribution is also limited in that there is not space to include a description of the ways in which teachers who are not designated as part of the careers team in a school nevertheless contribute through their classroom work in English, mathematics, social studies, and other subjects to the total preparation of young people for the aspects of adult life associated with earning a living.

19.2 A Careers Service view of inner London[1]

The range of employment available to young people in the County of London is almost all-embracing. The place of the City of London as a centre of trade and exchange is reflected in the amount of clerical employment there in professional and commercial work. Demand from the departmental stores and the dressmaking trades in the West End has been on a similar scale. There is a profusion of all the traditional crafts. Industries such as clothing abound in Bethnal Green and Stepney, furniture in Shoreditch, boot and shoe manufacture in Hackney. The Hatton Garden area of the City is internationally known for its jewellery industry. Greater in the labour force they employ are the more modern industries of various forms of engineering, food manufacture and processing and the like. Except for a few of the heavier and rural industries, there is no employment in the country which cannot be found in the County of London.

This excerpt from the first annual report of the London County Council Youth Employment Service represents the heyday of youth employment in the inner city. The 1950 description of the inner London job markets (broadly true until the mid-1960s would be regarded more as a fairy tale than as history by most of the *present* inner London school leavers and as scarcely credible by careers officers trained and coming into the London service since the mid-1960s.

'Profusion' has been replaced by an increasing shortage of skilled craft jobs of all kinds, whether traditional or modern, despite the Industrial Training Act 1968, which creditably improved the quality of training (and incidentally raised entry requirements) but not its quantity. The few firms left after the furniture- and shoe-manufacturing industries moved out of Shoreditch and Hackney can scarcely be recognised as significant in terms of providing employment and training opportunites. In every area of inner London a more serious change has been the reduction in the number of medium-sized expanding industrial firms that can be relied on each year to recruit and train a sizable group of young people in various occupations. The transplanting of these 'seedbed' firms (in terms of training opportunities for young people) to the outer ring of Greater London, to new towns, or to other development areas may have been desirable for many reasons, but it is certainly seen by careers officers as the major contributory factor leading to the continuing

[1]The author of this section, Robert Gourlay, died in 1977, and this section is reproduced by permission of Mrs Mary Gourlay. The employment situation described is therefore that existing in mid-1976.

impoverishment of the local inner-London job markets. Only in the very centre of London is the job profusion of the 1950s still perceptable. As described by Lomas in *The Inner City* study (1974), the city-forming services have kept the central job market strong. It is not generally understood that growth in the number of jobs that are available in financial, professional, and scientific services, in the public service, or in the commercial sector provides no answer to the problem of the less educationally well-qualified proportion of the school-leaving population. It has to be remembered also that entry requirements tend to rise as the number of employment opportunities decline; the entry levels of the 'hierarchic' job market of central London (open to all within commuting distance) move up or down a notch in response to the supply/demand state. The movement has in recent years continued upwards: from 'A' level General Certificate of Education (GCE) to graduate level entry; from 'O' level to 'A' level entry; from no educational qualifications to 'good Certificate of Secondary Education (CSE)'. This rise had added another dimension to the problem described in the 1974 report of the National Youth Employment Council entitled 'Unqualified, Untrained and Unemployed'.

Choice of employment in inner London remained a reality for most school leavers until the mid-1960s. From then until 1975 the narrowing range in the kinds of work that were available was masked by the continuing surplus of the total number of available jobs compared with the number of young people leaving school for employment.

Although the number of vacancies dealt with by the Careers Service cannot be regarded as a measure of total vacancies, a comparison of the figures for various dates at least give some indication of the changes in demand for young workers. Before a rather longer-term comparison can be made, and where, as in inner London, 'notified' demand has constantly exceeded the number of available young people, the underlying trend may also be indicated.

An examination of the total figures of vacancies dealt with annually by the inner-London Careers Service (covering the area of the former County of London) shows that demand for young people under the age of 18 remained fairly stable at about 50,000 from the late 1950s until the mid-1960s, declining to about 35,000 by 1970 and to 22,600 by 1974. The total for the year ended September 1975 was 15,300 after intensive canvassing of employers by staff of the Careers Service for vacancies for summer school leavers. The recession underlined the fact that no longer could it be taken for granted that the vast majority of inner-London school leavers would already have jobs to go to after the end of term or after their summer holidays. In the summer of 1975, out of about 22,000 pupils from the Inner Lindon Education Authority (ILEA) area who left school to enter employment, some 4,000 were still unemployed at the beginning of the autumn term. The slowness of the rate of absorption into employment can be judged from the fact that nearly 1,000 were still unemployed at Christmas, falling to about 500 at Easter.

Almost without exception these young people had left school at the earliest possible moment with little in the way of educational attainment and had been faced with a shrinking market in local jobs. Again, although the figures in Table 19.1 may not be a measure of the total unemployed, they represent young people who 'proved' unemployment by reporting at careers offices. They clearly indicate the trend. It can be seen that in the first three months of 1976 the number of registered unemployed school-leavers from inner London (serving the area of twelve inner-London boroughs) was greater than the number from the twenty outer-London boroughs.

Careers officers faced the summer of 1976, with its new early school-leaving date, with a backlog of about 1,000 ILEA school leavers still without jobs, since the 500 mentioned above had been joined on unemployment registers by another 500 (one-eighth of the Easter school leavers). The situation is always worse in the divisions south of the Thames, with twice as many young people registered unemployed as in the divisions north of the Thames, and

Table 19.1 Unemployment at careers offices, January – March 1976 (no. registered).

	January	*February*	*March*
ILEA area:			
Total register	2,537	2,352	2,102
School leavers in register	864	816	570
Outer London:			
Total register	2,776	2,410	2,064
School leavers in register	727	601	441
Greater London:			
Total register	5,313	4,762	4,166
School leavers in register	1,591	1,417	1,011

half the vacancies available. The total vacancies held by the Careers Service in May 1976 was nearly 5,900, of which 2,806 were held at the central-London careers office. Care must be taken not to equate the numbers unemployed with the number of vacancies unfilled. At times of high unemployment, entry requirements in respect of young people tend to rise; and this, together with the narrowing range of job opportunities as industry continues to move away from inner London, renders most vulnerable to unemployment those who are least competitive in terms of educational qualifications in the central-London job market, with increasing public transport fares as an added disincentive to compete.

It must be emphasised that during the term current vacancies are *immediate*, and employers are not prepared to consider for them those young people who are still at school or college. Most vacancies for summer leavers are obtained through canvassing of employers by staff of the Careers Service. Many small firms are obviously unable to plan their recruitment; and experience has shown that they are unlikely to respond to canvassing efforts, whether by letter, telephone, or visit, until nearer the time when young people are actually 'on the market' and available to start work. Even so, canvassing returns from divisional careers officers and from the central-London careers office in 1976 left no doubt that the overall situation was serious and that young people leaving school and college in the London area faced a far worse situation than those who left the previous year. In addition to a recruitment cutback in the private sector, increased financial stringency was severely affecting recruitment in the public sector.

The ILEA is determined to do all it can to ensure that the Education Service as a whole is as responsive as possible to the problems and needs of young people who have left school and cannot find jobs. The education officer has written to all heads of secondary schools and college principals on what can be done, despite the limitation on resources, through co-operation within the Education Service. An all-out drive is being intensified by the Careers Service to discover every job and training opportunity that is available. No doubt further alleviating measures can be expected from central government as the situation develops. At present this consists of Community Industry schemes, the Job Creation Programme, and certain activities of the Training Services Agency in setting up occupational selection courses for unemployed school leavers at their Skill centres.)

The question remains as to what can be done about causes as well as dealing with the symptoms? Apart from whatever may hopefully come from the attention currently being given to employment policies by Greater London Council and the inner London boroughs, the inherent uncertainties in employment trends in inner London suggest that a fundamental response is in terms of education that will fit young people for the various periods of training and retraining that will be necessary during their working lives. Experience in submitting school leavers for selection for present training schemes in employment emphasises that the prime need is for a secure foundation of basic educational skills in literacy and numeracy. Without this, vocational training schemes in, and associated with, employment will continue to affect only the small proportion of school leavers who can take advantage of them. These are the skills that employers complain about most often in recruitment and selection. It would be idealistic to suppose that the growth in the number of jobs in the financial, professional, scientific, and public services sectors and in commerce, and the decline in manual jobs in industry, could be totally compensated for by the greater adaptability (achieved through secondary education) of young people at work. This supports the view that, in the interests of the employment of inner-London school leavers and young workers, there is every reason for supporting action to reverse the trend for manufacturing industry to leave inner London and for supporting the policy of further encouraging the 'growth services' type of activity in inner London.

The importance of the development of the new initiatives in schools and colleges of further education already proposed, and of good practice in realistic and effective schemes of careers education and guidance, cannot be overemphasised now and for the future in all educational establishments in inner London. Without the full and informed co-operation of all teaching staff, success for these efforts will be doubtful, and pupils and students will be the losers in the competition for jobs and training opportunities.

19.3 Careers education and guidance

A reasonable definition of careers education is that it forms part of the curriculum of secondary school pupils and of students in colleges of further and higher education, is school or college based, is the responsibility of the teachers, is undertaken on a class or group basis, and desirably starts when the pupils are at the age of 14 and confronted with the first important educational decisions on the subjects that they will take throughout the fourth and fifth years leading up to CSE or 'O' level. Careers education is independent of the stage of 'vocational maturity' reached by individual boys and girls and of their own need for guidance as they progress through the education system into employment.

A course of careers education should be seen as applicable to all pupils, of both sexes and of the whole range of ability. It is as important for the academically able, who may not enter full-time employment until the age of 21 or even 25, as for those seeking work as soon as the law enables them to do so. It is as important for girls as for boys. It should be directed towards the acquisition of knowledge and skills and the development of attitudes that will help pupils to face adult life, irrespective of the stage at which they choose their own careers. It should contain a considerable amount of pupil participation, including written work and exercises, and not merely consist of the passive absorption of ideas from teachers and their various aids, such as films, television, or visiting speakers. It should actively assist pupils in the process of acquiring self-awareness and understanding and include practice in decision making as well as in the skills that are appropriate to the transition from school to work.

There are four main aims and objectives in the process of careers education and guidance. First, it should develop *educational awareness* through helping to enable pupils to understand the provisions in various educational institutions and courses and to appreciate the relationship between the requirements of various courses for further education and training for a career. It clearly includes some understanding of the relationship between academic subjects studied at school or college and the appropriate training for various occupations, whether this means the need for specific GCE passes at 'O' level and 'A' level in order to train as a doctor or lawyer or the amount of mathematical competence that will be expected of an apprentice whose day release is designed to lead to the sitting of a City and Guilds examination. Second, it aims to develop *career awareness* through pupils' understanding of the range of career opportunities that exist, the type of job openings that may be available to them locally or further afield, and the lifestyles associated with different types of work. Third, careers education develops *self-awareness* by helping young people to understand human differences in ability, aptitude, and competence, to appreciate the strength of their own interests to establish a system of values by which to determine their future path, and to achieve some knowledge of the characteristics of personality and temperament that will be important in planning to achieve their various educational and career aspirations. Lastly, it should help pupils to acquire the necessary *planning skills* of decision making, a knowledge of the procedures involved in making the transition from school to work or to further education, including the skills of self-marketing for a job or place, and a basis on which to achieve the capacity to cope with various life situations as they arise. These could include redundancy, examination failure, divorce, etc.

Having defined the purpose of careers education, it is necessary to establish some sort of ideal provision in a secondary school. Ideally, there should be a teacher who has the status of a head of department, who is responsible for organising the various activities that make up the syllabus or programme of careers education and for co-ordinating curricular contributions from other subject teachers (particularly English, social studies, and mathematics) and from careers officers and other extramural agents, such as lecturers from colleges of further and higher education and representatives of industry, commerce, and the public services. Pupils in the third, fourth, and fifth years of the secondary course should be timetabled for careers education on a basis that may be one period a week throughout the three years or blocks of time alternating with other non-examination subjects, such as health education, moral education, or political understanding. Teachers in the team undertaking careers education need also to be timetabled to take occasional classes for sixth-formers in preparation for university and college applications, and they also need to be freed from classroom teaching in sufficient proportion to enable them to interview each pupil annually from the fourth year onwards in order to monitor their educational progress and its relationship to changing career aspirations.

The ILEA has a specific policy endorsed by the schools subcommittee on 17 September 1974. It is:

(a) that every county and voluntary ILEA secondary school be encouraged to establish a post of head of department of careers guidance on a scale equivalent to that accorded to house or year heads;

(b) that district inspectors should encourage heads to make provision within the timetable for all pupils to have basic careers education during the main school years, and for the team of careers teachers to have adequate time to take classes of pupils on preparation for adult life as well as supervising the careers resource centre and organising a programme of activities in co-operation with careers officers;

(c) that general support should be given to teachers undertaking training for careers work by short in-service courses – many of which occur during school holidays – and by longer courses as these develop;

(d) that appropriate facilities should be provided for pupils, parents, and teachers in all secondary schools to have ready access to appropriate sources of information on careers and tertiary education, and for the establishment of pupil record systems to faciliate co-ordination between teachers with pastoral responsibilities within the school and careers officers and other agencies concerned with the welfare of young people; and

(e) that teachers should be encouraged to volunteer for inclusion in a school's careers team, especially if they have had industrial or commercial experience, in order to foster closer links between schools, further education, and employers.

There are within the ILEA area schools that exhibit virtually the whole spectrum. At one end of the scale are schools with a large team of teachers undertaking careers education according to their own special interests or aptitudes, led by a teacher with high status in the school's hierarchy and supported by a good careers resource centre, an adequate classroom equipped with appropriate materials, and an allowance to enable the teachers to get written work done by the pupils and to have stocks of classroom materials and audiovisual aids. There may also be an office in the school, provided with a telephone and suitable equipment, from which careers teachers and careers officers can organise the necessary introductions for pupils to appropriate outside agencies and which enables them to interview pupils and their parents in reasonable comfort and efficiency. At the other end of the scale are schools that make virtually no timetabled provision for careers education and where a few books and pamphlets are stored in the corner of the library and there is apparently little evidence of serious attention to this aspect of secondary school life.

Some of the issues faced by those who advocate an extension of the present provision for careers education include the usual one of resources, in that it is difficult in many schools to provide accommodation for a 'new' subject and financial restraints may limit the amount of special books and equipment that can be provided.

Many teachers question whether careers education would be more effective if it were seen by the pupils to be leading to an examination, while others firmly resist this suggestion. In practice some schools have evolved Mode III syllabuses for a CSE social studies examination.

In conditions of high unemployment many pupils of low scholastic achievement feel that careers education is irrelevant since they are not likely to get jobs anyway. This presupposes that the purpose of careers education is mainly to provide occupational information to assist pupils when they come to their vocational guidance interview with a careers officer. In fact the case can be made for the subject on a much broader basis, as providing education in lifestyles rather than crude information on jobs.

There are a few teachers who disapprove of careers education as being contributory to the perpetuation of capitalist society, while others claim that it vocationalises education and that pupils should study all subjects for purely academic reasons regardless of the vocational outcome. Occasionally, there is conflict between the respective views of their roles of the careers teacher and the careers officer, in that it is no longer a simple matter of careers teachers understanding pupils and careers officers knowing about jobs. As careers officers are to be found more and more on a regular basis in the schools they are seen by the pupils as being much more part of the total educational process. At the same time many teachers like to build up contacts with representatives of employment and are thus sometimes tempted to place their own pupils, who might have a wider choice of employers to apply to were they left to the activities of the careers officer.

The concept of *education for employability* has gained currency as a result of the complaints voiced by many employers about the standard of literacy and numeracy achieved by many young school-leavers applying for jobs. Employers complain that some youngsters are unable to communicate orally or in writing, cannot undertake simple calculations, and have behavioural characteristics that reflect an unsympathetic attitude towards work and the personal relationships involved in it. Teachers feel that these complaints are unfairly directed at them, and consequently they may themselves be less sympathetic to the broad aims of careers education within the curriculum.

Lastly, there is no doubt that careers education conducted on a mixed ability basis exemplifies the ideals of comprehensive schooling, because it can demonstrate the interdependence of all workers' contribution to society, regardless of their educational achievement levels. To have a class in which the future doctor and future ambulance driver work together on a project on the health service, or the potential tycoon studies local industry with classmates who are likely to be destined for the shopfloor, is wholly admirable on educational grounds; but undoubtedly many teachers find it difficult to achieve, partly because their own knowledge of industry and commerce may be limited but also because so few careers teachers have as yet had any significant amount of training for this difficult but highly rewarding and important task. In inner London, with all its present difficulties but its long tradition of challenging education, it is particularly important that keen and able teachers should be found to volunteer to become part of the team for careers education and guidance.

VII Perspectives on Industry and Employment in the Inner City

20 An Economist's Perspective

Alan Evans

20.1 Introduction

The Centre for Environmental Studies (CES) began organising the series of meetings, of which this book is one result, at a time when public concern was beginning to be expressed over the high level of unemployment in the inner areas of the larger cities. Despite this concern the precise nature of the inner city employment problem was not clear. Could the inner city be treated as merely another kind of region, or was the problem fundamentally different from the 'regional problem' of the 1960s? Should the long-standing national policies for the dispersal and decentralisation of jobs and population from the major cities be slowed, stopped or even reversed?

At that time, in 1975, there was a lack of empirical evidence on which to base informed, rather than intelligent uninformed, statements about the problem. The main reason for holding the conference and seminars and for publishing this book was to try to remedy this situation by bringing together the best work done on the problem in Britain in the last few years.

The reader will of course make up his own mind about the nature of the inner city problem and the policies that should be pursued. These two concluding chapters contain the personal views of the editors, arrived at after considering the conference and seminars at which over forty papers were presented and editing this book in which the final version of a selection of the papers are collected. Of course, just as the various contributors have presented conflicting views, so the editors disagree on some points with each other, and there is certainly no reason why the other contributors to the book should agree with the opinions expressed in these chapters.

20.2 A straw man

Let us start by setting up a straw man. There is a view of the inner city employment problem that is simplistic but tends to be the basis of much general discussion of the topic. On this view it is clear that inner city unemployment results from the decline in manufacturing industry in the inner cities: as the firms have closed, so the jobs have disappeared and the residents have become unemployed. This decline in manufacturing industry has been accelerated by planning policies to encourage housing, eliminate non-conforming uses, and promote decentralisation and dispersal to the regions. Modification, and to some extent reversal, of these policies is necessary to encourage industry to remain and expand in, or move back to, the inner city. To this end incentives of the kind that have proved reasonably successful in dealing with the regional problem should be used to encourage industry to the inner areas.

However, from the available evidence the problem appears to be more complex. In the first place, residents have in fact been moving out of the cities faster than the jobs, so that it is naive to claim that high unemployment is a result of the decline in jobs. Of course, it could be said that, although population may be declining faster than jobs in *aggregate*, this may not be true of particular areas of the city nor, more importantly, of particular skills. If both skilled and unskilled jobs have been declining but only the skilled have been able to move, unemployment will occur among the unskilled, who are tied to the inner city by the cost of moving, and the level of unemployment among the unskilled will be higher in the inner areas than in the suburbs. The evidence shows, however, that the probability of being unemployed for a person with given characteristics (i.e. skill level, age, marital status, etc.) does not vary very much within an urban area. Thus, although unemployment is high in the inner areas, this appears to be due to the fact that this is where the unskilled, who have a higher probability of being unemployed than the more skilled, tend to be concentrated. Thus, the high unemployment rate in the inner area is due to the characteristics of the residents, not to the characteristics of the area.

The basic disagreement here is about the operation of the labour market in an urban area. On one view, the urban area is a set of labour markets between which movement is for most people difficult and expensive. On the other, it is a single labour market in which changes in one part of the area lead to equilibrating movements as people commute to jobs in other areas, in the process possibly changing the occupation or industry in which they are employed. On this view the current high unemployment rates in the inner areas are due to the facts (a) that the national unemployment rate is high, since this results in very high levels of unemployment among the unskilled because their unemployment rates will always be higher than average, and (b) as already remarked, that in the inner city a higher proportion of the working population will be unskilled than in the suburbs. The problem is therefore unlikely to be solved by policies concerned only with the inner city. They must be either national policies that result in lower national unemployment rates or regional policies that encourage the mobility of work or workers between, rather than within, urban areas.

20.3 Manufacturing industry and the inner city

But let us begin at the beginning. Why should manufacturing industry be located in the inner area? What kind of manufacturing industry locates there? After all, a site in the inner area has in the past usually been considerable more expensive than a site in the suburbs. What benefits does such a location bring to compensate for the higher cost of space?

Some industries, of which the docks of London and Liverpool are obvious examples, are there because of the physical characteristics of the city's location. Other industries, however, are not tied to a particular site. Past investigation of these industries and the kinds of firms located in the inner areas has shown that they both appear to be particularly dependent upon what have come to be called the 'external economies' of the city. The firms in the inner area tend to be smaller than those outside, and they tend to be in industries with an unstandardised product that is subject to rapid change; the best examples are the manufacture of women's clothing and printing. This has been clearly shown by Cameron (Chapter 15). Location in the inner areas allows these firms to minimise the risks that are inherent in their trades. The capital invested can be minimised by using the services and supplies provided by other firms, so that the goods and services purchased can be changed as the firm's product changes. An inner city location allows transport costs to be minimised and the number of easily accessible suppliers to be maximised. At the same time the proximity of others in the same trade gives the firm ready access to a knowledge of changes in the industry.

It has been observed that large firms have 'internalised' these external economies, which then become economies of scale. The large firm, or rather the large plant, is thus unlikely to find its optimal location in the inner area of a large city. It will be found in the suburbs or in a smaller town. From the observation that small firms were generally located closer to the centre of a city than large firms, the hypothesis was developed that new firms would often be located *initially* in the inner city and, if successful, would migrate to the suburbs as they grew larger. The inner city is thus the incubator or nursery for new manufacturing firms. This is the hypothesis discussed by Cameron, who has found that the inner city does appear to be a favourable location for small firms and external economy industries, although the birthrate *per se* is higher in the outer areas of the conurbation (Chapter 15).

20.4 The decline of manufacturing industry in the inner city

The decline in employment, particularly in manufacturing industry, in the inner city is well known; but the causes of this decline are not transparently clear, probably because there are in fact a number of causes. All the explanations are to some extent true, and so no single explanation is self-evidently true.

The decline of employment in the inner city and its growth in the suburbs have been going on since the early days of the modern industrial city, although of course what were the suburbs have now become the inner areas. For example, Hall (1962) in his book on the industries of London has demonstrated the outward movement of many industries between 1861 and 1951. At a more general level Mills (1970) has shown that in the United States employment in all industrial classifications has been decentralising at least since the turn of the century, and in Chapter 1 Warnes has shown that in the United Kingdom it has been going on at least since 1921. Detailed investigation of the nature of this decentralisation has revealed that, although it is usually the outward movement of jobs (and by implication therefore the outward movement of firms) that is spoken of, in fact most of the decentralisation of employment does not result directly from the decentralisation of firms but occurs indirectly, through differences between the birthrates and deathrates of firms and between the growth rates of firms in different parts of the urban area (see Dennis, Chapter 2; Gripaios, Chapter 3).

The most obvious cause of the decline in inner city employment and the decentralisation of industry is the improvement in transport and communications. This process has been continuing for a long time. The railway and other nineteenth-century improvements in transport have not only led to an increase in the feasible size of cities in terms of population but also allowed an increase in terms of area, with inner area densities often declining on average. The improvements in transport and communication have reduced the necessity for physical proximity to other firms either in the same business or in other trades. It can be said either that the importance of the external economies of an inner city location has been reduced or, alternatively, that the external economies are available over a wider area. The transport improvements have also meant that firms do not have to stay close to their labour supply or on public transport routes and can economise by moving further from the centre, to the suburbs, possibly even to small towns outside the urban area.

The second probable cause of industrial decentralisation is the trend towards larger plants. Changes in technology have meant that the most economical means of production may now use mass production methods requiring large one-storey factories. In turn these require large areas of land, and such sites are not usually available in the inner areas of large cities. Thus, in order to obtain such sites firms develop on sites on the periphery or beyond, probably in new industrial estates. This pattern is shown by Massey and Meegan's study of industrial reorganisation in the electronics industries (Chapter 4). Of course, as said earlier, larger plants are anyway likely to be located further out than smaller plants because they have less need of external economies of an inner city location. Therefore, even if large sites were readily available in the inner city, the increase in the scale of manufacturing plants would still result in a decentralisation of industry.

The third possible cause of decentralisation is institutional. It is argued that the planning policies pursued by local authorities in the inner areas of British cities have been instrumental in leading to the decline of manufacturing industry in those areas. They have been concerned with housing rather than employment; while they have been required to be responsible for housing the population of their area, they have not been responsible for ensuring the availability of jobs. Since the war local authorities have attempted to clear away as much old low-standard housing as possible. The premises of small industrial firms were often mixed in with this housing; and since authorities went in for the construction of large-scale housing estates rather than small infill developments, these premises were demolished and not usually replaced. Even if they were replaced by new flatted factories, the new premises were usually too expensive for the old firms, which then went out of business. Therefore, both because of organisational attitudes and because of a desire to eliminate 'non-conforming' uses the area that is available for industrial use has been steadily reduced and limited to zones already predominantly occupied by industry. An extreme example, quoted by Gripaios (Chapter 3), is a study of the effect of redevelopment in Wandsworth; this has shown that out of 250 firms in areas redeveloped for housing only fourteen remained in business after development (Wandsworth, 1976). It could be said by the cynical that in order to provide homes for people their jobs have been destroyed. It could also be argued that such a policy discriminates against small firms, which are the most likely to be found scattered among housing and the least likely to be found in industrial zones. Since, as already noted, the inner city provides a more favourable environment for small firms than large, such a policy is therefore doubly destructive. Moreover, if there is any truth in the hypothesis that the inner city acts as a nursery for new firms, the elimination of premises in which they could be set up may have not only a short term effect on employment in the inner city but also a long term effect on the future growth of the city, the region, and the national economy. On policies to encourage small firms, see Falk (Chapter 16).

Of course to some extent the encouragement of decentralisation was deliberate rather than accidental. It was a generally accepted national policy that population should move from the large conurbations to new or expanded towns some distance from the parent conurbations. It was therefore also implied that their jobs should move with them. In practice, of course, only a small part of this ex-urban expansion took place in the new and expanded towns; most of the decentralisation took place in an unplanned way in other small towns surrounding the conurbations. Thus, as Dennis (Chapter 2) has noted, between 1966 and 1974 only 7 per cent of the decline in industrial employment in London was due to movement to new and expanded towns. A reduction in resources given to the latest generation of new towns will not necessarily lead to a regeneration of the inner city, as some seem to think and as the government, from current policies, appears to hope.

Moreover, it was also a generally accepted national policy that industrial employment should be moved, if possible, from the more prosperous regions of south England, the Midlands, Yorkshire, and Lancashire to the high unemployment areas in the North, Scotland, and Wales. Thus, these twin policies of decentralisation and dispersal may have worsened the inner-area employment problems of London, Birmingham, and possibly Manchester and Leeds, but they should not have directly affected Liverpool, Newcastle, and Glasgow. However, as Townsend (Chapter 6) has pointed out, New Towns in the Assisted Areas, e.g. East Kilbride near Glasgow and Washington near Newcastle, may have attracted plants that would otherwise have located nearer the large cities and may in this way have exacerbated the employment problems in these cities.

Finally, the process of decentralisation can be explained in terms of the differing industrial structure of the different parts of the urban area. It is argued that industries that have been declining nationally have tended to be concentrated in the inner areas of the big cities while industries that have been expanding have been located outside these areas. So, for example, Massey and Meegan (Chapter 4) have shown that industrial restructuring in the electronics industries has particularly affected employment in the major cities. The fact that the decentralisation of jobs is mainly caused by differences between the birthrates and deathrates of firms in different areas, and between their rates of growth rather than by the actual movement of firms, lends some support to this view.

Each of the four factors outlined above may be causing the outward movement of industry, but it may be very difficult indeed to disentangle their effects and determine their relative importance. As already observed, if changes in production methods lead to larger factories, the increase in the size of the plant will itself lead to a reduction in the need for proximity to other firms; hence, any outward movement may appear to be due – indeed, will also be due – to a reduction in the importance of external economies, as well as to a need for larger sites. Similarly, the scarcity of suitable sites in the inner city for large manufacturing plants may on the one hand be due to the characteristics of the existing pattern of development, but on the other hand it may be due to planners making no provision for such sites in their proposals for future development. Again, if firms in particular industries are concentrated in the inner areas and are being forced out of existence by redevelopment and the shortage of alternative sites, the decline in the importance of these industries will be indistinguishable from a decline caused by falling demand for the products of these industries – at least it will be if only national figures for employment or production are examined. Finally, the apparent discouragement of manufacturing industry by local authorities may not be effective; the reduction in the land area that is available to industry may merely anticipate, whether accidentally or deliberately, the decline in the land area demanded by industry as it moves out of the inner city for other reasons, e.g. because improvements in transport and communications make an inner area location uneconomic.

Although it is difficult to determine the relative importance of the four factors outlined above, because, as has been shown, the effects of each will be similar, a decision is necessary if it is intended to try to reverse the trend, since the economic costs of doing so will depend on the factor that is the predominant cause of decentralisation. Thus, if planning policy towards manufacturing industry is most important, it can easily be reversed or otherwise altered. If the scarcity of suitable large sites is the problem, public intervention may be able to make such sites available more quickly than if their provision is left to private initiative, and the social costs of this intervention should be relatively low. On the other hand, if it is no longer economic for manufacturing plants to be located in the inner city because transport improvements have eliminated the need for centrality, firms can only be induced to locate plants in the inner areas by subsidies and controls. Such policies might be expensive; and alternative policies that, say, encouraged the resident population to move out rather than firms to move in might be found to be cheaper in the long run, both economically and socially.

Despite the fact that many critics of British planning policy have argued that the loss of manufacturing jobs in the inner city is a result of that policy and of the way in which it has been applied, there is a large volume of evidence that the decentralisation of manufacturing industry has occurred, and is occurring, throughout the United States (Mills, 1970; Kain, 1968) and western Europe. In a survey article Wullkopf and Pearce (1977) have stated: 'by the end of the fifties the reconstruction of industrial plant and technical infrastructure was virtually complete in most European countries . . . Industrial programmes now sought to achieve economies of scale and, concentrating more on the few available open sites, helped simplify land acquisition' (p. 42); and 'Manufacturing trades decentralised to more spacious and accessible sites . . . The population of the city centre declined as many people traded city centre accessibility for more living space in suburban areas' (p. 43).

In view of the ubiquity of the process it seems certain that British planning policy has not been the most important factor in Britain and that relaxations of that policy are unlikely to bring manufacturing costlessly back to the inner city. Any policy that aims to reverse a worldwide trend is going to be expensive. On the other hand, if the aim is not to reverse the decline but rather to slow down the rate of decline, a more encouraging attitude by planning authorities towards manufacturing will probably have some effect, relatively cheaply. Moreover, as will be argued later, it is likely that a slowing down rather than a reversal may be all that is required.

It is not true, after all, that in the conurbations population is static and jobs are declining. Both population and jobs are decentralising. Therefore, in order to alter the balance between the two it is in fact not necessary to bring new employment into the inner areas – only to ensure that jobs decline at a slower rate than the population. Ensuring that local authority policies do not actually eliminate jobs may in that case be quite effective.

20.5 Problems created by industrial decentralisation

Three kinds of problem have been attributed to the decline of manufacturing industry in the inner areas. It is necessary to distinguish them because in many discussions they are treated as one single inner-city problem. In fact they need not necessarily co-exist.

First, it is argued that this decline leads to unemployment. People lose their jobs as these jobs disappear – as firms go out of business or move out of the central city. It is not clear, however, as stated earlier and as will be argued more fully later, that the resulting unemployment is anything other than temporary and is cancelled by the outward movement of population, which results in equivalent vacancies, thus ensuring that jobs are easier to come by than they would otherwise be if there were no population movement.

Second, the closure or outward movement of firms results in the premises or land that they occupied becoming vacant; and since few firms are coming into existence or moving into the area, these sites remain vacant. If a number of firms move out of a single area, large areas will become dead and increasingly derelict. It should be noted that this is particularly likely to occur at times of economic recession when neither other firms nor local authorities have the resources to rebuild these derelict areas, so that the phenomenon may be temporary. Also, the existence of vacant land need not be associated with an inner-city employment problem; indeed, vacant land is more likely to exist if both employment and population are moving out than if only one is.

Third, it is argued that the outward movement of firms reduces the revenue that local authorities can raise from a given rate poundage (i.e level of property tax), while not reducing the costs that they must bear to the same extent. As a result the tax rate is increased, thus providing a further incentive for firms and upper income households to move out of the area. In this way a cumulative cycle of decline may be set up. In the end the reduction in the property tax base may lead to a fiscal crisis of the kind that has faced New York City.

While this process appears feasible in American cities, the tax equalisation schemes that exist in Britain may make it unlikely here. A reduction in the property tax base will (generally) lead to an increase in the resources element of the rate support grant from central government. An increase in the proportion of the population that is dependent on welfare benefits as higher income households move out will (generally) lead to an increase in the needs element of the rate support grant. Moreover, in London an equalisation scheme reduces differences between the rate poundages of the thirty-two London boroughs, particularly differences between the poundages of the inner and the outer boroughs. Thus, while some commentators (e.g. Eversley, 1972) have expressed concern over the problem, it is unlikely to be as intractable in the United Kingdom as it is in the United States, where a tradition of civic independence, both from other cities and from state and federal governments, makes these kinds of schemes difficult to set up and to operate.

Once again it should be noted that a financial crisis in local government need not be associated with an inner city employment problem; indeed, it may be more likely to occur if both employment and population are moving out than if only one is.

20.6 The service industries

Given that employment in manufacturing industry is declining in the inner city, for whatever reason, can other industries provide alternative employment? Indeed, can employment in the head offices, sales offices, regional offices, etc. of manufacturing firms replace employment in the factories of those firms? Is employment in offices, in commerce, and in services in the central city growing fast enough to outweigh the decline in employment in manufacturing in the inner areas? The evidence is that it is not. Since the early 1960s employment in the British conurbation centres has been declining (Cameron and Evans, 1973); and although there is evidence that employment in the centre was increasing rapidly in the 1950s, although not as rapidly as was thought at the time (Evans, 1967), when employment in the surrounding inner areas was already declining rapidly, it is now clear that no major expansion of employment in the conurbation centres can be relied on. Any increase in employment in the urban area must take place, if it takes place at all, in the outer suburbs.

Townsend (Chapter 6) has shown that the kind of non-personal services usually located in the inner city outside the central business district have been declining for years.

20.7 Population decline

If employment can be expected to decline in the central city, will this result in unemployment in the same way that, at a regional level, the decline of the older industries (mining, shipbuilding, cotton) has resulted in high levels of unemployment in the regions in which these industries are concentrated – so-called structural unemployment? The political response to this latter problem has been a battery of controls and incentives designed to induce firms to move to or expand in, or at worst contract less slowly in, the depressed regions. This response has been categorised as 'taking work to the workers'; the alternative response, i.e. taking workers to the work, has also received some governmental support (see Salt, Chapter 11).

But can the inner city be regarded as merely another region? It seems that it cannot, the main reason for this view being that, while population movement between regions is relatively costly, population movement within a city or even within an urban region need not be. The social costs – the possibility of losing touch with friends and relatives, the problems of adjusting to life in a new place – are all considerably less. Moreover, migration into and out of the central city at different stages of the family lifecycle is continually occurring as the costs and benefits of particular locations change for people as their family circumstances changes.

The second reason for believing that the inner city employment problem is fundamentally different from the regional problem is that the relationship between population and employment is not the same. Because the region can be regarded as a single labour market or set of labour markets, the number of available jobs must equal, or be greater than, the number of people wishing to be employed in order for there to be no unemployment problem. Because the inner city is not a single labour market, in that people live there but work outside it and work there but live outside it, full employment does not require equality between those seeking work and the number of available jobs.

This difference is important. It is clear that the resident population of the inner city is falling as fast as, or possibly faster than, the number of jobs. However, this outward movement has tended to precede, and has not been caused by, the decentralisation of jobs (see Warnes, Chapter 1). Quite the reverse is probably true: that the reduction in the resident population of the inner city has caused a decline in the number of available jobs as the demand for personal services has fallen. The problem is thus fundamentally different from the regional problem, for in a region the outward movement of people will be expected to follow the outward movement of jobs as people move to regions with better employment prospects.

20.8 The labour market

Since the resident population is falling faster than the number of jobs, it follows that *in aggregate* there should be no general unemployment problem in the inner city. However, it is still possible that there may be localised unemployment problems, either in particular areas (e.g. if job closures are concentrated in one part of the inner city and population declines in another) or among particular skill groups (e.g. if the jobs that leave are relatively unskilled but the population that leaves is predominantly skilled). The first kind of localised unemployment could be expected to disappear over time as people found jobs in nearby areas, and by a chain of moves the localised vacancies in some other part of the city would be filled. The effect would be similar to throwing a stone in a pond; the disturbance is great at the point of impact, but it dissipates as it ripples outwards and finally disappears. The level of the pond will be permanently raised, however, even if by only a small amount, just as a factory closure in one part of the urban area will have a permanent effect on the labour situation over the whole urban area. Moreover, a continuing series of factory closures, like a series of stones thrown in the pond, may create a permanent disturbance in a particular area with no immediate possibility of a return to normal.

It seems true that the city can be treated as a single labour market or, at the very least, as a set of highly interconnected labour markets. This can be contrasted with the simplistic view that the city can be thought of as a set of virtually separate labour markets, so that unemployment in a particular part of it will persist since people will find it difficult to seek work in other parts of the city. This difference in the perception of the urban labour market is crucial. The major evidence that supports the single-labour-market view is the finding by Metcalf and Richardson (Chapter 8) that differences between the London boroughs in their average rates of unemployment could be largely explained (a) by differences in the proportion of the working population that was unskilled, and (b) by variations in average family characteristics. Differences in the total amount of manufacturing employment lost from each borough appeared to explain hardly any of the differences in the rates of employment. Thus, it seems that the characteristics of the population of an area are more important in determining the level of unemployment in that area than the characteristics of the area. Any person in a particular skill group and with a particular set of family responsibilities will have the same probability of being unemployed in whatever part of the urban area he lives, whether the inner city or the outer suburbs. This assertion is supported by the more detailed analysis of the London labour market by Evans (Chapter 9) and also by the analysis of unemployment in the other British conurbations by Corkindale (Chapter 7).

Not only will there be a high degree of intraurban spatial mobility, but there also appears to be a high degree of mobility between occupations and between industries when people change jobs. Thus, it is unlikely that 'mismatch' will occur as those who become unemployed are unable to find jobs in the industries or occupations that they have just left while the jobs that are available in other industries or occupations remain unfilled. This type of employment is unlikely to persist, since unless people's skills are both highly industry-specific and very highly paid they are likely to shift between industries and occupations, possibly gaining or losing skills in the process. Berthoud (Chapter 10) has shown one way in which this can happen by demonstrating that on average the population becomes more skilled up to the age of 40 and less skilled after the age of 50. Therefore, just as spatially localised concentrations of unemployment because of plant closures are unlikely to persist for long, so discrepancies between the skills offered and the skills demanded are also unlikely to persist. Thus, as Evans (Chapter 9) has shown, the unemployment records of the employment exchanges give little indication that unemployment is concentrated among those who have lost jobs in manufacturing industry.

A lack of mobility between cities and a high degree of spatial, occupational, and industrial mobility within cities can thus explain the way in which the probability of being unemployed for any person with particular skills will tend to be the same wherever he lives within the city. The average levels of unemployment will tend to vary between cities, however; the effects of a factory closure will be felt throughout an urban area, but spatial immobility will mean that the effects will be limited to that city. The impact of a weakening of the labour market will be felt most by the unskilled, however, since the more skilled can always retain employment by taking less skilled jobs, while the unskilled cannot. Moreover, the more skilled may be able and willing to travel to other cities, while the less skilled may not.

20.9 Policies

The interpretation made of the evidence presented in the chapters of this book is not merely of intellectual importance. It affects the policies that can be recommended; a policy that may be the most effective if one interpretation is correct will be ineffective if another is.

On one interpretation, inner city unemployment results from the closure of firms in the inner city areas. It can be cured by encouraging firms to move back to, or to open plants in, the inner city and by easing the planning restrictions that hinder this. Since the inner city is regarded as a nursery for small firms and new firms, one approach would be to encourage these in particular (Falk, Chapter 16; Aldrich, Chapter 17). Since those who have become unemployed will have skills that are suitable for manufacturing industries that no longer exist, a complementary policy would be to finance the retraining of the unemployed labour in order to encourage new factories to open in the area or to enable the unemployed to fill existing vacancies (Reid, Chapter 18).

However, the location of new firms in the inner city is unlikely to do much for unemployment in that area, for the effect will be dispersed over the whole conurbation. Moreover, it will be difficult to persuade plants to open there because the inner city is now an uneconomic location for manufacturing, although changes in local government policies may reduce the rate at which existing plants close. It is possible that this may discourage small firms less, but the impact of any increase in the number of small firms is likely to be small. Retraining may be of some use in enabling those out of work to get new jobs, but retraining schemes are unlikely to encourage new plants to locate there.

No policy is likely to be effective quickly. The lessening of restrictions on the mobility of workers is likely to have some effect in allowing people to move from their rented housing, whether private or public, in the inner city to other areas where jobs are available. Since the people who will thus be enabled to move are likely to be less skilled, this should bring down the average unemployment rate in the inner city in the long run. In the short run, however, the only policies that are likely to be effective are national policies aimed at bringing down the level of national unemployment, for the high rate of unemployment in the inner city is due to the concentration there of the unskilled, who are more likely to be laid off in any recession.

21 A Planner's Perspective

David Eversley

21.1 Recapitulating the historical development

The introduction to this volume, written from the standpoint of social planning, pursued an historical rather than a particularly analytical approach. The main theme of the chapters that followed was the anxiety about the amount of work that is available now, and will be available in future, for the inhabitants of the inner cities. (The term is used loosely and is not geographically exact; it includes many older industrial urban areas that are not the cores of large conurbations, and it excludes centrally located but economically advantaged populations.) The questions raised are those of the Inner Area Studies, published in the summer of 1977, and they are all concerned with the possible solutions to the problem of mismatch as it was seen in the early 1970s: rising unemployment on the one hand, and continued labour shortages, in both unskilled and highly skilled occupations, on the other. Therefore, apart from the economic analysis of the causes of the decline of employment opportunities and the desirability and feasibility of reversing this trend, the present concern is mainly with the possibility of finding work for those who are now unemployed or underemployed or receiving low wages: by education, training, and retraining; by enabling them to move to where there are vacancies; or by relying on future generations being willing and able to take up such chances as will present themselves owing to the growth of some selected occupations.

However, these are very recent preoccupations. Historically speaking, it is only in the very last stages of urban planning that the

United Kingdom has faced this set of questions, although it has long been familiar in the United States. For most of British urban-planning history the problem was that of containing the growth of the city. Urban areas grew, almost without interruption and at a very even pace, ever since the advent of the steam engine made manufacturing concentrations possible and even necessary; and at an increasing rate the towns became magnets for population from the countryside. With the advent of the railways urban areas assumed increasing regional significance; with the rise of the tertiary sector the growth of jobs accelerated even more, since offices required less land than industry per worker employed. Industry in cities meant environmental nuisance and even danger; the failure of the building industry to keep pace with employment growth meant increasing overcrowding, multioccupation, the 'classic slum', and greater distances travelled to work by those who were able to escape from the housing conditions of the older parts of the city.

For all these reasons industrial or employment planning meant, from its beginnings, the attempt to relieve the pressures by diverting employment away from its traditional locations. The voluntary examples of Cadbury at Bournville, Rowntree at New Earswick, and Lever at Port Sunlight were quickly followed by less celebrated and smaller scale examples. Official planning did not at first exert direct pressures; but by the increasing enforcement of legislation concerning smoke emission, atmospheric pollution, and effluent disposal it forced some types of firms to seek new locations. Then in the 1930s, almost imperceptibly the economics of location changed in the face of new technologies and new industrial organisation. Electric power, motor transport, the continuous assembly line, and the coming of space-intensive chemical, electroengineering, and vehicle-manufacturing industries led to a growing preference for greenfield locations on the edges of cities or altogether outside the traditional industrial areas.

The official mind was finally made up by the Barlow Report of 1940 (Board of Trade, 1940), with its emphasis on urban containment, help to the depressed (development) areas, the difficulties and dangers of urban congestion, and the need for greater industrial efficiency.

After the war the New Towns Act 1946, the Town and Country Planning Act 1947, green belt legislation, and then increasingly effective regional planning attempts combined to reinforce a trend that was in any case dictated by economic necessity. So, relative industrial growth in the cities was already much smaller in the period 1935–55 than it had been in the previous 100 years, i.e. since the start of the steam and railway age. There was still some growth in the traditional sector; but mostly there was the rapid rise of retailing, service industries, finance, banking and insurance, personal services, tourism, and entertainment – in short, all the concomitants of increasing real incomes and increased mobility, which ensured that the overall growth of employment continued even when manufacturing industry contributed much less. Cities still fulfilled the 'seedbed' function discussed in Chapters 15 and 16. Thus, in a period of generally low national unemployment not only London, Birmingham, and Manchester, but also the East Midlands cities and many smaller urban areas, had what now seem impossibly low unemployment rates – less than 1 per cent of the insured labour force in some cases.

Under these circumstances good planning meant, until the late 1960s, an intensification of official attempts to persuade industries to move out of cities, to new and expanded towns, to development areas, or in suitable cases to almost any location where land was zoned for industry and labour was either available or likely to be attracted. The emphasis between these types of location changed; the movement did not. Very gradually (and none of the contributors to this book have been able to pinpoint the threshold year), employment growth came to a halt. The inner cities had been losing population since the beginning of the century. The conurbations, defined in their wider sense – and in the case of London recognised in the London Government Act 1963, which created the Greater London Council (GLC) – reached their peak populations and their peak employment about the middle of the century and thereafter began to decline. In some cases, e.g. London, this peak was reached before the war, in others at some time between 1961 and 1966. The decline was not noticed at first, although Evans suggested as early as 1967 that growth might have gone into reverse. Different cities began to turn around at different dates; and as the downward movement accelerated, so it became visible as an increasing failure of workplaces and available labour to decline in phase with each other. As it happened, population growth slowed down after the mid-1960s, but the available labour force still grew (and will continue to do so for quite a few years despite the falling birthrate). Then, after about 1970, and increasingly since 1972, Britain's economic growth first declined and by now may have stopped altogether. Again, these movements were masked for some time. The tertiary sector, especially in public administration and services, continued to grow and therefore shielded the cities for some time from the effect of manufacturing decline. It was not until national unemployment rose to above 4 per cent that it was noticed that the difference in employment and earnings was no longer, if at all, in favour of the large cities as against other areas, quite apart from the long-recognised chronic problems of Liverpool and Glasgow, which had never shared the prosperity of even Birmingham, let alone London.

21.2 Industrial location policies questioned

Given this very long history of urban growth it is not surprising that the entire machinery of government, and of planning in particular, should have been devised with the reduction of urban employment in mind. The legislation enabling (indeed commanding) planning authorities at all levels to facilitate the movement of jobs out of the cities is still on the statute book, and there is as yet no legislation attempting to promote an opposite trend (assuming that the Inner Urban Areas Act 1978 mainly tries to arrest the prevailing tendency). However, Acts of Parliament apart, the attitude of mind created under the old regime will take a long time to die. It exists in the minds of all planners and is institutionalised both in pressure groups like the Town and Country Planning Association and in vested interests like the new towns administrations, the road transport industry, and of course the development areas themselves. Politically, all the votes still seem to be on the side of decentralisation and regional policies. (The charge that the inner cities policy is a 'vote-catching' device is simply silly; all the votes are on the other side.)

Thus, the attempts by planners to identify an 'inner city problem' have not been singularly successful. There were too many handicaps. Apart from any absence of clearcut ideas about the functions of the city there was (and as this book has demonstrated still is) no unanimity as to whether industry could survive in the big cities. Reliable statistics were not (and are not) available in a disaggregated and population-related form that would have made a meaningful analysis of the urban labour market feasible. As has been said, tradition, official policy, legislation, and vested interests all held out against the idea that something might be wrong. The generally moderately favourable underlying economic growth trends were still masking the deteriorating social situation in the late 1960s.

This can be illustrated from the successive stages of the ill-fated Greater London Development Plan (Greater London Council, 1970). From the *Report of Studies* published in 1970 and based on work undertaken by the London planners and economists in the three previous years, which hardly mentioned the possibility of a serious employment problem, to the final version approved by the Secretary of State for the Environment in 1976, the GLC moved by almost imperceptible stages from a whole-hearted endorsement of a dispersal strategy to strong opposition to such a policy. Central government did not accept the case put forward by London (and other large urban authorities) until later, and even then it paid lip service to the idea of reversal rather than taking action (which in any case was not open to it at a time of severe industrial recession). Under these circumstances it is not surprising that the change in planning opinion was neither smooth nor free from some serious aberrations. Research was commissioned but was seldom conclusive enough to settle the matter one way or another. Thus, the GLC was persuaded by some of its staff economists that certain industries were more efficient in London than elsewhere and that it was therefore in the national interest that they should be kept there. A firm of consultants was commissioned to investigate this point and came up with a lengthy and quite inconclusive report, but the idea remained in the text of the Plan through several revisions. Again, the GLC was in favour of flexibly regulating total employment according to the state of the available labour supply, and it thought that it could do this by legislating on the amount of additional industrial and commercial floorspace permitted each year. This device was both to regulate overall supply–demand relationships and to ensure the relocation of employment in specially designated favourable areas, mostly in outer London. This idea came in for sharp criticism at the Greater London Development Plan inquiry, and it was thrown out by the panel that inquired into the Plan. Indeed, the Layfield Report went further and virtually suggested that the volume of employment in London was not the concern of the GLC planners at all but a matter for central government. Therefore, the question of *how* to regulate employment did not arise; it was not the GLC's business, except in a narrow planning sense. That is, the GLC was allowed to see to it that new office and industrial building did not violate regulations devised to protect the environment, to prevent traffic nuisances, to separate residential from industrial zones, and to limit the height of buildings. In other words, Layfield took the view that planning was purely an activity concerned with land use and transportation planning, environmental protection, and the enforcement of building standards.

The difficulties did not end there. As already mentioned, the growth of the tertiary sector for a long time masked the decline of industry; and given the gradual change in the composition of the labour force, office growth was useful in taking care of that increasing proportion of school leavers who were not totally illiterate and in providing jobs for married women who wanted work. However, offices were a delicate issue politically. There were some notorious scandals; and finally the Labour Party decided on a policy of opposing office growth altogether, on the grounds that this type of development only served to make excessive profits for developers, increased the inequality of income, and provided no jobs for those who needed them most, as well as spoiling the townscape and aggravating traffic problems. This attitude persisted in the face of ample evidence that the labour force entrants of future years would find either employment in offices or none at all. Also, it was at variance with the views even of the Labour government, which in 1978 went so far as to instruct the specially created Location of Offices Bureau to change direction and encourage office developers to consider suitable sites in London, rather than concentrate solely on the policy to assist firms to leave London. Thus, the economic situation apart, the planners were facing great uncertainties.

Why then does the problem continue to figure so largely in the contemporary planner's repertoire? Why have the Home Office and the Department of the Environment initiated studies to see if these long-standing trends can be reversed? Why are local authorities experimenting in a variety of ways (demonstrated in some of the chapters in this book) to see if they can act as promoters of industrial activity or at least remove the supposed obstacles that prevent firms from taking up traditional locations?

If one wants to take a fairly narrowly political view of these questions, one could possibly find the answers in the White Paper *Policy for the Inner Cities*, published in June 1977 to coincide with the three Inner City Studies reports (Department of the Environment, 1977b). It claims to be the outcome of a 'major review of inner city policy announced by the Prime Minister on 10th September 1976' and proceeds to present the problem in terms suggesting a very recent discovery: that despite everything done for and in urban areas since the war, economic decline, physical decay, social disadvantage, and the problem of ethnic minorities dominate the scene to an increasing extent. This is not the place to discuss the analysis presented in the White Paper, nor its policy conclusions, nor the chances of implementing what is advocated. Whatever the current shifts in political emphasis, there are good planning reasons why it is necessary to pursue positive policies to arrest the decline (which is not now disputed). These reasons are independent of the conflicting views of the origin, extent, or future course of the economic changes discussed in this book. That is to say, from the point of view of the social planner the causes of decline and the future prospects of the revival of employment are relevant, in as much as they must be the basis of any action taken to arrest this decline, or even to reverse it. However, this analysis does not of itself provide the planning reasons for wishing to intervene in what most people regard as perfectly natural processes.

In fact the reasons lie partly in the established objectives of existing social policies and partly in the close connection between the level of economic activity, in as far as this affects the volume and composition of private and public incomes, and the possibility of urban renewal.

21.3 Work planning at the centre of strategic planning

Social objectives are described as 'existing', although they are nebulous and by no means universally agreed. As far as this can be demonstrated, since the war there has been something of a consensus in British society that at any rate the more glaring inequalities of incomes, life chances, and to a lesser extent wealth should be reduced. This lies at the root of the whole package of welfare policies, including taxation and the provision of social services in kind, together with insurance and other cash benefits. These policies have had their ups and downs, not all of which have been politically motivated or at any rate totally traceable to the political party in power. At the time of writing they are in fact being eroded, at least in some important respects, by public expenditure cuts. Nevertheless, it can be shown that in real terms the redistribution of real incomes is fairly substantial and has been achieved by a mixture of policies, of which land use planning and the allocation of public expenditure to the built environment have been a major part. This is true at the local level, in intraregional planning, and above all in inter-regional policies.

Therefore, if it can be demonstrated that *after* so many years of the operation of these policies (note that this is not to say *because* of these policies) the country is still faced with the phenomena described so many times – an increasing concentration of the unfit and overcrowded stock of dwellings in the inner areas of large urban concentrations, a deteriorating total environment, and a progressive failure of the transport and services infrastructure precisely in these areas – and if it can also be demonstrated that there is a close correlation between personal and environmental disadvantage, then the social policy component of planning has failed *prima facie* in this important respect. It may appear superfluous to state such simple facts. However, it is necessary, because unless this approach is used there will be a tendency to fall into the trap of approaching the problem one-sidedly: either as a purely physical one of poor structures that have to be improved, if necessary by grants and subsidies; or as an economic one, which may or may not be capable of being solved by the redistribution of activity. These extremes may now seem far-fetched, but they are not. For evidence of the first view it is only necessary to look at the original remit in 1972 from the Department of the Environment to its consultants for the Inner City Studies, which reads today like a demand for prescriptions for urban cosmetic operations; indeed, at that stage the consideration of employment and incomes was specifically excluded from the instructions. It took two years to persuade the Department that physical decay could not be seen in isolation. Even when it was conceded that these matters were important there was still a long way to go before it was possible to present these studies, as has now been done, as exercises in the investigation of the distribution of real incomes and life chances between groups and in geographical space. In other words, the idea that all planning is in fact related to overall social policy objectives (whether or not this is called social planning) is, if not of recent date, at any rate only lately accepted as respectable.

Therefore, the historical reversal of the accepted view of what policies are good for the large conurbations in a purely physical or functional sense has coincided with an altogether different view of what planning is about. That is not to say that the new view is universally accepted. In a recent document, *Planning and the Future* (Royal Town Planning Institute 1976), a working party composed of members of several professional organisations certainly seemed to favour the new approach, but it has not commanded general acceptance.

It is therefore immaterial whether the present situation is regarded as being the direct outcome of mistaken, or too intensely pursued, past policies (such as intra- and inter-regional ones), or as the product of recent economic growth failures, or as a concomitant of the demographic decline that appeared a few years ago, or as only a residual failure left after many years of successful planning and housing activities. Again, all these questions matter when considering the nature of solutions but not when discussing the approach to the problems as such.

To sum up this part of the reasons for considering the inner city problems, particularly employment, as an integral part of planning policy: if it is accepted that planning is an activity designed to assist in the redistribution of real incomes, the reduction of inequalities, and the removal of individual and group disadvantages, then it cannot be concerned solely with fabric and function but must turn to the problem of the level and allocation of incomes as an indispensable precondition of urban renewal.

21.4 Location planning at the regional and local scale

It has been said above that there is another historically conditioned reason for looking at inner city employment as a planning problem. When urban planners became no longer so much concerned with environmental pollution and other nuisances as central constituents of their attitude towards employment, it seemed at one time that only two questions remained for them to consider: whether the location of economic activity fitted into transportation plans (or whether these could be adapted to fit the changing pattern of activity), and the extent to which such activities could be relocated outside the metropolitan areas without decreasing productivity. This, as has been shown, was still a central point at the time of the Greater London Development Plan; but since no general theoretical or empirically tested answer could be found, the debate has tended to become, in the best sense, academic (and many chapters in this book are evidence of this), while employers, with or without official encouragement, have solved the unanswered question by relocating elsewhere.

So, what is there left for the planner to think about? Certainly the transportation question is still there, even though it is now less important. The movement of workers and goods still causes problems of congestion and high individual and social costs. However, most of the work opportunities that planners are seeking to create are in theory 'footloose', at least within a regional framework.

The central problem now is that, if individual incomes in any given definable area are too low, the chances of improving that area physically are also reduced. This bald statement requires definitions and qualifications. By 'too low' is meant generally that the level of disposable incomes is such as to keep a large part of the population at or below subsistence level (or supplementary benefit level – the two are not the same), and therefore a population having such incomes exercises insufficient demand for goods and services to tempt the private entrepreneur to contribute his share of total infrastructure renewal. More will be said about this later, but first let us refine the spatial definition. By the 'given area' is meant that whole or part of any settlement where the expenditure of local residents is crucial in determining the level of activity in non-basic industries and services. Clearly, if an inner city area happens to coincide with being a regional centre – or supraregional, national, or even international centre – for retailing, administration, education, entertainment, and so on, the spending power of the local population will not be of paramount importance (although, conversely, high prices due to the supralocal importance of such areas can affect the local population negatively, e.g. in tourist areas). However, the 'inner areas' as defined in these studies generally mean older mixed residential and industrial areas at a critical distance from the central business district (CBD). Crucial in this context is the fact that, whatever disposable incomes flow into the CBD, they may not touch the district and local centres of the disadvantaged areas. These depend on local custom. If this does not materialise, shops will close, as will professional offices, and there will be a lack of demand for every kind of personal service. Leisure activities will be restricted. If the local population has a high proportion of low-paid, unemployed, elderly, and handicapped household heads, it will be a poor proposition for the private investor. It will be an equally unrewarding location for publicly provided services, except for

those which are part of the welfare system; and these are by definition costly to run, yield no income, and normally do not offer much
employment to local people except that of the most unskilled variety. Resources such as public libraries or sports facilities may be
poorly used compared with possible suburban locations. All this is
by now common knowledge although it is rarely openly stated. The
point usually omitted, though, is that there is a direct connection
between low incomes and low demand for those public services
which might be called optional.

The other point is also familiar. It is that, if an area suffers from
low incomes, its yield in terms of rates (or any other source of public
income that might at some future point be adopted) will be low. In
other words, such areas will require additional public expenditure,
but they will yield decreasing public incomes. When to this are
added the difficulty that low-income owner-occupiers have in maintaining their dwellings, the possibility of widespread vandalism, the
vermin infestation that follows the abandonment of once-inhabited
buildings, and so on, the whole catalogue of urban blight that is
repeated in every analysis of the inner city is soon arrived at.

However, it is precisely at this point that planners enter the area
of dangerous subjective judgements. If this state of affairs is blamed
largely on some form of personal inadequacy (i.e. people are
blamed for being old, handicapped, black, or sick or for having poor
educational attainments and a low level of skills), the next step is
either to give up the attempt to renew the city or, alternatively, to
call for the removal of this feeble component of the total population
and its replacement by economically stronger sections of the population.

However, this approach is one-sided and has been largely discre-
dited (without, however, ruling out some alteration in the pattern of
settlement, as the Lambeth Inner Area Study (1976) advocates).
However, if the idea that low incomes are mainly due to personal
inadequacies is rejected, the only possible alternative must be
accepted: that opportunities for earning higher incomes do not (or
do no longer) exist within the reach of the residents of the inner city
area. The moment that this point is conceded it becomes necessary
to look at the changing size and composition of the labour market,
at the possibility of access to employment opportunities with a
tolerable expenditure of time, money, and energy, and at the
educational and training facilities that are available to that part of
population which could now (or in future) qualify for such
employment chances as there are (or may exist in future).

Thus, the argument has come full circle. Decline is progressive because it reduces private and therefore public incomes. The reduction of incomes reduces the stimulus to investment and maintenance. Deteriorating environment and poor services drive out remaining enterprises and able-bodied households. The higher the concentration of a disadvantaged residue, the less will be both total incomes and the local labour supply for remaining or potential enterprises.

If this analysis is accepted, the provision of sources of higher incomes will become a crucial component not only of social policy (as it could do anywhere in the country, including rural and development areas) but also of urban planning policy. If the problem is approached in this way, the question of the economic viability of enterprises that still exist, or that may in future be located in the inner city, will be only part of a larger social accounting problem. This is that expenditure on the physical renewal of the urban infrastructure and built fabric may be uneconomic in the sense that, unless the household incomes of the area are raised at the same time, not only will a high proportion of the operation fall on the public sector, but also there may be rapid deterioration again after a very short time. For proof of this it is necessary to look no further than those interwar or postwar estates on the edges of urban areas which were built to quite tolerable building specifications but which deteriorated rapidly once unemployment had reached a high level and the disposable incomes of those still at work had been reduced through low local wages or long journeys to more remunerative work (Kirkby in Liverpool, Ferguslie Park in Paisley, and numerous other examples).

From this it follows that the review of income levels is an integral part of the inner-city renewal planning operation. The improvement of the physical environment cannot be divorced from the social institutions and services provided, and both depend on the availability of sources of higher income. Theoretically, it could be argued that such incomes could be provided by social benefits and divorced from work; in practice nobody seriously considers this feasible either here and now or even under quite different economic circumstances.

To sum up, unless a substantially greater part of the population of the inner city has access to higher earned incomes, there is little chance of succeeding with other improvements. If it is agreed that this is a major concern to the planners of inner city improvement, the question must be asked: is there anything that can be done by government, at any level, to improve the present situation? The answers will depend on the analysis of the causes; and the essays in this book have demonstrated very clearly that, since there is little agreement on causes, remedies may also be elusive.

21.5 Ensuring income maintenance

First of all, if the main decline of well-paid employment, especially for manual workers, is due to the reduction of jobs in manufacturing industry (and it does not matter for this purpose whether this reduction is due to outward movement or to closures of old firms), it will be necessary to ask whether the creation of new industrial jobs (if this were considered possible) would cure the current problem of unemployment and low wages. Most of the contributors to this book have been sceptical about the possibilities of establishing large modern manufacturing concerns, with their opportunities for semi-skilled work leading to high earnings through overtime and piecework, in the old areas. There is some interest in smaller industrial estates, providing opportunities for craft workshops and small independent manufacturing operations. However, such developments, even if they were to take place within easy travelling distance of the potential workers, might not give many chances to the unskilled, the married women who would like to work but cannot do so, and the school leavers without minimal educational qualifications.

Second, if it is accepted that the main cause of the present situation is the growth of employment of a new kind, demanding precisely those workers who have left the city areas in search of a better environment, the emphasis will be on better education, retraining, and deliberate attempts to settle in the cities those who could take advantage of these openings. (This, from a planning angle, would be preferable to encouraging more people to travel into the city to work.)

Third, if it is maintained that the unemployed and poor are basically in some sense 'inadequate' workers who would not find jobs even if industry were to re-establish itself, let alone be suitable for training for the new kinds of vacancies that have arisen in increasing numbers, it will be necessary either to ensure that they have an adequate income in the city without working, or to supplement their earnings, or to enable them to a greater degree than hitherto to move to areas where they can live more cheaply and have access to jobs that they can do. Even if they were judged to be incapable of working, their dispersal to other areas where they would form relatively small deprived minorities might ease the urban renewal problem – if, that is, it were accepted that the concentration of large numbers of unemployed or badly paid people is in itself a bar to faster urban renewal. (We omit here all reference to the alternative view, already noted earlier and held by many Community Development Project authors, that the whole UK political system is so damaged by the ravages of capitalism that nothing short of a totally new social and economic structure can provide a remedy. We started, as have the majority of other investigators of inner city problems, from the assumption that remedies could be found by drastic, but fundamentally conventional, legislative and administrative processes leading to a further redistribution of people and workplaces spatially and to a redistribution of incomes and access to services for individuals and households.)

21.6 The preconditions for planning success

Even if there were some agreement about the principal causes of the present manifestations of decay and about the kind of solutions that would be appropriate (for there would certainly have to be more than one), it would be necessary to recall some other preconditions that will need to be fulfilled if remedial action is to have a chance to succeed. These have all been stated in the Inner Area Studies and are repeatedly referred to in the relevant chapters, but it may be convenient to summarise them again:

1. Sufficient funds It must be assumed throughout either (a) that the total amount of real resources available to public authorities increases at a faster rate than has been possible in the last few years, or (b) that it is politically possible to redistribute existing resources away from areas now benefiting from them towards the disadvantaged inner-city districts. The first condition is clearly not within sight. Indeed, public expenditure has been cut severely several times; and even if the gross national product were to grow again at the moderate rates that were taken for granted in the mid-1960s, it is unlikely that the proportion allocated to public expenditure would again be allowed to rise to the very high levels of the early 1970s. As for the second possibility, such a redistribution is obviously far more difficult at a time when real incomes are falling; but it should not be taken for granted that, even if they rose again, governments of any political complexion would find it easy in the long run to cut sharply the allocations to prosperous suburbs and new and growing settlements, let alone the still designated development areas, in order to divert more to the inner cities, over and above the now rising amounts for the Urban Aid Programme and the special allocations foreshadowed in the June 1977 White Paper.

2. *Devolution of decision making*   It is also necessary to see the problem in the context of the general desire for the devolution of powers from central government – the increasing demands for a restoration of decision-making powers to local authorities. The ideas now being seriously discussed will require some form of regional decision-making level and much more advanced forms of directly involving the local community in the processes of planning and redevelopment. Therefore, all ideas based solely on what central government departments can do (with the customary 'consultation' with the local authorities affected) must be rejected and the concept of 'partnership' substituted. The newly completed county-structure plans (in so far as they have been, or will be, approved by central government) cannot play any significant role in the process of reallocation that is seen as central to the new planning processes required. However, nobody has as yet realistically worked out by what new constitutional device central government intends to devolve real powers of decision making to regional or local, let alone community, governments, while underwriting the whole, or the vastly greater part, of the cost involved in the process of regeneration and while retaining the right to make the broad distributional judgements between regions with differing levels of absolute need. The partnership agreements are now being monitored to establish whether they provide an effective (i.e. flexible but robust) mechanism for resource allocation.

3. *Co-ordinated agency effort*   Although this is another point that by now should hardly need restating, it is not possible to conceive of any proposals being put into effect except by the operation of some form of corporate management in which the planning authorities play a leading, but not necessarily dominant, role. While economists tend to see the location of employment and residential settlement patterns largely in terms of land costs, transportation costs and facilities, relative locational advantages for manufacturing

industry and services, and other variables that are directly pertinent to the search for an optimal pattern of structures in the economic sense, the planning approach requires the decisions associated with the evolution of this new structure to be the outcome of a joint effort with all those who are responsible for every other aspect of urban (and regional) government. In the inner area context this means mainly housing, education, and social and health services. However, many other agencies are also involved, and it needs only to be reiterated here that the present pattern of functions and powers divided between different tiers of elected government, and statutory undertakers, has so far nullified all attempts to produce a rational new structure. The one exception, as critics will not be slow to point out, is seen in the new towns. Here, an all-agency effort could be mounted to produce something that may not always be aesthetically satisfying and has recently been open to criticism on the grounds of its inadequate contribution to the social problems of Britain; but at least it managed to combine all executive, managerial, and planning functions to a high degree and also persuaded those authorities which had an essential contribution to make to the provision of all the required services to function more or less in accordance with the master plan timetable. However, there are not to be any more new towns; the idea of urban development corporations has been ruled out (e.g. in the London docklands) as they offend against the principles listed in the second background point above. Consequently the fact remains that any plan to 'rescue our cities', however well conceived, will on present showing fail because of the inability of the agencies concerned to work together.

The main difference between the economic locational approach and the planning approach is probably just this: that the planner is no longer interested in two-dimensional solutions if they are incapable of being put into practice, whereas the economist can still analyse the problem in terms of either a free market solution or a planned end-state without worrying unduly about the mechanisms for implementation. Unfortunately, economic analysis increasingly tends to take place in a political vacuum, often ignores the short term constraints of public finance, and seldom is concerned with the social consequences of spatial rearrangements.

4. Support by social security agencies   The next background area is that of the personal social services and the income-maintaining activities of the Department of Health and Social Security and the Supplementary Benefits Commission. Throughout, this book has been concerned with individual poverty and deprivation. In this part of the conclusion an attempt has been made to show that there is likely to be a close connection between the level of individual and corporate incomes on the one hand and the prospects of urban renewal on the other. Underlying this approach has been the notion that the only way to achieve improvement is by raising the extent of active labour-force participation and the average level of earnings. There has been a deliberate omission of any consideration of the ways in which the public agencies deal with poverty, deprivation, discrimination, and the other manifestations of urban malaise (e.g. vandalism, mental disorders, community friction). It is taken for granted that those concerned with these matters will try to improve their performance in the interim period until something more permanent can be done – that they will recognise needs and dangers and act preventively and remedially. This may well be an unrealistic assumption, but it will have to do. Equally, it is assumed that these departments of state and local government, together with voluntary agencies, will always cope with any residual problems, however successful the urban regeneration process may be.

5. Necessity for interference   Lastly, in some contributions to the debate (although not often in the contributions to this book) there are undertones to the effect that there ought not to be any interference with free market forces, which alone can provide something like optimal locations for industry and services and satisfy the aspirations of individuals. Again, this is an argument that is likely to be advanced by academic economists, whether of the school of Milton Friedman in the United States or of the Institute of Economic Affairs in the United Kingdom. However true it may be in some abstract sense that the application of such an attitude could raise the gross national product fastest in the short run, no planner will accept this solution. The social costs are too high. It is tantamount to abandoning the cities. The progress of emigration has gone far, but there are still probably something like 5 million people living in inner city areas (and more than 30 per cent of the population live in conurbations as a whole). It would be totally irresponsible to abandon these people to their fate; and there is no doubt as to what this fate would be – living for the rest of their lives amid increasing dereliction and danger, unable to earn a wage enabling them to survive, increasingly dependent on the welfare services (if these can still operate) to save them from the grossest forms of deprivation, increasingly demoralised and quite possibly a very great danger to themselves and to others, as well as being the targets of attack. As it has so often been said, blight is contagious. It cannot be contained by barbed wire; and once the inner city has been allowed to decay completely the disease will spread, as it has begun to do in some British cities and has long done in North American ones.

It is therefore assumed that, however much certain interests may plead for 'grassing over the empty spaces' (either because they think that this is the best use for urban land or because they think that it will raise national income fastest), this is a solution expressly rejected by the Inner Areas Studies teams, by successive central and local governments, and by all planners in the field. It is a purely academic view and requires no further discussion in this book.

21.7 Conclusion

This is perhaps as far as it is necessary to go. The chapters themselves present their general and local analysis. They blame various agencies for what has happened, according to the local experience of the author, his political views, and his economic beliefs. Equally, the solutions that they advocate (if any) differ in the same manner. It has not been the purpose in this exercise to settle the question of new towns versus inner cities, development areas versus decaying conurbations, manufacturing industries versus the tertiary sector, and other artificial polarisations of policies. It is hardly necessary to stress the need for much more research – academics always want more money for research. However, now, following the Inner Area Studies reports, there is a very clear demand from the Department of the Environment itself for more research work to be done; and there is a long list of topics about which there still seems to be much ignorance, despite all the work already carried out. This book has presented only a fraction of what has been done, and the references contain much as yet unpublished work. Yet, it is only in the abstract models of the spatial analysts that neat formulae have emerged. The practitioners recognise that they do not know many of the simplest basic data that they need for a meaningful analysis for their own purposes; and they further recognise that many other topics are not susceptible to desk research techniques at all but require more action research, more monitored experiments, and more surveys of firms, individuals, and local organisations. If this seems a confession

478   *The Inner City: Employment and Industry*

of failure, it is not meant to be. Events have overtaken planners and economists alike. What were thought to be fixed parameters like continuous economic and demographic growth have become very uncertain, and on the political/psychological front there are even more fundamental and far-reaching changes. They have recognised this and are ready for a fresh beginning, to which this book forms an introduction.

Bibliography

ADAMS, W. and DIRLAM, J. (1966), 'Big steel, invention and innovation', *Quarterly Journal of Economics*, vol. 80, no. 2, May.

ALDRICH, H. (1973), 'Employment effects of white-owned businesses in the black ghetto', *American Journal of Sociology*, vol. 78, May.

ALDRICH, H. (1975), 'Ecological succession in racially changing neighbourhoods: a review of the literature', *Urban Affairs Quarterly*, vol. 10, March.

ALDRICH, H. (1976a), 'Ecological succession and middle man minorities: new Commonwealth origin shopkeepers in Wandsworth', paper presented at a Centre for Environmental Studies 'Inner City Employment' seminar.

ALDRICH, H. (1976b), 'Testing the middleman minority model of Asian entreprenurial behaviour: preliminanry results from Wandsworth, England', unpublished working paper (Oxford: Nuffield College).

ALDRICH, H. and REISS, A. J. Jr (1976), 'Continuities in the study of ecological succession: changes in the race composition of neighbourhoods and their businesses', *American Journal of Sociology*, vol. 81, January.

AMBROSE, P. and COLENUTT, R. (1975), *The Property Machine* (London: Penguin).

ATKINS, D. H. W. (1973), 'Employment change in branch and parent manufacturing plants in the UK: 1966–71', *Trade and Industry*, vol. 12, pp. 437–9.

BACON, R. and ELTIS, W. (1975), 'How we went wrong', *Sunday Times*, 2 and 9 November.

BAIN, J. S. (1966), *International Differences in Industrial Structure: Eight Nations in the 1950s* (New Haven: Yale University Press).

BANNOCK, G. (1976), *The Smaller Businesses in Britain and Germany* (London: Wilton House for the Anglo-German Foundation).

BERRY, B. J. L. and COHEN, Y. S. (1973), 'Decentralisation of commerce and industry: the restructuring of metropolitan America', in L. H. Masotti and J. N. Hadden, *The Urbanization of the Suburbs*, Urban Affairs Annual Reviews, vol. 7. (Beverly Hills, Cal.: Sage Publications).

BERRY, B. J. L., PARSONS, S. J., and PLATT, R. H. (1968), *The Impact of Urban Renewal on Small Business: the Hyde Park-Kenwood case* (Chicago: Centre for Urban Studies, University of Chicago).

BERTHOUD, R. (1978), *Training Adults for Skilled Jobs* (London: Policy Studies Institute).

BEYNON, H. (1973), *Working for Ford* (London: Penguin).

BIRCH, D., ATKINSON, R., SANSTRÖM, S. and STACK, L. (1974), *The New Haven Laboratory: A Test-bed for Planning* (Lexington, Mass.: Lexington Books).

BLUMENFELD, D. E. (1972), 'Effects of road system designs on congestion and journey times in cities', unpublished PhD thesis (London: University College).

BOARD OF TRADE (1940), *Report of the Royal Commission on the Distribution of the Industrial Population* under the chairmanship of Sir Montague Barlow (the Barlow Report), Cmnd. 6153 (London: H. M. S. O.).

BOARD OF TRADE (1963), *The North-East: A Programme for Development and Growth* (London: HMSO).

BOGUE, D. J. (1959), *The Population of the United States* (Glencoe, Ill.: Free Press).

BOLTON COMMITTEE (1971), *Report of the Committee of Inquiry on Small Firms* (London: HMSO).

BONACICH, E. (1973), 'A theory of middleman minorities', *American Sociological Review*, vol. 38, October.

BOSANQUET, N. and DOERINGER, P. B. (1973), 'Is there a dual labour market in Great Britain?', *Economic Journal*, vol. 83, no. 330, June, pp. 421–35.

BOSWELL, J. (1971), *The Rise and Decline of Small Firms* (London: Allen and Unwin).

BRAMLEY, G. R. (1979), 'The inner city labour market', in C. Jones (ed.), *Urban Deprivation and the Inner City* (London: Croom Helm).

BROWN, A. J. (1972), *'The Framework of Regional Economics in the United Kingdom*, National Institute of Economic and Social Research (Cambridge: Cambridge University Press).

BROWN, R.; HAYTON, J.; BROWN, P.; and SANDY, C.(1976), *Small Businesses: Strategy for Survival* (London: Conservative Political Centre).

BUCK, T. W. (1970), 'Shift and share analysis: a guide to regional policy?', *Regional Studies*, vol. 4, pp. 446–7.

BULL, P. J. (1978), 'The spatial components of intra-urban manufacturing change: suburbanisation on Clydeside, 1958–68', *Transactions of the Institute of British Geographers*, new series, vol. 3, pp. 91–100.

BURN, S. M. (1972), 'Local authority housing: implications for labour mobility', unpublished MPhil thesis (London: Department of Town Planning, University College).

BURNS, T. and STALKER, G. M. (1961), *The Management of Innovation* (London: Tavistock).

BUSSIERE, R. (1970), *The Spatial Distribution of Urban Population* (Paris: Centre de Recherche d'Urbanisme).

CAMERON, G. C. (1973), 'Intra-urban location and the new plant', *Papers and Proceedings of the Regional Science Association*, vol. 29, pp. 125–43.

CAMERON, G. C. (1977a), 'Economic renewal in the inner city: Glasgow', *Architects' Journal*, vol. 165, pp. 215–7.

CAMERON, G. C. (1977b), 'The economy of the inner city: some policy dimensions', paper presented to the Institute of British Geographers' annual conference, Newcastle upon Tyne, January.

CAMERON, G. C. and EVANS, A. W. (1973), 'The British conurbation centres', *Regional Studies*, vol. 7, pp. 47–55.

CAMERON, G. C. and REID, G. L. (1966), *Scottish Economic Planning and the Attraction of Industry*, University of Glasgow Social and Economic Studies, No. 6 (Edinburgh: Oliver and Boyd).

CAMINA, M. (1974), 'Local authorities and the attraction of industry', *Progress in Planning*, vol. 3, pp. 83–182 (Oxford: Pergamon Press).

CARNEY, J., HUDSON, R. and TAYLOR, C. C. (1975), 'Inner-city employment situations: the case of the North-East', paper presented at a Centre for Environmental Studies 'Inner City Employment' seminar.

CAVES, R. (1969), 'Market organisation, performance and public policy,' in *The Brookings Report on the British Economy* (Washington, DC: Brookings Institution).

CENTRAL STATISTICAL OFFICE (1974), *Social Trends*, no. 5, (London: HMSO).

CHAMPION, A. G. (1976), 'Evolving patterns of population distribution in England and Wales, 1951-71', *Transactions of the Institute of British Geographers*, new series, vol. 1, pp. 401-32.

CHESHIRE, P. C. (1973), *Regional Unemployment Differences in Great Britain*, National Institute of Economic and Social Research Regional Papers 2 (Cambridge: Cambridge University Press).

CHISHOLM, P. C. (1973), 'Regional policies in an era of slow population growth and higher unemployment', *Regional Studies*, vol. 10, no. 2, pp. 201-14.

CHISHOLM, M. and OEPPEN, J. (1973), *The Changing Pattern of Employment, Regional Specialisation and Industrial Localisation in Brtiain* (London: Croom Helm).

CLARK, C. (1964-65), 'The location of industries and population', *Town Planning Review*, vol. 35, pp. 195-218.

CLARK, C. (1967), *Population Growth and Land Use* (London: Macmillan).

COMMUNITY DEVELOPMENT PROJECT (1975a) – Canning Town, *Canning Town to North Woolwich: The Aims of Industry* (London: Community Development Project, Home Office).

COMMUNITY DEVELOPMENT PROJECT (1975b) – Newham, *The Aims of Industry?* (London: Community Development Project, Home Office).

COMMUNITY DEVELOPMENT PROJECT (1975c) – Saltley, *Workers on the Scrapheap* (London: Community Development Project, Home Office).

COMMUNITY DEVELOPMENT PROJECT (1976), *The Costs of Industrial Change* (London: Community Development Project, Home Office).

COMMUNITY RELATIONS COMMISSION (1974), *Unemployment and Homelessness* (London: HMSO).

COOPER, A. (1964), 'R & D is more efficient in small companies', *Harvard Business Review*, vol. 42, May–June.

CREAMER, D. B. (1935), *Is Industry Decentralising?* (Philadelphia, Penn.: University of Pennsylvania).

CRIPPS, F. and TARLING, R. (1974), 'An analysis of the duration of male unemployment in Great Britain, 1932–73', *Economic Journal*, vol. 84, no. 2, June, pp. 289-316.

CULLINGWORTH, J. B. (1965), *English Housing Trends*, Occasional Papers on Social Administration, No. 13 (London: London School of Economics).

CULLINGWORTH, J. B. (1969), *Housing and Labour Mobility* (Paris: Organisation for Economic Co-operation and Development).

DALTON, M. and SEAMAN, J. M. (1973), 'The distribution of new Commonwealth immigrants in the London borough of Ealing, 1961–1966', *Transactions of the Institute of British Geographers*, vol. 58.

DANIEL, W. W. (1972), *Whatever Happened to the Workers in Woolwich?*, PEP Broadsheet 537 (London: Political and Economic Planning).

DANIEL, W. W. (1974), *A National Survey of the Unemployed* (London: Political and Economic Planning).

DANIEL, W. W. (1975), 'The PEP survey on inflation', unpublished paper.

DARLEY, G. and SAUNDERS, M. (1975), 'Conservation and jobs', *Built Environment Quarterly*, vol. 1, no. 3, September.

DARLEY, G. and SAUNDERS, M. (1976), 'Save report: conservation and jobs', *Built Environment Quarterly*, vol. 2, no. 3, September, pp. 211–27.

DEPARTMENT OF EMPLOYMENT (1970), *New Earnings Survey* (London: Department of Employment).

DEPARTMENT OF EMPLOYMENT (1974a), 'Vacancy study', *Department of Employment Gazette*, March, p. 223.

DEPARTMENT OF EMPLOYMENT (1974b), *New Earnings Survey* (London: Department of Employment).

DEPARTMENT OF EMPLOYMENT (1974c), 'Characteristics of the unemployed', *Department of Employment Gazette*, March.

DEPARTMENT OF EMPLOYMENT (1975), *The Changing Structure of the Labour Force*, Unit of Manpower Studies Project Report (London: Department of Employment).

DEPARTMENT OF EMPLOYMENT (1976a), 'The changed relationship between unemployment and vacancies', *Department of Employment Gazette*, vol. 74, no. 10, pp. 1093–9.

DEPARTMENT OF EMPLOYMENT (1976b), *New Earnings Survey* (London: Department of Employment).

DEPARTMENT OF EMPLOYMENT (1977), *New Earnings Survey* (London: Department of Employment).

DEPARTMENT OF INDUSTRY (1975), *Regional Development Incentives* (London: HMSO).

DEPARTMENT OF INDUSTRY (1976), 'The direct impact of the relocation of manufacturing firms from London to new and expanding towns', unpublished research paper.

DEPARTMENT OF THE ENVIRONMENT (1975), *The Manning of Public Services in London* (London: Department of the Environment).

DEPARTMENT OF THE ENVIRONMENT (1976), *British Cities: Urban Population and Employment Trends, 1951–71*, Research Report, No. 10 (London: Department of the Environment).

DEPARTMENT OF THE ENVIRONMENT (1977a), *Inner Area Studies: Liverpool, Birmingham and Lambeth: Final Reports* (London: HMSO).

DEPARTMENT OF THE ENVIRONMENT (1977b), *Policy for the Inner Cities*, Cmnd 6845 (London: HMSO).

DICKEN, P. and LLOYD, P. E. (1978), 'Inner metropolitan industrial change, enterprise structures and policy issues: case studies of Manchester and Merseyside', *Regional Studies*, vol. 12, pp. 181–98.

DOCKLANDS DEVELOPMENT TEAM (1975), *Work and Industry in East London* (London: Greater London Council).

DONNISON, D. V. (1964), 'The movement of households in England', in D. V. Donnison *et al.*, *Essays on Housing*, Occasional Papers on Social Administration, no. 9 (London: London School of Economics).

DUGMORE, K. (ed.) (1975), *The Migration and Distribution of Socio-economic Groups in Greater London*, GLC Research Memorandum 443 (London: Greater London Council).

DUNNELL, K. and HEAD, E. (1975), *Employers and Employment Services*, SS 1012 (London: Social Survey Division, Office of Population Censuses and Surveys.

DURHAM COUNTY COUNCIL (1976), *County Structure Plan: Report of Survey* (Durham: Durham County Council).

ECONOMY GROUP, SOUTH-EAST JOINT PLANNING TEAM (1976), *Report* (London: Department of the Environment).

EDWARDS, M. (1977), 'Vagaries of the inner city land market', *Architects' Journal*, vol. 165, pp. 206–7.

ELEY, P., FALK, N., WILLIAMS, B., and WORTHINGTON, J. (eds) (1978), 'Use of redundant buildings for small enterprises', *Architects' Journal*, vol. 31, no. 168, August.

EVANS, A. (1967), 'Myths about employment in London', *Journal of Transport Economics and Policy*, vol. 1, no. 2, May, pp. 1–12.

EVANS, A. (1973), *The Economics of Residential Location* (London: Macmillan).

EVERSLEY, D. E. C. (1971), 'Population changes and regional policies since the war', *Regional Studies*, vol. 5, pp. 211–28.

EVERSLEY, D. E. C. (1972), 'Rising costs and static incomes: some economic consequences of regional planning in London', *Urban Studies*, vol. 9, no. 3.

EVERSLEY, D. E. C. (1973), 'Problems of social planning in Inner London', in D. V. Donnison and D. E. C. Eversley (eds.), *London: Urban Patterns, Problems and Policies* (London: Heinemann).

EXPENDITURE COMMITTEE (1973), *Trade and Industry Sub-Committee, Minutes of Evidence*, July, (London: HMSO).

FAGG, J. J. (1973), 'Spatial changes in manufacturing employment in Greater Leicester, 1947–70', *East Midland Geographer*, vol. 5, part 8, pp. 440–15.

FALK, N. (1974), 'Community as developer', *Built Environment*, February.

FALK, N. (1978a), *Think Small*, Fabian Tract 453.

FALK, N. (1978b), *Forming a Centre for Small Enterprise in Covent Garden* (London: Urbed Research Trust).

FALK, N. (1975), 'Conservation: another industrial revolution?', *Built Environment Quarterly*, vol. 1, no. 3, September.

FALK, N. and MARTINOS, H. (1975), *Inner City: Local Government and Economic Renewal*, Fabian Research Series 328 (London: Fabian Society).

FIRN, J. R. (1975), 'External control and regional development: the case of Scotland', *Environment and Planning*, vol. 7, pp. 393–414.

FIRN, J. R. (1976), *Economic Microdata Analysis and Urban-Regional Change: The Experience of GURIE in 'Establishment-based Research: Conference Proceedings'*, Urban and Regional Discussion Paper, No. 22 (Glasgow: Department of Social and Economic Research, University of Glasgow).

FIRN, J. R. and HUGHES, J. T. (1973), 'Employment growth and decentralisation of manufacturing industry: some paradoxes', *Papers from the Urban Economics Conference 1973*, Centre for Environmental Studies Conference Paper No. 9. vol. 2, pp. 483–518, (London: Centre for Environmental Studies).

484   *Bibliography*

FIRN, J. R. and SWALES, J. K. (1978), 'The formation of new manufacturing establishments in the central Clydeside and West Midlands conurbations, 1963–72: a comparative analysis', *Regional Studies*, vol. 12, pp. 199–214.

FOREMAN-PECK, J. S. and GRIPAIOS, P. A. (1977), 'Inner city problems and inner city policies', *Regional Studies*, vol. 11, pp. 401–12.

FOSTER, C. and RICHARDSON, R. (1973), 'Employment trends in London in the 1960s and their relevance to the future', in D. V. Donnison and D. E. C. Eversley (eds), *London: Urban Patterns, Problems and Policies* (London: Heinemann).

FOY, N. (1977), 'Greenwich: friend of the small company', *The Times*, 20 June.

FRANKLIN, M. and STAFFORD, F. (1977), 'Building for inner city industry', *Architects' Journal*, vol. 165, no. 2, February, pp. 209–14.

FRAZIER, E. F. (1957), *Black Bourgeoisie* (Glencoe, Ill.: Free Press).

FRIEDLANDER, D. and ROSHIER, R. J. (1967), 'A study of internal migration in England and Wales, Part II: Recent internal migrants: their movements and characteristics', *Population Studies*, vol. 20, pp. 45–59.

GALBRAITH, J. K. (1957), *American Capitalism* (London: Hamish Hamilton).

GALBRAITH, J. K. (1967), *The New Industrial State* (London: Hamish Hamilton).

GILJE, E. K. (1975), *Migration Patterns in and around London*, GLC Research Memorandum 470 (London: Greater London Council).

GODDARD, J. B. and SPENCE, N. A. (1976), 'A national perspective of changes in the occupational and industrial structure of employment in urban labour markets', paper presented at a CES seminar in York.

GOERING, J. M. (1978), 'The London ghetto?', *Comparative Urban Research*, vol. 5, pp. 2–3.

GORDON, D. M. (1972), *Theories of Poverty and Underemployment: Orthodox, Radical and Dual Labor Market Perspectives* (Lexington, Mass.: D. C. Heath).

GOULD, P. R. and WHITE, R. R. (1968), 'The mental maps of British school learners', *Regional Studies*, vol. 2, pp. 161–82.

GREATER LONDON COUNCIL (1970), *Greater London Development Plan: Report of Studies*, (London: Greater London Council).

GREATER LONDON COUNCIL (1971–72), 'Greater London transportation survey: home interview survey', unpublished survey.

GREATER LONDON COUNCIL (1973), *Greater London Development Plan: Report of the Panel of Inquiry*, under the chairmanship of Frank Layfield (the Layfield Report), (London: HMSO).

GREATER LONDON COUNCIL (1974), *Strategic Housing Plan: Report of Studies* (London: Policy Studies Unit, Greater London Council).

GREATER LONDON COUNCIL (1975), *Employment in Greater London and the Rest of the South-East Region*, Submission to Strategy for the South-East Review (London: Greater London Council).

GREATER MANCHESTER COUNCIL (1975), *County Structure Plan: Report of Survey, Employment and the Economy* (Manchester: Greater Manchester County Planning Department).

GRIPAIOS, P. A. (1977a), 'The closure of firms in the inner city: the south-east London case, 1970–75', *Regional Studies*, vol. 11, pp. 1–6.

GRIPAIOS, P. A. (1977b), 'Industrial decline in London: an examination of its causes', *Urban Studies*, vol. 14, pp. 181–90.

GRIPAIOS, P. A. (1977c), Review of 'Employment in Southwark: a strategy for the future', *Regional Studies*, vol. 11, p. 69.

HADJIFOTIOU, N. and ROBINSON, H. (1972), *Employment and Housing Conditions in Four Selected Labour Market Areas in England and Wales*, Housing and Labour Mobility Study Working Paper, No. 5 (London: Department of Geography, University College).

HALL, P. (1962), *The Industries of London since 1861* (London: Hutchinson).

HALL, P. (1964), 'Industrial London', in J. Coppock and H. Prince (eds), *Greater London* (London: Faber).

HALL, P. (1975), 'Migration', *New Society*, vol. 31, no. 644, 6 February.

HALL, P.; GRACEY, H.; DREWETT, R.; and THOMAS, R. (1973), *The Containment of Urban England, Vol. I: Urban and Metropolitan Growth Processes* (London: Allen and Unwin).

HALL, R. E. (1970), 'Why is the unemployment rate so high at full employment?' *Brookings Papers on Economic Activity*, No. 3, pp. 369–402 (Washington, DC: Brookings Institution).

HARRIS, A. I. and CLAUSEN, R. (1967), *Labour Mobility in Great Britain: 1953–63* (London: HMSO).

HARRIS, D. F. and TAYLOR, F. J. (1976), *The Service Sector: Its Changing Role as a Source of Employment* (Leeds: Leeds Regional Office, DOE).

HARTSHORN, T. A. (1971), 'Inner city residential structure and decline', *Annals of the Association of American Geographers*, vol. 61, pp. 72–96.

HEDGES, B.; BERTHOUD, R.; BISSONET, D.; and WILSON, M. (1974), *Housing in Westminster in 1972* (London: Westminster City Council/Social and Community Planning Research).

HENDERSON, R. A. (1974), 'Industrial overspill from Glasgow, 1958–68', *Urban Studies*, vol. 11, pp. 61–80.

HILL, M., HARRISON, R. M., SARGEANT, A. V. and TALBOT, V. (1973), *Men Out of Work: A Study of Unemployment in Three English Towns* (Cambridge: Cambridge University Press).

HOLTERMANN, S. (1975), 'Areas of urban deprivation in Great Britain: the analysis of 1971 census data', *Social Trends*, no. 6, pp. 33–47 (London: HMSO).

HOLTERMANN, S. (1978), 'Unemployment in urban areas', *Urban Studies*, vol. 15, pp. 231–3.

HOOVER, E. M. (1975), *An Introduction to Regional Economics*, 2nd edn (New York: Alfred Knopf).

HOOVER, E. M. and VERNON, R. (1959), *Anatomy of a Metropolis: The Changing Distribution of People and Jobs Within the New York Metropolitan Region* (Cambridge, Mass.: Harvard University Press).

HOOVER, E. M. and VERNON, R. (1960), *The New York Regional Study Plan* (Cambridge, Mass.: Harvard University Press).

HORWOOD, E. M. and BOYCE, R. P. (1959), *Studies of the Central Business District and Urban Freeway Development* (Washington, DC: University of Washington Press).

HOWARD, R. S. (1968), *The Movement of Manufacturing Industry in the United Kingdom, 1945–65* (London: HMSO).

HUDSON, R. with JOHNSON, M. R. D.; BRETT, D. V.; MACOURT, M. P. A.; PATTISON, D.; ROBINSON, J. F. F.; and TOWNSEND, A. R. (1976), *New Towns in North-East England*, 2 vols (Durham: North-East Area Study, University of Durham).

HUNTER, L. C. and REID, G. L. (1968), *Urban Worker Mobility* (Paris: Organisation for Economic Co-operation and Development).

IBM/URBED (1977), *Creating Work through Small Enterprise*, seminar report (obtainable from URBED, 12–13 Henrietta Street, London WC2).

ISLINGTON PLANNING DEPARTMENT (1975), *Employment*, Topic Paper, No. 6 (London: Borough of Islington, November).

JACOBS, J. (1972), *The Economy of Cities* (London: Pelican).

JAMES, F. J. and HUGHES, J. W. (1973), 'The process of employment change: an empirical analysis', *Land Economics*, vol. 49, pp. 404–13.

JEWKES, J.; SAWERS, D.; and STILLERMAN, R. (1969), *The Sources of Innovation* (London: Macmillan).

JOHNSON, J. H.; SALT, J.; and WOOD, P. A. (1974), *Housing and the Migration of Labour in England and Wales* (Farnborough: Saxon House).

JONES, P. E. and JUDGES, A. V. (1935), 'London population in the seventeenth century', *Economic History Review*, vol. 6, pp. 58–62.

KAIN, J. F. (1968), 'The distribution and movement of jobs and industry', in J. Q. Wilson (ed.), *The Metropolitan Enigma* (Cambridge, Mass.: Harvard University Press); reprinted in J. F. Kain (1975), *Essays on Urban Spatial Structure* (Cambridge, Mass.: Ballinger).

KEEBLE, D. E. (1968), 'Industrial decentralisation and the metropolis: the north-west London case', *Transactions of the Institute of British Geographers*, vol. 44, pp. 1–54.

KEEBLE, D. E. (1969), 'Local industrial linkage and manufacturing growth in outer London', *Town Planning Review*, vol. 40, pp. 163–88.

KEEBLE, D. E. (1971), 'Employment mobility in Britain', in M. Chisholm and G. Manners (eds), *Spatial Problems of the British Economy* (Cambridge: Cambridge University Press).

KEEBLE, D. E. (1975), 'Industrial mobility: in which industries has plant location changed most?: a comment', *Regional Studies*, vol. 9, pp. 297–9.

KEEBLE, D. E. (1976), *Industrial Location and Planning in the United Kingdom* (London: Methuen).

KEEBLE, D. E. (1977), 'Spatial policy in Britain: regional or urban?', *Area*, vol. 9, pp. 3–8.

KITAWEGA, E. M. and BOGUE, D. J. (1955), *Suburbanisation of Manufacturing Activities within Standard Metropolitan Areas* (Oxford, Ohio: Scripps Foundation, Miami University).

KITCHING, J. (1967), 'Why do mergers miscarry?', *Havard Business Review*, vol. 45, no. 6 (November–December); reprinted in *Harvard Business Review* Mergers and Acquisitions series (reprints from *Harvard Business Review*, Boston, 1961–68) (Boston, Mass.: Graduate School of Business Administration, Harvard University, 1973).

LADINSKY, J. (1967), 'Occupational determinants of geographical mobility among professional workers', *American Sociological Review*, vol. 32, no. 2, April, pp. 253–64.

LAMBERT, C. (1977a), *Inner Cities*, Bibliography No. 194 (London: Department of the Environment).

LAMBERT, C. (1977b), *Inner Cities*, Bibliography No. 194, Supplement No. 1 (London: Department of the Environment).

LAMBERT, C. (1978), *Inner Cities*, Bibliography No. 194, Supplement No. 2 (London: Department of the Environment).

LAMBETH INNER AREA STUDY (1975a), *Changes in Socio-economic Structure*, IAS/LA/2 (London: Department of the Environment).

LAMBETH INNER AREA STUDY (1975b), *Labour Market Study*, IAS/LA/4 (London: Department of the Environment).

LAMBETH INNER AREA STUDY (1975c), *Poverty and Multiple Deprivation*, IAS/LA/10 (London: Department of the Environment).

LAMBETH INNER AREA STUDY (1976), *London's Inner Area: Problems and Possibilities* (London: Department of the Environment).

LAMBETH INNER AREA STUDY (1977a), *Local Employers' Study*, IAS/LA/16 (London: Department of the Environment).

LAMBETH INNER AREA STUDY (1977b), *Second Report on Multiple Deprivation*, IAS/LA/15 (London: Department of the Environment).

LANSING, J. B. and MORGAN, J. N. (1967), 'The effect of geographic mobility on income', *Journal of Human Resources*, vol. 2, no. 4, pp. 449–60.

LAWTON, R. (1968), 'The journey-to-work in Britain: some trends and problems', *Regional Studies*, vol. 2, pp. 27–40.

LEE, T. R. (1977), *Race and Residence: The Concentration and Dispersal of Immigrants in London* (Oxford: Clarendon).

LEIBENSTEIN, H. (1966), 'Allocative efficiency vs "x" efficiency', *American Economic Review*, vol. 56, no. 3, June, pp. 391–415.

LEONE, R. (1971), 'Location of manufacturing in the New York manufacturing region', unpublished PhD thesis (New Haven, Connecticut: Yale University).

LEONE, R. and STRUYK, R. J. (1976), 'The incubator hypothesis: evidence from five SMSAs', *Urban Studies*, vol. 13, no. 3, pp. 325–32.

LESSEM, R. (1977), 'Fruits of conservation', *Accountancy Age,* vol. 8, no. 46, 19 November.

LEVER, W. F. (1972), 'Industrial movement, spatial association and functional linkages', *Regional Studies*, vol. 6, pp. 371–84.

LEVER, W. F. (1974), 'Manufacturing linkages and the search for suppliers and markets', in F. E. Hamilton (ed.), *Spatial Perspectives on Industrial Organisation and Decision-making* (London: Wiley).

LICHTENBERG, R. M. (1960), *One-tenth of a Nation* (Cambridge, Mass.: Harvard University Press for the Regional Plan Association).

LITTLE, A. D. (1977), *New Technology-based Firms in the United Kingdom and Federal Republic of Germany* (London: Wilton House).

LIVERPOOL INNER AREA STUDY (1977a), *Social Area Analysis*, IAS/LI/22 (London: Department of the Environment).

LIVERPOOL INNER AREA STUDY (1977b), *Change or Decay: Final Report of the Liverpool Inner Area Study* (London: HMSO).

LIVERPOOL INNER AREA STUDY (1977c), *Economic Development of the Inner Area*, IAS/LI/21 (London: Department of the Environment).

LIVERPOOL INNER AREA STUDY (1977d), *Getting a Job*, IAS/LI/20 (London: Department of the Environment).

LLOYD, P. E. and MASON, C. M. (1978), 'Manufacturing industry in the inner city: a case study of Greater Manchester', *Transactions of the Institute of British Geographers*, new series, vol. 3, pp. 66–90.

LOGAN, M. I. (1966), 'Locational behaviour of manufacturing firms in urban areas', *Annals of the Association of American Geographers*, vol. 46, no. 3, pp. 451–66.

LOMAS, G. (1974), *The Inner City* (London: London Council of Social Services).

McDERMOTT, P. J. (1977), 'Regional variations in enterprise: electronics firms in Scotland, London and the outer metropolitan area', unpublished PhD thesis (Cambridge: University of Cambridge).

McDERMOTT, P. J. (1978), 'Changing manufacturing enterprise in the metropolitan environment: the case of electronics firms in London', *Regional Studies*, vol. 12, no. 5, pp. 541–50.

MACKAY, D. A. *et al.* (1971). *Labour Markets under Different Employment Conditions* (London: Allen and Unwin).

MACKAY, D. I. and REID, G. L. (1972), 'Redundancy, unemployment and manpower policy', *Economic Journal*, Vol. 82, no. 328 (December).

MACKAY, R. R. and SEGAL, N. (1976), *United Kingdom Regional Policy: The Northern Region and the EEC*, Newcastle Discussion Papers in Economics, No. 17 (Newcastle: Department of Economics, University of Newcastle).

McKEAN, R. (1975), *The Impact of Comprehensive Development Area Policies on Industry in Glasgow*, Urban and Regional Studies Discussion Paper, No. 15 (Glasgow: Department of Social and Economic Research, University of Glasgow).

MANNERS, G. (1976), 'Reinterpreting the regional problem', *Three Banks Review*, no. 111.

MANPOWER SERVICES COMMISSION (1976), *Towards a Comprehensive Manpower Policy* (London: Manpower Services Commission).

MANPOWER SERVICES COMMISSION (1977), *Young People and Work* (the Holland Report) (London: Manpower Services Commission).

MANPOWER SERVICES COMMISSION (1978), *Training for Skills: A Programme for Action* (London: Manpower Services Commission).

MANSFIELD, E. (1963), 'Size of firm, market structure and innovation', *Journal of Political Economy*, vol. 71, December, pp. 556–76.

MARTIN, J. E. (1957), 'Industry in inner London', *Town and Country Planning*, vol. 25, pp. 125–8.

MARTIN, J. (1966), *Greater London: An Industrial Geography* (London: G. Bell and Sons).

MARTIN, J. (1969), 'Size of plant and location of industry in Great Britain', *Tijdschrift voor Economische en Sociale Geografie*, vol. 60, no. 6, pp. 369–74.

MARTIN, J. and SEAMAN, J. M. (1975), 'The fate of the London factory: twenty years of change', *Town and Country Planning*, vol. 43, November, pp. 492–5.

MASSEY, D. B. and MEEGAN, R. A. (1979), 'The geography of Industrial reorganisation: the spatial effects of the restructuring of the electrical engineering sector under the Industrial Reorganisation Corporation', *Progress in Planning*, vol. 10, Part 3 (Oxford: Pergamon).

MERRETT, A. J. and LEHR, M. E. (1971), *The Private Company Today: An Economic Investigation into the Economic Position of the Unquoted Company in the United Kingdom* (London: Gower Press).

MERSEYSIDE COUNTY COUNCIL (1975a), *Merseyside Structure Plan: Draft Report of Survey, Economic* (Liverpool: Merseyside County Council).

MERSEYSIDE COUNTY COUNCIL (1975b), *Merseyside Structure Plan: Stage One Report* (Liverpool: Merseyside County Council).

MILLAR, J. and MELLON, T. (1970), 'Manchester: survey of a city's industry', *Journal of the Town Planning Institute*, vol. 56, pp. 384–8.

MILLS, E. S. (1970), 'Urban density functions', *Urban Studies*, vol. 7, no. 1, February, pp. 5–20.

MINISTRY OF HOUSING AND LOCAL GOVERNMENT (1965), *Report of the Committee on Housing in Greater London* (the Milner Holland Report) (London: HMSO).

MINISTRY OF HOUSING AND LOCAL GOVERNMENT (1969), *Council Housing: Purposes, Procedures and Priorities*, Central Housing Advisory Committee (London: HMSO).

MOBBS, G. N. (1976), *Industrial Investment: A Case Study in Factory Buildings*, Slough Industrial Estates, February.

MOORE, B. and RHODES, J. (1973), 'Evaluating the effects of British regional policy', *Economic Journal*, vol. 83, pp. 87–110.

MOORE, B.; RHODES, J.; TARLING, R.; and WILKINSON, F. (1978), 'A return to full employment?', *Economic Policy Review*, no. 4, pp. 22–76 (Cambridge: Department of Applied Economics, University of Cambridge).

MORTLOCK, D. (1972), 'Employment changes in Greater London', *Quarterly Bulletin of the Intelligence Unit, Greater London Council*, no. 20, September, pp. 16–26.

MORTON-WILLIAMS, J. and STOWELL, R. (1974), *Small Heath, Birmingham: An Inner Area Study* (London: Department of the Environment).

MOSES, L. and WILLIAMSON, H. (1967), 'The location of economic activity in cities', *American Economic Review*, vol. 57, May, pp. 211—22.

MUKHERJEE, S. (1972), *Making Labour Markets Work* (London: Political and Economic Planning).

MUKHERJEE, S. (1974), *There's Work to be Done: Unemployment and Manpower Policies* (London: Manpower Services Commission).

MUKHERJEE, S. (1976), *Government and Labour Markets* (London: Political and Economic Planning).

NELSON, R. R. (1969), 'The economics of invention: a survey of the literature', *Journal of Business*, vol. 32, April.

NORTHERN REGION STRATEGY TEAM (1975), *The Characteristics of the Unemployed in the Northern Region, 1966–74*, Technical Report, No. 6 (Newcastle upon Tyne: HMSO, September).

NORTHERN REGION STRATEGY TEAM (1976), *Causes of the Recent Improvement in the Rate of Unemployment in the Northern Region Relative to Great Britain*, Technical Report, No. 11 (Newcastle upon Tyne: HMSO).

NORTHERN REGION STRATEGY TEAM (1977), *Strategic Plan for the Northern Region*, 5 vols (Newcastle upon Tyne: HMSO).

O'CLEIREACAIN, C. (1974), 'Labour market trends in London and the rest of the South-East', *Urban Studies*, vol. 11, no. 3, October, pp. 329–39.

OFFICE OF POPULATION CENSUSES AND SURVEYS (1973), *Census 1971: England and Wales: County Reports: Greater London* (London: HMSO).

OFFICE OF POPULATION CENSUSES AND SURVEYS (1975), *General Household Survey: 1972* (London: HMSO).

OFFICE OF POPULATION CENSUSES AND SURVEYS (1975), *General Household Survey: 1972* (London: HMDO).

OI, W. (1962), 'Labour as a quasi-fixed factor', *Journal of Political Economy*, vol. 70, December, pp. 538–55.

ORGANISATION FOR ECONOMIC CO-OPERATION AND DEVELOPMENT (1974), *Year Book of Labour Statistics* (Paris: OECD).

PENNANCE, F. G. and GRAY, H. (1968), *Choice in Housing* (London: Institute of Economic Affairs).

PRAIS, S. J. (1976), *The Evolution of Giant Firms in Great Britain* (Cambridge: Cambridge University Press).

REDDING, B. G. (1971), *A Study of Industrial Traffic Generation in London*, GLC Research Memorandum 292 (London: Department of Planning and Transportation, Greater London Council).

REDER, M. (1955), 'The theory of occupational wage differentials', *American Economic Review*, vol. 44, pp. 833–52.

REEDER, L. (1954), 'Industrial location trends in Chicago in comparison to population growth', *Land Economics*, vol. 30, pp. 177–82.

REES, A. R. (1966), 'Information networks in labor markets', *American Economic Review*, vol. 45, pp. 559–66.

REES, A. R. and SHULTZ, G. (1970), *Workers and Wages in an Urban Labour Market* (Chicago, Ill.: University of Chicago Press).

REEVE, D. E. (1974), 'An industrial geography of Greater Manchester with particular reference to recent changes', unpublished MA thesis (Manchester: University of Manchester).

RILEY, R. C. (1973), *Industrial Geography* (London: Chatto and Windus).

ROCHDALE METROPOLITAN BOROUGH (1974), *Obsolete Industrial Areas* (Rochdale: Borough of Rochdale).

ROLT, L. T. C. (1970), *Victorian Engineering* (London: Penguin).

ROSE, K. E. (1976), 'The economic situation in the West Midlands', paper presented at a Regional Studies Association conference on 'The Economic Crisis and Local Manufacturing', July.

ROY, D. (1974), *State Holding Companies*, Young Fabian Pamphlet 40 (London: Fabian Society).

ROYAL TOWN PLANNING INSTITUTE (1976), *Planning and the Future*, Discussion Paper prepared by a working group under the chairmanship of Sylvia Law (London: RTPI).

SAMUELS, J. M. and SMYTH, D. J. (1968), 'Profits, variability of profits and firm size', *Economica*, vol. 35, May.

SANT, M. (1975), *Industrial Movement and Regional Development: The British Case* (Oxford: Pergamon).

SCHERER, F. M. (1965), 'Firm size, market structure, opportunity and the output of patented inventions', *American Economic Review*, vol. 55, no. 5, pp. 1097–25.

SCHNORE, L. F. and KLAFF, V. Z. (1972), 'Suburbanisation in the sixties: a preliminary analysis', *Land Economics*, vol. 48, pp. 23–9.

SCHUMACHER, E. F. (1974), *Small is Beautiful* (London: Sphere Books).

SCIENCE OF SCIENCE FOUNDATION (1970), *Technological Innovation and the Economy*, proceedings of a Science of Science Foundation symposium on 'Technological Innovation and the Growth of the Economy', edited by M. Goldsmith (Chichester: Wiley Interscience).

SCOTTISH DEVELOPMENT DEPARTMENT (1963), *Central Scotland: A Programme for Development and Growth* (Edinburgh: HMSO).

SHANKLAND, G.; WILLMOTT, P.; and JORDAN, D. (1977), *Inner London: Policies for Dispersal and Balance: Final Report of the Lambeth Inner Area Study* (London: HMSO).

SHEPHERD, J.; WESTAWAY, J.; and LEE, T. (1974), *A Social Atlas of London* (Oxford: Clarendon).

SIMMONS, D. A. (1976), *Economic Power* (Northolt, Middlesex: Gemini).

SIMON, H. (1960), 'The corporation: will it be managed by machines?' in *Management and Corporations*, 1935 (New York: McGraw-Hill); reprinted in H. J. Leavitt and L. R. Pondy (eds), *Readings in Managerial Psychology* (Chicago), Ill.: University of Chicago).

SIMON, N. W. H. (1977), 'The relative level and changes in earnings in London and Great Britain', *Regional Studies*, vol. 11, pp. 87–98.

SMITH, B. M. D. (1974), *Employment Opportunities in the Inner Area Study Part of Small Heath, Birmingham, in 1974*, Centre for Urban and Regional Studies Research Memorandum, No. 38 (Birmingham: Centre for Urban and Regional Studies).

SMITH, B. M. D. (1975), *Youth Employment in Birmingham in 1972: An Exploration of the Statistics and their Implications*, Centre for Urban and Regional Studies Research Memorandum, No. 45 (Birmingham: Centre for Urban and Regional Studies).

SMITH, B. M. D. (1977a), *The Inner City Economic Problem: A Framework for Analysis and Local Authority Policy*, Centre for Urban and Regional Studies Research Memorandum, No. 56 (Birmingham: Centre for Urban and Regional Studies).

SMITH, B. M. D. (1977b), *Premises in Manufacturing and Related Uses in the Small Heath Planning District, Birmingham 1958–75*, Centre for Urban and Regional Studies Research Memorandum No. 59 (Birmingham: Centre for Urban and Regional Studies).

SMITH, B. M. D.; RUDDY, S. A.; and BLACK, J. (1974), *Industrial Relocation in Birmingham*, Centre for Urban and Regional Studies Research Memorandum, No. 31 (Birmingham: Centre for Urban and Regional Studies).

SMITH, D. J. (1974), *Racial Disadvantage in Employment* (London: Political and Economic Planning).

SOUTH-EAST JOINT PLANNING TEAM (1971), *Strategic Plan for the South-East: Studies*, Vol. 5: *Report of Economic Consultants Ltd* (London: HMSO).

SOUTH-EAST JOINT PLANNING TEAM (1976), *Strategy for the South-East: 1976 Review* (London: HMSO).

SOUTHWARK TRADES COUNCIL and ROBERTS, J. C. (1976), *Employment in Southwark* (London: Southwark Trades Council).

STONE, P. A. (1970), *Urban Development in Britain: Standards, Costs and Resources* (Cambridge: Cambridge University Press).

STONE, P. A. (1975), 'The implications for the conurbations of population changes (with particular reference to London)', paper presented at a Regional Studies Association conference on 'Population Decline', July.

STRATHCLYDE REGIONAL COUNCIL (1976a), *Strathclyde Regional Report* (Glasgow: Strathclyde Regional Council).

STRATHCLYDE REGIONAL COUNCIL (1976b), *Development Strategy* (Glasgow: Strathclyde Regional Council).

STRATHCLYDE REGIONAL COUNCIL (1976c), *Economic Policy* (Glasgow: Strathclyde Regional Council).

STRUYK, R. J. and JAMES, F. J. (1975), *Intrametropolitan Industrial Location* (Lexington, Mass.: Lexington Books).

TARVER, J. D. (1964), 'Occupational migration differentials', *Social Forces*, vol. 43, no. 2, December, pp. 231–41.

THOMAS, R. (1968), 'Journeys to work', *Planning*, PEP Broadsheet 504 (London: Political and Economic Planning).

THOMPSON, T. E. (1933), *Location of Manufacturers, 1899–1929: a study of the tendencies toward concentration and toward dispersion of manufacturers in the United States* (Washington: U.S. Bureau of the Census).

TOWNSEND, A. R. and GAULT, F. (1972), 'A national model of factory movement and resulting employment', *Area*, vol. 4, no. 2, pp. 92–8.

TOWNSEND, A. R. and TAYLOR, C. C. (1975), 'Regional culture and identity in industrialised societies: the case of north-east England', *Regional Studies*, vol. 9, no. 4, pp. 379–93.

TOWNSEND, R. (1970), *Up the Organisation* (New York: Knopf).

TRAINING SERVICES AGENCY (1974), *Vocational Preparation for Young People* (London: Manpower Services Commission).

TREASURY (1976), *Economic Progress Report*, February.

TYNE AND WEAR COUNTY COUNCIL (1976), *Structure Plan: Report of Survey* (Newcastle upon Tyne: Tyne and Wear County Council).

UNITED STATES TEMPORARY NATIONAL ECONOMIC COMMITTEE (1941), *The Problem of Small Business* (Washington, DC: United States Temporary National Economic Committee).

URBED (Urban and Economic Development Group) (1977), *Industrial Estates and the Small Firm* (London: URBED).

URBED (1978a), Employment and the Small Firms, survey by S.C.P.R. (London: URBED).

URBED (1978b), *College and the Community: fostering new enterprises* (London: Urbed).

VALLIS, E. A. (1972), 'Urban land and building prices, 1892–1969', *Estates Gazette*, vol. 222, pp. 1406–7.

VERNON, R. (1960), *Metropolis 1985* (Cambridge, Mass.: Harvard University Press).

VOORHEES, A. M. and ASSOCIATES: COLIN BUCHANAN and PARTNERS (1973), *Tyne-Wear Plan: Urban Strategy* (Newcastle: Tyne-Wear Plan).

WACHTER, M. L. (1974), 'Primary and secondary labour markets: a critique of the dual approach', *Brookings Papers in Economic Activity*, no. 3, pp. 637–80, (Washington, DC: Brookings Institution).

WANDSWORTH, London Borough of (1976), *Prosperity or Slump? The Future of Wandsworth's Economy* (London: Borough of Wandsworth).

WARNES, A. M. (1972), 'Estimates of journey-to-work distances from census statistics', *Regional Studies*, vol. 6, pp. 315–26.

WARNES, A. M. (1975), 'Commuting towards city-centres: a study of population and employment density gradients in Liverpool and Manchester', *Transactions of the Institute of British Geographers*, vol. 64, pp. 76–96.

WARRINGTON DEVELOPMENT CORPORATION (1975), *New Environments for Technology and Administration*, seminar, Warrington, 2 October.

WEATHERITT, D. and LOVETT, A. (1976), *Manufacturing Industry in Greater London*, GLC Research Memorandum 498 (London: Greater London Council).

WEBER, A. F. (1899), *The Growth of Cities in the Nineteenth Century* (Ithaca, NY: Cornell reprint, 1963).

WEST CENTRAL SCOTLAND PLAN (1974), *The Regional Economy*, Supplementary Report 1 (Glasgow: West-central Scotland Plan).

WESTERGAARD, J. H. (1957), 'Journeys-to-work in the London region', *Town Planning Review*, vol. 28, pp. 37–62.

WEST MIDLANDS REGIONAL STUDY (1972), *A Developing Strategy for the West Midlands, Technical Appendix 3: Economic Study 3 (Industrial Mobility)* (Birmingham: West Midland Regional Study).

WILLIS, J. (1968), *Population Growth and Movement*, Working Paper 12 (London: Centre for Environmental Studies).

WILSON, H. and WOMERSLEY, L.; SCOTT and WILSON, KIRKPATRICK and PARTNERS (1969), *Teesside Survey and Plan*, 2 vols (London: HMSO).

WILSON, H. and WOMERSLEY, L. and ASSOCIATES (1976), *Inner Area Study: Liverpool, Fourth Study Review*, IAS/LI/12. (London: Department of the Environment).

WOOD, P. A. (1974), 'Urban manufacturing: a view from the fringe', in J. H. Johnson (ed.), *Suburban Growth* (Chichester: Wiley).

WOOD, P. A. (1976), 'Inter-regional migration in western Europe: a re-appraisal', in J. Salt and H. D. Clout (eds), *Migration in Post-war Europe* (London: Oxford University Press).

WOODBURY, C. (1953), *The Future of Cities and Urban Redevelopment* (Chicago, Ill.: University of Chicago Press).

WOOLF, M. (1967), *The Housing Survey in England and Wales: 1964* (London: HMSO).

WRIGLEY, E. A. (1967), 'A simple model of London's importance in changing English society and economy', *Past and Present*, vol. 37, pp. 44–70.

WULLKOPF, U. and PEARCE, A. E. (1977), 'Some views on long-term trends in urban and regional research in western Europe', *Urban Studies*, vol. 14, no. 1, February, pp. 41–50.

ZIMMER, B. (1964), *Rebuilding Cities: The Effects of Displacement and Relocation* (Chicago, Ill.: Quadrangle).

Subject Index

Author Index